ROUTLEDGE

INTENSIVE DUTCH COURSE

ROUTLEDGE INTENSIVE LANGUAGE COURSES

Other books in the series

Routledge Intensive Italian Course
Anna Proudfoot, Tania Batelli-Kneale, Anna Di Stefano and Daniela Treveri Gennari
ISBN 0-415-24080-8

Routledge Intensive Italian Workbook
ISBN 0-415-24079-4

Routledge Intensive Italian CDs
ISBN 0-415-24081-6

Coming soon

Routledge Intensive Russian Course
by Robin Aizlewood
ISBN 0-415-22300-8

Routledge Intensive Russian CDs
ISBN 0-415-22301-6

Routledge Intensive German Course
by Paul Hartley
ISBN 0-415-25346-2

Routledge Intensive German CDs
ISBN 0-415-25347-0

ROUTLEDGE INTENSIVE DUTCH COURSE

Gerdi Quist
Christine Sas
Dennis Strik

Routledge
Taylor & Francis Group
LONDON AND NEW YORK

First published 2006 by Routledge
2 Park Square, Milton Park, Abingdon, Oxon OX14 4RN

Simultaneously published in the USA and Canada
by Routledge
711 Third Avenue, New York, NY, 10017, USA

Routledge is an imprint of the Taylor & Francis Group, an informa business

Typeset in DIN and Rotis by
Florence Production Ltd, Stoodleigh, Devon

British Library Cataloguing in Publication Data
A catalogue record for this book is available from the British Library

Library of Congress Cataloging in Publication Data
Quist, Gerdi.
Routledge intensive Dutch course/Gerdi Quist, Christine Sas, Dennis Strik. – 1st ed.
p. cm. – (Routledge intensive language courses)
Includes bibliographical references and index.
1. Dutch language – Textbooks for foreign speakers – English. 2. Dutch language – Self-instruction. I. Sas, Christine, 1971–. II. Strik, Dennis. III. Title. IV. Series.
PF112.5.Q587 2005
439.318'2421 – dc22 2005005255

ISBN10: 0-415-26191-0 (coursebook)
ISBN10: 0-415-26192-9 (CDs)

ISBN13: 9-78-0-415-26191-3 (coursebook)
ISBN13: 9-78-0-415-26192-0 (CDs)

Printed in Canada

CONTENTS ROUTLEDGE INTENSIVE DUTCH COURSE

ACKNOWLEDGEMENTS

The authors would like to acknowledge the following people for their support or inspiration, or for simply allowing their work to be quoted:

Michel de Bakker
Hester van Kruijssen
Django de Bakker
Sylt Steen
Nico Quist
Niesje Quist-Mars
Jac Groot
Han en Gré Strik
Helen Stanbridge
Chris, Kim and Remi Bumstead
Filip, Cato and Doris Vermeiren
Wim Wouters
And last, but not least, past and present students at UCL and the FCO.

PERMISSIONS AND COPYRIGHT

The authors would also like to thank the following copyright holders for giving permission to use their work:

Piet de Geus (Anders Reizen), Baby Boardrent, Ministerie van Verkeer en Waterstaat, Reclamebureau Roorda, Waanders Uitgevers, Anno, R. van Rijswijk, Vrij Nederland, Politiek-Actie.net/Steven de Jong, Jonge Socialisten in de PvdA/T. Rottinghuis & G.J. van Midden, Wablieft, Jan G. Elburg (Bezige Bij), Goed Gevoel, www.vdab.be, www.floor.nl, Youp Van't Hek (Hekwerk Theaterproducties), www.fgov.be, Jeroen Brouwers (Arbeiderspers), Marko Heijl (Van Halewijck), Steven De Foer (Balans uitgeverij), Tom Lanoye (Prometheus), Walter Van Den Broeck (Bezige Bij), Weekblad Weekend, Anne Morelli (EPO), Patricia Carson (Lannoo uitgeverij), Men's Health, Janny Groen (de Volkskrant), Raymond van het Groenewoud (Debbel Debbel Produkties NV), Geert Mak, Frank Ligtvoet (NRC Handelsblad), Karel Vosskuehler (NRC Handelsblad), Mar Oomen (Vrij Nederland), Natuurbehoud, De Standaard, De Telegraaf, de Volkskrant, Volkskrant magazine, One, Opzij, NRC Handelsblad, Vrij Nederland, Algemeen Dagblad, Trouw, Dagblad de Limburger.

HOW TO USE THIS BOOK

Level and target audience

This course in Dutch as a Foreign Language is aimed at users in higher education or evening classes. The course is designed to be used in a classroom context. However, the key and the explanations on grammar do make it possible to use the book for self-study, even though (occasional) assistance from a teacher is advisable.

The book is an accelerated course; it starts completely from scratch and takes you up to a level of competence where you can understand complex language, and where you can express yourself fluently in many different situations. As well as learning practical language skills, you will learn communicative strategies, such as how to adapt your style and tone according to who you are communicating with. And finally, you will gain some knowledge and understanding of Dutch and Flemish culture.

Common European Framework

In terms of practical language skills the course is on a par with level B2 of the Common European Framework for Languages. In terms of intellectual competences, such as manipulating language stylistically and language awareness, the course goes beyond this level. The four domains described by the Common European Framework are all present here. Topics and language skills at the start of the course focus on the private domain, i.e. your immediate surroundings in a private context, and increasingly look outwards towards activities in the public domain. In the latter part of the course you will practise skills which are relevant to the world of work and educational contexts, such as holding a debate, writing an argument or giving a presentation. Topics become increasingly abstract and challenging and include areas such as lifestyles, your place in society and national identity.

Approach

The distinctive approach of this course lies in its integration of learning the language in relation to its cultural context. The course looks at language in a critical way and asks questions such as: How is language used in particular contexts? Why is it used this way? What are the effects of using certain language structures or certain words? In addition, you will find information on cultural aspects of the Netherlands and Flanders throughout the course, with a particular focus on modern day Flanders and the Netherlands in the last three units.

This course is also distinctive in its approach to the progress of language skills: starting from simple grammar only, while encouraging authentic language use from the start. This ensures that you will learn to manipulate patterns correctly. Focusing initially on simple grammatical patterns only will give you the chance to quickly build up a body of vocabulary.

Structure

The book has 11 units. Progress is carefully structured in terms of language skills and topics. Topics move from the personal to the public, from the practical to the abstract. The tasks you will be asked to do also become increasingly challenging.

You are encouraged right from the start to think about style, so you develop 'a feel' for the language very quickly. For this reason, for instance, modal particles, the little words that colour communicative interaction, are introduced early on, although initially you only need to recognise the meaning of these receptively.

All units contain reading texts and listening texts, called **Tekst**, and texts for closer analysis, called **A closer look**. The latter are designed either to look at certain strategies the writer may have used, to recognise the implied messages in texts or to recognise the stylistic impact of certain ways of writing. Each unit also has sections on grammar, called **Structuren**; on language functions and issues of style and social communications, called **Communicatie**; and some informative sections explaining the cultural references in the texts, called **Cultuur**.

In addition, each unit has a plethora of exercises which allow you to practise all the skills. The exercises are designed to progress from guided and controlled exercises, practising particular grammar structures or language functions, to increasingly less-guided exercises in which you learn to manipulate language for specific contexts and purposes. Revision exercises are included throughout the course, revisiting previously learnt vocabulary or language patterns.

Units are subdivided into sections, each starting with a text or dialogue, followed by a vocabulary list and information on grammar, functions and social communication found in that particular text.

On the Routledge website (www.routledge.com/intensive/dutch), you can find a self-evaluation form, so that you can keep track of your progress throughout the course. You can photocopy this form and fill it in after you have completed each unit. The answer key can also be found on this website.

How to use the course

As mentioned the course is designed for use in a classroom situation, but can be used – with assistance – as a self-study course. The key to the exercises helps you with this. However, you should note that in the case of questions which ask for an interpretation, the answer in the key is the interpretation of the authors. Your or your teacher's answers may differ, but may be just as valid.

In a university context the course will take approximately 160 contact hours to complete. In addition to these contact hours you will need to spend the same amount of time on preparation and homework.

Further guidance on how to use this book can be obtained from the teacher notes on the Routledge website.

Unit 1
Hier ben ik

In this unit you will learn to talk about yourself and how the ways in which you use the language also give away something about yourself (and others). You will also learn about various conventions used when greeting people. We will look at what you actually 'do' when you use language: which functions and tasks you perform, and what strategies you can use for writing, depending on what impression you want to achieve.

TOPICS

- Talking about yourself
- Describing people
- Numbers to 100
- Formal and informal forms of address
- Writing: style to fit context
- Strategies for writing

FUNCTIONS

- Introducing yourself
- Saying what you like
- Saying what you like from a relationship
- Stating where you live and work
- Greeting people and saying goodbye
- Directly addressing someone
- Talking about characteristics of a person
- Making a compliment
- Checking the information you have is correct
- Stating that something is correct
- Inviting someone to expand on something
- Expressing surprise
- Adverbs to modify meaning
- Expressing that you are making an assumption

GRAMMAR

- Finite verb
- Stem of verb
- Infinitive
- Place of finite verb in sentence
- Regular and irregular verbs
- Prepositions
- Articles
- Nouns
- Plural nouns
- Use of the present tense: **nu**, **al**, **pas**, **nog maar**
- Personal pronouns
- Imperative

Tekst 1 Telefoon-dating

We'll begin this unit by listening to several people introducing themselves. They are two men and two women, who have registered with a dating agency 'Telefoon-dating Nederland'.

For each of the candidates, try and write down

1 their name,
2 where they live and
3 what they do for a living.

Welkom bij Telefoon-dating Nederland

Man 1: Goedemiddag, Dirk Fransen is de naam. Ik ben directeur bij een marketingbedrijf. Ik ben 51 jaar. Ik woon in Den Haag en ik zoek een intelligente vrouw, tussen de 35 en 45 jaar. Ik hou van lezen en reizen. Goedendag.

Vrouw 1: Hoi. Ik ben Angelina. Ik woon in Delft. Ik ben 34 jaar en ik werk voor een modebedrijf. Ik zoek intimiteit, spontaniteit en een beetje magie. Ik praat graag, ik lach veel en ik geniet van het leven. Jij ook? Doei!

Man 2: Hallo. Ik heet Rutger. Ik werk in de informatica. Ik zoek een spontane meid en wat romantiek. Ik heb een goed gevoel voor humor en een hond. Ik woon in Haarlem. O ja, ik ben 29. Hoi!

Vrouw 2: Dag, mijn naam is Harriëtte. Ik ben 42 jaar oud. Ik woon in Brabant. Ik ben secretaresse bij een exportbedrijf. Ik hou van koken en muziek. Ik wil een serieuze relatie met een charmante man. Ik vind spiritualiteit en respect belangrijk. Dag.

Key vocabulary

een beetje magie	a little magic
belangrijk	important
bij	at/with
een charmante man	a charming man
directeur	director
en	and
een exportbedrijf	an export company
een goed gevoel voor humor	a good sense of humour
graag	(I) like to . . .
een hond	a dog
informatica	I.T.
een intelligente vrouw	an intelligent woman
intimiteit	intimacy
jij ook?	you too?
koken	to cook
het leven	life
lezen	to read

een marketingbedrijf	a marketing company	**een serieuze relatie**	a serious relationship
mijn	my	**een spontane meid**	a spontaneous woman
een modebedrijf	a fashion company	**spontaniteit**	spontaneity (informal)
muziek	music	**tussen**	between
reizen	to travel	**veel**	a lot
secretaresse	secretary	**wat romantiek**	a little romance

Structuren

VERBS: THE PRESENT TENSE

Listen to the following speech patterns taken from the texts, and repeat each of the phrases.

Ik ben Rutger.
I am Rutger.

Ik heet Rutger.
I'm called/My name is Rutger.

Ik werk voor een bank.
I work for a bank.

Ik werk in Amsterdam.
I work in Amsterdam.

Ik woon in Haarlem.
I live in Haarlem.

Ik heb een hond.
I have a dog.

Ik zoek een vrouw.
I'm looking for a woman.

Ik wil een man.
I want a man.

Ik vind respect belangrijk.
I think/find respect (is) important.

Ik praat veel.
I talk a lot.

Ik lach veel.
I laugh a lot.

Ik geniet van vakanties.
I enjoy holidays.

Ik hou van dansen.
I love/like dancing.

The four speakers introducing themselves in the texts above use the present tense throughout. As you can see, you can use the present tense to give information about yourself (**Ik woon in Utrecht.** 'I live in Utrecht.') and to give an opinion (**Ik vind spiritualiteit belangrijk.** 'I think spirituality is important.')

Infinitive

All verbs have an infinitive form – in English this is the form preceded by 'to': to work, to live, to swim. In Dutch the infinitive of most verbs ends in **-en**: **werken**, **leven**, **zwemmen**.

Finite verb

A verb tells you what's happening in a sentence (whether the subject is working, living, swimming, etc.), but one of the verbs in a sentence (usually the first) also changes its form to indicate person (i.e. who is performing the action) and tense, i.e. it tells you whether you are talking about the past, present or future. This verb is called the finite verb.

Place of finite verb

The finite verb in statements always comes at the second place in the sentence.

Ik **werk** in de informatica.
Ik **zoek** een beetje magie.

Stem

The form of the finite verb depends on the subject of the sentence. Most verb forms are based on a basic form called the stem of the verb. The stem is the form of the verb which goes with '**ik**'. You can usually find the stem of regular verbs by taking away **-en** from the infinitive. Here are some examples:

infinitive	*stem*	
werken	**werk**	work
leven	**leef**	live
zwemmen	**zwem**	swim
zingen	**zing**	sing

As you can see, the spelling of certain verbs may change when forming the stem. Check the spelling rules in Appendix 1.

Irregular verbs

Irregular verbs do not follow rules to form their different forms like regular verbs. It is best to simply learn the various verb forms of irregular forms by heart. You will find an appendix with irregular verbs and their forms at the back of the book.

Oefening 1

Look up the meaning of the following verbs in a dictionary and give the stem of each of these verbs.

1	vergaderen	____________	6	lunchen	____________
2	helpen	____________	7	tekenen	____________
3	denken	____________	8	luisteren	____________
4	rekenen	____________	9	fietsen	____________
5	kijken	____________	10	typen	____________

Oefening 2

As before, look up the meaning of these verbs and give the stem. Note that with the following verbs, the spelling changes. You can look up the spelling rules in Appendix 1.

1	geven	____________	6	slagen	____________
2	koken	____________	7	adviseren	____________
3	schrijven	____________	8	liggen	____________
4	maken	____________	9	voetballen	____________
5	lezen	____________	10	horen	____________

Oefening 3

Fill in the appropriate form of the verb in brackets and translate the sentences.

1 Ik ____________ een relatie. (**willen**)
2 Ik ____________ veel. (**lachen**)
3 Ik ____________ Mark. (**heten**)
4 Ik ____________ 25 jaar oud. (**zijn**)
5 Ik ____________ in Nederland. (**wonen**)
6 Ik ____________ een goed gevoel voor humor. (**hebben**)
7 Ik ____________ een man. (**zoeken**)
8 Ik ____________ in Maastricht. (**werken**)
9 Ik ____________ spontaniteit belangrijk. (**vinden**)

Oefening 4: Introductions

Complete the following introductions by filling in the correct form of the verbs in brackets. Look up the meaning of verbs which you do not know.

1 Hallo, ik ______________ (zijn) Hassan Remers. Ik ______________ (werken) bij een internetbedrijf. Ik ______________ (ontwerpen) internetsites. Ik ______________ (zijn) 24 jaar oud en ik ______________ (houden) van sporten en televisie kijken.

2 Dag, ik ______________ (zijn) Katlijn Verhaege. Ik ______________ (zijn) manager bij een grote bank. Ik ______________ (werken) erg hard en erg lang. Maar ik ______________ (lachen) ook veel, en ik ______________ (verdienen) veel geld!

3 Hoi, ik ______________ (heten) Safina. Ik ______________ (studeren) economie aan de universiteit in Nijmegen. Ik ______________ (hebben) een vriend. Ik ______________ (wonen) in een studentenflat met twee vriendinnen. Ik ______________ (houden) van koken. En van mijn vriend natuurlijk.

Communicatie

STATING YOUR PROFESSION

Leave out *a/an* when giving your job title in Dutch:

Ik ben directeur.
I am a director/manager.

Add *the* when saying what industry you work in:

Ik werk in de informatica.
I work in I.T.

You can work **voor** 'for' or **bij** 'at/with' a company:

Ik werk voor een bank.
I work for a bank.

Ik werk bij een modebedrijf.
I work at a fashion company.

Oefening 5

State your profession or where you work, using the information below.

Example

computerbedrijf **Ik werk voor een computerbedrijf.**

1	uitgever	*publisher's*	____________
2	secretaresse	*secretary*	____________
3	internetcafé		____________
4	transportbedrijf		____________
5	financieel directeur	*finance director*	____________
6	advertentiebureau	*advertising agency*	____________

FORMAL AND INFORMAL

In Dutch you make a distinction between addressing people in a formal way (e.g. **goedendag** 'good day') or an informal way (e.g. **hoi** 'hi').

a) Whether language is perceived as formal or informal, depends on the context and the situation, but generally more formal or neutral ways of greeting people are:

goedendag good day
goedemorgen good morning
goedemiddag good afternoon
goedenavond good evening

Hallo 'hello', is fairly neutral, but **hoi** 'hi' is more informal.

b) A neutral way of saying goodbye is: **tot ziens** 'goodbye'

More formal are:

goedendag good day **dag** bye

More informal are:

doei bye (not used in Flanders)

hoi bye (very informal, used esp. amongst those young 'at heart')

c) There are also other ways of being more or less formal, for instance by using more formal or informal words (**meid** is more informal than **vrouw**), or using shorter or longer sentences (longer sentences usually make language more formal.)

Oefening 6

How would you greet the following people, and say goodbye to them?

1 your boy/girlfriend (in the afternoon)
2 your boy/girlfriend's mother (in the morning)
3 a neighbour (in the evening)
4 the Vice-President of your company (when popping in for a visit)
5 a friend of your younger brother (any time of day)
6 an elderly aunt (in the afternoon)

INTRODUCTIONS

There are various ways of introducing yourself. Here are some examples:

Ik ben Marloes.	I am Marloes.
Ik heet Jonah.	My name is Jonah. (literally: I'm called Jonah.)
Mijn naam is Martijn.	My name is Martijn.

A more formal way of introducing yourself is:

Karelsen is de naam.	literally: Karelsen is the name.

You can only use this structure when including your last name.

Oefening 7

Use different ways of introducing yourself to as many fellow students as possible.

NUMBERS 1–100

1	een	11	elf	21	eenentwintig
2	twee	12	twaalf	22	tweeëntwintig
3	drie	13	dertien	23	drieëntwintig
4	vier	14	veertien	24	vierentwintig
5	vijf	15	vijftien	25	vijfentwintig
6	zes	16	zestien	26	zesentwintig
7	zeven	17	zeventien	27	zevenentwintig
8	acht	18	achttien	28	achtentwintig
9	negen	19	negentien	29	negenentwintig
10	tien	20	twintig		

30	dertig	36	zesendertig
40	veertig	49	negenenveertig
50	vijftig	52	tweeënvijftig
60	zestig	65	vijfenzestig
70	zeventig	73	drieënzeventig
80	tachtig	84	vierentachtig
90	negentig	97	zevenennegentig
100	honderd		

AGE

To say how old you are in Dutch you simply mention the number of years with or without the word **jaar** 'year' (always singular).

Ik ben 24.	I am 24.
Ik ben 18 jaar.	I am 18 years old.

You can also add the word **oud** 'old':

Ik ben 54 jaar oud.	I am 54 years old.

Oefening 8

How old are you? Read out the following sentences with the numbers in full.

1 Ik ben 20 jaar.
2 Ik ben 40.
3 Ik ben 32 jaar.
4 Ik ben 95.
5 Ik ben 3 jaar oud.
6 Ik ben 5.
7 Ik ben 9 jaar oud.
8 Ik ben 15 jaar.
9 Ik ben 69.
10 Ik ben ______________ .
(fill in your own age)

LIEFDE ('LOVE')

A particular liking or love for something or someone is expressed in Dutch with:

Ik houd van . . .
I love/like . . .

Note that you have to use the preposition **van** (literally 'of') in this structure.

Oefening 9

Work in small groups or pairs. Tell each other (at least) two things that you like (doing). If necessary, use a dictionary or ask the teacher.

Oefening 10

Fill in the missing words.

1 Ik werk ______________ een internetbedrijf.
2 Ik heb ______________ hond.
3 Ik hou ______________ muziek.
4 Ik ______________ Joris.
5 Mijn ______________ is Anoek.

Oefening 11

Look at the following diagram and use the information given to pretend you are the people whose name is given in the left-hand column and introduce yourself, following the example. Add an appropriate greeting for each person and also say goodbye.

Example

Hoi. Ik heet Jaap. Ik ben 23 jaar oud en ik woon in Heerlen. Ik werk in Eindhoven. Ik hou van lezen. Ik vind spontaniteit belangrijk. Doei.

name	*age*	*lives in*	*works*	*likes*	*thinks important*
Jaap	23	Heerlen	in Eindhoven	lezen	spontaniteit
Annelies	54	Lelystad	*for a bank*	werken	respect
Francesca	36	Leiden	in Den Haag	koken	een beetje magie
Ricardo	27	Gent	*in I.T.*	romantiek	intimiteit
you	?	?	? (town)	lezen, romantiek or werken?	respect, spontaniteit *or* een beetje magie?

Cultuur

You have already seen what you can say when greeting people, from the informal **hoi** to the more formal **goedemorgen**, for instance. However, to a large extent, greeting other people consists of non-verbal communication, usually with its own strict conventions.

In the Netherlands, people usually shake each other's hand, both when they're meeting and when they're saying goodbye. This is true when you are meeting someone for a business meeting, but also when you're visiting friends and relatives or attending a party. Friends usually kiss each other (**kussen** or **zoenen**) at the same time: always three kisses (**kusjes** or **zoenen**), starting on the right cheek. Again, kisses are also exchanged when saying goodbye. In Flanders people often only give one another one kiss.

A CLOSER LOOK

Vragen bij tekst 1 ('Questions')

Listen again to the four introductions in Tekst 1 and look at the different ways in which the people present themselves by answering the following questions.

1 Which of the four people is the most informal and which is the most formal? How can you tell?

2 For each person, write down the words which tell you something about their personality.

3 How would you characterise the personality of each of the four people?

Tekst 2 Mini-dialogen

Listen to the following mini-dialogues and complete the box to indicate in which situations the participants 'A' in the dialogues are doing the following:

Functie	**Situatie** (e.g. 1, 2, etc.)
a Checking information is correct	
b Giving a compliment	
c Criticising	
d Inviting to expand	

1 **De ene taalstudent tegen de andere.** One language student to another.
A: Jij spreekt goed Nederlands!
B: Dank je.

2 **Een vriendin tegen haar vriend.** A girlfriend to her boyfriend.
A: Je doet soms zo raar!
B: Jij toch ook?

3 **Op een sollicitatiegesprek.** At a job interview.
A: Je werkt momenteel bij een verzekeringsbedrijf en je wilt nu een andere baan?
B: Ja, dat klopt.
A: En je hebt ervaring met computers?
B: Jazeker.

4 **Bij de douane op het vliegveld.** At customs at the airport.
A: U bent meneer Davids?
B: Ja.
A: En u bent hier op vakantie?
B: Nee, voor zaken.

5 **Inschrijving op een conferentie.** Registration at a conference.
A: U bent zeker meneer Hulst?
B: Ja, inderdaad.

6 **Radio-interview met een Engelse immigrante.** Radio interview with a (female) English immigrant.
A: Mevrouw Van Hameren, u woont in Zoetermeer?
B: Ja, inderdaad.
A: En u bent nogal actief hier.
B: Ja, dat klopt. Ik help de bejaarden.
A: U helpt de bejaarden?
B: Ja, ik help met boodschappen doen.

Key vocabulary

een andere baan	another job
de bejaarden	old age pensioners
bij een verzekeringsbedrijf	at an insurance company
boodschappen doen	do the shopping
dat klopt	that's right/correct
ervaring	experience
goed	good/well
hier	here
inderdaad	that's right
jazeker	yes (indeed)
met	with
momenteel	at the moment
Nederlands	Dutch
nogal actief	quite active
nu	now

op vakantie	on holiday	**zaken**	business
soms	sometimes	**zo raar**	so strange
u bent zeker. . .	I expect you are . . .		

Oefening 12

Listen carefully to the tone used in the dialogues above. Repeat the dialogues with a fellow student and try and copy the tone of the speakers on the recording. It helps if you exaggerate as much as you can. If you can, record yourselves and listen to your recording to check whether you sound authentic.

Structuren

U/JE/JIJ + VERB

U woont in Zoetermeer? You live in Zoetermeer?
Je werkt in Leiden? You work in Leiden?
Jij ook? You too?

Practise the following patterns by listening to them on the recording and repeating them.

	informal	*formal*
regular	Jij/Je spreekt Nederlands. *You speak/are speaking Dutch.*	U spreekt Nederlands.
	Jij/Je helpt bejaarden. *You help/are helping pensioners.*	U helpt bejaarden.
	Jij/Je maakt een grapje. *You make a joke/are joking.*	U maakt een grapje.
	Jij/Je leest een boek. *You read/are reading a book.*	U leest een boek.
	Jij/Je woont in Nederland. *You live/are living in the Netherlands.*	U woont in Nederland.

	informal	*formal*
	Jij/Je werkt hard. *You work/are working hard.*	U werkt hard.
irregular	Jij/Je bent gek. *You are crazy/mad.*	U bent gek.
	Jij/Je hebt ervaring. *You have experience.*	U hebt/heeft ervaring.
	Jij/Je doet veel. *You do/are doing a lot.*	U doet veel.
	Jij/Je wilt een huis. *You want a house.*	U wil/wilt een huis.

	unstressed	*stressed*
formal	**u**	**u**
informal	**je**	**jij**

In general you address people informally if you are on a first-name basis with them.

Oefening 13

Compare the patterns of **je/jij/u** with the **ik**-pattern you studied at the start of this unit. What do you think the rule is for forming the verb patterns with **je/jij/u** for regular verbs? Fill in this table:

	regular verbs, present tense	***zijn***	***hebben***
ik	stem	________	________
je/jij/u	stem + ________	________	________

Oefening 14

Fill in the correct form of the verb in brackets.

1 U ______________ in Engeland? (wonen)
2 Jij ______________ samen met Ellie, hè? (werken)
3 Je ______________ ook Engels? (spreken)

4	U ______________	zeker de Telegraaf?	(lezen)
5	Je ______________	altijd zo direct.	(zijn)
6	Je ______________	leuke kinderen	(hebben)

Key vocabulary

samen	together	**altijd**	always
Engels	English	**leuke kinderen**	nice children

Oefening 15

Work with a partner to create 5 mini-dialogues in which you check information about one another.

Example

A: **Jij woont zeker in Londen?**
B: **Ja, inderdaad.**

Answer in the affirmative in as many different ways as you can. You can use the dialogues above for inspiration.

After you have written down the dialogues practise them out loud.

Communicatie

JE/JIJ/U

You normally address people directly with **je/jij/u** to ask a question or to give an order. In both cases this will have consequences for word order (see Unit 2). However, as you have seen, **je/jij/u** + a verb can also be used for various other functions including:

a) Directly addressing someone about his/her characteristics, behaviour or standard of work. Often this will take the form of a compliment:

Je spreekt goed Nederlands.	You speak Dutch well.

But it is not uncommon for people to criticise directly as well:

Je doet soms zo raar.	You behave so weird sometimes.

b) Checking the information you have is correct (when reading from a CV for instance):

U bent meneer Davids?	You are Mr Davids?

c) Inviting someone to expand by repeating information as a question:

U helpt de bejaarden?	You help the elderly?

d) Expressing surprise (expressed through tone of voice):

Jij werkt bij de Hema?!	You're working at the Hema?!

Oefening 16

You are in a generous mood. Compliment a friend using the expressions given below. Remember to follow the correct pattern with the verb in second position (the verbs are underlined).

Example

altijd leuke kleren dragen **Je draagt altijd leuke kleren.**	to wear nice clothes

altijd	always

1	mooi *zingen*	to sing beautifully
2	in een schitterend huis *wonen*	to live in a fantastic house
3	altijd lekker *koken*	to be a good cook
4	nogal actief *zijn*	to be quite active
5	altijd vriendelijk zijn; altijd een praatje *maken*	to be friendly; to have a chat
6	mooi haar *hebben*	to have beautiful hair
7	snel *antwoorden*	to respond promptly

Oefening 17

Work in pairs. One of you interviews several different people (all played by the other student). The interviewer wants to encourage the interviewees to expand by repeating their statements. How will you address them? Formally or informally?

Example

A radio presenter interviews mevrouw Aarts about her job. She organises events (**evenementen organiseren**).

Interviewee:	**Ik organiseer evenementen.**
Interviewer:	**U organiseert evenementen?**

1 A market researcher interviews an older person in the street who says she speaks seven languages. (**zeven talen spreken**)

2 A boss interviews a 16 year old for a Saturday job who says he is attending school. (**op school zitten**)

3 A journalist interviews a popstar who says he earns enough money. (**genoeg geld verdienen**)

4 A radio presenter interviews Mr Bomhof about going on a holiday. He says he always gets homesick. (**altijd heimwee krijgen**)

WAYS OF STATING THAT INFORMATION IS CORRECT

dat klopt	that's correct
ja, inderdaad	yes, that's right
jazeker	yes (indeed)

Oefening 18: Role play

Work with a partner. Write on a note what your name is (make up names in order to be able to do this exercise more than once), where you live, where you work, how old you are and which languages you speak.

Give the note to your partner and check with one another that the information is correct. Respond appropriately, using one of the phrases you have learnt.

Example

A: **U bent meneer Mailing?** or: **Jij bent Jack?**
B: **Ja, dat klopt.**

WORDS TO MODIFY MEANING

In some of the situations given on page 12 adverbs have been added to make the statements less crude and to qualify them to some extent. Often these adverbs add a time element:

Jij doet soms zo raar.
You act strangely sometimes.

Je wilt nu een andere baan?
You want another job now?

U bent nogal actief.
You are quite active.

CHANGING MEANING: ZEKER

Other words like **zeker** can change the meaning and intention of a statement or question:

a) To check that an assumption is correct:

U bent zeker de moeder van Jaap? I expect you are the mother of Jaap?

b) to assume (sarcastically) that someone/something has a particular characteristic:

Jij leest zeker de Telegraaf? I bet you read the Telegraaf.

Oefening 19

Modify the following questions expressing surprise to an assumption:

Example

Jij kijkt naar soaps?
Jij kijkt zeker naar soaps!

1 Jij stemt op Groen Links?
2 Jij volgt een dieet?
3 Jij houdt van voetbal?
4 Jij oefent vaak?
5 Jij fietst graag?

Key vocabulary

stemmen	to vote
een dieet volgen	to be on (follow) a diet
vaak	often
fietsen	to cycle

Structuren

EXTENDING PATTERNS

The basic pattern of **je/jij/u** + verb can be expanded by all sorts of different kinds of word patterns. Many word patterns start with a preposition (prepositional phrases):

in Zoetermeer in Zoetermeer
bij een verzekeringsbedrijf at/with an insurance company
op vakantie on holiday

Prepositions

Prepositions generally show the relationship between things in a sentence. Frequently this relationship is one of time, place or direction, but many prepositions are also part of a fixed expression. Frequently these expressions in English don't even use a preposition, or if they do, the use of these does not correlate with their use in Dutch. It helps therefore if you memorise these fixed prepositions as part of an expression. Here are some examples:

houden van	to like, to love
denken aan	to think of
ervaring hebben met	to have experience with
kijken naar	to look at/to watch
rijden in	to drive in

Oefening 20

Link the two columns by choosing the most appropriate prepositional phrase:

1	Jij helpt	a	in een Ferrari?
2	Jij kijkt	b	in de politiek?
3	U rijdt	c	met boodschappen doen?
4	Ik zit	d	op de Partij van de Arbeid?
5	Ik heb ervaring	e	op school.
6	Je bent nogal actief	f	naar Top of the Pops?
7	Jij stemt	g	met computers.

NOUNS AND ARTICLES

Dutch has three articles: **de, het, een**

Indefinite

Een means 'a/an' and is the indefinite article. All nouns used without an article or with the indefinite article **een** are called indefinite nouns.

Ik heb een nieuwe laptop.
I have a new laptop.

Computers zijn erg duur.
Computers are very expensive.

Definite

De and **het** both mean 'the'. All nouns used with **de** are common nouns, and all nouns used with **het** are neuter nouns. There are no easy rules for finding out whether a noun takes **de** or **het**, except that:

all plural nouns take **de**
all diminutives (see Unit 4) take **het**
all nouns referring to people take **de**

There are roughly twice as many **de**-words as **het**-words.

It helps if you memorise the articles with the nouns. You can also look up the article in a good dictionary. In Dutch dictionaries, the gender of nouns is often indicated with a single letter:

neuter nouns with **o** for **onzijdig** 'neuter';
common nouns with **v** for **vrouwelijk** 'feminine' or **m** for **mannelijk** 'masculine'.

PLURAL NOUNS

Most nouns take -**en** in the plural:

singular	*plural*	
het feest	**de feesten**	party
de meid	**de meiden**	girl
de boterham	**de boterhammen**	sandwich

Nouns with a schwa (e.g. those ending in **-el**, **-em**, **-en**, **-er**, **-je**) in the last syllable take **-s**:

singular	*plural*	
de nachtclub	**de nachtclubs**	nightclub
de tafel	**de tafels**	table
de computer	**de computers**	computers

Nouns ending in a vowel take **'s**:

singular	*plural*
de euro	**de euro's**
de baby	**de baby's**

Oefening 21

Look up the meaning of the following nouns in a dictionary and indicate whether they take **de** or **het**.

1 vader
2 belasting
3 meisje
4 geluidsinstallatie
5 boodschap
6 kaars
7 oma
8 potlood
9 onderwerp
10 boterham

Oefening 22

Make the nouns of the previous exercise plural, adapting the spelling where necessary.

Tekst 3 Persoonsbeschrijvingen

Read and listen to the following descriptions of people and answer the questions below the descriptions.

1 Een artikel over een art director:

> Hij is jong, aantrekkelijk
> en rijk. Hij woont in een groot grachtenhuis in
> hartje Amsterdam.

2 Karina praat over haar vriendje:

> Ja joh, hij is hartstikke lief en sexy.
> Hij heeft echt veel geld en hij woont in een ontzettend
> groot huis, midden in Amsterdam.

3 Een memo over een functioneringsgesprek:

> Anita de Bakker werkt nu 3 maanden
> op de afdeling. Ze is verantwoordelijk voor de
> administratie. Ze is accuraat en doet haar werk
> met enthousiasme. Ze heeft goede
> communicatieve vaardigheden.

Key vocabulary

de afdeling	the department
het artikel	article
echt	really
het functioneringsgesprek	job appraisal
goede communicatieve vaardigheden	good communication skills
het grachtenhuis	house situated at the side of a canal in a town (usually a very prestigious house)
groot	big
hartje	in the centre
hartstikke	very, really (very informal)
jong, aantrekkelijk, rijk	young, attractive, rich
lief	sweet
met enthousiasme	with enthusiasm
midden in	in the middle/in the centre
ontzettend	very, terribly, extremely
praten over	to talk about
het vriendje	boyfriend
haar werk	her work
ze is verantwoordelijk voor de administratie	she is responsible for the administration

Vragen bij tekst 3

1 The first two descriptions are about the same person and refer to the same attributes. How do the two descriptions differ?
2 The style of the description of Anita de Bakker differs from the two previous descriptions. How?

Oefening 23

Karina, who talked about her boyfriend in one of the texts above, is Anita de Bakker's colleague. How do you think Karina might talk about Anita's work? Re-write the last two sentences in Text 3 as Karina might say it. You can use Text 1 for inspiration.

Structuren

HIJ/ZIJ/HET

Hij/zij/het are Dutch words for 'he/she/it'. These are the various forms:

stressed	*unstressed*	
hij	**(ie)**	he
zij	**ze**	she
het	**('t)**	it

When speaking you mostly use the unstressed forms. In writing, or if you want to indicate contrast when speaking, the stressed forms are used.

The unstressed forms in brackets are generally considered too informal to use in writing.

HIJ/ZIJ/HET + PRESENT TENSE

Look at the examples. How do you think the verb form for **hij/zij/ze** is formed in the present tense? Fill in the table below the examples.

regular	**Hij/Zij/Ze werkt bij een bank.**	He/She works/is working at a bank.
	Hij/Zij/Ze woont in Engeland.	He/She lives/is living in England.
irregular	**Hij/Zij/Ze is I.T.-manager.**	He/She is I.T. Manager.
	Hij/Zij/Ze heeft een hond.	He/She has a dog.
	Hij/Zij/Ze doet veel.	He/She does a lot/is doing a lot.

Oefening 24

	regular verbs, present tense	***zijn***	***hebben***
ik	stem	________	________
je/jij/u	stem + ________	________	________
hij/zij/het	stem + ________	________	________

Oefening 25

Fill in the correct form:

1 Hij ______________ altijd hoge cijfers. (krijgen)
2 Zij ______________ morgen. (komen)
3 Hij ______________ veel. (praten)
4 Hij ______________ gevoel voor humor. (hebben)
5 Ze ______________ van het leven. (genieten)
6 Zij ______________ Petra. (heten)

hoge cijfers	good grades
komen	to come
morgen	tomorrow

Oefening 26

Fill in the correct form of **zijn** or **hebben**.

1 Mijn moeder _______________ 56 jaar oud.
2 Richard _______________ nog niet thuis.
3 Ik _______________ een nieuwe secretaresse.
4 Je _______________ tien minuten te laat.
5 Mijn hond _______________ een internetpagina.
6 Je _______________ een mooie televisie.
7 Ik _______________ verantwoordelijk voor de administratie.
8 Maria _______________ de sleutels.
9 U _______________ een huis in Londen?
10 Je _______________ erg lief.

Oefening 27

Complete the sentences with one of the following verbs:

doen gaan gaan komen lachen werken werken wonen zijn zoeken zijn

1 Ronneke _______________ in augustus op vakantie.
2 Ik _______________ in Amsterdam maar ik _______________ in een groot huis in Edam.
3 Haar vriend _______________ ook op het feest.
4 U _______________ naar Amerika, hè?
5 Ik _______________ al mijn financiën op de computer.
6 Shalom _______________ een vriendin.
7 Doeshka _______________ een leuke meid, ze _______________ veel.
8 Je _______________ te veel, dat _______________ niet goed voor je.

Communicatie

USE OF THE PRESENT TENSE

a) The present tense is also used to talk about the past when it includes the present. Compare how this is done in English:

Ze werkt nu drie maanden op de afdeling.
She has been working in the department for three months (now).

Instead of **nu**, the words **al** or **pas**, **nog maar** can also be used.

nu	now	**pas**	only
al	already (for as long as)	**nog maar**	only

b) The pattern **hij/zij** +verb is used in the descriptions on page 21 to respectively describe characteristics of people, to give information and an evaluation about them and their activities.

Oefening 28

The sentences below are not correct because one of the following words must be inserted:

al nu pas nog maar

Example

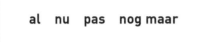

Johan woont 2 jaar in Heerlen. (you think that's quite long)
Johan woont al 2 jaar in Heerlen.

1 Heleen werkt 5 maanden in Brussel. (you don't think this is very long)
2 Peter werkt 15 jaar bij de televisie. (that's quite long)
3 Lieve is 2 maanden verantwoordelijk voor de administratie. (neutral)
4 Gabi woont 1 jaar in Londen. (not very long)
5 Theo werkt 9 jaar in de mode. (quite long)
6 Marlies heeft 3 maanden een relatie met die jongen. (not very long)

Oefening 29

Work in groups. Say how long you have been living where you live and working where you work. Exchange this information with as many fellow students as possible.

DESCRIBING PEOPLE

a) When you attribute various characteristics to someone, people often list these together in a sentence. This makes the discription sound snappy and/or read easily. Stating three attributes sounds better than stating two or four.

b) When you are writing an appraisal, for instance, you will want to sound as neutral as possible. Often short sentences and few descriptive words are used. Convention tends to dictate which descriptive words are considered to be acceptable in this context. A few examples:

accuraat	accurate	**zorgvuldig**	conscientious
enthousiast	enthusiastic	**zelfstandig**	independent

c) Talking or writing about people informally allows for a much greater range of patterns and vocabulary to be used.

Oefening 30

Work in pairs.

1 Describe the following people to each other, using the information below.

naam	**leeftijd**	**enkele karakteristieken**	**woonplaats of woonsituatie**	**extra informatie**
	age	*some characteristics*	*town or living situation*	*extra information*
Hans	32	zelfverzekerd	Rotterdam	heeft weinig geld/ academicus
Marijke	46	creatief	met haar man en 2 kinderen	part-time lerares/houdt van rust
Tamara	18	intelligent	bij haar ouders in Leiden	secretaresse/ spaart voor een wereldreis
someone you know		[give a positive characteristic]	[give the town where they live]	[say what he/she likes]
you		[give a positive characteristic]	[give the town]	[say whether you are spontaneous or not]

2 Write full sentences about these people.

Make sure you use the correct verbs and the correct form of the verbs.

Key vocabulary

bij haar ouders	with her parents
lerares	teacher (female)
haar man	her husband
rust	peace and quiet
sparen voor een wereldreis	to save up for a trip around the world
weinig	little
zelfverzekerd	self-assured, confident

EMPHASIS

hij heeft echt veel geld
he really has a lot of money

hij woont in een ontzettend groot huis
he lives in a terribly big house

hij is hartstikke lief
he is really sweet

Emphasising something with words like **echt, ontzettend** and **hartstikke** tends to be done more in spoken than in written language and only in informal situations. It can give the impression that you are exaggerating.

Oefening 31

Write an introduction of a few sentences for an article about each of the people in Oefening 30 above, as if you were introducing them in a company magazine.

You can choose words and phrases from the vocabulary list below and decide what information you leave out or keep in, in order to make your introduction sound more snappy and fluent.

Key vocabulary

charmant	charming
geliefd zijn bij haar leerlingen	popular with her pupils
jong	young
knap	good looking
mooi	beautiful
op een gerenommeerde universiteit werken	working at a renowned university
open	open
spontaan	spontaneous
van avontuur, cultuur en andere vrouwen houden	to like adventure, culture and other women

Oefening 32

Write about the same people, but write as a teenager would say it.
Choose information which seems most appropriate to you.
Here are some more words:

arrogant	arrogant
brutaal	brazen, bold
populair	popular

As in English you can leave out the pronoun when you repeat the same pattern in one sentence. This sounds snappier:

Ze is accuraat en (ze) doet haar werk met enthousiasme.
She is accurate and (she) does her work with enthusiasm.

Tekst 4 Mededeling

Read and listen to the following text and then answer the question below.

Een mededeling in een fitnesscentrum

Fitnesscentrum
Gezond & Fit

Wij helpen jullie – helpen jullie Gezond & Fit?

We staan altijd klaar voor de gym en onze leden. Maar helpen jullie de gym ook: **hou de gym schoon**!

Key vocabulary

altijd	always	**de mededeling**	notice
gezond	healthy	**onze leden**	our members
hou . . . schoon	keep clean	**we staan klaar**	we're there
jullie	you (plural) (for you)		

Vraag by tekst 4

What is the purpose of this notice?

Structuren

WIJ/JULLIE/U/ZIJ

Wij, jullie, u, zij are Dutch words for 'we', 'you' (plural) and 'they'. There are several forms:

stressed	*unstressed*	
wij	**we**	we
jullie	**(je)**	you (plural, informal)
u	**u**	you (plural, formal)
zij	**ze**	they

As with the other pronouns, when speaking you mostly use the unstressed forms. In writing, or if you want to indicate contrast when speaking, the stressed forms are used. The unstressed form **je** for **jullie** is only used when it has been clearly established who you are speaking about.

Oefening 33

Look at the examples. How do you think the verb forms for **wij/jullie/u/zij** are formed in the present tense? Fill in the box below the examples.

regular	**Wij helpen jullie.**	We help you.
	Jullie helpen Gezond & Fit.	You help Gezond & Fit.
	U werkt te hard, mevrouw.	You work too hard, madam.
irregular	**We staan altijd klaar voor de gym.**	We're always there for the gym.
	Jullie hebben een groot huis.	You have a big house.
	Heren, wilt u koffie?	Gentlemen, would you like some coffee?

	regular verbs, present tense	***zijn***	***hebben***
ik	stem	________	________
je/jij/u	stem + ________	________	________
hij/zij/het	stem + ________	________	________
wij	________	________	________
jullie	________	________	________
zij	stem + ________	________	________

POSSESSIVE PRONOUNS

These are the Dutch possessive pronouns.

	stressed	*unstressed*	
singular	**mijn**	**(m'n)**	my
	jouw	**je**	your (informal)
	uw		your (formal)
	zijn	**(z'n)**	his
	haar	**(d'r)**	her
plural	**ons/onze**		our
	jullie	**je**	your (informal)
	uw		your (formal)
	hun		their

When speaking you mostly use the unstressed forms. In writing, or if you want to indicate contrast when speaking, the stressed forms are used.

Dit is niet jouw project maar mijn project.
This isn't your project but my project.

The unstressed forms in brackets are generally considered too informal to use in writing.

Ons is used with het-words, and **onze** with **de**-words.

IMPERATIVE

The imperative is a verb form which is mainly used in commands and instructions:

Hou	**de gym schoon.**	Keep the gym clean/tidy.
Help	**ons.**	Help us.
Kom	**naar ons feest.**	Come to our party.

The imperative is formed with the stem of the verb only.

Oefening 34

You work as a volunteer for a local charity. You write a leaflet to try and get as many people as possible to help out for the annual fundraising event. In this leaflet you suggest how they can help. You have written down the list below, but you want to give your suggestions more impact, so you rewrite the following statements using imperatives.

Example

U kunt uw oude CDs geven.
Geef uw oude CDs.

1 U kunt een cake bakken.
2 U kunt de zaal versieren.
3 U kunt een spel organiseren.
4 U kunt oude kleren verzamelen.
5 U kunt uw oude boeken geven.
6 U kunt iets koken.
7 U kunt een lied zingen.

Key vocabulary

bakken	to bake	**oude**	old
geven	to give	**het spel**	game
kleren	clothes	**versieren**	to decorate
kunt	can	**verzamelen**	to collect
het lied	song	**de zaal**	hall

Oefening 35

Fill in the correct possessive pronoun.

1 Is dit ______________ sleutel?
Is this my key?

2 Waar is ______________ auto?
Where is your car? (plural/informal)

3 De buren hebben ______________ kat weer.
The neighbours have their cat again/back.

4 Misha heeft ______________ fiets in Gouda gekocht.
Misha bought his bike in Gouda.

5 Heeft Moira ______________ moeder al gebeld?
Has Moira called her mother yet?

6 Ik heb ______________ pen hier.
I have your pen here. (singular/informal)

7 Hoe oud is ______________ hond?
How old is your dog? (singular/formal)

8 Wij hebben ______________ vakantie geboekt in januari.
We booked our holiday in January.

9 Hakan kan ______________ belastingformulier niet vinden.
Hakan cannot find his tax form.

10 U mag ______________ auto hier niet parkeren.
You are not allowed to park your car here. (singular/formal)

A closer look

The organiser of a childeren's summer festival, **Zomerkriebels**, in Leiden wrote to all parents in the city to inform them about and raise interest in this festival. This is how the letter began:

Zomerkriebels

We verwachten ten minste 3000 kinderen mét hun ouders op zondag 21 juni in de binnenstad van Leiden. Zij nemen deel aan **Zomerkriebels**, een festival voor en door kinderen. Een uitbundig programma staat hun te wachten met muziek, workshops, circus, theater en een kunstzinnige aankleding van de binnenstad rond de Burcht, Bibliotheek en Hooglandse Kerk. Kortom: een fantasierijk festival voor de jeugd in en rond Leiden.

naar: Michel de Bakker

Key vocabulary

aankleding	decoration
de bibliotheek	library
de binnenstad	town centre
de Burcht	(old) fortress
fantasierijk	imaginative
de jeugd	youth
kortom	in short
kriebels voelen	itching to do something (to go out/travel/dance/etc.)
kunstzinnig	artistic
nemen deel aan	take part in
staat hun te wachten	awaits them
uitbundig	exuberant
verwachten	to expect
zomerkriebels	the summer itch

Oefening 36

The author has used various strategies to make parents enthusiastic about this event.

Fill in the work sheet with examples of the following strategies used by the author:

1 Making positive and direct statements, instead of saying things like: we hope that . . ./we aim to . . .

2 Emphasizing children in the text rather than the parents themselves;

3 Creating an atmosphere of fun and expectation (list the words that contribute to this):

Strategies to create a lively, creative and fun image of festival	Examples from the text
Positive and direct statements	
Emphasising children	
Atmosphere of fun and expectations	

Vraag

The author says in which city the festival takes place, but doesn't give the name of the exact area, or the names of streets where the festival is located. Instead, he identifies the area by mentioning significant buildings. Why do you think he does that?

Unit 2
Samenleven

In this unit you are encouraged to think about the tone in which you talk, and how it conveys messages in its own right. This unit focuses on communications between people living together and the practical issues which arise when people interact. In this unit you will also learn about the little words that colour your language use and can change or modify meaning.

TOPICS

- Use of tone
- Communicative styles between friends and people living together
- Foodstuffs
- Numbers over 100
- Ordinal numbers
- Domestic chores
- Activities

FUNCTIONS

- Talking about food
- Asking for things
- Asking for more
- Asking open and closed questions
- Using a website for recipes
- Ordering in a restaurant or café
- Using language in different interpersonal contexts and styles
- Giving advice
- Talking cooperatively
- Using modal particles to indicate different meanings and functions
- Talking about dividing the domestic chores
- Qualifying something
- Writing in different styles

GRAMMAR

- Modal particles: **even**, **wel**, **nu**, **maar**, **echt**, **weer**, **hoor**, **toch**
- Negation: **geen** and **niet**
- Yes/no questions
- Questions with a question word
- Inversion
- Modal verbs
- Separable verbs
- Adverbs
- Use of **zou** in polite requests
- Use of **zou** in uncertain statements

1 In een studentenwoongroep

Nienke joins Harry at the kitchen table over breakfast.

Nienke	Mag ik de melk even?
Harry	De melk is op.
Nienke	Alweer? Dat is nu de tweede keer deze week.
Harry	Dan moet je maar vroeger opstaan. Dan is er nog wel een vol pak melk.
Nienke	Hmmm. Ik neem wel brood. Is er ook geen hagelslag meer?
Harry	Nee sorry, ook op.
Nienke	Wat is er dan wel?
Harry	Kaas. En aardbeienjam.

Key vocabulary

de aardbeienjam	strawberry jam
alweer	again
het brood	bread
de hagelslag	chocolate sprinkles
is er geen . . . meer?	is there no more . . .
de kaas	cheese
nemen	to have; to take
op	*here*: finished
opstaan	to get out of bed
het pak	*here*: carton
de studentenwoongroep	shared student flat
vol	full
vroeger	earlier

Oefening 1

Listen several times to the dialogue and write down what Nienke had wanted for her breakfast and what she has for breakfast in the end.

Oefening 2

Work with a fellow student and read the dialogue out loud, trying to match the intonation of the speakers. It helps if you exaggerate as much as you can. If you can, record yourselves and see whether your intonation sounds authentic.

Vragen bij tekst 1

1 Why does Harry not hand Nienke the carton of milk?

2 By listening to the tone in Nienke's voice, what can you deduce about her reaction? She is:

- ☐ surprised
- ☐ not surprised
- ☐ annoyed
- ☐ accepting

Tick the boxes that apply.

3 Which word particularly shows Nienke's reaction?

4 Do you feel that Harry is sympathetic to Nienke's plight? Explain your answer.

Cultuur

Breakfast in the Low Countries is frequently a 'contentinental' style breakfast with bread, cheese, **vleeswaren** (in Belgium: **charcuterie**) 'cooked meats' and a variety of sweet or savoury spreads and toppings. One of these includes **hagelslag**, but others are **pindakaas,** 'peanutbutter', **jam** or **appelstroop**, a sticky treacle-like spread made from apples.

Of course people eat a variety of things for breakfast and **yoghurt** and **muesli** or **cornflakes** are equally common.

ETEN *FOOD*

enkele voorbeelden a few examples

ontbijt	breakfast	**tussen de middag**	lunch	**avondeten**	dinner
een sneetje brood	slice of bread	bolletje	soft roll	groenten	vegetables
het roggebrood	pumpernickel bread	puntje	hard roll	aardappelen	potatoes
wit/bruin brood	white/brown bread	salade	salad	spruitjes	Brussels sprouts
ham	ham	tosti	toasted sandwich	bloemkool	cauliflower
kaas	cheese	soep	soup	sperziebonen	green beans
hagelslag	chocolate hundreds and thousands			courgettes	courgettes
een eitje (gebakken of gekookt)	an egg (fried or boiled)				

gerechten	dishes
nasi	an indonesian rice dish
pasta met groenten	pasta with vegetables
gehaktballetjes in tomatensaus	meatballs in tomato sauce
Marokkaanse kipschotel	Moroccan chicken dish

tussendoortjes	snacks	**zoetigheid**	confectionery	**dranken**	drinks
zakje chips	bag of crisps	koekje	biscuit	thee	tea
patat/friet	chips/fries	gebakje	cake	koffie	coffee
fruit	fruit	stroopwafel	toffee waffle	frisdrank	soft drink
sinaasappels	oranges	gevulde koek	almond cake/ biscuit	wijn	wine
aardbeien	strawberries	appelgebak	apple pie	bier/pils	beer/lager
		taart	cake		

specifiek Vlaamse woorden	specific Flemish words
pistolet	roll
croque monsieur	toasted sandwich
hesp	ham
smos kaas/ hesp	baguette with cheese or ham with lettuce, tomato and egg
patisserie	luxury cakes and tarts
pint(je)	beer, lager

Oefening 3

Re-enact the following dialogue three times, substituting the underlined vocabulary depending on what meal you are eating.

Nienke	Mag ik de melk even?
Harry	De melk is op.
Nienke	Hmmm. Ik neem wel brood.
Harry	Sorry, ook op.
Nienke	Wat is er dan wel?
Harry	Kaas. En aardbeienjam.

Do this for breakfast, lunch and dinner.

Oefening 4

You can do this exercise in pairs or on your own. You (and your partner) have invited some friends for dinner. Create a menu of what you'd like to cook and make a shopping list of the items you need to buy to cook the dishes you have selected. Make use of websites for inspiration about dishes and finding out the names of the ingredients. You can use www.ah.nl and click on **eten & drinken** and then on **recepten** 'recipes'. You should also use a good and up-to-date dictionary. For more recipe ideas you can do a search using (**hollandse**) **gerechten** or **recepten** as search terms.

Communicatie

1 VRAGEN OM MEER *ASKING FOR MORE*

Is/zijn er nog . . .?	Is there/are there still . . .?
Nee, er is/zijn geen . . . meer.	No, there is/are no more . . .
Is er geen . . . meer?	Is there no more . . .?
Nee, de/het . . . is/zijn op.	The . . . is/are finished.

Example

Is er nog kaas?	Nee, er is geen kaas meer/Nee, de kaas is op.
Zijn er nog aardappelen?	Nee, er zijn geen aardappelen meer/ De aardappelen zijn op.

2 VRAGEN OM IETS *ASKING FOR SOMETHING*

Mag ik de melk even?
Could you pass me the milk, please?

Mag ik een koffie?
Could I have a coffee, please?

Both questions ask for something, yet their respective meaning differs through the use of the word **even.** In this context **even** makes the question more polite and also assumes that you are asking for something to be passed to you. When you order in a restaurant you would simply say: **Mag ik een pilsje?** Alternatively you could say:

Een koffie, alstublieft.

Compare

Mag ik een glas melk?
Could I have a glass of milk, please?

Mag ik de koffie even?
Could you pass me the (pot of) coffee, please?

Oefening 5: Work in pairs

You are encouraging your guests to have a little more of the dishes you (virtually) prepared in the previous exercise. Use the following phrase:

Wil je nog een beetje (wijn/saus/pasta/couscous/etc.)?

The guest can accept or decline gracefully:

Ja, graag.	OR:	**Een klein beetje, graag.**
Nee, dank je.	OR:	**Nee, dank je, ik zit vol.**
	OR:	**Nee, dank je. Het was lekker.**

Key vocabulary

een klein beetje	just a little	**ik zit vol**	I'm full
graag	please	**nee, dank je**	no thanks
het was lekker	it was nice	**de saus**	sauce

Note that the expression 'ik zit vol' is very common in the Netherlands, but sounds rather rude in Belgium.

Oefening 6

The meal was clearly delicious and all the food has been finished. But the guests would love to have a little more. Act out a few dialogues with your partner using the following phrases:

Is er nog een beetje . . . / Zijn er nog wat . . . / Mag ik nog wat . . .?
Sorry, de . . . is op. / Er is geen . . . meer. / Er zijn geen . . . meer.

Oefening 7

Write out two different dialogues based on the two previous exercises. Each of the dialogues should contain some encouragement from you, as the host, to urge your guests to have a little more food. Each of the dialogues should also contain at least one question from one of your guests asking for some more.

Oefening 8

1 Take turns with your partner to place your order in a restaurant and, respectively, to ask for something to be passed to you at the dinner table.

Iets bestellen in een restaurant 'Ordering something in a restaurant'	**Thuis aan tafel** 'At home during the meal'
1. een pilsje	de rijst
2. nummer 72 (bij een Chinees restaurant)	de kroepoek/de ketjap
3. de [name of dish]	de sla
4. een sapje	de wijn
5. een Italiaans bolletje	het zout

2 Write out your orders and your questions during the mealtime.

Structuren

NUMBERS OVER 100

Tellen boven de 100

101	honderdeen	2000	tweeduizend
102	honderdtwee	10 000	tienduizend
150	honderdvijftig	100 000	honderdduizend
200	tweehonderd	1000 000	een miljoen
1000	duizend	1000 000 000	een miljard

Oefening 9: In pairs or groups

Take turns to count up or down:

1 from 105 to 120
2 from 275 to 260
3 from 1986 to 1999

ORDINAL NUMBERS

1e	eerste	11e	elfde	22e	tweeëntwintigste
2e	tweede	12e	twaalfde	34e	vierendertigste
3e	derde	13e	dertiende	51e	eenenvijftigste
4e	vierde	14e	veertiende	87e	zevenentachtigste
5e	vijfde	15e	vijftiende	100e	honderdste
6e	zesde	16e	zestiende	101e	honderd(en)eerste
7e	zevende	17e	zeventiende	120e	honderd(en)twintigste
8e	achtste	18e	achttiende	730e	zevenhonderd(en)dertigste
9e	negende	19e	negentiende	1000e	duizendste
10e	tiende	20e	twintigste	1000.000e	miljoenste

Oefening 10

Below is a list of the placings some local school children achieved at a district sports competition. As you are the editor of the school magazine you write out where each of the pupils ranked in the competition.

Example

Anna Bruin (2)
Anna Bruin kwam tweede.

1 Mieke Host (5)
2 Nina Vogel (7)
3 Bas Arend (11)
4 Jenny Dewitte (17)
5 Ron Waterman (23)
6 Wim Cosemans (48)
7 Peter van de Velde (52)

Oefening 11

Ask your fellow students what day of the month their birthdays are. Then write out each of them.

Example

Nicola is jarig op de zestiende.
John is jarig op de eenendertigste.

GEEN/NIET

To make a sentence negative you would normally use either **niet** or **geen.**

niet	not
geen	not any/not a/no

You use **geen** when you refer to an indefinite noun (i.e. a noun which refers to something general rather than something specific). In all other situations you use **niet**:

Ik ga niet naar huis.	I am not going home.
Ik heb geen geld.	I have no money.
Ik drink geen alcohol.	I don't drink any alcohol.
Ik drink die wijn niet.	I don't drink that wine.

Oefening 12

Ask one another the following questions and answer in the negative with either **niet** or **geen** as appropriate.

1 Heb je veel geld?
2 Drink je nu wijn?
3 Eet je hagelslag op brood?
4 Werk je hard?
5 Ga je naar huis?
6 Mag ik een koffie?
7 Kijk je naar voetbal?
8 Heb je een auto?
9 Woon je in Haarlem?
10 Werk je bij een modebedrijf?

Communicatie

TONE

A tone of voice can also be reflected in writing. There are no rules for which words express which tone; we can only recognise a tone, e.g. annoyed, unfriendly or rude in context. In the context of the dialogue in Tekst 1 **alweer** indicates Nienke is annoyed. And in the same context **Dan moet je maar vroeger opstaan** indicates that Harry doesn't really care about Nienke's breakfast. In fact, he implies it's her own fault anyway: she should have got up earlier.

The short conversation between Nienke and Harry would have carried a more friendly tone if Nienke had asked something like:

Is er geen melk meer? O, wat jammer.
Is there no milk any more? What a shame.

Harry would have shown a bit more sympathy if he had said:

Neem dan wat anders, joh.
Why don't you take something else?

Or:

Misschien kun je iets anders nemen?
Maybe you can take something else?

Note that **Joh** tends to emphasise a sense of a bond between friends. English equivalents would be 'man', 'mate', 'girl', 'baby' depending on the context.

Oefening 13: Work in pairs

You and your partner are in a bad mood and you take it in turns to complain and give one another brusque advice. First listen to the recording and then read out the following exchanges, taking care to use the appropriate tone and expression. Create a piece of drama out of it by exaggerating as much as you can.

Partner 1	*Partner 2*
Er is alweer geen koffie.	Dan moet je maar koffie kopen.
Ik heb alweer een slecht cijfer.	Dan moet je maar hard werken.
Ik heb alweer een pukkel op mijn gezicht.	Dan moet je maar Clearasil gebruiken.
De treinen waren alweer vertraagd vandaag. En ik was dus weer te laat op mijn werk.	Dan moet je maar vroeger van huis gaan.
Ik ben alweer natgeregend.	Dan moet je maar een paraplu meenemen.

Key vocabulary

het cijfer	mark	**de pukkel**	spot
gebruiken	to use	**slecht**	bad
het gezicht	face	**te laat**	too late
kopen	to buy	**de trein**	train
meenemen	to take with you	**vertraagd**	delayed
natgeregend zijn	to be wet/soaked	**vroeger**	earlier
de paraplu	umbrella		

Oefening 14

1 Now do the same again, but think about 'complaints' and advice yourself. Use a dictionary if needed.

2 Write out at least 3 of the dialogues you have created.

Oefening 15

Act out the situations of **Oefening 13** again, but this time you speak in a friendlier and more supportive manner. Listen to the recording first. Again make it as expressive as you can by exaggerating the tone of voice.

Partner 1	*Partner 2*
Er is geen koffie.	Neem wat anders, joh. Kun je niet wat anders nemen?
Ik heb een slecht cijfer.	O jee, hoe komt dat?
Ik heb een pukkel op mijn gezicht.	O jee, doe er wat make-up op. Misschien kun je er wat make-up op doen?
Ik was alweer te laat op mijn werk.	Misschien moet je iets vroeger opstaan?
Ik ben alweer natgeregend.	Kun je geen paraplu meenemen?

Key vocabulary

hoe komt dat?	how come?
o jee	oh dear
opstaan	to get up in the morning

Oefening 16

Look at the situations you created in **Oefening 14** and create dialogues in which you are supportive rather than too direct. Write out these dialogues.

Communicatie

SMALL WORDS WITH BIG MEANINGS

In real-life communication we often use small words, modal particles, which can subtly change the meaning of what you're trying to say. The meaning of these words depends largely on the context in which you use them, and they are particularly important in creating a certain tone. They can make you sound more polite or annoyed, or they can help to 'oil' the conversation. They can help to establish contact, or they make an order into a question, or the other way round. They can also emphasize or even de-emphasize something. When used appropriately, these words will make you sound more authentic, so it is important to be aware of them and use them when you can. Sometimes these words can only be conveyed in English through a change in your tone of voice.

Oefening 17

Listen to the following words and how they can change the whole intonation of the sentence. How do you think you would convey this in English?

1	**wel**	
	Wat is er dan?	Wat is er dan **wel**?
2	**nu**	
	Dat is de tweede keer.	Dat is **nu** de tweede keer.
3	**maar**	
	Dan moet je een paraplu meenemen.	Dan moet je **maar** een paraplu meenemen.
4	**even**	
	Mag ik de ketjap?	Mag ik de ketjap **even**?

Oefening 18

The word **wel** can indicate a myriad of meanings. In the conversation between Nienke and Harry it is used three times, and each time with a different meaning. Listen again to the dialogue and see whether you can figure out from the tone of voice which of the meanings below were intended, by linking the two columns. How would you convey that same meaning in English?

1	Dan is er nog wel een vol pak melk.	a	To express acceptance
2	Ik neem wel brood.	b	To emphasize contrast with a touch of impatience
3	Wat is er dan wel?	c	To emphasize contrast

Oefening 19

The words **nu** and **maar** also can indicate various meanings. What do you think they mean in Tekst 1? Choose from the list below, but note that not all the meanings given in the box are appropriate in this context. How would you convey the appropriate meaning in English?

to emphasise contrast   to express irritation   to express doubt to soften a statement   to give brusque advice

1 Dat is nu de tweede keer deze week.
2 Dan moet je maar vroeger opstaan.

Tekst 2 Een stel op zaterdagochtend

Listen to the dialogue of this couple. What is their main topic of conversation?

Jenny	We moeten vandaag echt het huis weer eens schoonmaken. 't Is zo'n troep! Wat doe jij liever? Stofzuigen of de badkamer schoonmaken?
Mark	Sorry hoor, ik moet de stad in. Ik heb nieuwe sportschoenen nodig.
Jenny	Ja, dus ik kan het weer mooi in m'n eentje doen. Ik ben ook altijd de pineut!
Mark	Weet je wat? Ik neem je vanavond mee uit eten. Dan hoef je niet te koken.
Jenny	*Jij* neemt *mij* mee uit eten? En wie betaalt?
Mark	Wat maakt dat nou uit? We doen toch alles samen?

Key vocabulary

alles	everything
altijd	always
de badkamer	bathroom
betalen	to pay
in m'n eentje	on my own
koken	to cook
liever (doen)	rather; prefer to (do)
mee uit eten nemen	to take out for dinner
niet hoeven	not having to
nieuw	new
nodig hebben	to need
de pineut zijn	to be the one to suffer
samen	together
schoonmaken	to clean
de sportschoenen	trainers
de stad in	up to/down town
het stel	couple
stofzuigen	to do the vacuum cleaning
vanavond	tonight
vandaag	today
wat maakt dat nou uit?	what difference does that make?
zaterdagochtend	Saturday morning
zo'n troep	such a mess

Oefening 20

Read the dialogue aloud several times and keep on practising, taking great care over the intonation till you feel you sound authentic.

Vragen bij tekst 2

(a) Answer questions 1–4 in Dutch. The start of each answer has already been given.

1 Waarom wil Jenny het huis schoonmaken? Het is ____________

2 Wat gaat Mark doen? Hij moet ____________

3 Hoe zie je dat Jenny het huis niet in haar eentje wil schoonmaken? — Zij zegt: ik ben ook ______________

4 Hoe wil Mark het goedmaken met Jenny? — Hij neemt Jenny ______________

goedmaken	to make up	**willen**	to want
waarom	why		

(b) The dialogue between Jenny and Mark, though a little stereotypical, contains many assumptions and implied messages. Jenny and Mark convey these as much through *what* they say as through *how* they say it and the tone they use. The questions below are meant to make you think about this. Discuss the questions in small groups.

1 Does Jenny seek Mark's opinion on whether to clean the house today? Explain your answer.

2 Mark doesn't state explicitly that he doesn't want to do the cleaning. How does he convey the impression that he will not take part in this?

3 How can you tell that both Mark and Jenny assume that she will be the one to do the cleaning on her own? Explain your answer by referring to what they say.

4 Which words and sentences give you the idea that Jenny is responsible for domestic tasks in general?

5 What can you say about Jenny and Mark's different interpretations about equality?

Tekst 3 Een moeder en haar zoons op zaterdagochtend

Listen to this dialogue between a mother and her sons. Are the boys cooperative?

Marian	Kees, doe jij de afwas?
Kees	Maar ik moet altijd afwassen. Waarom kan Jasper het niet doen?
Marian	Jasper kan papa helpen met de zolder opruimen.
Jasper	Wat? Nee hoor, ik ga met Patrick en Michel de stad in. Dat heb ik gisteren afgesproken.

Key vocabulary

de afwas doen	to do the dishes
dat heb ik gisteren afgesproken	I arranged that yesterday
gisteren	yesterday
de moeder	mother
opruimen	to clear/tidy up
papa	dad
de zolder	the attic
de zoon	son

Oefening 21

Read the dialogue out loud several times and keep on practising, taking great care with the intonation till you feel you sound authentic.

Vragen bij tekst 3

Answer the questions below in Dutch. The start of each answer has already been given.

1 Waarom wil Kees de afwas niet doen?
Hij moet ______________

2 Wat wil Marian dat Jasper doet vandaag?
Jasper kan ______________

3 Waarom wil Jasper de zolder niet opruimen?
Hij gaat ______________

Communicatie

MEER KLEINE WOORDJES (MORE SMALL WORDS (MODAL PARTICLES))

Modal particles are very difficult to learn, especially because these small words can have many different meanings, depending on the context. The exercise below lists some more frequently used modal particles, although only one context is given, so only one meaning is referred to. At this stage you don't have to be able to use these words correctly, it simply helps if you are aware of them. It might help if you learn these words initially in relation to the context and situation where you encountered them. Gradually you will feel more confident in using them and you will enjoy sounding more authentic.

Oefening 22

Listen to the intonation of these particles in the sentences listed below. Repeat these sentences until you have really got the intonation right.

1	**echt** **Ik moet nu echt weg.**	I really need to go now.
2	**weer** **Ik kan het dus weer in m'n eentje doen.**	So I can do it on my own, again!
3	**hoor** **Sorry hoor!**	So sorry!
4	**hoor** **Nee hoor.**	No, not at all./Don't worry.
5	**toch** **We doen toch alles samen?**	But we're doing everything together, aren't we?

Oefening 23

What do you think the modal particles in the sentences above add to the meaning? Choose from the following:

> to add a sense of urgency
> to reassure the other speaker after a yes/no question
> to show an expectation that the other speaker will agree
> to show irritation
> to sound more friendly or chummy

Structuren

WORD ORDER IN QUESTIONS AND INVERSION

Yes/no question

When asking a yes/no question, you simply reverse the word order of subject and finite verb. The subject comes after the finite verb. This reverse word order is called: inversion.

Mag ik de melk even?	Can you pass me the milk, please?
Doe jij de afwas?	Will you do the dishes?

Note that you need to drop the **-t** at the end of the verb when you reverse **je/jij** with the verb. This only happens with **je/jij**:

Jij komt morgen.	You are coming tomorrow.
Kom jij morgen?	Are you coming tomorrow?

Oefening 24

Change these statements into questions using the same subject.

Example

Bert komt ook naar het feestje.
Komt Bert ook naar het feestje?

1 Natalie heeft een pukkel op haar gezicht.
2 Stefan is niet echt aardig.
3 Daan werkt bij een computerbedrijf.
4 Jij neemt Jenny mee uit eten.
5 Ze doen alles samen.
6 Jij doet het huishouden in je eentje.
7 Papa ruimt morgen de zolder op.
8 Ik kook graag Indonesische gerechten.
9 Jij bent alweer te laat op je werk.
10 Wij gaan lekker uit eten vanavond.

Oefening 25

Change these questions into statements using the same subject.

Example

Betaal jij?
Jij betaalt!

1 Kom je morgen?
2 Vind je spontaniteit belangrijk?
3 Zit je nog op school?
4 Heb je vaak heimwee?
5 Heb je veel ervaring?
6 Is Jaap verantwoordelijk voor de administratie?
7 Heeft Anouska goede communicatieve vaardigheden?
8 Gebruik je veel make-up?
9 Ben je alweer natgeregend?
10 Sta je vroeg op?

Questions starting with a question word

In open-ended questions the question word is followed by the finite verb and then the subject. In other words, inversion also takes place in these kind of questions:

Wie heeft gewonnen?
Who has won?

Wat doe jij zaterdag?
What are you doing on Saturday?

Waar ligt Amsterdam?
Where is Amsterdam?

Hoe kom je naar de universiteit? Met de bus of met de trein?
How do you get to the university? By bus or train?

Waarom kan Jasper het niet doen?
Why can't Jasper do it?

Wanneer begint de les?
When does the lesson start?

Welke kleur vind je mooi? Rood of groen? [*de* kleur]
Which colour do you like? Red or green?

Welk boek lees je? [*het* boek]
Which book are you reading?

Oefening 26

Fill in the correct question word in the questions below.
Choose from the box below.

wie wat waar hoe wanneer welke waarom

1	______________ is de koningin van Nederland?	Koningin Beatrix.
2	______________ groot ben jij?	Ik ben 1.72m.
3	______________ is mijn pen?	In je tas.
4	______________ begint de voorstelling?	Om 8 uur.
5	______________ studeer je Nederlands?	Mijn vriendin is Nederlands.
6	______________ sport vind jij het leukst?	Voetbal.
7	______________ is de hoofdstad van Vlaams Brabant?	Leuven.

Key vocabulary

groot	big
de hoofdstad	capital city
de koningin	queen
om 8 uur	at 8 o'clock
de tas	bag
de voorstelling	performance

Oefening 27

Take turns asking the following questions. Your fellow students have to answer with simple statements. You can make this into a quiz. The first person to answer correctly gets a point.

1 Wat is de hoofdstad van Nederland?
2 Wie is de president van Frankrijk?
3 Wie is de premier van het Verenigd Koninkrijk?
4 Welke film heeft dit jaar de oscar voor beste film gewonnen?
5 Wanneer is het oudejaarsavond?
6 Welke schilder schilderde zonnebloemen?

Key vocabulary

dit jaar	this year
gewonnen	won
de oudejaarsavond	new year's eve
de premier	prime minister
de schilder	painter
schilderde	painted
de zonnebloem	sunflower

Oefening 28

Ask the questions which might lead to the following answers using either a question word question or a yes/no question as appropriate.

Example

Ik zoek intimiteit en een beetje magie.
Wat zoek je (in een relatie)?

1 Ik werk bij een exportbedrijf.
2 Rutger woont in Almere.
3 Nee, hij woont in een vrij klein huis.
4 Ik wil een lieve hond.
5 Ja, ik heb zelfs vrij veel ervaring met computers.
6 Nee, ik hou niet echt van koken.
7 Nee, Sam is niet echt arrogant, maar hij heeft wel erg veel zelfvertrouwen.
8 Nee, hij krijgt niet altijd hoge cijfers. Soms zijn zijn cijfers heel slecht.

veel zelfvertrouwen hebben	to have a lot of self confidence

Inversion in statements

Inversion doesn't only occur in questions, but also in statements. If a sentence starts with any word other than the subject, there will automatically be an inversion of the finite verb position and the subject position:

Dan moet je maar vroeger opstaan.	Then you'll have to get up early.
Dan hoef je niet te koken.	Then you won't have to cook.

Note that the finite verb remains in second position in the sentence.

Oefening 29

Rewrite the following sentences, starting with the word(s) given in brackets.

Example

Jij moet wat aardiger zijn tegen je vriendin. (voortaan)
Voortaan moet je wat aardiger zijn tegen je vriendin.

1	Ik hou niet van scherp eten.	(meestal)
2	Wij ontbijten altijd in de keuken.	(vanaf morgen)
3	Je moet wat minder drinken.	(misschien)
4	Ik ga naar het feestje van Marleen.	(morgen)
5	Je komt ocht?	(straks)

Key vocabulary

meestal	mostly	**straks**	in a little while
ontbijten	to have breakfast	**vanaf morgen**	from tomorrow on
scherp	spicy	**voortaan**	from now on

Modal verbs

Modal verbs express meanings such as whether you can, want, must, should or have to do something. Modal verbs are normally combined with another verb, which is put at the end of the sentence in its full infinitive form:

moeten	**Ik *moet* altijd afwassen.**	I always have to do the dishes.
mogen	**Ik *mag* ook nooit wat.**	I am never allowed anything.
willen	***Wil* jij afwassen?**	Do you want to do the dishes?
kunnen	**Jasper *kan* papa helpen.**	Jasper can help dad.
zullen	**Ik *zal* het wel doen.**	I will do it.

However, most modal verbs can also be used on their own, without another verb:

Dat kan.	That's possible.
Dat moet helaas.	That's necessary, unfortunately.

Here are the forms of the modal verbs.

	zullen	*willen*	*kunnen*	*mogen*	*moeten*
ik	zal	wil	kan	mag	moet
je/jij/u	zal/zult	wil/wilt	kan/kunt	mag	moet
hij/zij/het	zal	wil	kan	mag	moet
wij	zullen	willen	kunnen	mogen	moeten
jullie	zullen	willen	kunnen	mogen	moeten
zij	zullen	willen	kunnen	mogen	moeten

Note that:

- The forms **zult**, **wilt** and **kunt** are more formal and used much less often.
- **U** is the polite form of address, both for singular and plural.

Oefening 30

Use the list of activities below to write down statements about what you have, must, can and want to do. Try and use contrasting statements between what you want or can do and what you must do or are (not) allowed to do

You can think up more statements if you like. You can add extra little words to make the statements sound more authentic:

Ik wil straks *eigenlijk* mijn foto's bekijken, maar ik moet *eerst* mijn kamer opruimen.

eigenlijk	actually	**eerst**	first

Activiteiten

de tuin doen	mijn kleren wassen
mijn nieuwe huis schilderen	een souvenir voor mijn moeder uit Namibië meebrengen
een nieuwe computer kopen	voor mijzelf een Afrikaanse drum kopen
eerst mijn collegegeld betalen	een echt Hollands gerecht koken
geen nieuwe boeken meer lenen	een patatje bij de snackbar halen
eerst mijn oude boeken terugbrengen	
naar de kroeg gaan	

Oefening 31

Interview your partner and ask what his/her plans are for the coming week or coming year.

Wat wil hij/zij doen de komende week/komend jaar.
Wat moet hij/zij doen?

Oefening 32

Write a short text about your partner's plans and his/her tasks.

Oefening 33: Wie doet wat bij jou thuis?

Take turns to ask your partner who does what at your home.

Examples

vraag:	**stofzuigen** **Wie stofzuigt bij jou thuis?** **de afwas doen** **Wie doet bij jou thuis de afwas?**
mogelijke antwoorden:	**Dat doe ik alleen.** **Dat doen we samen.** **Dat doet mijn man/zus/vrouw/partner enz.** **Dat doen we om de beurt.**

1	de tuin doen	to do the gardening
2	de was doen	to do the laundry
3	de boodschappen doen	to do the shopping
4	de vuiniszak buiten zetten	to put out the bin/garbage
5	koken	to cook
6	strijken	to iron
7	de vakantie regelen	to arrange the holiday
8	de financiële beslissingen nemen	to take the financial decisions
9	de loodgieter bellen	to phone the plumber
10	de kinderen naar de kinderopvang brengen	to take the children to the nursery/childminder

enz. [enzovoort]	etc., and so on
iets om de beurt doen	to take turns doing something

Oefening 34

Arrange who is going to do what by re-enacting the following dialogue, substituting the underlined words using the vocab lists of activities in previous exercises, or by using a good and up-to-date dictionary.

Example

Wat doe jij liever? **Stofzuigen** of **de badkamer doen**?
Ik **doe de badkamer** wel.

Structuren

SEPARABLE VERBS

Separable verbs are verbs which are made up of two separate words which are sometimes separated.

Examples of separable verbs:

schoonmaken opruimen afwassen meebrengen terugbrengen opbellen uitgaan

When to separate

In the present tense when the separable verb is the finite verb, the two parts are split. The prefix of the separable verb moves to the end of the sentence.

Ik *maak* morgen het huis *schoon*.
Amina *ruimt* altijd haar kamer *op*.
Ik *was* wel *af*.
***Breng* je de boeken vandaag *terug*?**
Jullie *gaan* wel vaak *uit*, hè?

When not to separate

When the separable verb is used as an infinitive, for instance with a modal verb, you do not split the two parts:

Ik moet morgen het huis *schoonmaken*.
Je moet vandaag echt de boeken *terugbrengen*.

Note the following points:

- There are more rules for splitting or not splitting up the separable verb. You will come across these later on in the book in units 4, 8 and 9.
- Not all verbs which seem to be made up of two words are separable, e.g. stofzuigen.

Oefening 35

Fill in the correct form of the separable verb and separate where necessary.

1	Morgen ______________ ik mijn kamer ______________ .	**opruimen**
2	Maar eerst moet ik even ______________ .	**uitrusten**
3	Wanneer ______________ je je moeder ______________ ?	**opbellen**
4	Je moet je geld niet aan die nonsens ______________ .	**uitgeven**
5	______________ je geld toch niet aan die nonsens ______________ .	**uitgeven**
6	Hij ______________ er nog even over ______________ .	**nadenken**
7	Maar hij moet er niet te lang over ______________ .	**nadenken**
8	Ik ga vanavond een nieuw Grieks recept ______________ .	**uitproberen**

9 ______________ jij dan dat Marokkaanse recept ______________ ? **uitproberen**

10 ______________ je de ex-vriendin ook ______________ ? **uitnodigen**

Key vocabulary

nadenken over	to think about	**uitproberen**	to try out
uitgeven	to spend	**uitrusten**	to rest
uitnodigen	to invite		

Oefening 36

(a) **Wie doet wat?**
You have made a list of tasks that need to be done today. Take turns with your partner to suggest you do one task if he/she is doing the other one.

Example

de keuken schoonmaken/afwassen
Ik maak de keuken wel schoon. Was jij dan af?

1 de garage opruimen/de loodgieter opbellen

2 boeken terugbrengen/belastingformulier invullen

3 brief aan de gemeente afmaken/vrienden uitnodigen

het belasting formulier	tax form	**de gemeente**	council

(b) Write out the suggestions you made.

Communicatie

STRAIGHT TO THE POINT

In the Netherlands the tone in which people conduct their everyday communication tends to be fairly direct, the Dutch do not beat about the bush. In Flanders on the other hand, the tendency is to be more polite. Naturally these observations are generalisations and, as in all communities, the tone of how you communicate depends on many different factors, such as who you are talking to and what your relationship is with these people, what you want to achieve, and why you want to achieve that. In the dialogue below, the three friends adopt a less direct tone with one another and they are more cooperative than the dialogues we have seen so far in this unit.

Tekst 4 Drie vriendinnen bereiden een feestje voor

Hanne	Hebben we nog genoeg wijn?
Karin	Ja, Elsa zou 10 flessen kopen.
Elsa	Zou jij dat niet doen?
Karin	Nee, ik heb de kratjes pils gekocht.
Elsa	O jee, wat vervelend. Sorry hoor. Gewoon vergeten. Ik ga dan nu nog even snel naar de Aldi . . . Hebben we nog wat anders nodig?
Hanne	Misschien nog wat meer kaarsen?
Elsa	Ja, of nee . . . waxinelichtjes misschien. OK. Staat op mijn lijstje. Tot zo.

Key vocabulary

de Aldi	*name of a cheap supermarket chain*
gekocht	bought
genoeg	enough
gewoon vergeten	(I) just forgot
de kaars	candle
het kratje pils	crates of beer (lager)
het lijstje	(shopping) list
o jee	oh dear
snel	quickly
tot zo	see you in a bit
voorbereiden	to prepare
de vriendin	female friend
wat vervelend	*here*: oh no/oh dear (*lit*: what a nuisance)
het waxinelichtje	tea light
zou jij dat niet doen?	were you not going to do that?
zou . . . kopen	was going to buy . . .

Oefening 37

Listen to the dialogue above. Is the tone between the three friends curt or cooperative?

Oefening 38

Re-enact the dialogue aloud several times and keep on practising taking great care over the intonation till you feel you sound authentic.

Vragen bij tekst 4

Beantwoord de vragen in het Nederlands. Hou de zinnen heel simpel.

1 Wat zou Elsa kopen?

2 Wie zou dat doen volgens Elsa?

3 Wat heeft Karin gekocht voor het feestje?

4 Wat is Elsa's oplossing voor het probleem?

5 Wat wil Elsa kopen in plaats van kaarsen?

in plaats van	instead of	**volgens**	according to
de oplossing	solution		

Oefening 39

List all the words and expressions in the dialogue that show that the three friends are careful to conduct their conversation in an egalitarian tone.

Oefening 40

You and two of your friends were going to prepare a picnic. Write out the dialogue below in Dutch following the patterns in the text above.

You	1	Ask whether we have enough bread.
André	2	Say yes; Brigitte was going to buy rolls.
Brigitte	3	Ask André whether he wasn't going to do that.
André	4	Say no, you bought the cake.
Brigitte	5	Express your dismay, apologise and say you just forgot.

Communicatie

MEER KLEINE WOORDJES

nog Hebben we **nog** genoeg wijn?

Misschien **nog** wat meer kaarsen?

nu nog even Ik ga dan **nu nog even** snel naar de winkel.

Note that many of the modal particles can be combined and tend to occur in a fixed order in the sentence: **nu/nou nog even**.

Oefening 41

Listen to the intonation in the following sentences. What do you think **nog** adds to the communicative meaning of the statements or questions below? Link the expressions with the meanings in the box. How would you convey the meanings in English?

a to ask for more time
b to indicate you refer back to a previous conversation where this topic was discussed
c to indicate impatience
d to indicate something surpasses expectation
e to indicate it's early (days) yet
f to indicate friendly encouragement.

1 Ben je nou nog niet klaar?
2 Even wachten. Ik moet dit nog afmaken.
3 Heb je hem nog gevraagd voor een avondje uit?
4 Ga nog even bij hem langs.
5 Het was nog leuker dan ik dacht
6 Het is nog maar in een beginstadium.

het beginstadium an early stage of development

TO SAY YOU THOUGHT SOMEONE ELSE WOULD DO IT

Elsa *zou* 10 flessen kopen.

Dat *zou* jij toch doen?

TO ASK SOMETHING POLITELY AND IN A FRIENDLY MANNER

***Zou* jij dat even willen doen?**

***Zou* jij dat even kunnen doen?**

Note that when a modal verb is used as an infinitive and is combined with another infinitive, the modal verb always comes before that other infinitive:

We zullen onze vakantie vroeg *moeten boeken*.

Ik zal mijn huiswerk morgen *kunnen afmaken*.

Oefening 42: Work in pairs

(a) Ask your partner in a friendly way to do a few things for you. Answer, equally nicely, by saying you are too busy.

Example

koffie zetten
Zou jij even koffie willen zetten?
Ik ben nu even bezig, maar ik doe dat straks wel.

1 melk halen
2 dit voor mij nakijken
3 dit voor mij vasthouden
4 die e-mail sturen
5 de wijn kopen
6 kijken of we nog genoeg glazen hebben
7 de vuilniszak buiten zetten

Key vocabulary

het glas (*plural*: **glazen**)	glass	**nog genoeg**	still enough
koffie zetten	to make coffee	**vasthouden**	to hold
nakijken	to check		

(b) Look at the list of domestic chores in Oefening 33. Write out the questions you would ask you partner (again in a friendly way) to do the various chores.

Oefening 43

You and your partner are organising another dinner for some friends. Write out a dialogue between you and your partner in which you ask him/her to do the tasks involved. Use your experience of planning such an event in oefening 4. You can also make use of the vocab below or look up words in the dictionary. Try to vary the answers your partner will give, (e.g. **nee, dank je, sorry hoor**, etc.) but remain polite and friendly to one another.

[de groenten] snijden   de . . . koken   de . . . in de pan doen
de tafel dekken   de kaarsjes aandoen

A closer look

The following texts come from a chat line of a women's magazine, inviting women to respond to the question: who does the chores in your house? As with all chat texts, the style in which these contributions are written is a combination between written and spoken language.

Anneke, 28 jaar

Ik kan heel kort zijn. Niet verdelen, maar uitdelen. Aan het begin van de week deel ik de taken uit. En wat schetst mijn verbazing: het werkt. Hij vindt het fijn zegt-ie: 'Dit is tenminste duidelijk. Jij zegt wat ik moet doen en ik doe het.' Klaar. Probleem opgelost.

duidelijk	clear	**uitdelen**	to distribute
opgelost	solved	**verdelen**	to share
de taak	task	**wat schetst mijn verbazing**	to my own amazement
tenminste	after all		

Ria, 45 jaar

Nou misschien leef ik nog in de middeleeuwen, maar ik doe alles alleen. Ik kook, ik was, ik strijk, ik poets en ik boen. Maar ik vind het niet erg. Hij brengt het inkomen binnen en soms neemt hij een bloemetje voor me mee. Heerlijk toch?

boenen	to scrub/to clean	**de middeleeuwen**	the Middle Ages
het inkomen	income	**poetsen**	to polish/to clean

Lieve, 32 jaar

Mijn man werkt 40 uur en ik 34 uur. Hij helpt behoorlijk in het huishouden. Veel vrienden, collega's en familie vinden dat hij ontzettend veel doet. Maar wij vinden het een eerlijke verdeling. Het is toch redelijk dat je het huishouden samen doet?

behoorlijk	quite a bit	**ontzettend veel**	an awful lot
eerlijk	fair	**redelijk**	reasonable

Vragen bij de tekst

Beantwoord de vragen in het Nederlands, voor zo ver mogelijk.

1 Welke woorden en zinnen in de teksten doen denken aan spreektaal?
2 Hoe komt het volgens Anneke dat haar man huishoudelijke taken doet?
3 Vindt Ria het erg dat ze alles alleen moet doen? Waarom wel/niet?
4 Denk jij dat Lieve en haar man een volkomen gelijke verdeling hebben of heeft één van beiden de verantwoordelijkheid?

één van beiden	one of them	**de verantwoordelijkheid**	responsibility
het erg vinden dat . . .	to be upset by . . .	**volkomen**	completely
de spreektaal	spoken language		

Oefening 44

Rewrite the second sentence of Ria's contribution and use the verb **moeten**. What different feeling does that create in comparison with the original version?

Oefening 45

Bespreek in kleine groepjes wat je eigen situatie is wat betreft het doen van huishoudelijke taken. Bespreek ook wat je ideale situatie is. Stel de volgende vragen:

1 Verdelen jullie de taken eerlijk?
2 Wie deelt de taken uit?
3 Wie doet de taken in jouw ideale situatie?

Communicatie

QUALIFYING SOMETHING

To give extra information about to what degree something is happening, or about how the speaker feels about what is happening, people often use adverbs. These adverbs can be used for toning down or emphasizing the information you are giving.

Toning down

Ik ben daar redelijk tevreden over.
Hij helpt behoorlijk mee.

Mijn cijfers zijn vrij goed.
Dat is enigszins overdreven.

Emphasizing

Hij is ontzettend lief.
Dat is geweldig leuk.

Ik vind dat dat echt niet kan.
Ik ben er verschrikkelijk blij mee.

Lieke is (heel) erg gemotiveerd.

Note that the adverb **enigszins** is quite formal. Most of the adverbs that emphasize something, on the other hand, tend to be used more in spoken than in written language.

Oefening 46

Write a contribution yourself to the chat line in which you discuss who does what in your (fictional) home. Use a direct style of writing similar to that of the other contributions. You might want to use adverbs to emphasise the points you are making. Don't create complicated sentences though: stick to grammar patterns you are familiar with.

Oefening 47

You now want to send your contribution to a newspaper where the same topic is debated. Reading through the text you wrote for the previous exercise, you decide you want to tone some of your statements down. Also make sure that you are using complete sentences, but again, stick to language patterns you know.

Unit 3
Op straat

In this unit you will learn practical functions of everyday activities in the outside world. You will see that even in simple and straightforward conversations and activities such as shopping for clothes, the language you use conveys more than you think.

TOPICS

- Everyday activities
- Referring to days and times
- Shopping
- Money
- Bank holidays
- Countries, inhabitants, languages
- The weather
- Clothes, sizes and prices
- Colours

FUNCTIONS

- Making a telephone call
- Arranging to meet up
- Asking how people are and answering
- Buying a ticket
- Ordering coffee
- Shopping for clothes
- Talking about the weather
- Small talk
- Reading strategies
- Telling the time

GRAMMAR

- Object pronouns
- Use of the adverb **graag**
- **Liggen, zitten, staan, hangen**
- Prepositions
- Expressing the future
- Adjectives
- Infinitive constructions
- Expressing duration

Tekst 1 Bellen naar Rob

Saskia, a 23 year-old actress, who lives in Amsterdam, is calling 24-year-old Rob, who is retraining to be a psychologist and who lives in Tilburg. They used to study together, but haven't seen each other for a while.

Rob	Met Rob.
Saskia	Hoi Rob, met Saskia.
Rob	Goh, Sas, da's lang geleden! Hoe gaat het met jou?
Saskia	Goed! Ja! En met jou?
Rob	Goh, ja, ook goed . . .
Saskia	Zeg, ik kom zaterdag naar Tilburg. Ben jij er 's avonds toevallig?
Rob	Ja, ik ben gewoon thuis. En ik heb nog geen plannen. Zullen we iets afspreken?
Saskia	Nou, weet je, ik was eigenlijk van plan om naar de nieuwe adaptatie van 'Vrijdag' van Hugo Claus te gaan. Mijn vriendin Claudia speelt Jeanne. Heb je zin om mee te gaan?
Rob	Ja, leuk. Reserveer jij de tickets?
Saskia	Doe ik. Ik bel je nog wel zaterdagmiddag.
Rob	OK, prima. Dan zie en hoor ik je zaterdag, daaag!
Saskia	Doeg, tot dan!

Key vocabulary

afspreken	to arrange (to meet)
da's	that's *colloquial speech*
eigenlijk	actually
gewoon	just
goh	*expresses hesitation, surprise*
iets	something
lang geleden	a long time ago
reserveren	to book
thuis	at home
toevallig	coincidental, *here*: by any chance
was van plan	was planning
zin hebben in (iets)/ om (iets te doen)	to feel like something/ doing something

Vragen bij tekst 1

Beantwoord vragen 1 and 2 in het Nederlands.

1 Wanneer komt Saskia naar Tilburg?
2 Wat gaan Saskia en Rob doen?
3 How does Rob react to Saskia's call? Is he happy? How do you know? Do you think they know each other well?

Oefening 1

Work in pairs

(a) Listen to the dialogue a few more times and re-enact it with a fellow student, making sure you capture the right tone and intonation.

(b) Create another dialogue together, using one of the situations below. Write out the dialogue in full and practise the intonation until you get it right.

1 You call an old friend from school or college and arrange to meet up.
2 You call a close friend or your partner and decide what to do this evening.
3 You call an older relative and arrange a visit.

(c) If possible, perform your dialogue in front of your fellow students, who will need to figure out which situation you are acting out.

REFERRING TO DAYS AND WEEKS

maandag
dinsdag
woensdag
donderdag
vrijdag
zaterdag
zondag

eergisteren
the day before yesterday

gisteren
yesterday

vandaag
today

morgen
tomorrow

overmorgen
the day after tomorrow

volgende week
next week

vorige week
last week

de morgen
the morning

's morgens
in the morning

vanmorgen
this morning

de middag
the afternoon

's middags
in the afternoon

vanmiddag
this afternoon

de avond the evening	**'s avonds** in the evening	**vanavond** this evening
de nacht the night	**'s nachts** at night	**vannacht** tonight
	's zaterdags on Saturdays	

Oefening 2

Create mini-dialogues with a fellow student. Try to do this spontaneously, without planning it first.

You phone a friend and say you are coming to town. Ask him or her whether s/he happens to be around and whether s/he fancies doing one of the following:

1 naar de film gaan
2 naar de klasreünie gaan
3 naar een tentoonstelling (van . . .) gaan
4 iets gaan drinken (in . . .)
5 iets gaan eten (in . . .)
6 gaan wandelen in het park

You can use the following phrases:

Heb je zin om ______________ . (**te**+infinitive)?	Do you feel like ______________ (doing something)?
Heb je zin in ______________ (noun)?	Do you feel like ______________ (something)?
Zullen we ______________ (infinitive)?	Shall we ______________ ?
Laten we ______________ (infinitive).	Let's ______________

Then agree and say goodbye.

de klasreünie	class reunion	**wandelen**	to walk
de tentoonstelling	exhibition		

Oefening 3

Kijk naar de agenda van Rob en beantwoord de vragen.

maandag	cursus psychopathologie 2–4u
dinsdag	mama op bezoek 11.30u + lunch [kamer opruimen!]
woensdag	tennissen met Mario 7u
donderdag	therapie 3u
vrijdag	eten met flatgenoten, koken (?!)
zaterdag	Saskia! toneel stadstheater
zondag	uitslapen

1	Wanneer heeft Rob les?	Op ______ , van ______ tot ______
2	Wanneer komt zijn moeder op bezoek?	Op ______
3	Wat gaat hij op dinsdagmorgen eerst doen?	Hij gaat ______
4	Waar gaat Rob naartoe op donderdag?	Hij ______
5	Wat doet hij op vrijdag?	Hij ______ en hij ______
6	Sport Rob?	Ja/nee, hij ______
7	Op welke dag doet hij niets?	Op ______

de agenda	diary
het bezoek	visit
de cursus	course
de flatgenoot	roommate
naartoe	to*
opruimen	to tidy up
sporten	to play sports
het toneel	stage *here*: play
uitslapen	to have a lie-in
van . . . tot	from . . . until . . . *to indicate time span*

* If no place is mentioned when you say you are going somewhere, you need to use **naartoe** instead of **naar**.

EVERYDAY ACTIVITIES

slapen	to sleep
lopen	to walk
luisteren (naar)	to listen (to)
gaan (naar)	to go (to)
winkelen	to shop
praten	to talk
drinken	to drink
denken	to think
lezen	to read
werken	to work
koken	to cook
kijken (naar)	to look (at)
eten	to eat
geven	to give
schrijven	to write

Oefening 4

Interview a fellow student about his/her daily whereabouts. Try and use the verbs you have learned so far. You can of course look up some more in a dictionary, but don't try to use verb forms you haven't studied yet.

You could also write down your answers and have them checked to see whether you have spelled your verbs correctly.

Example

Wat doe je 's zaterdags?
Goh, ik slaap, eet, drink en kijk naar voetbal op TV.

Wat doe je meestal 's avonds?
Ik speel met mijn kinderen en ga vroeg naar bed.

meestal mostly, *here*: usually

Structuren

OBJECT PRONOUNS

	stressed	*unstressed*
Hij geeft *mij (me)* een horloge voor mijn verjaardag.	mij	me
Ik bel *jou (je)* nog op zaterdagmiddag.	jou	je
Ik stuur u die brief morgen.	u	
Ik breng een bos rozen voor *haar (d'r)* mee.	haar	(d'r)
Ik geef *hem ('m)* elke morgen een kus.	hem	('m)
[het boek] Ik geef *het ('t)* morgen aan Karin.	het	('t)
[de krant] Geef *hem* eens hier!	hem	('m)
Denk aan *ons*!	ons	
We geven *jullie* drie minuten om na te denken.	jullie	
Nederlands is een heel moeilijke taal voor *hen (ze)*.	hen	ze

Function

Object pronouns *refer to the object* of a sentence. This could be people, things or ideas.

Form

Most object pronouns in Dutch have both a *stressed* and an *unstressed* form. In writing, people use the stressed forms more often. The unstressed forms are more used in spoken language.

Emphasis and contrast

You also use the *stressed form* if you want to emphasize the person or object you are referring to.

Ik geef *jou* met plezier een cadeautje, maar hij krijgt niets!
I will gladly give you a present, but he doesn't get anything!

Goh, dat is lang geleden, hoe gaat het met *jou*?
Gosh, it's been a long time, how are *you*?

In English, you do this through intonation only 'Hey, how are you?'

Refer to an object

If you are referring to an object, rather than a person, you can use either **het** or **hem** in the singular and **ze** in the plural.

The plural **hen** is only used to refer to people.

	de-words		**het-words**	
singular	hem	Ik koop de auto. Ik koop hem.	het	Ik koop het boek. Ik koop het.
plural	ze	Ik koop de bloemen. Ik koop ze.	ze	Ik koop de boeken. Ik koop ze.

In speech, the demonstrative pronoun **die** is often used instead of **hem** and **ze**.

De nieuwe film van Michael Moore is uit.
Michael Moore's new film has been released.

Ja, *die* wil ik heel graag zien.
Yes, I would love to go and see it.

Oefening 5

Replace the object by an object pronoun in the following sentences.

Example

Ik geef Paul een horloge voor zijn verjaardag.
Ik geef hem een horloge voor zijn verjaardag.

1 Wij wachten al de hele middag op Joris en Karel.
2 Ik ken Karin al acht jaar.
3 Hij heeft het boek bijna uit.
4 Leg je jas maar op de bank.
5 Hij gaat zijn vader roepen.
6 Zij zet de borden op tafel.
7 Dora haalt de kinderen op.
8 Ik schrijf het artikel morgen wel.
9 Jan emailt zijn broer elke dag.
10 Hij doet zijn hemd aan.

een boek uit hebben	to finish a book	**het hemd**	the shirt

Oefening 6

Answer the following questions using an object pronoun.

Example

Wanneer zie je *Rob*? (op zaterdag)
Ik zie hem op zaterdag.

1. Wat koop je voor <u>Rita</u>? (bloemen)
2. Bel je naar <u>je moeder</u>? (ja, morgen)
3. Heb je <u>nieuwe schoenen</u>? (nee, al twee jaar)
4. Ben je een fan van <u>Marco Borsato</u>? (ja, grote fan)
5. Wanneer bezoek je <u>je kinderen</u>? (volgende week zaterdag)
6. Koop je dat cadeautje voor <u>mij</u>? (ja, met plezier)
7. Geloof je <u>de minister</u> of <u>zijn minnares</u>? [pick one]
8. Wat geef je <u>Karel en Jan</u> voor hun verjaardag? (een nieuwe fiets)
9. Lees jij <u>de krant</u>? (ja, elke morgen)
10. Vind je <u>het huis</u> mooi? (ja, heel mooi)

Communicatie

ASKING HOW PEOPLE ARE

There are different ways of asking people how they are and of answering this question, depending on the degree of formality of the situation and how well you know people.

very formal:	Hoe maakt u het?
formal:	Hoe gaat het met u?
neutral:	Hoe gaat het met jou? Hoe gaat het ermee? Hoe gaat het?
informal:	Alles goed? Hoe is 't?

ANSWERING HOW YOU ARE

On a scale from good to bad:

+++	uitstekend/geweldig/fantastisch
++	heel goed/prima
+	goed

±	het gaat wel, zozo
–	niet zo goed/best
– –	slecht

If you want to thank someone for asking you how you are, you can say: **Heel goed, dank je/u**. Generally, a typical casual conversation would go as follows:

Hallo, hoe gaat het (ermee)?
Goed, (dank je,) en met jou?
Ja, prima, dank je.

Oefening 7

Listen to the following short conversations and try to figure out what the relationship is between these people, by looking at pronouns and ways of talking.

Match the dialogues in the first column with the relationships in the second.

1	Hallo Hans, hoe gaat het? Goed joh, en met jou?	(a)	verpleegster 'nurse' en patiënt
2	Goedemorgen meneer Damsma, hoe gaat het met u? Prima Karin, dank je, en met jou?	(b)	twee vrienden in een bar
3	Goedemorgen mevrouw Verschueren, hoe gaat het met u vandaag? Nou ja, kan beter.	(c)	secretaresse en haar baas
4	Dag mevrouw Vermeiren, hoe gaat het met u? Uitstekend, dank u, en met u?	(d)	buren (formeel) 'neighbours'
5	Hoi Mark, alles goed? Gaat wel, gaat wel, jij? Ja, goed ja. Sigaret?	(e)	twee vrienden op straat

Oefening 8

Now listen to the previous dialogues again and the intonation in particular. Next, act them out with another student. You can record them if you like, so you can listen to your own intonation. Did you capture the right tone? It helps if you exaggerate as much as you can.

Tekst 2 Een kaartje kopen

On Saturday morning, Saskia goes to **Amsterdam Centraal Station** to catch the train to Tilburg. Listen to the dialogue without reading the transcript and answer the questions.

Saskia	Een weekend retour Tilburg, graag.
Loketbediende	Dat is €26.10 alstublieft.
Saskia	Ik heb alleen een briefje van €100.
Loketbediende	Geen probleem. Dat is dan €73.90 terug en uw kaartje, alstublieft.
Saskia	Dank u wel, wanneer is de eerstvolgende trein?
Loketbediende	Die vertrekt over 10 minuten van spoor 8.
Saskia	Dank u wel.
Loketbediende	Graag gedaan.

Key vocabulary

eerstvolgende	the first/next
geen probleem	no problem
gepast geld	exact change
graag	here: please
graag gedaan	you're welcome
het kaartje	ticket
over 10 minuten	in 10 minutes
retour	return
het spoor	platform
vertrekken	to leave

Vragen bij tekst 2

Beantwoord vragen 1 tot en met 3 in het Nederlands.

1 Hoe veel kost het kaartje?
2 Heeft Saskia gepast geld?
3 Wanneer en waar vertrekt de trein?
4 How do you say 'please' and 'thank you'?

MONEY (HET GELD)

The currency in Belgium and the Netherlands is the euro. It used to be the **frank** in Belgium and the **gulden** in the Netherlands. There are still a number of expressions in the language relating to this old currency, using words such as **kwartje** (25 cent or one quarter of a guilder) and **dubbeltje** (10 cents). Examples are:

zijn frank valt niet	he doesn't get it
voor een dubbeltje op de eerste rij willen zitten	to want the best for little money
een kwartje voor je gedachten	a penny for your thoughts

If you look up **dubbeltje** and **kwartje** in a monolingual dictionary, you will find many more.

This is how you refer to prices:

€3.50 = drie (euro) vijftig *or* drie en een halve euro
€3.05 = drie (euro) vijf

Oefening 9

You are at **Amsterdam Centraal Station** and you ask about ticket prices. Take turns with a fellow student to play either the salesperson or the traveller, using the price table below. All prices are in euros.

Amsterdam – Tilburg			*Amsterdam – Den Haag*		
	vol	*reductie*		*vol*	*reductie*
enkel	14.60	8.70	enkel	8.90	5.30
retour	26.10	15.60	retour	16.70	10.00
Amsterdam – Groningen			*Amsterdam – Nijmegen*		
	vol	*reductie*		*vol*	*reductie*
enkel	26.00	15.60	enkel	15.30	9.10
retour	37.90	22.60	retour	27.20	16.30

Example

retour Tilburg met reductie

A Hoeveel kost een kaartje naar Tilburg?
B Enkel?
A Nee, retour.

B Heeft u korting?
A Ja, ik ben student.
B Dan is het 15 (euro) zestig, alstublieft.

Note that **korting** is the same as **reductie** and is Dutch for 'discount'.

1 enkel Nijmegen – vol
2 retour Den Haag – vol
3 enkel Groningen – reductie (onder de 18)
4 enkel Tilburg – vol
5 retour Groningen – reductie (student)

If you are travelling to the Netherlands or Belgium and you need more information on the railways, you can find timetables, prices and more on www.ns.nl (Nederlandse Spoorwegen) or www.nmbs.be (Belgische Spoorwegen).

Communicatie

GRAAG

The word **graag** can be used for different functions:

1 to be polite:

Wat wilt u drinken?	What would you like to drink?
Een koffie, graag.	A coffee please.

2 to say you like something:

Ik speel graag piano.	I like playing the piano.

3 in the expression **graag gedaan**, meaning 'you're welcome'/'it's my pleasure'.

Oefening 10

Take turns with your partner in creating mini-dialogues. Respond to the questions or statements below using the word **graag**.

Example

Hou je van sport?
Ja, ik tennis en zwem graag.

1 Wil je iets drinken?
2 [in a bar] Wilt u bestellen?
3 Dank je wel voor je hulp.
4 Wat eet je graag?
5 Wat drink je graag?
6 Wat doe je graag in het weekend?
7 Wat doe je graag 's avonds?
8 Dank u wel.
9 Wilt u melk of suiker in de koffie?
10 Doe je aan sport?

aan sport doen	to play a sport	**bestellen**	to order

Oefening 11

Some more practice with asking questions

Match the question with the correct answer. Think of a few more questions and quiz the general knowledge of your classmates.

1	Waar staat manneken pis?	(a)	Om tien uur.
2	Wanneer begint de film?	(b)	Brussel
3	Ga jij naar Amsterdam?	(c)	Ja, op de Lange Voorhout.
4	Woon jij in Den Haag?	(d)	In Brussel.
5	Wie heeft *Het meisje met de parel* geschilderd?	(e)	Op 25 december.
6	Wat is de hoofdstad van België?	(f)	Nee, naar Brussel.
7	Werk je vaak?	(g)	Een nieuwe fiets.
8	Waar wonen de Toearegs?	(h)	Maxima
9	Kook je graag?	(i)	Nee, alleen op maandag.
10	Wie is de vrouw van kroonprins Willem-Alexander?	(j)	Vermeer
11	Wanneer is het Kerstmis?	(k)	Ja, ik doe het elke dag.
12	Wat wil je voor je verjaardag?	(l)	In de Sahara.

manneken pis	(statue of a peeing boy in the centre of Brussels, more information on www.manneken-pis.com)		
het meisje met de parel	girl with the pearl earring		
schilderen	to paint	**de verjaardag**	birthday

Cultuur

BANK HOLIDAYS IN THE NETHERLANDS AND BELGIUM

Bank Holidays, **feestdagen**, are mostly related to (Christian) religious holidays in both countries. As you can see, Belgium has more official holidays than the Netherlands.

maand	*Nederland*	*België*	
1 **januari**	Nieuwjaar	Nieuwjaar	New Year's Day
februari	–	–	
maart	–	–	
maart/**april**	Goede Vrijdag	–	Good Friday
maart/april	tweede paasdag	paasmaandag	Easter Monday
30 april	Koninginnedag	–	Queen's Birthday
1 **mei**	–	dag van de arbeid	Labour Day
half mei	Hemelvaart	Hemelvaart (40 dagen na Pasen)	Ascension Day
eind mei	tweede pinksterdag	pinkstermaandag (10 dagen later)	Pentecost Monday
juni	–	–	
21 **juli**	–	Nationale Feestdag	National holiday
15 **augustus**	–	Maria-Hemelvaart	Assumption
september	–	–	
oktober	–	–	
1 **november**	–	Allerheiligen	All Saints day
11 november	–	Wapenstilstand	Remembrance day
25 **december**	eerste kerstdag	Kerstmis	Christmas
26 december	tweede kerstdag	–	Boxing Day

Please note that days of the week and months of the year are *not* written with a capital letter.

Oefening 12

Beantwoord vragen 1 tot en met 4 in het Nederlands en stel je medestudenten vragen 6 tot en met 8.

Example

Wanneer is het Kerstmis?
Op 25 december.

1 Wanneer is het Pasen?
2 Wat vieren de Nederlanders op 30 april?
3 Wat vieren de Belgen op 15 augustus?
4 Welke Belgische feestdagen zijn geen Nederlandse feestdagen?
5 Look at your answer to question 4. What impression do you get about values in Belgian society?
6 Zijn Kerstmis en Pasen ook officiële feestdagen in [your country]?
7 Vieren jullie ook andere religieuze feestdagen?
8 Hebben jullie nog andere feestdagen?

andere	other	**vieren**	to celebrate

COUNTRIES, INHABITANTS AND ADJECTIVES

land/regio	*inwoner (man/vrouw)*	*adjectief/taal*
Nederland	Nederlander/Nederlandse	Nederlands
België	Belg/Belgische	Belgisch
Vlaanderen	Vlaming/Vlaamse	Vlaams
Frankrijk	Fransman/Franse	Frans
Groot-Brittannië	Brit/Britse	Brits
Duitsland	Duitser/Duitse	Duits
de Verenigde Staten	Amerikaan/Amerikaanse	Amerikaans
Canada	Canadees/Canadese	Canadees
Australië	Australiër/Australische	Australisch
Engeland	Engelsman/Engelse	Engels
Schotland	Schot/Schotse	Schots
Ierland	Ier/Ierse	Iers
Wales	–	Wels

As you can see, there are no hard and fast rules as to what to call the inhabitants of a country, so you will have to look this up. Some dictionaries (such as Van Dale's *Pocketwoordenboek Nederlands als Tweede Taal*) contain a separate list of all nationalities and related words.

The adjective relating to a country is the same word as the respective language, which always ends in an **-s**.

Although there are male and female words for the inhabitants of a country, many people prefer to use the adjective, simply saying: **Ik ben Nederlands**, instead of: **Ik ben een Nederlander/Nederlandse**.

Oefening 13

Answer the following questions, using the appropriate word, whether it is the name for a country, inhabitant or adjective/language. You may have to look up a few words in a dictionary. Make up some of your own questions to ask your fellow students.

Example

Waar komt Arnold Schwarzenegger vandaan?
Hij komt uit Oostenrijk.

1 Welke taal/talen spreken de Belgen?
2 Wat is de nationaliteit van de popgroep Abba?
3 Waar komt Madonna vandaan?
4 Waar komen de frieten vandaan?
5 Welke talen spreken de Zwitsers?

6 Waar komt ______________ vandaan?
7 Welke taal spreekt ______________ ?
8 Wat is de nationaliteit van ______________ ?
9 Wat is de origine van ______________ ?
10 ______________ ?

Cultuur

DE NEDERLANDSE TAAL

Dutch is spoken by sixteen million Dutch and six million Flemish people. This makes it the tenth language in Europe, after Russian, German, English, Turkish, French,

Italian, Ukrainian, Polish and Spanish. Dutch belongs to the family of Germanic languages and in the language family tree it is related to contemporary German as well as to English.

The Dutch language was standardised in the seventeenth century. One of the most important books to spread this standard language was the 'Statenbijbel' (Dutch authorised version of the Bible), which was translated from the original Greek and Hebrew. The standard language was heavily influenced by the various dialects spoken in Amsterdam, as this was the most dominant and prosperous city at the time. Amsterdam was also rich in dialects from Brabant and Flanders, because some of its wealthy and educated citizens had fled the strict Catholic Spanish rule in the South to settle in the more tolerant North.

Tekst 3 Koffie bestellen

Saskia has arrived in Tilburg and decides to have a coffee first, before going into town to do some shopping and buy theatre tickets. She orders a coffee in a small coffee shop outside the station. Listen to the conversations without reading the text and try to answer the questions below.

Vragen bij tekst 3

Beanwoord vragen1 tot en met 4 in het Nederlands.

1 Wat bestelt Saskia?
2 Neemt ze suiker in haar koffie?
3 Wat vraagt ze aan de ober?
4 Waar praat de man over?
5 Is Saskia interested in his conversation? How do you know?
6 Do you think Saskia is a little bit sarcastic? Explain

ober waiter

Discuss your answers with a fellow student. Then listen again. Did you get all the answers between the two of you?

Saskia	Een koffie en een croissant graag.
Ober	Alstublieft, dat is €3.50 samen.
Saskia	Waar staat de suiker?
Ober	Suiker en melk staan op tafel.

Saskia gaat zitten en drinkt haar koffie. Ze leest de krant. Een man in fietsoutfit komt binnen. Hij gaat zitten aan het tafeltje naast Saskia en begint een praatje.

Man	Mooi weer vandaag, hè?
Saskia	eh, mm . . .
Man	Ja, het weerbericht was nogal slecht; regen, wind, buien. Maar je ziet! Stralende zon, blauwe lucht en geen wolkje te zien! Ideaal fietsweer.
Saskia	Eh, mm. Nou, fijn voor je.
Man	Ja, het weerbericht klopt nooit, hè? Ik ga een dagje fietsen, en jij?
Saskia	Euh, nee, ik niet, nee, ik blijf in Tilburg.

Key vocabulary

binnen	inside
de bui	shower (rain)
de fiets	bicycle
de kast	cupboard
kloppen	to be correct/right
de krant	newspaper
de lucht	air
de melk	milk
de muur	wall
nogal	quite
het praatje	chat
de regen	rain
samen	together
stralend	radiant
de suiker	sugar
de tafel	table
tegen	against
het weer	weather
het weerbericht	weather report
de wind	wind
de wolk	cloud
de zon	sun

Oefening 14

Read or act out the conversation with your partner. Make sure you capture the tone. This will take some practice. Again, exaggeration is the key.

Communicatie

INDICATING WHERE THINGS ARE

Dutch has a preference for using the words **zitten**, **liggen**, **staan** and **hangen** to indicate where things or people are, rather than **zijn**, as you would in English. For example:

Waar is het boek?
Where's the book?

Het ligt op tafel.
It is on the table.

Waar zijn de kinderen?
Where are the kids?

Die zitten op zolder.
They are in the attic.

Waar is de witte wijn?
Where is the white wine?

Die staat in de ijskast.
It is in the fridge.

Waar is de foto?
Where is the picture?

Die hangt aan de muur.
It is on the wall.

So it is all right to use **zijn** in the questions, although it is also perfectly possible to use **zitten/liggen/staan/hangen**. In the answers however, it would sound very odd if you used **zijn**.

PREPOSITIONS

In order to indicate location and place, you need prepositions. As in any language, it is not always easy to know which preposition to use where and, again, a dictionary might come in handy.

Oefening 15

Look at the drawing below and answer the questions. You can work in pairs and take turns in asking and answering.

Example

Waar zijn de servetjes? (de toonbank)
Die staan op de toonbank.

1 Waar is Saskia? (de stoel, de tafel)
2 Waar zijn de kranten? (het rek, de muur)
3 Waar is de kinderstoel? (het raam)
4 Waar is Saskia's tas? (de stoel)
5 Waar is Saskia's mobieltje? (de tas)

de toonbank	counter

Oefening 16

You take a personal object (pen, umbrella, coat, book, etc.) and put it somewhere in the classroom, where it is still visible. You then tell your fellow students you have lost your pen, umbrella etc. and ask them whether they know where it is. Walk around the class to talk to as many people as possible.

Example

Ik ben mijn pen kwijt, waar is hij/die?
I have lost my pen, where is it?

Jouw pen zit in je tas.
Your pen is in your bag.

Tekst 4 Het textielmuseum

Saskia has picked up a leaflet on the Textile museum and she is reading it while drinking her coffee. She would like to visit this museum this Saturday afternoon, is this possible?

Het **Nederlandse Textielmuseum** ligt in het hart van Brabant, in de voormalige textielstad Tilburg. Het museum is gevestigd in een voormalige textielfabriek. U kunt er met de auto of het openbaar vervoer makkelijk komen. Het gezellige stadscentrum met winkels, café's, restaurants, Schouwburg en Concertzaal ligt op loopafstand.

Bezoekadres
Nederlands Textielmuseum
Goirkestraat 96
5046 GN Tilburg
Telefoon algemeen 013 5367 475
Bezoekersinformatie 013 5494 564

Open
Dinsdag tot en met vrijdag van 10 tot 17 uur.
Zaterdag en zondag van 12 tot 17 uur.
Tweede paasdag, tweede pinksterdag, tweede kerstdag en hemelvaartsdag van 12 tot 17 uur.

Gesloten
Elke maandag, eerste paasdag, eerste kerstdag, eerste pinksterdag, koninginnedag, 5 mei en 1 januari.

naar: www.textielmuseum.nl

Key vocabulary

algemeen	general
het centrum	centre
gesloten	closed
gevestigd zijn	to be located
gezellig	nice, pleasant
het hart	heart; centre
de loopafstand	walking distance
makkelijk	easy
het openbaar vervoer	public transport
de stad	city
tot en met	to (and including)
voormalig	former

Vragen bij tekst 4

1 Is het museum open op zaterdagmiddag?
2 Is het museum in de buurt van de Schouwburg?
3 Wat is er nog meer in de buurt?
4 Is het museum open met Kerstmis?
5 Welk nummer bel ik voor meer informatie?

in de buurt	around/near
wat is er nog meer	what else is there?

Communicatie

The information on the textile museum in the previous text was not very hard to decipher. This is due to the fact that you are familiar with this type of text. You know what kind of information it probably holds and where to look for it. So even if you don't know a language at all, it is likely you will still be able to understand a fairly simple leaflet.

This strategy can also be used for different types of text. It is therefore important to know what kind of publication a text comes from and who it is aimed at. This context, together with the title and subtitles will give you an idea of what the text is about.

When you read a text in a foreign language, you should always try to get a general idea of the context first. In the case of a short article, such as the one you will read next, the best thing to do is to read through the whole thing first, before looking up any words.

There is a Belgian newspaper, called *Wablieft*, which is aimed at people with reading difficulties. The language is fairly easy. You can read this weekly newspaper on the website http://bop.vgc.be/tijdschriften/wablieft/.

Oefening 17

Read the following short article, which is taken from *Wablieft*. Look for familiar words but don't try to understand every single word! Read through the whole text a few times, before looking at the vocabulary. Then discuss with your fellow students – in English – what you think the text is about. Together you will be able to make sense of it.

Broodje Vet

Elke dag hamburgers van McDonald's eten is ongezond. Dat wou een man uit Amerika bewijzen. Daarom at hij elke dag een hamburger met frieten als ontbijt. 's Middags lag er nog eens hetzelfde op zijn bord. En 's avonds nog eens. Dat hield hij een maand vol. De man maakte er een film van. In die maand werd hij 11,5 kilo dikker. Hij kreeg in die tijd 13,5 kilo suiker binnen. En 5,5 kilo vet. Zijn dokter was ongerust. Want de man werd er echt ziek van. Heel wat mensen gingen naar de film kijken in Amerika. Maar McDonald's was woest. 'Deze man overdrijft. En dat is altijd fout', zei het bedrijf.

uit: Wablieft, juli 2004

Key vocabulary

bewijzen	to prove	**overdrijven**	to exaggerate
het broodje	sandwich	**vet**	fat
dikker	fatter	**volhouden**	to keep up
hetzelfde	the same	**woest**	furious
ongerust	worried	**wou**	wanted
ongezond	unhealthy	**ziek**	ill

This text makes use of the past tense. Even though you haven't dealt with this yet, this doesn't stop you from understanding the general gist.

Oefening 18

1 Have a look at the *Wablieft* website and look for a short article that interests you. Use the same strategy as you did earlier.

2 Bring this article to class and discuss what you found hard about it. You can then exchange strategies about how to deal with obstacles.

3 Tell your fellow students a few lines about your article, in Dutch. You start with:

Dit artikel gaat over _______________ This article is about _______________

4 Write a short summary in Dutch. When you write, it is important to stick to what you know. So write in the present tense and keep it simple.

Tekst 5

IN DE KLEDINGZAAK (1)

Saskia is strolling around the city centre and she passes a traditional looking clothes shop. It is not the kind of shop she would usually buy clothes in, but she is tempted by a big sign saying **uitverkoop**. She has seen a pair of trousers that she likes. Does she buy them in the end?

Listen to the text without looking at your book. Check your answer with another student and then listen again.

Saskia	Pardon mevrouw, hebt u deze broek ook in een maat 40? Hier hangen alleen 38'jes.
Verkoopster	Ja, een ogenblikje. . . . Ziezo, hier is een 40. Wilt u hem passen?
Saskia	Ja, maar ik kijk nog even rond. Ik zoek eigenlijk ook nog een leuk T-shirt of een topje voor de zomer.
Verkoopster	We hebben hele mooie linnen bloezen in aardekleuren, die staan mooi bij die broek. Eens kijken, ja, hier is nog een maatje 40 in bruin en beige. Wilt u die passen?
Saskia	Ja, waar zijn de paskamers?
. . .	
Verkoopster	En? Zitten ze goed?
Saskia	Mmm, de broek is een beetje groot, maar de bloes past perfect. Hoeveel kost die?
Verkoopster	De bloezen kosten nu maar €18, ze zijn afgeprijsd van €25.
Saskia	Mmm, ik denk er nog even over na.

Key vocabulary

afprijzen	to reduce in price	**mooi**	beautiful/pretty
alleen	only	**het ogenblik**	moment
de bloes	the blouse	**de paskamer**	changing room
de broek	trousers	**passen**	to try on/to fit
bruin	brown	**rondkijken**	to look around
goed zitten	to fit nicely/comfortably	**staan bij**	to match
ik denk er nog even over na	I'll think about it	**het topje**	top
de kleur	the colour	**de uitverkoop**	sale
de maat	the size	**zoeken**	to look for

IN DE KLEDINGZAAK (2)

Saskia passes another shop. Loud music is streaming outside. Again this is not her usual kind of shop, but she is nevertheless tempted to go inside. She tries to attract the attention of the female shopping assistant who seems to be engaged in deep conversation with a young man. Does she buy the trousers in this shop?

Saskia	Hallo . . . eeh . . . hallo . . . Heb je deze broek ook in een 40?
Verkoopster	. . . (*She looks Saskia up and down*) Veertig? Weet je het zeker?
Saskia	Eh ja, ik draag meestal een 40.
Verkoopster	O, ik zal er een voor je zoeken. Nee, we hebben ze niet meer in 40. Hier heb je wel een 42. O, en kijk, een maat 44.

Saskia past de broeken.

Verkoopster	En? . . . zitten ze goed?
Saskia	Ja, ik neem deze.
Verkoopster	(*Speaking loudly*) Toch de 44 hè? Zie je nou wel!

Key vocabulary

dragen	to wear	**zal**	shall
maat 40	[UK] size 12, [US] size 10	**zeker weten**	to know for sure
meestal	mostly	**zie je nou wel!**	see? I knew it!
toch	after all		

Vragen bij tekst 5

1 List the differences in how the two shop assistants approach Saskia and how she approaches them.

2 Who comes across as the stronger person in the customer–salesperson relationship in each dialogue? How come? Refer to the actual language used.

Kleren

de das	tie	**de rok**	skirt
het hemd	shirt	**het pak/het kostuum**	suit
het T-shirt	t-shirt	**de jurk**	dress
de trui	jumper	**de jas**	coat
de schoenen	shoes	**de sokken**	socks
het ondergoed	underwear		

Oefening 19

1 Listen to the two dialogues above a few times.

2 When you feel confident with the phrases and the different styles, team up with another student and write your own dialogue, using one of the situations below.

(a) a male customer with the saleswoman in the second dialogue;
(b) a critical salesman and an intimidated customer;
(c) a pedantic customer and a shy salesperson.

Make sure you are aware of your role when you are writing and performing.

3 If possible, perform your dialogue in front of your fellow students who will need to figure out which situation you have chosen.

Structuren

TALKING ABOUT THE FUTURE

The most common way of talking about the future is by using the *present tense*:

Ik *blijf* gewoon thuis deze zomer.	I will just stay at home this summer.
Ik *speel* morgenmiddag tennis.	I will play tennis tomorrow afternoon.
Wij *zijn* volgende week niet thuis.	We won't be at home next week.

You can also use a form of **gaan** + *infinitive*. The infinitive will then take the final position in the sentence.

Wat *ga* je morgen *doen*?
Ik *ga* mijn tante in Utrecht *bezoeken*.

Wat *ga* je in het weekend *doen*?
Ik *ga* uitslapen en lekker *ontbijten*.

Finally you can use a form of **zullen** + *infinitive*. The infinitive will take the final position in the sentence. Although this is the future tense 'proper', it is not used very often. It also carries the meaning of a suggestion, an intention or a promise as you can see in the examples below.

Zullen we een datum afspreken?
Shall we set a date?

Ik zal mijn best doen.
I'll do my best.

Oefening 20

Fill in the correct form of **gaan** and select an appropriate infinitive to fit the following sentences.

bezoeken kijken doen werken lezen uitslapen studeren winkelen drinken

Paul en Linda zijn studenten en flatgenoten. Het is donderdagavond en zij zijn thuis.

Paul	Heb je al plannen voor het weekend? 1 _______ je iets spannends _______ ?
Linda	2 Ik _______ mijn ouders in Tilburg _______ en een beetje _______ voor mijn examens.
Paul	3 Ja, ik _______ ook _______ . Ik heb geld nodig voor mijn vakantie. 4 Ik _______ vrijdagavond een pilsje _______ met wat vrienden en zaterdagmorgen _______ ik _______ . Blijf je heel het weekend in Tilburg?
Linda	Ja, ik kom maandag terug. 5 Ik _______ dan _______ want ik heb een nieuwe jas nodig.
Paul	Mmm. 6 Ik _______ nog een beetje _______ .
Linda	7 Ik ben te moe voor een boek, ik _______ nog wat TV _______ in mijn kamer.
Paul	Slaapwel.

kamer	room	**spannend**	exciting
nodig hebben	to need	**thuis**	at home
slaapwel	sleep well/goodnight		

Note that **slaapwel** is common in Flanders, in the Netherlands people use the expression **welterusten**.

Oefening 21

Interview a fellow student about his or her plans for the weekend or the holidays. Then tell the rest of the class what s/he is going to do.

Example

Wat ga jij in het weekend doen / in de vakantie doen?
Ik ga naar Oxfordshire, mijn ouders bezoeken, en jij?
Ik blijf in Londen dit weekend.

Hij gaat zijn ouders in Oxfordshire bezoeken.
Zij blijft in Londen.

THE ADJECTIVE

de leuke film	**een leuke film**	**de film is leuk**
het goede boek	**een goed boek**	**het boek is goed**

You add an **-e** to the adjective if it is placed before the noun, as you can see above. The only instance when you don't add an **-e** is when a '**het**-word' is used with the indefinite pronoun **een**.

Note that adjectives referring to materials always end in -en. For example: een leren handtas, een gouden ring, de wollen trui, een linnen broek, het zijden hemd.

Oefening 22

Fill in the correct form of the adjective. Don't forget to check the spelling!

1 'De ________ prins' is een populair boek voor kinderen. — klein
2 Ik heb ________ ________ schoenen voor vanavond. — mooi rood
3 Designerkleren zijn heel ________ . — duur
4 De ________ mosselen zijn heel lekker. — klein
5 Ik heb thuis het ________ boekje. — groen
6 Zij geven een ________ feest voor hun kind. — groot
7 Rob heeft een ________ appartement. — gezellig
8 Saskia heeft een ________ carrière. — succesvol

9	Ik hou van ________ ________ mannen/vrouwen.	lang slank
10	________ mensen zijn heel open.	Nederlands

slank slim

KLEUREN

blauw	blue
grijs	grey
rood	red
zwart	black
geel	yellow
wit	white
groen	green
bruin	brown
oranje	orange
donkergroen	dark green
paars	purple/violet
lichtblauw	light blue

Oefening 23: Fashion showtime!

Describe what another student is wearing and make sure you name all the colours and possibly some materials of the garments and put them in the right form. Prepare this in writing. Use a dictionary if you need the words for items of clothing not listed earlier.

Example

Doris draagt vandaag een groene wollen rok met een rood katoenen hemd. Ze heeft ook een oranje leren handtas.

Oefening 24: One more exercise on numbers and prices!

Work in pairs. You are in a shop and ask for prices. You will alternately take the role of the salesperson and the customer. Each student takes 2 pieces of paper. On each piece of paper, you write down a number between 100 and 100 000 and a consumer item that might cost that much. Your tutor collects the pieces of paper and redistributes them. Look up the Dutch word for the consumer item on your papers and share this information with your partner. Now you can enact the following roleplay.

Example

item: een breedbeeldtelevisie [wide screen television]
price: €1899

klant	Sorry,/Zeg, hoeveel kost een breedbeeldtelevisie?
verkoper 1	Nou, deze hier kost duizend achttienhonderd negenennegentig euro.
klant	Hoeveel??
verkoper 2	Duizend achttienhonderd negenennegentig euro.
klant	O, dat is duur/veel/goedkoop/weinig.

duur	expensive	**veel**	a lot
goedkoop	cheap	**weinig**	little

Tekst 6 Rob bellen

Saskia has finished shopping and has managed to get the theatre tickets. She now calls Rob.

Saskia	Hoi Rob, met mij.
Rob	Hoi. Waar zit je?
Saskia	Ik sta op het Stadhuisplein. Wat ben jij aan het doen?
Rob	Ik was aan het lezen en lag wat naar muziek te luisteren. Zeg, heb je tickets voor vanavond?
Saskia	Ja, het begint om acht uur. Zullen we eerst iets gaan eten?
Rob	Ja, is goed. Ik kom wel naar jou toe. Er is daar in de buurt een leuk Italiaans restaurantje, aan de Oude Markt.
Saskia	OK, tot straks.

Key vocabulary

aan	at	**is goed**	colloquial abbreviated form of **Dat is goed**
de buurt	area	**lag**	past tense of **liggen**
iets	something		

Vragen bij tekst 6

Beantwoord in het Nederlands.

1 Waar is Saskia?

2 Wat doet Rob?

3 Hoe laat begint het toneel?

4 Wat gaan ze samen doen?

samen	together	**het toneel**	the play

TELLING THE TIME

Het is tien uur.	It is ten o'clock.
Het is kwart over tien.	It is a quarter past ten.
Het is twintig over tien. (VL)	It is twenty past ten.
Het is half elf.	It is half past ten.
Het is vijf over half elf.	It is twenty five to eleven.
Het is tien over half elf. (NL)	It is twenty to eleven.
Het is elf uur.	It is eleven o'clock.

het half uur	half an hour	**de minuut**	minute
het kwartier	fifteen minutes	**het uur**	hour

N.B. Twenty to and twenty past are expressed as **tien over/voor half**, particularly in the Netherlands. In Flanders, **twintig voor/over** is also possible.

Oefening 25

Match the digital times with the written ones

1	vijf over half tien 's avonds	(a)	03.00 uur
2	kwart over acht 's morgens	(b)	15.30 uur
3	drie uur 's nachts	(c)	19.45 uur
4	half vier 's middags	(d)	04.30 uur
5	twintig voor tien 's morgens	(e)	21.35 uur
6	kwart voor acht 's avonds	(f)	14.10 uur
7	half vijf 's morgens	(g)	08.15 uur
8	tien over twee 's middags	(h)	11.30 uur
9	twintig over tien 's avonds	(i)	09.40 uur
10	half twaalf 's morgens	(j)	22.20 uur

Oefening 26

Fill in the right time-related preposition. You can choose from the options in the box below.

op om na in tot (2x) van voor over

1 Het nieuws op TV1 begint _______ 19u.
2 _______ het nieuws is er een kwisprogramma.
3 Dat duurt _______ kwart voor _______ kwart over acht.

4 _______ maandag moet ik nooit werken.
5 Mijn oma is geboren _______ 1900.
6 Die radio dateert van _______ de Tweede Wereldoorlog.
7 Je moet wachten _______ ik klaar ben.
8 _______ drie weken moet zij bevallen.

bevallen	to give birth	**klaar zijn**	to be ready
dateren van	to date from	**het nieuws**	news
duren	to last		

Oefening 27

Browse to http://gids.omroep.nl and print out the Dutch and/or Flemish television programme. Make a list of the names of 5 programmes you would like to watch and the channels they are on. Work in pairs. One person checks the programme and the other one asks when a programme starts and how long it lasts. If you are working on your own, you can write down question and answers in the same format.

Example

A Hoe laat is het nieuws op Nederland 1?
B Er is een journaal om vier en vijf uur 's middags, en ook om acht uur 's avonds.
A Hoe lang is het journaal van acht uur?
B Dat duurt een half uur.

het journaal	news broadcast	**het kanaal / de zender**	channel

Structuren

IT'S HAPPENING NOW

To indicate that something is happening right now you use **zijn** + **aan het** + infinitive. For example:

Ik ben een boek aan het lezen.
I am reading a book.

Hij is koffie aan het drinken.
He is drinking coffee.

You can also use a form of the verbs **zitten/liggen/staan** + **te** + infinitive. You translate **zitten/liggen/staan** in these contexts with 'to be' in English. For example:

Hij zit de krant te lezen.
He is reading the newspaper. [while he is sitting down]

Hij ligt naar muziek te luisteren.
He is listening to music. [while he is lying down]

OTHER INFINITIVE CONSTRUCTIONS

As in the examples above, many other verbs can be supplemented by **te** + infinitive. The most common ones are **proberen**, **beginnen**, **hoeven** and **vergeten**. For example:

Ik probeer al jaren Frans te leren.
I have been trying to learn French for years.

Morgen beginnen we te werken.
We will start working tomorrow.

Je hoeft niet te wachten, hoor.
You don't have to wait, you know.

Hij vergeet altijd de vuilnisbak buiten te zetten.
He always forgets to put the bin outside.

Please note that **hoeven** is always used in the negative and implies there is no obligation, which makes it the opposite of **moeten**.

There are a number of verbs that don't take **te** before the infinitive. The most common ones are the modal verbs, **gaan**, **komen**, **zijn**, **laten**, **blijven**, **zien** and **horen**. For example:

Hij kan heel mooi zingen.
He can sing very well.

Ze zullen me het boek opsturen.
They will send me the book.

Ik kom je morgen helpen.
I will come and help you tomorrow.

Erik is even melk halen.
Erik is getting milk.

Ik laat mijn hemden strijken.
I have my shirts ironed.

Oefening 28

Give two possible answers to these questions and make use of the following infinitives.

huilen praten bellen wachten lezen kijken

Example

Wat is het kind aan het doen?
Het kind ligt te huilen. / Het kind is aan het huilen.

1 Wat zijn de tieners aan het doen?
2 Wat doet de jonge man?
3 Waar is de oude man?
4 Wat doet de jonge vrouw?
5 Wat is de oude vrouw aan het doen?

Oefening 29

Finish the following sentences with an infinitive construction. You can choose an infinitive from the list below or think of one yourself.

tennissen luisteren iets drinken optreden **voetballen werken eten knippen zijn fluiten halen** **kopen discussiëren feest vieren koken praten**

Example

Ik kan heel goed ______________ .
Ik kan heel goed tennissen.

1 Hij zal vanavond laat ______________
2 Ga jij dit weekend ook ______________ ?
3 Komt Erik morgen mee ______________ ?
4 Ik kan heel goed ______________ .
5 Ik zie Marco Borsato graag ______________ .
6 Laat jij elke maand je haar ______________ ?
7 Wij willen eigenlijk liever niet ______________ .
8 Waarom moet je altijd zo direct ______________ ?
9 In de keuken hoor je 's morgens de vogels ______________ .
10 Mijn vriend is even naar de bakker brood ______________ .

fluiten	*here*: to sing	**optreden**	to perform
halen	to get		

Oefening 30

Complete the sentences in column 1 by using the most appropriate information given in column 2.

1	Karin ligt ______________	(a)	rustig de krant te lezen.
2	Hij zit ______________	(b)	morgen koffie drinken.
3	De docent gaat ______________	(c)	aan het koken.
4	De student probeert ______________	(d)	de essays nakijken.
5	De kleine Jef hoort ______________	(e)	TV te kijken.
6	Mijn tante komt ______________	(f)	niet elke dag spruiten te eten.
7	Mijn flatgenoten zijn ______________	(g)	zijn vader thuiskomen.
8	De dokter begint ______________	(h)	een essay te schrijven.
9	De kinderen hoeven ______________	(i)	vanavond een toespraak houden.
10	De minister zal ______________	(j)	mij te onderzoeken.

nakijken	to check, *here*: to mark	**de toespraak**	speech
onderzoeken	to examine		

Oefening 31

Some more practice with asking questions. Fill in the gaps with the right question word. Ask your fellow student these questions after you have finished.

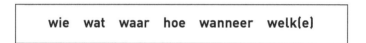

wie	**wat**	**waar**	**hoe**	**wanneer**	**welk(e)**

Example

__________ groot ben je?
***Hoe* groot ben je?**

1 __________ staat de Eiffeltoren?
2 __________ ver is Londen van Brussel?
3 __________ is de minister-president van Nederland?
4 __________ heet de koning van België?
5 __________ talen spreek jij?
6 __________ is het Koninginnedag?
7 __________ is jouw favoriete acteur?
8 __________ boeken lees je graag?
9 __________ is het jouw verjaardag?
10 __________ oud ben je?

Oefening 32

Team up with another student and create a mobile phone dialogue between the two of you. Arrange to meet up this evening. Discuss *what* you are going to do, and *when* and *where* you are going to meet. If possible, perform your dialogue in front of the other students and take care to use authentic intonation. Your fellow students need to take notes of *what* you are going to do and *where* and *when* you are going to meet.

A closer look

Have a look at the following three texts about clothes shops. The first one is about one particular shop in Antwerp, whereas the other two are Dutch chains: *C&A* which can be found all over Europe and *De Bijenkorf*, a department store with branches in many major Dutch town centres. Read through the texts first before you start looking up any words you don't know. Try to find out who the texts are aimed at. What kind of customer do you think they appeal to?

Tekst 7 Shopping tips

Fish & chips

In de Kammenstraat in Antwerpen vind je een shoppingtempel voor jonge trendy mensen: de Fish & Chips! Op de beats van hippe DJ's kan je in de streetwear rondsnuffelen. In de basement vind je de '*fucking new underground shoe corner*', waar – de naam zegt het al – de schoenen zijn. Je komt er met de trap of met de glijbaan. Als je naar boven gaat zie je de DJ aan het werk. Je kan in de zithoek uitblazen.

Key vocabulary

aan het werk	at work	**de trap**	stairs
de glijbaan	slide	**uitblazen**	have a rest
rondsnuffelen	to browse	**de zithoek**	sitting area

Vragen bij tekst 7, fish & chips

1 This text is fairly easy to understand after a first reading, why is that?

2 Which audience is this shop aimed at? What makes you think so? Refer to the text.

3 What kind of atmosphere is created? Which words indicate this?

C&A

Mode voor jong en oud. Mode die voor elke gelegenheid en voor ieder type de juiste kleding heeft. Op die manier maakt C&A het leven voor miljoenen klanten aangenamer. Al meer dan honderd jaar biedt C&A in Europa haar klanten kwaliteitskleding tegen een betaalbare prijs.

Key vocabulary

aangenaam	pleasant, convenient	**ieder**	every
betaalbaar	affordable	**juist**	right
bieden	to offer	**het leven**	life
elke	each	**de mode**	fashion
de gelegenheid	occasion		

Vragen bij tekst 7, C&A

1 Are C&A looking for a niche market? Explain.

2 What is their motto?

3 How do they create an image of soundness and reliability? Which words indicate this?

De Bijenkorf

De Bijenkorf is een inspirerende, trendsettende en dynamische warenhuisformule. In het assortiment van de Bijenkorf vindt u internationale topmerken en eigen merken op het gebied van mode, cosmetica, accessoires, wonen, media, sport en reizen. Als vooraanstaand warenhuis hebben wij vaak een voortrekkersrol. Onze waarden en normen moeten daarom in onze activiteiten te zien zijn.

Key vocabulary

belangrijk	important	**reizen**	travel
daarom	therefore	**vooraanstaand**	prominent
eigen	own	**de voortrekkersrol**	role of pioneer
horeca	catering business	**waarden en normen**	values and norms
het merk	brand	**het warenhuis**	department store
op het gebied van	which has to do with		

Vragen bij tekst 7, De Bijenkorf

1 Make a list of the adjectives used to describe this store.

2 Is the reader addressed directly and if so, how?

3 What kind of market is this store aiming at, you think?

4 The text claims the Bijenkorf has a pioneering function. Does it specify what this function consists of?

5 Why does the Bijenkorf mention their **normen en waarden**, do you think?

Oefening 33

Write two short texts (100 words each) for the website of a popular magazine, describing

1 a very young and fashionable bar or restaurant;

2 a more conservative, reliable restaurant.

Look at the internet for inspiration. Try and find a website for two restaurants that fit the description above. Start off with making a list of nouns, adjectives and verbs. Make use of a dictionary where necessary. Write a short introduction and continue in question and answer format.

Example

Wat voor mensen eten hier? Yups met veel poen!
Waar ligt het? Tussen de trendy en hippe bars op de Nieuwmarkt.

Bear in mind the following:

(a) whether to address the reader directly and if so, how;
(b) whether to talk about yourself (as the restaurant reviewer) using **ik** or not;
(c) whether to use English words or not;
(d) the connotation of words you are using, how they add up to an image.

Keep your text simple. Don't try to use grammatical structures that you haven't studied yet.

Unit 4
Groepsgedrag

In this unit you will look at ways in which language is used in specific, set ways within particular groups, such as families, particularly in the context of group gatherings and celebrations. In this unit you will also learn how official texts are written in order to get the point across to certain groups of people.

TOPICS

- Family celebrations (birthdays and new baby)
- Government campaign to stop drink-driving
- Recipe for cake
- Politeness
- Family relations

FUNCTIONS

- Congratulating people
- Ways of greeting people at a family party
- Thanking for a present
- Offering/accepting food and drinks
- More and less formal ways of addressing people
- Talking about driving
- Talking about the past
- Talking about children using terms of endearment
- Changing a topic
- Expressing an opinion
- Talking about family
- Writing for different purposes and audiences

GRAMMAR

- Present perfect
- Verbs of motion
- Subclauses
- Indirect statements
- Indirect questions
- Word order in main and subclauses
- Diminutives

Tekst 1 Joert is jarig

Listen to the dialogue a few times without reading along. Then answer the recorded questions in **Oefening 1**. Then study the dialogue more closely by reading along and looking up difficult words.

Joert is celebrating his birthday. Family and friends are gathering, and are sitting around Joert's living room in a big circle. Joert's sister Anneke and her husband Ashgar arrive.

Joert	Hoi. Gezellig, joh. Kom binnen.
Anneke	Dag, Joert. Kom hier. Nou, gefeliciteerd met je verjaardag.

[She kisses him three times on the cheek.]

Ashgar	Ja, jarige Job, van harte. Alsjeblieft.

[He shakes hands with Joert and gives him an envelope. Anneke is going round the circle, greeting everyone by shaking their hand and kissing them on the cheek, three times. Ashgar follows her, shaking everyone's hand.]

Anneke	Dag, tante Janet. Gefeliciteerd met Joert.
Tante Janet	Dag, kindje. Jij ook gefeliciteerd, hoor.
Anneke	En oom Berend ook gefeliciteerd met Joert.
Oom Berend	Jij ook, Anneke.

[While they go round, Joert opens the envelope.]

Joert	Een boekenbon, wat leuk. Hartstikke bedankt, jongens!
Ashgar	Graag gedaan. Dan kun je zelf een boek kopen dat je mooi vindt.
Joert	Willen jullie koffie?
Anneke	Graag.
Joert	Met kwarktaart of appelgebak?
Anneke	Appel voor mij.
Ashgar	Ik heb liever kwark.
Joert	Prima. Komt eraan.

Key vocabulary

het appelgebak	apple pie
de boekenbon	book token
gefeliciteerd	congratulations
de kwarktaart	cheese cake
van harte	congratulations

Oefening 1

Beantwoord de vragen in het Nederlands.

1 Wie is jarig?
2 Wat geven Anneke en Ashgar aan Joert voor zijn verjaardag?
3 Wil Anneke appelgebak of kwarktaart?
4 Wat neemt Ashgar?

voor zijn verjaardag for his birthday

Listen to the second part of the dialogue at the birthday. First try to answer the questions again before reading along.

Ashgar and Anneke have had their coffee. Joert is offering everyone something else to drink.

Joert	Wat wil je drinken, Ashgar?
Ashgar	Ik weet niet. Rij jij of rij ik, Anneke?
Anneke	Ik heb vorige keer gereden. Toch?
Ashgar	Nee, jij hebt vorige keer niet gereden. Ik heb gereden. We hebben er nog ruzie over gehad.
Anneke	Ja, je hebt gelijk. Verleden week heb jij gereden. Nou, dan rij ik.
Ashgar	Dan wil ik een pilsje, alsjeblieft, Joert.
Joert	Prima. Jij een Spa rood, An?
Anneke	Ja, doe maar. Ik Bob wel.
Tante Janet	Wat bedoel je met Bob?
Anneke	Heeft u nog nooit van Bob gehoord? Dat is een campagne van de overheid: 'Bob jij of Bob ik?' De persoon die niet drinkt, is Bob.
Tante Janet	O, zeg je dat zo? Daar heb ik nog nooit van gehoord.
Anneke	Echt? Oom Berend, kent u Bob? Heeft u de reclame op TV niet gezien?
Oom Berend	Ja, hoor. Die heb je toch wel gezien, Janet? Het is zo vaak op TV geweest. En ik heb het ook op de radio gehoord.
Ashgar	En wie is Bob, bij jullie?
Tante Janet	Ja, wie is Bob bij ons, Berend?

Key vocabulary

erover	about it
de overheid	state/government
de reclame	commercial/advert
de ruzie	fight/argument
toch?	haven't I?

Oefening 2: Luistervragen

Beantwoord vragen 1 tot en met 7 in het Nederlands.

1 Wie rijdt naar huis, Ashgar of Anneke?
2 Wie heeft de vorige keer gereden?
3 Wat drinkt Anneke?
4 Waar zie en hoor je reclame voor 'Bob jij of Bob ik?'
5 Kent tante Janet 'Bob jij of Bob ik?'
6 Kent oom Berend de campagne?
7 Wie rijdt naar huis, oom Berend of tante Janet?
8 How do Ashgar and Anneke address their uncle and aunt? Do they address Joert in the same way? What is the difference?
9 How do the uncle and aunt address Anneke and Ashgar? What does that say about their relationship?
10 How does tante Janet greet Anneke? What does that say about their relationship?
11 How does Joert thank Anneke and Ashgar for their present? What does that say about his relationship with them?

Oefening 3

Read the dialogues out loud (in a group if possible). Try and capture the appropriate tone. Exaggerate as much as you can.

Oefening 4

Listen to the sentences and choose a word from the box to fill in.

alsjeblieft bedankt binnen gefeliciteerd ik niet

1 ______________ 4 ______________

2 ______________ 5 ______________

3 ______________ 6 ______________

Oefening 5

Look up the ingredients from the recipe below. To get into a Dutch celebratory mood, you may want to try and make this pie.

RECEPT

KWARKTAART VAN TANTE LIEN

Ingrediènten

500 g kwark (in Flanders this is called 'platte kaas')
7 blaadjes gelatine
1 blikje mandarijnen
lange vingers
0,5 l room
150 g suiker
citroensap van 3 citroenen
likeur (Grand Marnier)

Bereiding

Meng de kaas, de suiker en het citroensap. Warm het sap van de mandarijnen op en los de gelatine hierin op. Klop de room. Meng het sap plus de room door het kaasmengsel, maar hou een klein beetje room over voor de garnering. Zet het mengsel in de koelkast. Bedek een taartvorm met lange vingers en besprenkel die met likeur. Giet het mengsel uit de koelkast erover heen. Laat dit ongeveer 4 uur opstijven in de koelkast. Garneer met mandarijntjes en room.

Structuren

TALKING ABOUT THE PAST

Look at the following sentences from the two texts above. All describe events that refer to the past. Try and describe the pattern which is used to talk about the past in Dutch.

Ik *heb* vorige keer *ge*reden.
I drove last time.

Jij *hebt* vorige keer niet *ge*reden.
You didn't drive last time.

We *hebben* ruzie *ge*had.
We had an argument about it.

Verleden week *heb* jij *ge*reden.
Last week you drove.

Daar *heb* ik nog nooit van *ge*hoord.
I've never heard of it.

***Heeft* u de reclame *ge*zien?**
Have you seen the (TV) commercial?

***Heeft* u de reclame op TV niet *gezien*?**
Haven't you seen the (TV) commercial?

Die *heb* je toch wel *gezien*?
Surely you've seen it?

Ik *heb* de reclame *gehoord*.
I've heard the (radio) commercial.

Het *is* zo vaak op TV *geweest*.
It has been on TV (so) often.

THE PRESENT PERFECT

Form

The pattern or tense used to describe events in the past – which have now finished – is the (present) perfect tense. The present perfect is formed with an auxiliary (a form of **hebben** or **zijn**) and a past participle

hebben/zijn + past participle

Past participle

The past participle of regular verbs is formed by prefixing the stem of the verb with **ge** and adding a final **t** or **d**.

ge + stem + **t/d**

If the last letter of the stem is one of the following: s, f, t, k, ch, p, (you can use 'soft ketchup' as a mnemonic) then a **t** is added. In all other cases a **d** is added.

Note that **ge** is not added to the past participles of verbs starting with **be**, **ge**, **her**, **er**, **ont** or **ver**, so the past participle of **vertellen** (to tell), for instance, is **verteld**.

With the past participle of separable verbs, **ge** is placed between the prefix and the verb. For example:

opbellen	**opgebeld**	to telephone
schoonmaken	**schoongemaakt**	to clean

Hebben or **zijn**

Most verbs take **hebben** in the past participle. However, some verbs take **zijn**. For example:

hebben **Ik heb een computer gekocht.**
I've bought a computer.

Heeft u gisteren tv gezien?
Did you watch TV last night?

zijn **De prijs van olie is gestegen.**
The price of oil has gone up.

Ze is om vijf uur vertrokken.
She left at five o'clock.

Most verbs that take **zijn** indicate a change of place or state (or its opposite, like **blijven**). Here are some examples:

blijven	to stay	**gaan**	to go
komen	to come	**zijn**	to be
worden	to become	**beginnen**	to begin
stoppen	to stop		

Oefening 6

1 Underline the elements of the present perfect tense in the following text.

> Ik heb gisteren m'n verjaardag gevierd. Het was erg druk en erg gezellig. 's Middags m'n familie en 's avonds m'n vrienden. Ik heb voor een kleine groep van zo'n 12 man ook eten gekookt. Niets bijzonders, alleen pasta met een sausje plus salade en brood, maar toch lekker. Ans en Amina hebben me gelukkig met de afwas geholpen. 's Avonds was er een man of 25. We hebben flink wat gedronken. Later op de avond hebben we ook gedanst. De meesten zijn rond een uur of één naar huis gegaan, maar een kleine groep is tot laat gebleven. De laatste – Miriam natuurlijk! – ging pas om vier uur naar huis.

2 Look up the infinitives of the verbs which you've found. Also look up the meaning of other words which you don't know.

Oefening 7

Fill in the correct form of **hebben**.

1 We _______ gisteren samen onze verjaardag gevierd.
2 Ik _______ een nieuwe mobiele telefoon gekocht.
3 Jurgen en Lisette _______ een vakantie naar Marokko geboekt.
4 Waarom _______ je moeder nog niet gebeld?
5 Mijn computer _______ nooit echt goed gewerkt.

Oefening 8

Fill in the correct form of **hebben** or **zijn**.

1 Zo'n lelijke bank _______ ik nog nooit gezien.
2 Hoe laat _______ Ans en Amina naar huis gegaan?
3 _______ de directieleden de agenda al gehad?
4 Dirk-Jan _______ vanochtend met de trein naar zijn werk gegaan.
5 Twee van mijn vriendinnen _______ verleden jaar 50 geworden.
6 Ik _______ voor volgende week een afspraak met mijn tandarts gemaakt.
7 Wie _______ nog nooit in Amsterdam geweest?
8 We _______ afgelopen weekend een avondje naar Antwerpen gegaan.

directieleden	members of the board	**nog nooit**	never

Oefening 9

You're telling a colleague about your weekend. Use the following information to make sentences in the present perfect.

Example

ik / op het strand / wandelen
Ik heb op het strand gewandeld.

1 ik en mijn vriend / naar de stad / fietsen
2 we / in een restaurant / lunchen
3 mijn vriend Antonio me / zondagochtend / bellen
4 hij / over zijn vakantie / vertellen
5 ik / zaterdagmiddag / in de sportschool / trainen
6 ik / zaterdag op de markt / samen met mijn moeder / boodschappen doen
7 we / met de taxi naar huis / gaan
8 wat / jij / in het weekend / doen?

Oefening 10

Answer the following questions in the negative (with 'not').

1 Heb je gisteren gewerkt?
2 Heeft Sander je op zijn verjaardag uitgenodigd?
3 Hebben jullie Antwerp-Cercle Brugge zaterdagavond op de TV gezien?
4 Ben je al in het nieuwe Japanse restaurant geweest? (Note: use **nog niet** 'not yet' in your answer.)
5 Zijn jullie naar de verjaardag van opa gegaan?

6 Heeft papa al een nieuwe auto gekocht? (Note: use **nog geen**)
7 Ben je afgelopen donderdag op kantoor geweest?
8 Heb je je auto aan Felipe verkocht?

afgelopen	last	**het kantoor**	(the) office

Oefening 11

Answer these questions from a questionnaire in the present perfect tense.

1 Hoeveel uur heb je afgelopen week televisie gekeken?
2 Hoe vaak ben je verhuisd?
3 Wanneer ben je voor het laatst naar de film geweest?
4 Welke film heb je toen gezien?
5 Waar heb je dit boek gekocht?
6 Wanneer ben je voor het laatst uitgeweest?
7 Waar ben je toen geweest?
8 Wat voor keuken heb je nog nooit gegeten? (bijvoorbeeld Indonesisch of Turks, etc.)

verhuizen	to move house	**wat voor keuken**	what type of cuisine
voor het laatst	the last time		

Hebben and **zijn** + verbs of motion

Look at the following examples:

We hebben vandaag drie uur gefietst.
We cycled for three hours today.

We zijn vandaag naar Lisse gefietst.
We cycled to Lisse today.

Verbs indicating motion, such as **fietsen** 'cycle', **lopen** 'walk', **rennen** 'run' and **rijden** 'drive' can take either a form of **hebben** or **zijn** in the present perfect. A form of **zijn** is used when a destination is given, such as in the second example above. Otherwise a form of **hebben** is used, like in the first example.

Oefening 12

Fill in the correct form of **hebben** or **zijn**.

1 We ______ vanmorgen om half zeven naar Schiphol gereden.
2 Tante Hennie ______ gisteren de hele dag in de stad gelopen.
3 Ik ______ in de regen naar m'n vriendin gefietst.

4 Hafid ______ nog nooit in een vrachtwagen gereden.
5 Masha is bang voor onweer, dus ze ______ razendsnel naar huis gerend.
6 We ______ op vakantie om de dag een eind gejogd.
7 Haar zoontje ______ in z'n eentje helemaal naar de andere kant van het zwembad gezwommen.
8 Tjeerd en Mark ______ van Sydney direct naar Zaventem gevlogen.

om de dag	every other day	**het onweer**	thunder and lightning

Cultuur

BELEEFD 'POLITE'

As you know from Unit 1, when greeting people in the Netherlands or Flanders, you always shake hands. Handshakes are also exchanged when parting.

Men and women, who know each other well, kiss each other three times on the cheek. Women also kiss each other, and although less common, it is now also acceptable for two men to kiss. Again, this ritual is also performed when leaving each other.

VERJAARDAG 'BIRTHDAY'

Birthdays are celebrated in many different ways in the Netherlands or Flanders. However, many people still opt for a traditional Dutch **verjaardagsfeestje** 'birthday party' as outlined in the dialogues above.

People gather for after-dinner coffee, usually around 7 or 7.30pm at the home of the person who is celebrating their birthday. Everyone sits around the edge of the living room in a circle, and first has coffee with cake. Every new person arriving at the party will first congratulate the host(ess) on his/her birthday, and then goes around the circle, greeting everyone else – see **beleefd** above – congratulating them on the host(ess)'s birthday. Only after everyone has had a cup of coffee or two, does the host start serving alcoholic drinks. When leaving, everyone will go round the circle, saying goodbye to everyone individually, finishing with the host(ess), who will see them to the door.

In Flanders, guests will be invited for dinner first (with a cake for desert), followed by drinks in the evening.

In both countries the person celebrating their birthday will treat colleagues at work or school to something sweet, like a piece of cake or chocolates, although for school children parents often choose a healthier alternative. Treating other people in this way is called **trakteren**.

Communicatie

EEN VERJAARDAG

Anil is jarig.	It's Anil's birthday. / Anil is celebrating her birthday.
gefeliciteerd	congratulations
gefeliciteerd met je verjaardag	congratulations on your birthday
gefeliciteerd met Anil	congratulations with Anil (said to someone at Anil's birthday)
Hoe oud ben je?	How old are you?
Hoe oud ben je/u geworden?	How old have you become?
Mag ik vragen hoe oud je/u bent geworden?	May I ask how old you are now?
Ik ben . . . (jaar) geworden	I am . . . (years old).

Oefening 13

Pretend it's everyone's birthday today. Choose three fellow students and congratulate them on their birthday in Dutch.

Oefening 14

Choose three other students to congratulate them on their (imaginary) sister's birthday (**je zus**).

Oefening 15

Discuss with fellow students the differences between the Dutch way of celebrating birthdays and congratulating people, and your own.

ADDRESSING PEOPLE

Different groups of people (older/younger, employee/employer, teacher/student, customer/staff) address each other in different ways. A sister will address her brother with **je/jij**, use neutral or informal vocabulary, and sentences which may be less complex and/or incomplete (**weet niet** 'don't know'; **waarom niet?** 'why not?'; **misschien** 'perhaps').

Oefening 16

Now make an inventory of how other people might address each other, for instance a **neef** 'nephew' to his elderly **tante** 'aunt'; and a **werkgever** 'employer' to her **werknemer** 'employee'. Discuss the differences which might occur from person to person and from situation to situation.

	neef *to* ***tante***	***werkgever*** *to* ***werknemer***
direct form of address: **u/je/jij**? first names? **meneer/mevrouw**?		
vocabulary: formal/informal?		
sentences: long/short?		
complex/simple: complete/incomplete?		

Oefening 17

To make this more practical, write (very) short dialogues, in which the **neef** greets the **aunt**, and the **werkgever** the **werknemer** (use a dictionary if necessary.) Also do this for:

1 a pupil greets his/her teacher;
2 a teacher greets his/her pupils;
3 a husband greets his wife.

Do the same for these people when thanking each other for a present, and saying goodbye.

Cultuur

A BABY IS BORN

Hoera, we eten beschuit met muisjes,
want wij hebben een zoon met twee kleine knuistjes,
twee oogjes, twee oortjes, een neusje en een mond,
tien kleine teentjes en kerngezond.

from: http://www.babyboardrent.nl/gedichten/gedichten.shtml

Key vocabulary

de beschuit	Dutch crisp bakes	**de knuist**	fist
kerngezond	in perfect health	**muisjes**	aniseed comfits

To celebrate the birth of a new baby, Dutch people eat **beschuit met muisjes**, a type of toasted bread (or crisp bread) with blue and white aniseed sprinkles on top if a boy has been born, and pink and white ones if a girl has been born. In Belgium people give each other **doopsuiker**, coloured sugar coated almonds (blue and white for boys, pink and white for girls).

Vraag

Note the use of the word **knuistjes** 'little fists'. Why do you think this word was used, instead of for instance **handjes** 'little hands'?

Tekst 2 Kraambezoek

Listen to the dialogue a few times without reading along. Then answer the recorded questions in **Oefening 18**. Then study the dialogue more closely by reading along and looking up difficult words.

Mila has just had a baby boy. Bente, a friend of Mila's, is visiting.

Bente	Wat een poepie, zeg.
Mila	Een scheetje, hè? Onze kleine Joep.
Bente	Het is een plaatje. Hoe oud is hij nou?
Mila	Hij is twee weken geleden geboren.
Bente	Wil je dat ik de koffie inschenk?
Mila	Als je het niet erg vindt, graag! Alles staat in de keuken. Trouwens, heb jij nog van Eline gehoord? Ze is nog niet op bezoek geweest.
Bente	Weet je dat ze zwanger is?
Mila	Nee, echt? Wat leuk voor ze.
Bente	Ja. Ze zijn zo blij. Tom zegt dat ze al heel lang een baby willen.
Mila	Geweldig voor ze. En Merel en Martijn? Merel wil toch ook een baby?
Bente	Ja, maar ze is nog niet zwanger omdat Martijn geen kinderen wil.
Mila	Goh, dat wist ik niet. Denk je dat het binnen hun relatie voor problemen zorgt?
Bente	Wie weet?

Key vocabulary

als je het niet erg vindt	if you don't mind
goh	gee, golly
inschenken	to pour
het kraambezoek	visit to the new baby and mother
op bezoek geweest	visited
het plaatje	little beauty
het poepie	little darling
het scheetje	little sweetie
voor problemen zorgen	to cause problems
zwanger	pregnant

Note that **poepie** and **scheetje** are not used in Belgium. Instead **schatje** or **schattebolleke** might be used.

Oefening 18: Vragen

Beantwoord de vragen 1 tot en met 4 in het Nederlands.

1 Wanneer is Joep geboren?
2 Wie schenkt de koffie in?
3 Heeft Bente van Eline gehoord? Wat heeft Bente gehoord?
4 Willen Merel en Martijn kinderen?
5 List the words used to describe the newborn baby. What feeling do they create?

Oefening 19: Roleplay

In groups, make up a roleplay where you're visiting a mother and her newborn baby. Use as many terms of endearment as possible to describe the baby. First write down the roleplay on paper, and then play it out in front of the whole group.

While listening, the others should write down all the different terms of endearment.

Oefening 20

In the text above, Mila suddenly changes the topic. She does this by using the word **trouwens** 'by the way'. Pretend that you're talking to a friend, and change the topic using **trouwens**.

Example

Ik heb Annette in de stad gezien.
Trouwens, ik heb Annette in de stad gezien.

1 Mijn broer en zijn vrouw hebben een baby.
2 Ik heb 25 euro in de lotto gewonnen.
3 De buren komen vanavond eten.

4 Die nieuwe CD van George Michael vind ik helemaal niet zo goed.
5 Jos belde vrijdag. Dat was zo onverwacht.
6 Weet je al dat er een nieuwe film van Coppola is?
7 Mijn laptop is kapot.
8 We moeten niet vergeten eerst boodschappen te doen.

Oefening 21

Repeat Oefening 20 in pairs, making short conversations (answer plus reply). Repeat the **trouwens** sentences from Oefening 20 and then choose an appropriate response from the list of possible answers in the box (or make up one of your own).

Example

Trouwens, ik heb Annette in de stad gezien.
O ja? Wat leuk!

O ja? Goh, wat vervelend! O jee, wat erg!
Wat interessant, zeg! Gezellig, hoor! Inderdaad!
Wat leuk! Te gek, joh! O nee?

Structuren

You have learnt that the finite verb in Dutch sentences always comes at the second place in the sentence (except in yes/no questions and the imperative). However, this is only the case if the sentence is a main clause. In some sentence parts (a subclause and relative clause) the finite verb comes at the end of that clause. Look at the place of the verbs in the following sentences.

Wil je *dat* ik de koffie *inschenk*?
Would you like me to pour the coffee?

***Als* je het niet erg *vindt*.**
If you don't mind.

Weet je *dat* ze zwanger *is*?
Do you know that she's pregnant?

Tom zegt *dat* ze al heel lang een baby *willen*.
Tom says they've been wanting a baby for a long time.

Ze is nog niet zwanger *omdat* Martijn geen kinderen *wil*.
She isn't pregnant yet because Martijn doesn't want any children.

Denk je *dat* het voor problemen *zorgt*?
Do you think it gives problems?

Note that in separate verbs the two parts are written as one.

SUBCLAUSES

Subclauses start with special linking words, subordinating conjunctions. After a subordinating conjunction word order changes: Whereas in main clauses the finite verb takes up the second place in the clause, in a subclause all verbs are moved to the end of the clause. For example:

Ik kom niet. Ik moet morgen werken.
I'm not coming. I have to work tomorrow.

Ik kom niet *omdat* ik morgen *moet werken*.
I'm not coming because I have to work tomorrow.

Indirect statements and questions

Often, subclauses start with **dat** or **of** (whether), frequently after verbs like **zeggen**, **vragen**, **weten**, **geloven**, **vertellen**. In these cases the subclause functions as an indirect statement or question. For example:

Martijn is erg laat vertrokken.
Martijn left very late.

Zij zegt *dat* Martijn erg laat *is vertrokken*.
She says that Martijn left very late.

Is jouw baan zwaar?
Is your job tough?

Ze vraagt *of* jouw baan zwaar *is*.
She asks whether your job is tough.

Word order

MAIN CLAUSE

subject	verb	object
Terminator 3	is	een leuke film.
Ik	hou van	actiefilms.
Die modeontwerper	kreeg	een prijs voor zijn bontcollectie.

SUBCLAUSE

(main clause)	subject	object	last verb position	final position
Ik denk dat	Terminator 3	een leuke film	is.	
Ik vind die leuk omdat	ik	van actiefilms	hou.	
Ik geloof dat	die modeont-werper	een prijs	kreeg	voor zijn bontcollectie.

Note that sometimes other sentence elements can come after the final verb position in the sentence. Prepositional phrases are one of these elements.

Oefening 22

Turn the following statements into opinions.

1 Rood is een mooie kleur voor de woonkamer.
 – Ik vind dat ______________

2 Het leven in de stad is veel te druk.
 – Ik hou niet van leven in de stad omdat ______________

3 Actiefilms zijn een goede ontspanning.
 – Ik vind dat ______________

4 Indonesische rijsttafels zijn heel lekker.
 – Janet vindt dat ______________

5 Moderne meubels zijn koel en lelijk.
 – Ik vind dat ______________

Oefening 23

Make the following statements a little less certain by rewriting them, starting with

Ik denk dat ______________

1 Joanna verdient meer dan Klaas.
2 Meisjes werken harder dan jongens.
3 Amerikanen werken langer dan Europeanen.
4 Cricket is geen interessante sport.
5 De meeste mensen wonen het liefst in de stad.
6 E-mail is een goede manier van communiceren op het werk.
7 September en oktober zijn goede vakantiemaanden.
8 Het is vandaag druk in de stad.

het liefst	prefer to

Oefening 24

You're compiling questions for a survey. You want to check what people in the street think of the following statements; make questions of them, starting with **Vindt u dat** ______________ **?**

1 Het koningshuis is goed voor Nederland.
2 Een rookverbod in bars en cafés is goed.
3 Benzine is te duur.
4 De euro is goed voor de Europese economie.
5 De belastingen moeten omhoog.
6 De universiteit moet gratis voor iedereen zijn.
7 De overheid in Nederland moet tolwegen introduceren.
8 Criminaliteit is een groot probleem.

omhoog moeten	need to go up	**de tolweg**	toll road
de overheid	government		

Oefening 25

Interview each other, using the questions from the previous exercise. Possible answers:

Dat vind ik niet.
I don't think so.

Dat vind ik wel.
I do think so.

Ik vind dat . . .
I think that . . .

Dat vind ik ook.
I think so too.

Daar ben ik het (niet) mee eens.
I (don't) agree.

Oefening 26

Combine the following two sentences, making a conditional link between them using **als**.

Example

Ik ga op vakantie. Ik heb genoeg geld.
Ik ga op vakantie als ik genoeg geld heb.

1 Petra moet direct naar huis. We zijn klaar met vergaderen.
2 Ik bel je. Ik heb tijd.
3 Ik ga het nieuwe boek van Rushdie lezen. Ik heb dit boek uit.
4 Hij ruimt het altijd op. Zijn hond poept op de stoep.
5 Je moet een nieuwe batterij kopen. De batterij in de afstandsbediening is leeg.
6 Ik boek zelf mijn reizen. Mijn secretaresse is ziek.
7 Wij verzorgen de poezen. Onze buren zijn op vakantie.
8 Ik kijk altijd eerst op het internet. Ik wil een boek of een CD kopen.

de afstandsbediening	remote control	**uit**	finished
opruimen	to clear away	**vergaderen**	to have a meeting

Oefening 27

Do the same as in the previous exercise, now starting with the second sentence.

Example

Ik ga op vakantie. Ik heb genoeg geld.
Als ik genoeg geld heb, ga ik op vakantie.

Oefening 28

You've been invited to a party but you don't like the person who's throwing the party. Use the following sentences to make up excuses, starting each sentence with **Ik kan niet omdat** . . .

Example

Mijn auto is kapot.
Ik kan niet omdat mijn auto kapot is.

1 Ik moet werken.
2 Ik moet naar een andere verjaardag.
3 Ik ben ziek geweest.
4 Mijn schoonouders komen op visite.
5 Ik moet een vergadering voor morgen voorbereiden.

voorbereiden	to prepare

Oefening 29

Express an opinion with **omdat** using the information below. The start of the sentence is already given.

Example

(Ik ga op vakantie naar Florida) omdat (ik lig graag op het strand in de zon).
Ik denk dat ik op vakantie naar Florida ga, omdat ik graag op het strand in de zon lig.

1 (The Rolling Stones zijn een goede band) *omdat* (veel albums verkopen).
Ik vind dat ______________

2 (Globalisatie is een groot probleem) *omdat* (de kloof tussen arm en rijk wordt groter).
Ik denk dat ______________

3 (De economische crisis snel zal eindigen) *omdat* (de koopkracht bij de normale man vergroot).
Ik geloof dat ______________

4 (De nieuwe film van Spielberg is spannend) *omdat* (de film heeft succes in de VS).
Ik denk dat ______________

5 (Thais eten is lekker) *omdat* (ik hou van kokosmelk).
Ik vind ______________

eindigen	come to an end
de kloof	gap
de kokosmelk	coconut milk
de koopkracht	spending power
spannend	thrilling, exciting
vergroten	enlarge, increase

Oefening 30

You're going on holiday to Tunisia with a group of friends. You and a close friend have organised the trip abroad. One of the others, Eelco, wants to know what you have arranged and has asked all kinds of questions. You are discussing them with your fellow organiser.

Working in pairs, take turns asking each other indirect questions, following the example.

Example

Waar vliegen we naartoe?
Eelco vraagt waar we naartoe vliegen.

Eelco's questions:

1 Waarom hebben we de vliegtickets nog niet ontvangen?
2 Hoe laat vertrekt het vliegtuig?
3 Hoeveel bagage mogen we meenemen?
4 Hoe lang duurt de busrit van het vliegveld naar ons hotel?
5 Hebben we tweepersoonskamers?
6 Is de prijs van het hotel inclusief ontbijt?
7 Welke bezienswaardigheden gaan we bezoeken?
8 Wanneer maken we een dagtocht naar Carthago?

de bezienswaardigheid	sight	**de dagtocht**	day trip
de busrit	coach journey		

Diminutives

Diminutives can indicate that something is small (**boom** 'tree', **boompje** 'little tree'), but they can also indicate that something is:

• fun	**een lekker dagje uit**	a nice day out/outing
• sweet	**een schattig mannetje**	a sweet little boy
• to show contempt or irritation	**een vervelend zaakje**	an irritating business
	een vreemd ventje	weird (little) man
• not important	**een foutje**	a/one mistake

The basic ending of diminutives is **-je**. However, to aid pronunciation, different endings have developed. Here are some guidelines:

-tje afer a long vowel (plus **-(e)l**, **-(e)r**, **-(e)n**)	**traantje, kereltje**
-pje after a long vowel plus **-m**	**boompje, kraampje**
-etje after a short vowel plus **-l**, **-m**, **-n**, **-r**, **-ng**	**pilletje, dingetje**
-kje sometimes after **-ng**	**koninkje, beloninkje**

Oefening 31

Look at the poem earlier in this Unit, celebrating the birth of a baby (taken from a card announcing the birth) on page 113. Identify the diminutives in this text. Then find out their meaning and the stems from which they derive. How do the diminutives affect the meaning of what is being said?

Do the same with the diminutives from the dialogue **kraambezoek** on page 114.

Oefening 32

Make diminutives of the following nouns (use a dictionary if necessary).

1 kop
2 auto
3 mobiel
4 kom
5 raam
6 ring
7 bar
8 rivier

Oefening 33

Read the following text about someone's idea of a lazy summer holiday. To give the text the right feeling of summer sun and enjoyment a lot of words need to be made into diminutives. (Don't forget diminutives are **het**-words.) Note that with some nouns it is not appropriate to change them into a diminutive.

Zomergevoel

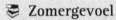

's Zomers ontbijt ik graag in de tuin. Heerlijk tussen de bloemen en de bijen met een croissant, een ei, een kop koffie en m'n krant. 's Middags een wandeling langs het strand en dan in de zon een bier op een terras drinken.

's Avonds eten met goede vrienden in een Frans restaurant. Een biefstuk met friet, en een lekkere wijn natuurlijk. Een likeur toe. Hemels!

Present perfect revisited

Look at the present perfect from the dialogue:

Hij is twee weken geleden geboren.
Heb jij nog van Eline gehoord?
Ze is nog niet op bezoek geweest.

Oefening 34: In paren

Geef antwoord (eerst mondeling, dan op papier).

1 Wanneer ben je voor het laatst op vakantie geweest? Waar naartoe?
2 Heb je dit jaar je verjaardag gevierd? Zo ja: Heb je een groot feest gegeven?
3 Heb je weleens Nederlandse of Vlaamse televisie gezien?
4 Heb je vanochtend ontbeten?
5 Heb je de afgelopen kerst kerstkaarten verstuurd?
6 Heb je kerstkaarten gekregen?
7 Heb je weleens geskied?

Oefening 35

Ask each other about what you've been doing recently. Examples:

- What films, plays (**toneelstukken**) and/or exhibitions (**tentoonstellingen**) have you seen recently?
- What books have you read?
- What meals have you cooked?
- What kinds of shopping have you done?

Communicatie

FAMILIE

The people referred to in the announcement of the newly born baby are called **een gezin** in Dutch, i.e. parents plus their children. Family in a wider context, for instance including aunts, uncles, nieces, nephews and cousins, is called **familie**.

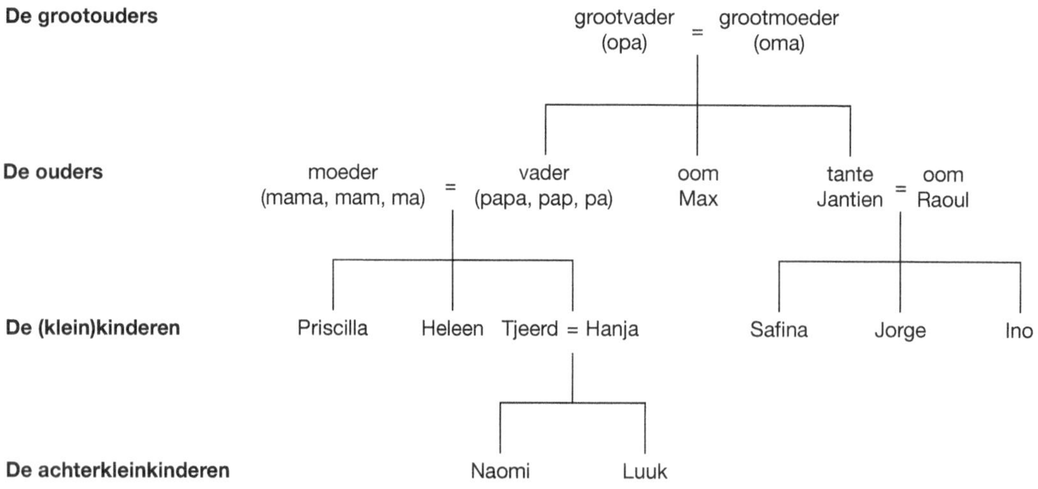

Oefening 36

Listen to the recorded text, in which Priscilla talks about her family, and answer the questions below. You might want to check the family tree while listening.

1 Hoeveel neven hebben oom Raoul en tante Jantien?

2 Hoeveel neven heeft Tjeerd?

3 Hoeveel nichten heeft Safina?

4 Hoeveel neefjes en nichtjes heeft oom Max (en hoeveel achterneefjes en -nichtjes?)

5 Hoeveel zwagers heeft moeder?

6 Hoeveel zwagers heeft tante Jantien?

7 Wie is de schoonzus van oom Max?

8 Hoeveel ooms en tantes hebben Safina, Jorge en Ino?

father-in-law **schoonvader**	mother-in-law **schoonmoeder**	in-laws **schoonouders**		
stepfather **stiefvader**	stepmother **stiefmoeder**	step-parents **stiefouders**	stepsister **stiefzus**	stepbrother **stiefbroer**
boyfriend **vriend**	girlfriend **vriendin**	married **getrouwd**	divorced **gescheiden**	single **alleenstaand**

Sirit en Jamal wonen samen.
Sirit and Jamal live together/ cohabit.

Mijn opa leeft nog.
My granddad is still alive.

Mijn oma is dood.
My grandma/granny is dead.

In Flanders a **zwager** is called **schoonbroer**, and an **oom** is often called **nonkel**.

Oefening 37

Describe your own family in as much detail as you can. Write down how many brothers, sisters, nieces, nephews, etc. you have. If you'd rather not discuss your own family, simply describe someone else's family as if it were your own.

Oefening 38

Ask other students about their family. Try and find out who has the largest and who has the smallest family.

Poem

Je hebt van twee mama s twee oma s gemaakt,
vervulde hun tederste dromen.
Je hebt van twee papa s twee opa s gemaakt,
alleen maar door bij ons te komen.

from: http://www.babyboardrent.nl/gedichten/gedichten.shtml

A closer look

TEKST 3

Bob jij of Bob ik?

WIE IS BOB?

Da's nou het mooie: iedereen kan de Bob zijn.

De ene keer jij, de andere keer één van je vrienden of vriendinnen en de volgende keer weer een ander.

Gewoon een kwestie van vooraf afspreken dus.

En natuurlijk bijhouden wie er aan de Bob-beurt is.

WAT IS BOB?

In België is Bob al jaren een fenomeen. Bob is degene die nuchter blijft, zodat de rest veilig thuiskomt.

Na een feestje bijvoorbeeld. Of de 3e helft in de sportkantine.

Of een nacht doorhalen in de kroeg.

WAAROM?

We kruipen in Nederland nog te vaak met een slok op achter het stuur. Met alle onnodige gevolgen: zie het aantal slachtoffers. In België is dat aantal gedaald sinds de invoering van de Bob-gedachte. Met andere woorden:

Bob werkt!

www.bobjijofbobik.nl

Key vocabulary

aan de beurt	whose turn	**een nacht doorhalen**	to make a night of it
het aantal	number	**de ene keer**	one time
achter het stuur kruipen	go behind the wheel	**de invoering**	implementation/start
al jaren	for years	**de kroeg**	bar/pub
bijhouden	keep track	**het mooie**	the beauty of it
de Bob-gedachte	the notion of Bob	**nuchter**	sober
da's	that's	**het slachtoffer**	victim
degene	the one	**vooraf**	beforehand

Oefening 39: Vragen

Answer in Dutch where possible.

1 'Bob jij of Bob ik?' is een campagne. Wat probeert de overheid met deze campagne te bereiken?

2 Zijn de zinnen in de tekst lang en complex, of relatief kort en eenvoudig?

3 Is het woordgebruik formeel of juist informeel? Geef voorbeelden.

4 Welke grammaticale tijden worden in de tekst gebruikt? Wat is het effect daarvan?

5 Aan wie is deze tekst uit de campagne gericht, denk je? Met andere woorden, wat is de doelgroep van deze tekst en van de campagne? Leg uit waarom je dat denkt.

Tekst 4 De kater komt later

ALCOHOLPREVENTIE VOOR JONGEREN

Op 3 juli vorig jaar ging de voorlichtingscampagne alcoholmatiging voor jongeren van start. Het Nationaal Instituut voor Gezondheidsbevordering en Ziektepreventie (NIGZ) organiseert deze campagne jaarlijks. De campagne 'De kater komt later' richt zich op alle jongeren in Nederland tussen de 12 en 20 jaar met als doel de bewustwording en kennistoename van alcoholgebruik en de gevolgen daarvan om zo het minder drinken te bevorderen.

Gedurende juli en augustus vorig jaar bezochten getrainde jongeren campings, stranden en evenementen in Nederland. Ze spraken met jongeren over hun alcoholgebruik en deelden voorlichtingsmaterialen uit met informatie, testjes en fun over alcohol. Deze voorlichting voor jongeren, door jongeren bleek de afgelopen jaren zeer effectief te zijn.

De campagne loopt door tot en met eind oktober dit jaar. De campagne wordt gevoerd met:

- 'free publicity' in doelgroepbladen;
- Postbus 51 televisie- en radiospots;
- posters op NS-stations, in cafés en strandtenten;
- een jongerenbrochure;
- internetsites.

www.postbus51.nl

Key vocabulary

alcoholmatiging	reduced alcohol intake
de bewustwording	becoming aware
bladen	magazines
bleek	turned out to be
de doelgroep	target audience
het gebruik	consumption
gedurende	during
de gezondheids-bevordering	promotion of public health
de kater	hangover
de kennistoename	increased knowledge
de radiospot	radio commercial
de strandtent	beach bar
de voorlichtings-campagne	information campaign
wordt gevoerd met	is conducted with

Oefening 40

Answer in Dutch where possible.

1. 'De kater komt later' is een overheidscampagne. Wat probeert de overheid met deze campagne te bereiken?
2. Wat gebeurt er bij deze campagne?
3. Van wanneer tot wanneer loopt de campagne?
4. Op wie is de campagne gericht? Dus: wat is de doelgroep van de campagne?
5. Vind je de tekst moeilijker of makkelijker dan de eerste tekst? Hoe komt dat denk je?
6. Zijn de zinnen in de tekst lang en complex, of relatief kort en eenvoudig, in vergelijking met tekst 3?
7. Is het woordgebruik formeler of informeler dan in de eerste tekst?
8. Welke grammaticale tijden worden in de tekst gebruikt? Zijn dat er meer of minder dan in de vorige tekst? Wat is het effect daarvan?
9. Aan wie is deze tekst (dus niet de campagne!) gericht, denk je? Met andere woorden, wat is de doelgroep van deze tekst? Leg uit waarom je dat denkt.
10. Wat is het doel van deze tekst?
11. Vat de verschillen tussen de twee teksten samen.

Oefening 41

You're working on a campaign to stop people dropping their **kauwgom** 'chewing gum' on the street right in front of the main university building. You've been asked to write two different texts. Split up into two groups. Group 1 will write a text to be printed on posters to be displayed inside and outside the university. Group 2 will write an e-mail to each of the departments of the University, informing them about the campaign.

Use the following information.

	poster	*e-mail*
aims(s)	stopping people throwing gum in the street; raising awareness of problem and consequences of problem	informing about campaign aims, strategies, etc.; asking for support
target audience	anyone dropping gum in street around university (mainly students?)	departmental staff
language to be used	you want people to change their behaviour, so appeal to the target audience in their own language (snappy, appealing, informal, short sentences)	appropriate for addressing members of staff (includes the 'powers that be')

In writing these, or any other type of texts, you may find it helpful to think of questions the target audience may want to find answers to in the text. Base your text on the answers to these questions.

	poster	*e-mail*
mogelijke vragen	wat is het probleem?	waar gaat dit over?
	waarom is het een probleem?	wat is het probleem?
	wat moet/kan ik doen?	wat is het doel van de campagne?
	waarom moet ik iets doen?	waarom is het belangrijk voor mij?
	wat kun je bereiken?	moet ik iets doen?
	etc.	kan ik iets doen?
		etc.

Unit 5
Ik en mijn wereld

This unit looks at how people express their identity and their view of the world through what they like and what they do. We will look at how different types of texts, for instance from a serious film magazine or a popular weekly magazine, use different kinds of language. Finally, we will look at some strategies for reading.

TOPICS

- Lifestyle; living preferences
- Shopping habits
- Town and country
- Low countries design
- Advertising language
- Films: general
- Films: evaluation and nuances in reviews
- Going out
- Role models and gender stereotypes

FUNCTIONS

- Expressing preference
- Describing your environment
- Talking about favourite books, actors, films, etc.
- Describing people and characteristics
- Asking for preferences and reacting
- Expressing an opinion
- Reading strategies
- Planning an evening out

GRAMMAR

- Use of **er**; indefinite subject
- Use of **er**; reference to place
- Use of **er**; reference to number
- Comparative and superlative
- Demonstrative pronouns
- Compound words

Tekst 1 Eigen stijl

Read the following quotes from a life-style magazine by a female artist talking about herself. What is your first impression of her?

Kunstenares Carmen Defee (43) woont in een groot en licht atelierhuis in Arnhem.

'Mijn zusje kocht in Alicante een schilderijtje van een vissersboot bij zonsondergang. Lichtje erboven, gouden lijstje eromheen. Zulke kitsch vind ik grappig.'

'Ik heb geen CD-speler. Muziek leidt af. Het geluid van regen, wind of vogels is genoeg.'

Key vocabulary

afleiden	to distract
het atelier	studio
eromheen	around it
het geluid	the sound
grappig	funny, amusing
de kunstenares	artist (female)
het schilderijtje	(small) painting
de zonsondergang	sunset
zulke	such

Now read the following extract from the same article and answer the questions.

Lievelingsobject?

De armband die mijn geliefde in Tunis door een astroloog heeft laten maken. Die heb ik altijd aan. En lippenstift. Zonder ga ik de deur niet uit.

Winkelen?

Ik hou van Marokkaanse en Turkse winkeltjes. De buitenlandse sfeer van groente en fruit voor de deur vind ik heel gezellig.

Wat zou je willen veranderen?

Ik zou directer contact willen met de natuur. Mijn vorige huis had veel ramen die vaak helemaal open stonden.

Eten buiten de deur?

Liever thuis. Ik kook graag zelf. Mediterraan, zoals Provencaalse tomaten met peterselie, knoflook en olijfolie uit de oven.

Onthaasten?

In een knus hoekje met een boekje voor de open haard.

Key vocabulary

de deur uitgaan	to leave the house	**de lippenstift**	lipstick
de geliefde	the lover	**onthaasten**	to de-stress
helemaal open	wide open	**de open haard**	the open fire
de (knof)look	garlic	**de peterselie**	parsley
knus	cosy	**veranderen**	to change
liever	rather	**zonder**	without

Vragen bij tekst 1

1 What does Carmen really value in her environment?

2 Make a list of the words that typify this woman, according to you.

3 Do you think Carmen presents herself as a woman who wants to conform or does she want to stand out? What makes you think this?

4 The text gives you the impression that Carmen likes things exotic and different. Which words create that impression?

Oefening 1

1 Write down five questions about preferences in living environment and life style, similar to the artist's portrait above. You can use a dictionary if necessary.

Example

[eten/koken] **Kook je graag zelf of eet je liever in een restaurant?**
[wonen] **Wil je in een villa aan de kust wonen of liever in een flat in de stad?**

2 Interview a fellow student and make up a list of his/her answers. There is no need to put them into full sentences; a list of adjectives, nouns and verbs is fine.

3 If possible, redistribute these lists among your fellow students, who will read them out loud. The other students then have to guess whose preferences are described.

Structuren

THE USE OF ER

Er is a small word that can have several functions. You have probably noticed this already in the texts you have read so far. We will deal with the most common uses in this unit.

Indefinite subject

You use **er** in sentences with an indefinite subject, such as **drie stoelen en een tafel** in the example below. This use of **er** can be translated as **there is/there are**.

Er staan drie stoelen en een tafel in de keuken.
There are three chairs and one table in the kitchen.

Er zit een boek in mijn handtas.
There is a book in my handbag.

Note that the position verbs **zitten/liggen/staan/hangen** are often used in conjunction with this **er**. As you have learned in Unit 3, these are mostly translated as **to be** in English.

Place

You use **er** to refer to a location mentioned earlier. This usually translates into 'there' in English.

Note that locative **er** is put immediately after the finite verb in the main clause.

[message on answerphone]
Sorry, wij zijn er niet. Spreek een boodschap in na de biep.
Sorry, we're not at home, leave a message after the beep.

Ben je al in New York geweest?
Have you ever been to New York?

Nee, ik ben er nog nooit geweest.
No, I have never been there.

In the latter example, you can also use **daar** instead of **er**, if you want to stress this particular place. In this case, **daar** often assumes the first position in the sentence.

Ben je al in New York geweest?
Nee, daar ben ik nog nooit geweest. Ik ben al wel in Chicago geweest.

Number

You use **er** when combining the reference with a number. **Er** is not translated in English.

Hoeveel kinderen heb je?
How many children have you got?

Ik heb er twee.
I have got two.

Ik heb er sinds februari twee.
I have two since February.

Note the position of **er** in the sentence, which is the same as locative **er**, right next to the finite verb in the main clause.

Heb je de essays al gelezen?
Have you read the essays?

Ik heb er gisteren snel twee gelezen.
I have quickly read two yesterday

Oefening 2

1 Look around your classroom or a room in your house, and describe what you see. Write down a description using '**Er is /ligt/ staat/ zit** . . . .'

2 Look up a still life painting in an art book or on the Internet and describe it as before. Bring your picture and its description to class. Display all the pictures and read out your description. The other students guess which picture you are talking about.

Oefening 3

(a) Work in pairs and interview one another about your shopping habits. Use **er** in your answers.

Example

Komt u wel eens bij de Colruyt?
Ja, ik kom er een keer per week, voor de grote boodschappen. Je vindt er goedkope merkproducten.
Nee, daar kom ik nooit.

1 Doet u uw boodschappen in de buurtwinkel?
2 Koop u wel eens bij Turkse, Marokkaanse of andere buitenlandse winkeltjes?
3 Winkelt u graag in het centrum?
4 Koopt u uw krant in de krantenwinkel op de hoek?
5 Koopt u soms dingen op het internet?
6 Komt u dagelijks in de supermarkt?
7 Gaat u ook soms naar de markt?

(b) Write out the mini-dialogues you have created.

de buurtwinkel	the neighbourhood shop (grocer)
de Colruyt	name of Belgian supermarket chain
dagelijks	daily
de krantenwinkel	the newsagent
de markt	the street market
het merkproduct	brand name
de supermarkt	the supermarket

Oefening 4

Replace the underlined words by referring to them with **er** in Jan's replies in the interview below. The first one has already been done for you.

dokter	Hoeveel sigaretten rookt u per dag?
Jan	Ik rook vijf sigaretten per dag. Ik rook er vijf.
dokter	Hoeveel glazen alcohol drinkt u per week?
Jan	Euhm, ik drink een glas elke dag, dus dat zijn zeven glazen per week.
dokter	Hoeveel pijnstillers neemt u?
Jan	Ik neem geen pijnstillers.
dokter	OK, neemt u vitaminepillen?
Jan	Ja, ik neem elke ochtend een vitaminepil.
dokter	Zozo, eet u appels?
Jan	Ja, ik eet elke middag een appel.
dokter	Eet u ook hamburgers?
Jan	Ja, ik eet zeker drie hamburgers per week.
dokter	Mmm, misschien moet u wat minder hamburgers eten.
Jan	Maar ik eet al minder hamburgers dan mijn vrienden. Die eten wel zeven hamburgers per week!

Tekst 2 Stadgenoot van Jan G. Elburg (1960)

The artist in text 1 said she loved nature, even though she lived in a city. The following poem is about a city dweller and his/her relation to nature.

Hij is het licht vergeten
en het gras vergeten
en al die kleine levende kevertjes
en de smaak van het water en het waaien

hij is de geur vergeten
van het hooi de grijze vacht van de schapen
de varens de omgelegde aardkluiten

zijn binnen is geen nest zijn buiten
geen buiten zijn tuin een vaas

hij is ook
de bliksem vergeten de rauwe
hagel op zijn voorhoofd

hij zegt niet: graan meel brood
hij ziet de vogels niet weggaan
en de sneeuw niet komen

Key vocabulary

de aardkluit	lump of earth
de bliksem	lightning
de geur	smell, the scent
het graan	grain
de hagel	hail
het hooi	hay
de kever	beetle
het meel	flour
omleggen	to turn over
de smaak	taste
de stadgenoot	fellow townsman/woman
de tuin	garden
de vacht	fur
de varen	fern
vergeten	to forget
het voorhoofd	forehead
het waaien	blowing of the wind

Vragen bij tekst 2

Beantwoord vragen 1 tot en met 5 in het Nederlands.

1 Waarom heet het gedicht *stadgenoot*, denk je?
2 Wat is hij of zij vergeten?
3 Syntactically the text is not complete, after stanza 1, it simply continues. Insert 'en' and main verbs where you can, so the text reads more fluently.
4 Welke zintuigen beschrijft de dichter? (horen – zien – proeven – ruiken – voelen)
5 Welke woorden gebruikt hij om te refereren aan de stad en het platteland? Wat merk je?

Answer the following questions in English.

6 The repetition of 'hij is . . . vergeten' does not appear in the last stanza. Instead the poet says: 'hij zegt niet: graan meel brood'? What do you think he means?
7 How does that relate to the next two lines?
8 What point about city life is the poet making, do you think? How does the use of the word 'vaas' illustrate this point?

de dichter	poet	**proeven**	to taste
het gedicht	poem	**ruiken**	to smell
merken	to notice	**het zintuig**	sense
het platteland	countryside		

Oefening 5: Revision of the adjective

Fill in the correct form of the adjective. Don't forget to check the spelling.

1 Het meisje met het (rood) ____________ haar is een (bekend) ____________ (Nederlands) ____________ film.

2 Cees Nooteboom is een (beroemd) ____________ schrijver uit Nederland.

3 Dat nieuwe Italiaanse restaurant ziet er heel (lekker) ____________ uit.

4 (*Vals*) ____________ *licht* is een boek van Joost Zwagerman.

5 Ik hou van (romantisch) ____________ films, maar mijn partner kijkt liever naar actiefilms.

6 Henk houdt van (modern) ____________ dans, maar ik ga liever naar (klassiek) ____________ ballet.

7 Mijn ouders gingen vaak naar het (plaatselijk) ____________ theater, omdat ze de acteurs daar (goed) ____________ vonden.

Structuren

COMPARATIVE EN SUPERLATIVE

Deze film is *leuk*,	**die is *leuker*,**	**maar de nieuwe Bond is de *leukste*.**
Deze jurk is *mooi*,	**die rode vind ik *mooier*,**	**maar die van Dior is de *mooiste*.**
Dit eten is *lekker*	**dat van jou is *lekkerder*,**	**maar dat van mama is het *lekkerst(e)*.**
Mijn jas is *duur*,	**die van jou is *duurder*,**	**maar die van de popster is de *duurste*.**

There are a few exceptions, such as:

Ik eet *graag* nasi, maar ik eet *liever* spaghetti en het *liefst(e)* eet ik noedels.
Mulisch is *goed*, maar ik vind Reve *beter* en Hermans het *best(e)*.
Ik lees *weinig*, mijn broer nog *minder*, maar mijn man leest het *minst(e)*.
Mijn man kijkt *veel* TV, mijn broer *meer* en ik het *meest(e)*.

The comparative is often used in the following construction:

***hoe* meer *hoe* beter**
the more the better

***hoe* groter het huis *hoe* duurder het wordt**
the bigger the house the more expensive it becomes

TE ('TOO')

If you want to express 'too + adjective' in English, you do this in a very similar way in Dutch, by using '**te** + adjective'.

Die broek is veel *te lang*.
Sorry hoor, maar dit is echt *te gek*.

Oefening 6

Fill in the correct form of the comparative or superlative as appropriate.

1 Je plaatselijke supermarkt is misschien goedkoop, maar Aldi is zeker (goedkoop).

2 Ik woon graag in het centrum, maar mijn man woont (graag) op het platteland.

3 A: Het (mooi) schilderij van Van Gogh vind ik nog steeds zijn Zonnebloemen.
B: O, nee, dat vind ik niet. Ik vind zijn zelfportretten (mooi).

4 De (groot) schrijver aller tijden is volgens velen Shakespeare.

5 De (veel) vrouwen houden van vrouwentijdschriften, maar (veel) en (veel) mannen lezen ze nu ook.

6 A: De (goed) film van het afgelopen jaar is ______________ .
B: Nou, nee hoor, ik vind ______________ (goed).

7 Hoe (veel) politie op straat, hoe (weinig) criminaliteit; dat is de opinie van velen.

8 Hoe (moeilijk) de oefening, hoe (frustrerend) het is voor de student.

Oefening 7

Discuss your favourite film/actor/writer/book with one of your fellow students. Try to use a mixture of adjectives, comparatives and superlatives.

Example

A Ik vind Tom Cruise een heel goede acteur

B Mm, ja, maar ik heb Brad Pitt liever, vooral in *Seven Years in Tibet*.

A Goh nee, ik vind hem beter in *Snatch*.

B Echt? Nee, ik niet, ik vind hem te melig in die film. In welke film vind je Tom Cruise het best?

A Hij is het subliemst in *Magnolia*, denk ik.

B Oh nee, daar is hij te irritant.

liever hebben	to prefer	**melig**	corny

Cultuur

DUTCH AND BELGIAN DESIGN

Design is big in the Netherlands and it contributes a great deal to the international design scene. If you visit a designer furniture or homeware shop anywhere in the world, you will come across many Dutch names. Think of Gerrit Rietveld's famous chair, the milk bottle lamp by Droog design or the Bugaboo buggy. In architecture the Dutch are fairly prominent as well with architects such as Rem Koolhaas. The city of Rotterdam, largely rebuilt after the bombings of the second world war, has become a homage to modern Dutch architecture. For more information on architecture and design in the Netherlands, you can go to www.holland.com/architectuur.

The Belgians have claimed a remarkable place in the world of designer fashion. Designers such as Walter Van Beirendonck, Ann Demeulemeester, Dirk Bikkembergs, Martin Margiela, Dries Van Noten and Raf Simons are familiar names among fashionistas. Antwerp now owns a state of the art fashion institute and museum, which are well worth a visit.

Designer furniture and fashion are rather expensive and the Netherlands wouldn't be the Netherlands if they hadn't come up with a cheap and cheerful version of it all. Every Dutch town centre has a HEMA, an affordable shop that sells everything from liquorice and cakes to bath foam, baby clothes and well-designed household objects, such as cutlery, glasses and lamps. HEMA also has shops in Flanders, where it is becoming increasingly popular.

Tekst 3 Starck stoel

Read the description of a design chair, taken from the Flemish lifestyle magazine *Goed Gevoel*, and answer the questions below.

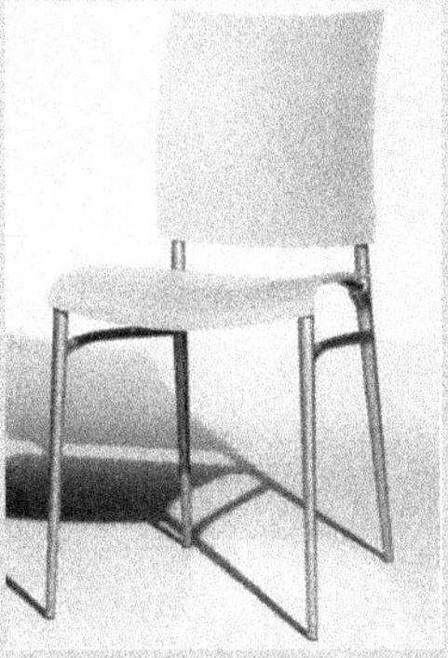

Philippe Starck vindt zijn nieuwe stoel sexy. Ze is als een vrouw, ze zit lekker, heeft smalle benen en een mooi profiel. En zoals heel veel vrouwen heeft ze ook een geheim: ze kan namelijk plooien! Ideaal om bij een feestje van achter de kast te toveren.

Key vocabulary

het feestje	the party
het geheim	the secret
de kast	the cupboard
plooien	to bend (in Flanders only; in the Netherlands: **vouwen**)
smal	narrow *here*: slender
toveren	to do magic

Vragen bij tekst 3

Beantwoord de volgende vragen in het Nederlands.

1 Maak een lijst van alle adjectieven (adjectives) die de stoel beschrijven.
2 Zijn dit typische adjectieven om een stoel te beschrijven? Waarmee vergelijkt de auteur de stoel?
3 Vind je de vergelijking effectief? Waarom (niet)?
4 Zou je de stoel kopen? Waarom (niet)?

Oefening 8

Categorise the following adjectives into what are generally considered to be 'male' and 'female' characteristics. Discuss your choice with your fellow students in Dutch. You can use the sample phrases below.

Note that the discussion is not just about whether you personally believe certain characteristics to be male or female, but about whether there is a pervading belief in society whether this is the case or not. You may of course disagree with this general consensus.

ambitieus – prestatiegericht– competitief – gevoelig – warm – zacht – hard – rationeel – emotioneel – communicatief – afhankelijk– onafhankelijk – snel – sexy – vriendelijk – afstandelijk – fysiek – sportief – stijlvol – comfortabel – veilig – persoonlijk – individualistisch – gevaarlijk

You can use the following patterns:

Veel mensen vinden rationaliteit een typisch mannelijke eigenschap.
Vrouwen zijn vaak emotioneel. Nou ja, emotioneler dan mannen.
Het is een algemeen aanvaarde opvatting dat mannen prestatiegericht zijn en vrouwen niet.

Ja, dat vind ik ook.
Nee, dat vind ik niet, want . . .

afhankelijk	dependent
afstandelijk	distant
de algemeen aanvaarde opvatting	generally accepted view
gevoelig	sensitive
onafhankelijk	independent
persoonlijk	personal
prestatiegericht	achievement-oriented
snel	fast
stijlvol	stylish
veilig	safe

Oefening 9

(a) Which word is the odd one out?

1 zacht – gevoelig – warm – hard
2 emotioneel – sportief – rationeel – ambitieus
3 comfortabel – gevaarlijk – veilig – stijlvol
4 prestatiegericht – competitief – individualistisch – afhankelijk

(b) Match the following words with their opposite:

1 ambitieus	(a) goedkoop
2 afstandelijk	(b) hard
3 zacht	(c) lui
4 aardig	(d) ongemotiveerd
5 sportief	(e) ongezond
6 sexy	(f) onvriendelijk
7 emotioneel	(g) ouderwets
8 duur	(h) persoonlijk
9 gezond	(i) rationeel
10 modern	(j) saai

Oefening 10

1 Write a short advertisement (100 words) for a car, using some of the adjectives of **Oefening 9** and **10**.

2 If possible, work in pairs and look at one another's advertisement. Have you used more 'male' or 'female' adjectives? Discuss – in English – whether you would have done it differently if you'd had a specific male or female target audience in mind. Explain.

Tekst 4 Naar de film

Erik (26), an insurance broker, and his girlfriend Els, who works at a travel agent, want to spend a night at the movies.

In the first listening round, don't look at the text and answer question 1 below. Then listen to the discussion a few more times, read it and answer the other questions.

Erik	Els, wil je nou nog naar de film?
Els	Ja, jij toch ook?
Erik	Welja, weet je al wat er draait?
Els	Er speelt een of andere Braziliaanse film, en die nieuwe van Lars Von Trier. Euhm, *Maid in Manhattan* met Jennifer Lopez draait ook, en natuurlijk ook *The Matrix Reloaded*.
Erik	Te gek, zo'n actiefilm. Dat vind jij toch ook leuk? Wat zeggen ze in de recensies?
Els	Nou, die film van Lars Von Trier en die Braziliaanse film zijn erg zwaar en psychologisch en zo.
Erik	Getver, ik heb geen zin in een serieuze film, hoor. Ik wil liever iets spannends. Vinden ze *The Matrix* niet goed?
Els	En een romantische film?
Erik	Nou, ik weet het niet. Wil jij dat dan?
Els	Ja, *Maid in Manhattan* lijkt me wel leuk . . .

Key vocabulary

draaien	*here*: showing	**zin hebben in**	to feel like
lijken	to seem	**zwaar**	heavy

Vragen bij tekst 4

Beantwoord de vragen in het Nederlands.

1 Wat voor soort films ziet Els graag? En Erik?
2 Naar welke film gaan ze uiteindelijk kijken, denk je?
3 Welke adjectieven gebruiken Els en Erik om de films te beschrijven? Maak een lijstje.

uiteindelijk finally

Listen to the dialogue one more time and pay special attention to the intonation. Then read it out loud, if possible with a fellow student, and try to capture the right tone.

Communicatie

ASKING FOR PREFERENCE

Wil jij nog naar de film?

Dat vind jij toch ook leuk?

Vinden ze *The Matrix* niet goed?

Kijk je graag naar actiefilms?

Heb je zin in een romantische film?

Heb je zin om naar de film te gaan?

POSSIBLE REACTIONS

Te gek!

Oh ja, leuk/lekker/gezellig/. . .

Ja, geweldig!

Ja, *Maid in Manhattan* lijkt me (wel) leuk.

Nou, ik weet het niet.

Nee, eigenlijk niet.

Nou, (nee) niet echt.

Ik heb geen zin in een serieuze film, hoor.

Oefening 11

Work in pairs. Respond to the following questions and make use of the expressions above. Try to use an authentic intonation and vary your responses beween positive and negative ones. Think of a few more questions yourself.

1 Wil je graag een avondje naar de opera?
2 Vind jij de schilderijen van Picasso mooi?
3 Jij vindt David Beckham toch zo'n knappe jongen?
4 Heb je zin om iets te gaan drinken?
5 Heb je zin in een kopje koffie? Koekje?
6 Lees jij graag detectiveromans?
7 Wil je naar die nieuwe film van Tarantino gaan kijken?
8 Heb je zin in een nieuwe haring?
9 Vind jij zoute drop lekker?
10 Vind jij ______________ ?
11 Heb je zin om ______________ ?

Oefening 12

You and your fellow students are going out for the evening and you discuss what you will do. Write a short dialogue (125 words) about this and make use of some of the expressions you have learnt. If possible, perform this in front of your fellow students and make sure you also capture the right tone. This will need some practice. Don't just read from the page. Your fellow students will have to make notes of your plans, so you can discuss them afterwards in the wider group.

Structuren

DEMONSTRATIVE PRONOUNS

Form

Deze and **dit** are used for the English 'this'. **Die** and **dat** for the English 'that'.

Deze/Die with a **de**-word: **Deze pen is van mij en die is van jou.**
This pen is mine and that one is yours.

Dit/Dat with a **het**-word: **Dit boek is van Hans en dat van Els.**
This book is Hans's and that one Els's.

Note that all plural words are **de**-words, so they need to be referred to with **deze/die**. For example:

Deze boeken en die pennen zijn van de zaak.

Use

Demonstratives can be used in front of a noun, just as in English. When it is clear what you are referring to, **deze**, **die**, **dit**, **dat** can also be used on their own. In English, you often translate this with 'this one' or 'that one'. For example:

Gaat deze trein naar Keulen?
Does this train go to Cologne?

Nee, *deze* gaat naar Brussel.
No, this one goes to Brussels.

Other functions

Die and **dat** are also used to refer to a person or an object. In English, you would normally use a personal pronoun here. For example:

Waar is moeder? **Die is in de keuken**	Where is mother? She is in the kitchen.
Waar zijn de kranten? **Die liggen op de tafel.**	Where are the newspapers? They are on the table.
Waar is mijn boek? **Dat ligt op je bureau.**	Where is my book? It is on your desk.

Dit and **dat** are used to introduce people or things. For example:

Dit is mijn vriend. **Dat is mijn vriend.**	This is my (boy)friend. That is my (boy)friend.
Dit zijn mijn kinderen. **Dat zijn mijn kinderen.**	These are my children. Those are my children.

Note that **deze** and **die** are not used in this last function!

Oefening 13

Fill in **deze**, **die**, **dat**, or **deze** in the following sentences. Sometimes both **deze/die** or **dit/dat** are possible, depending on whether you are pointing 'here' or 'there'.

Example

Welke bloemen vind jij het mooist, ______ hier of ______ daar?
deze die

1 Hé Bram, leg jij ______ boeken even terug in de kast?
2 Wil je ______ stuk taart of ______ ?
3 Van wie zijn ______ schoenen?
4 We moeten ______ huizen bekijken.
5 Ik wil graag in ______ huis wonen.
6 Ik hou wel van ______ pastelkleuren.
7 Wij gaan op vakantie naar Mauritius. Oh, ______ is leuk!
8 Waar zijn de kinderen? ______ zitten op zolder.
9 Waar ligt mijn jas? ______ hangt in de kast.
10 Koopt u normaal jonge kaas? Nee, ______ is te zacht voor mij.

Oefening 14

Fill in **deze/die/dit/dat** in the following e-mail. Please look at the context carefully.

Hoi Fred,

Hoe gaat het met je? Het is lang geleden sinds (1) ______ barbecue bij Karel! (2) ______ was een leuke avond, (3) ______ moeten we nog eens doen. Trouwens, ik heb (4) ______ boeken voor je, weet je nog, over auto-onderhoud. Is (5) ______ nog altijd je grote hobby?

Gisteren zag ik Martine, ken je haar nog? (6) ______ was heel erg moe. Haar kinderen slapen niet goed, maar ja, (7) ______ zijn ook nog heel jong. (8) ______ is maar een fase, zei ik haar, ze worden wel groot.

Maar, ik schrijf je eigenlijk omdat (9) ______ rekening van Karels cadeau nog niet betaald is. Zou jij (10) ______ niet doen? Ik had jou toch (11) ______ cheque gegeven? Zou je (12) ______ snel willen doen, want ik kreeg gisteren telefoon van de wijnhandel waar we (13) ______ flessen gekocht hebben.

Goed, (14) ______ was het zo'n beetje. Ik hoop dat alles verder goed met je is en tot horens,

Bart

het auto-onderhoud	car maintenance
de fase	phase
nog weten	to remember
de rekening	the bill
de wijnhandel	wine merchant

Tekst 5

Hans (38), who works in advertising and Simon (42), an unemployed actor, are queuing for tickets at the cinema. They are discussing films.

Hans	Heb jij *Dogville* al gezien?
Simon	Ja, je weet dat ik een grote fan ben van het oeuvre van Von Trier.
Hans	Een fascinerend cineast met een revolutionaire visie. Toch vind ik niet al zijn werk even geslaagd. Hij is niet altijd even subtiel.
Simon	Je hebt gelijk. Hij kan z'n protagonisten vrij hard in beeld brengen. Maar z'n films zijn ook vaak nogal humoristisch. Kan je je vinden in zijn humor?
Hans	Soms wel, maar niet altijd. Hij heeft een droog en cynisch gevoel voor humor. Daardoor spreken zijn films me niet altijd aan.
Simon	Nou, laten we hopen dat je je niet gaat ergeren! Let ook vooral op de onverwachte aanwezigheid van Nicole Kidman in deze prent. Ze overtreft zichzelf.
Hans	Ik ben benieuwd. Zij heeft zich al eerder bewezen in *The Hours*, maar ik associeer haar toch nog altijd met holle Hollywood glamour.

Key vocabulary

aanschuiven	to queue
aanspreken	to appeal to
de aanwezigheid	presence
benieuwd	curious
de cineast	film maker/director
even	*here*: equally
hol	empty, without content
in beeld brengen	to show, to portray
in de rij staan	to stand in line
onverwacht	unexpected
overtreffen	to exceed
de prent	a print; *here*: a film
slagen	to succeed
zich bewijzen	to prove oneself
zich ergeren aan iets	to be annoyed at something
zich vinden in iets	to relate to something

Vragen bij tekst 5

Beantwoord vraag 1 tot en met 4 in het Nederlands.

1 Wat vinden Hans en Simon van de Von Trier films?

2 Welke adjectieven gebruiken ze om de films te beschrijven? Maak een lijstje.

3 Vergelijk dit lijstje met het lijstje van Els en Erik in de vorige dialoog.

4 Is deze dialoog formeel of informeel? Waarom?

5 How would you characterise the way that Hans and Simon talk about films?

NAAR DE FILM

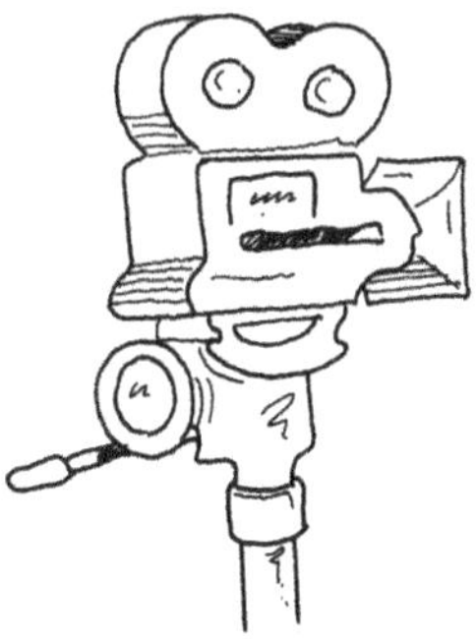

een film draait/speelt	a film is playing
een film gaat over	a film is about
de bioscoop	cinema [*the Netherlands*]
de cinema	cinema [*Flanders*]
ga je mee naar de film?	are you coming to the movies
de actiefilm	action film
de romantische film	romantic film
de komedie	comedy
de thriller	thriller
de tragikomedie	tragicomedy
de filmklassieker	film classic
de documentaire	documentary
de acteur	actor
de filmster	film star
de producent	producer
de zwart-witfilm	black and white movie
de actrice	actress
de regisseur	director
het scherm	screen

Oefening 15

Listen to the review of a film called *Napoleon Dynamite* and fill in the missing words. You can pick them from the list below. Read through the text before you start listening, so you get an idea of what you should be listening for.

cineast personages set satire verhaal
gaat over figuren bekijken acteerprestaties
gespeeld kapsel in beeld heeft gebracht

Gisterenavond ben ik gaan kijken naar *Napoleon Dynamite*, een ongewone film van onafhankelijk (1) ___________ Jared Hess. De film (2) ___________ *Napoleon Dynamite*, een humeurige tiener, (3) ___________ door John Heder.

Veel gebeurt er niet, maar dat is net de bedoeling, geloof ik. Het (4) ___________ speelt zich af in een dorp in Idaho, waar allerlei gekke maar toch herkenbare (5) ___________ rondlopen. Op het eerste gezicht een niet erg boeiend thema, maar door de (6) ___________ en de ongewone figuren toch echt de moeite waard. Er figureert bijvoorbeeld een humeurige lama op de (7) ___________ , en ook de nevenpersonages zoals Napoleons broer, oom en oma zijn hilarisch! Een deel van de film speelt zich af op de school van de jongen, waar je de gebruikelijke (8) ___________ tegenkomt; de populaire jongens en de sukkels die kibbelen in de gang. Napoleon zelf is verlegen, niet bijzonder populair, heeft een vreemd (9) ___________ en een permanent openhangende mond.

Al met al vind ik dat Hess een mooie (10) __________ heeft gemaakt en het zielloze stadje mooi (11) __________ . Een aanrader dus voor deze week!

Je kan hem gaan (12) __________ in de alternatievere bisocopen.

de aanrader	something worth recommending
de bedoeling	intention
figureren	to appear, to be an extra
gebruikelijk	usual
herkenbaar	recognisable
humeurig	moody
kapsel	hairdo
kibbelen	to bicker
de moeite waard	worth (seeing)
het nevenpersonage	side character
onafhankelijk	independent
ongewoon	unusual
openhangende mond	open mouth
de sukkel	loser
verlegen	shy

Communicatie

EXPRESSING AN OPINION

Ik vind . . .

Ik vind Terminator een hartstikke spannende film.
Zij vindt actiefilms maar niks.
Zij vindt romantische films leuk.

EXPRESSING PREFERENCES

Ik hou (veel–meer–het meest) van . . .
Ik zie/eet (graag–liever–liefst) . . .
Ik vind X (goed–beter–het best) . . .

Ik hou *meer* van een karakteracteur zoals John Malkovich of Willem Dafoe.
Ik eet *liever* bij de Italiaan dan bij de Chinees.
Ik heb *graag* veel licht en weinig meubels in mijn huis.

Oefening 16

(a) Turn the following statements into opinions:

1 Rood is een mooie kleur voor de woonkamer – Ik vind __________
2 Het leven in de stad is veel te druk – Ik hou niet van leven in de stad omdat __________

3 Actiefilms zijn een goede ontspanning – Ik vind ____________

4 Indonesische rijsttafels zijn heel lekker – Ik eet ____________

5 Moderne meubels zijn koel en lelijk – Ik vind dat ____________

(b) Compare the opinions above to your own, by using the comparative and superlative.

Example

Ik vind rood een mooie kleur voor de woonkamer, maar ik vind groen mooier.
Ik vind rood minder mooi voor de woonkamer, maar beter voor de slaapkamer.

Oefening 17

Think of three questions you can ask your fellow students about his or her lifestyle preferences and interview several students. Next, present your most interesting findings to the wider group.

Example

Hou jij van behang?
Ja, ik vind psychedelisch seventiesbehang en grote bloemen geweldig, maar ik vind effen kleuren wel praktischer.

het behang	wallpaper	**effen**	plain

Structuren

COMPOUND NOUNS

Compound nouns are nouns that consist of two or more words of which at least the last one is a noun. In Dutch this is written as one word. This can result in very long words. For example:

verzekeringsmakelaarskantoor insurance broker's office

A compound noun can consist of:

(a) noun + noun

de verzekering + de makelaar	=	**de verzekeringsmakelaar**
de video + de camera	=	**de videocamera**
de thee + het glas	=	**het theeglas**
de krant + het artikel	=	**het krantenartikel**

Note that the compound noun takes the article of the final noun.

(b) stem of verb + noun

lezen + de tekst = de leestekst

(c) (other) + noun

achter + deur = achterdeur

Oefening 18

Combine the following nouns to create a compound noun.

1. het strand + het huis
2. de telefoon + de rekening
3. de kop + de telefoon
4. het toilet + het papier
5. de televisie + het programma
6. de tand + de pasta
7. de sport + de schoen
8. het bad + de kamer
9. de politie + de auto
10. de muziek + het festival

de kop	head	**de tand**	tooth
het strand	beach		

Oefening 19

Make up as many compound nouns as you can from the columns below:

Example

werk + kamer = de werkkamer

1	werk (< werken)	het raam
2	de winkel	de deur
3	voor	het boek
4	eet (< eten)	het woord
5	na	de tafel
6	woorden	de kast
7	de keuken	de kamer
8	de school	het uniform

Oefening 20

Combine the following nouns by linking them with **-en-**, **-s-** or **-e-**. You may want to use a dictionary.

1 de tijd + het verschil
2 het verkeer + het bord
3 de koningin + de dag
4 de pan + de koek
5 de wet + het voorstel
6 de kip + het ei
7 de sleutel + de bos
8 de drugs + het beleid
9 het lichaam + het deel
10 de student + de kamer

het beleid	policy
het bord	sign
de bos	bundle, bunch
het lichaam	body
het verkeer	traffic
het verschil	difference
het voorstel	proposal
de wet	law, legislation

Oefening 21

Look up a common word in a dictionary such as **dood**, **bloem**, **hand**, **hoofd**, **handel**, **keuken**, **school**, **woord** and see how many compound words (not always nouns) are listed under the entry.

Pick one noun and list 5 compound words that you think are useful. Put them in a sentence and present these to your fellow students.

Tekst 6 Filmrecensies

You are going to read the reviews of the films that were discussed in the previous dialogues. These texts are not easy and may seem a bit daunting. However there are a number of strategies that can help you deal with this.

Communicatie

READING STRATEGIES

(a) It is generally a good strategy to take a moment before reading a text to think about *what you expect to find* in that text. Often the title and subtitles give you an indication. In the case of the film reviews below, you probably already have a set of expectations about the texts, because you are familar with the genre of film reviews. You would therefore expect to find at least some of these things:

- a short description of the film;
- a general opinion about the film;

- an opinion or description about the acting;
- an opinion or description about the directing or film technique;
- a recommendation about whether to go and see the film or not.

(b) Now read through the text to see if you *get the gist*. Do you indeed get the kind of information you were expecting to find, or do you need to adjust your expectations after a first reading? Using your expectations helps you in constructing what a text is 'doing'. For example:

'This paragraph or sentence tells me the positive points of a text, whereas the next sentence gives contrasting negative points.'

(c) You should by now have a broad idea of, or at least the gist of, the main points or ideas of the text. This should help you in trying to understand the text in more detail. Even if you don't know specific words, you are by now likely to realise which words in a sentence are *key words*. You can look these up in a dictionary. Many words which are new to you, you might recognise anyway, as they will be similar to English words (or French words you know).

(d) Finally, *grammar* can help you understand a text. Complicated texts tend to use complicated grammatical patterns. If you struggle, try to reconstruct a complicated sentence into smaller parts. You can do this by looking for:

- What are the main and subclauses?
- Is there more than one verb in the sentence and which is the finite verb?
- In what tense has the sentence been written?
- What is the subject and the object of the sentence?

Oefening 22

Look at the following sentence which comes from one of the reviews below.

De opvallende en nerveuze camerabewegingen zijn ook van een hoog niveau, en bevestigen Von Trier nog maar eens als een uitzonderlijke cineast.

1 What do you think the sentence is about?
2 How many clauses are there to the sentence?
3 What is/are the subjects of the sentence?
4 Look for the finite verb(s) in the sentence (parts).
5 Is the finite verb used on its own or with another verb construction, such as an infinitive?

You should by now have a good idea what the sentence is about. Look up any words which you think are key to understanding the sentence completely, but you have probably already found that you can guess the meaning of at least some of them.

Tekst 6

The Matrix Reloaded

Lang verwacht, maar nu hebben we ook wat. Vette film, sterke filosofie. Genoeg om een week door te lullen met vrienden. Minpuntje, te veel personages. Toch een echte must voor fans van actiefilms. Gave special effects, en alles ziet er onwijs cool uit.

Key vocabulary

doorlullen	**here*: to go on about	**onwijs cool**	*super cool
gaaf	*wicked/cool	**verwachten**	to expect
het minpunt	negative point	**vette**	*great, cool

* *very colloquial*

Cidade de Deus

Dit meesterwerk is het best te omschrijven als een superlatieve mix van *Amores Perros* en Martin Scorseses *Goodfellas*, maar dan in Tarantino-stijl. Het scenario is ingenieus, de tijdsreconstructie briljant, de karaktertekeningen psychologisch ragfijn, het camerawerk hyperkinetisch, de montage dynamisch, de soundtrack functioneel, de vertolkingen gedreven, en de mise-en-scène virtuoos. Wel laat de film meer provocerend en bruut geweld zien dan de meeste gemiddelde magen aankunnen.

Key vocabulary

gedreven	passionate	**omschrijven**	to describe
het geweld	violence	**ragfijn**	subtle/detailed
hyperkinetisch	hyperactive	**de vertolking**	performance
de karaktertekening	characterisation	**wat de gemiddelde magen aankunnen**	what the average person can stomach
laten zien	to show		
het meesterwerk	masterpiece		

Maid in Manhattan

De rijke Ralph Fiennes wordt verliefd op Jennifer Lopez. Maar zij is kamermeisje in een hotel. En als hij erachter komt wie zij echt is . . . zal hij dan nog van haar houden? Zal de pers zijn politieke carrière kapot maken? En welke rol speelt Jennifers schattige zoontje Ty? Een erg leuke en vooral ook romantische film! Fiennes en Lopez spelen hun rol heel overtuigend. Enkele hartverwarmende scènes maken de film compleet. Een aanradertje!

Key vocabulary

het aanradertje	a must/highly recommended	**kapot maken**	to destroy, to wreck
erachter komen	to find out	**overtuigend**	convincing
hartverwarmend	heartwarming	**de pers**	press
het kamermeisje	chambermaid	**verliefd worden op**	to fall in love with

Dogville

Dit minimalistische drama bestaat uit een proloog en 9 hoofdstukken. Von Trier brengt zowel symbolisch als analytisch de wreedheid van het mensdom vlijmscherp in beeld. De enscenering is fascinerend, net als het spel met de natuurelementen. De opvallende belichting en nerveuze camerabewegingen zijn ook van een hoog niveau, en bevestigen Von Trier nog maar eens als een uitzonderlijke cineast.

Key vocabulary

bestaan uit	to consist of	**opvallend**	remarkable
bevestigen	to confirm	**uitzonderlijk**	exceptional
de beweging	movement	**vlijmscherp**	razor sharp
de enscenering	staging, direction	**de wreedheid**	cruelty
het mensdom	mankind		

Vragen bij tekst 6

Werk in paren en bespreek de vragen in het Nederlands.

1 Wat denken de filmcritici van deze films? Hoeveel sterren zouden ze deze films geven, denk je?

*	=	zwak
**	=	niet slecht als je niets beters te doen hebt
***	=	de moeite waard
****	=	sterk
*****	=	schitterend, moet je zien

2 Uit wat voor verschillende publicaties komen deze recencies, denk je? Waarom denk je dat? Bijvoorbeeld:

een serieus filmblad
een tienerblad
een populair weekblad
een kwaliteitskrant

3 Zou je zelf naar deze film gaan. Waarom wel/niet?
4 Vat de recensies samen in enkele zinnen, in een neutrale stijl.

bespreken	to discuss	**verschillend**	different
samenvatten	to summarise		

Oefening 23

Write a review (150 words) about a film that you thought was either really good or really bad. Choose a particular publication to write for (e.g.: popular weekly, teenage magazine, quality newspaper, etc.).

Oefening 24

1 You and two or three other students want to go out one evening in Ghent or Groningen. You will have to look at the websites listed to make a choice from the three options below.

optie 1: naar de film gaan
optie 2: naar een restaurant gaan
optie 3: iets anders

website Ghent: www.gent.be
website Groningen algemeen: www.groningen.nl
website 'uit in Groningen': www.dsg.nl

2 Once you have decided what to do, you have to discuss in Dutch which film, restaurant or other venue you will go to. Discuss the criteria listed below to help you make an informed choice.

Optie 1: Jullie besluiten om naar de film te gaan. Bekijk het filmprogramma op de website of gebruik films die momenteel bij jou in de buurt draaien. Bespreek je criteria bij je keuze: acteurs – regisseur – thema – fotografie – het verhaal – de schrijver – recensies die je hebt gelezen.

Optie 2: Jullie besluiten om naar een restaurant te gaan. Bespreek in je criteria bij de keuze: keuken – kwaliteit – locatie – design – sfeer – dienst – publiek.

Optie 3: Misschien wil je liever iets anders gaan doen. Er staat heel veel informatie op de websites van beide steden. Bespreek samen je criteria en je keuze.

3 If possible, present your choice to the group. Make sure you explain well which criteria were important to you and why you chose that particular film, restaurant or event.

Oefening 25

One of your fellow students is running for mayor. You are going to interview him or her about his/her personal preferences and write an introduction of 200 words about him or her for a local newspaper. Your aim is to inform your readers about the person behind the public figure. Make sure you include information about:

(a) where he wants to live/where he lives
(b) food
(c) hobbies/leisure activities

A closer look

Read the following two texts, taken from the comments page of a popular newspaper website, where two people express rather opposing views on the masculinity of footballer David Beckham.

As the texts below are quite difficult, use the reading strategies outlined earlier.

Note that the title should give you an indication of what you can expect in the text.

Tekst 7 David Beckham

Metroseksueel met een geniale voet

Door Henk

Ik hoorde zijn iele stem, voelde zijn charisma en was onder de indruk van zijn enorme rust. Zijn bijna Zen-achtige uitstraling.

Hij is de enige topvoetballer die in een sarong durft te lopen en ook zijn huid injecteert met stoere tatoeages. Nagels lakken, wenkbrauwen epileren; net zo normaal voor het lichaamsonderhoud als je spieren opwarmen voor de wedstijd.

Hij is de ultieme metroseksueel, las ik. Dat zijn mannen die evenveel van auto's als van gezichtscrème houden. De bevrijde, postmoderne, stedelijke Renaissance-man.

Een watje, maar wel een mooi watje

Door Josefien

David Beckham is een mooie man, daar is geen discussie over mogelijk. Een perfect gezicht, een betoverende lach, altijd bezig met zijn uiterlijk.

Maar ook Beckham is niet perfect. En niet alleen door die rare, hoge stem, die menig vrouw ieder lustgevoel ontneemt.

Nee, die stem is niet eens het ergste. Het is iets anders. David Beckham is een watje. Zo, dat is er uit. Een man die om het minste of geringste in tranen uitbarst. Een gewonnen wedstrijd, een verloren wedstrijd. De geboorte van zijn kinderen, de scheiding van zijn ouders.

In de Verenigde Staten komen ze massaal uit de kast. Deze mannen doen wat ze willen, kopen wat ze willen en genieten van wat ze willen. Ze trekken zich niets aan van wat de wereld om hen heen 'mannelijk' vindt. Een rolmodel voor mannen én vrouwen.

Het past ook totaal niet bij het beeld dat ik heb van voetballers. Onverschrokken kerels. Mannen die liever hun eigen tong zouden inslikken dan de buitenwereld hun tranen te tonen. Soms zou ik willen dat Beckham ook zo was. Zou ik hem wel eens flink door elkaar willen schudden om hem dat duidelijk te maken. Wees nou eens een vent!

Naar: *Algemeen Dagblad*

Key vocabulary

-achtige	-like
betoverend	mesmerising
bevrijd	liberated
bezig	busy, working on
door elkaar schudden	to shake
durven	to dare
de geboorte	birth
genieten van	to enjoy
het geringste	the least
het gezicht	face
de huid	skin
iel	thin
in tranen uitbarsten	to burst into tears
inslikken	to swallow
de kerel	bloke
het lichaam	body
het lustgevoel	libido
menig	many a
mogelijk	possible
nagels lakken	to polish nails
onder de indruk zijn	to be impressed
onderhouden	to maintain, to look after
ontnemen	to take away
onverschrokken	fearless
raar	strange
de rust	peace
de scheiding	divorce
de spier	muscle
stedelijk	urban
stoer	tough
tonen	to show
uit de kast komen	to come out of the closet
het uiterlijk	the appearance
de uitstraling	radiance, *here*: aura
de vent	a bloke, *here*: a real man
verliezen	to lose
het watje	softie *(this term has negative overtones)*
de wedstrijd	game
wees	imperative of to be
wenkbrauwen epileren	to depilate eyebrows
zich (n)iets aantrekken van iets	(not) to be bothered by something

Vragen bij tekst 7

Beantwoord vraag 1 tot en met 5 in het Nederlands.

1 Waarom houdt Henk van Beckham en Josefien niet?
2 Hoe definiëert Henk een 'metroseksueel'?
3 Zowel Henk als Josefien zeggen iets over Beckhams stem, maar met een andere interpretatie. Leg uit.
4 Maak een lijstje met de woorden die Beckhams uiterlijk beschrijven in beide teksten. Vergelijk het beeld dat ze creëren.
5 Doe nu hetzelfde voor zijn persoonlijkheid.

Answer questions 6 to 8 in English.

6 Looking at the lists you have made, which aspects of Beckham's appearance and character does each writer focus on? Does this relate to their view on masculinity?
7 What is the difference between the ideal of the **metroseksueel** (Henk) and the **voetballer** (Josefien) ?
8 Can you point at a number of phrases and words which indicate the writer's preference for either ideal and their dislike for the opposite?

Oefening 26

What do you think? Is Beckham 'een rolmodel voor mannen en vrouwen' or 'geen echte vent' or something in between?

1 Write a reaction to the two texts above for the website of one of the following magazines:

(a) een roddelblad
(b) een feministisch maandblad
(c) een vrouwenblad
(d) een voetbalmagazine
(e) een mannenblad

mannenblad	men's magazine	**roddelblad**	gossip magazine

2 Bring your text to class and compare with other students. Look at the following aspects:

How did your target audience influence your writing?
How did this affect your choice of words?
How did you select your content, which aspects did you choose to focus on?
Which stylistic devices did you use (e.g.: very short sentences, exclamations, enumerations, affirmative sentences, questions) and to what effect?

Unit 6
Werkklimaat

This unit focuses on the world of work. You will study the way people talk about work and the various modes of communication at work such as e-mails. This unit looks at how style and language use reflect relations at work: between employer and staff and between company and customer. We also look at ways of inviting people and how these reflect professional relationships. In addition, the unit offers an opportunity to talk about personal development in a work context. Finally, some differences between Dutch as spoken in the Netherlands and in Flanders are discussed.

TOPICS

- Names of professions
- Aspects of work situation
- Some aspects of Flemish Dutch
- Regional variations of Dutch
- Work habits
- Invitations, ways of addressing people
- E-mails
- Professional development and training
- Job adverts
- Personality traits

FUNCTIONS

- Talking about work experience
- Expectations and preferences
- Writing e-mails with a clear focus and target audience
- Addressing people
- Inviting people
- Complimenting people
- Expressing criticism
- Phrasing criticism in the form of advice
- Talking about your strengths and weaknesses
- Reading satire

GRAMMAR

- Use of '**er**'; with a preposition
- Verbs and expressions with a fixed preposition
- Subclauses of time
- Subclauses of contrast
- Subclauses of comparison
- Subclauses of condition
- Subclauses of reason
- Relative clauses
- Sentence structure, main and subclauses: revision
- Position of adverbials

Tekst 1 Maandagmorgen in de tram

Luister naar de volgende dialoog tussen Arie en Marianne.

Arie (28) en Marianne (30) komen elkaar 's morgens tegen in de tram. Arie werkt sinds kort als teamleader in een callcenter en Marianne werkt al 6 jaar op het ministerie van landbouw, als administratief medewerker.

Arie	Hoi Marianne, tsjonge, jij ziet er moe uit!
Marianne	Ben ik ook, Arie. Ook goeiemorgen trouwens. Ik heb een zwaar weekend gehad.
Arie	Vertel!
Marianne	Pff, Arie, ik ben echt te moe. Vertel jij eens over je nieuwe baan.
Arie	O, het is eigenlijk heel leuk. Ik was bang dat het wat saai zou worden, maar we hebben een hartstikke leuk team en een sympathieke manager. We gaan altijd iets drinken op vrijdag en dat werkt ook goed. Wist je trouwens dat ik met een avondcursus begonnen ben?
Marianne	Eh, wat dan?
Arie	Ik studeer er nog bedrijfskunde bij. Zo kan ik binnen dit bedrijf makkelijker hogerop, zie je. Ik krijg het trouwens merendeels terugbetaald door mijn werk, dus dat is ook meegenomen.
Marianne	Klinkt allemaal geweldig. Ik zit nog steeds te suffen daar op het ministerie, maar het is wel goed betaald en lekker makkelijk. Ik ken het klappen van de zweep, heb leuke collega's en kan elke dag op tijd naar huis.
Arie	Nou, als ik jou was, zou ik toch ook naar iets anders uitkijken. Kan je niet op kosten van het ministerie iets bijstuderen? De regering loopt daar toch altijd over te roepen?
Marianne	Ik geloof wel dat dat mogelijk is; ik moet er eens naar vragen. Ik zou eigenlijk wel liever iets met meer menselijk contact doen, communicatiewetenschappen of marketing of zoiets.
Arie	Doen, zou ik zeggen. Je bent nooit te oud om te leren! Je kan toch niet tot je zestigste op diezelfde stoel blijven zitten!
Marianne	Nee, nee, waarschijnlijk niet. Je hebt gelijk. Nou, ik ben er, hier moet ik eruit. Arie, jongen, tot ziens!

Key vocabulary

bijstuderen	to continue one's studies	**eruitzien**	to look like
dat is meegenomen	that is an added benefit	**hogerop**	higher up

het klappen van de zweep kennen	to know the way things work somewhere, *literally*: to know the sound of the whip
de medewerker	staff
op kosten van	paid by
suffen	to fall asleep, to be drowsy
tegenkomen	to meet
tsjonge	wow, my oh my
de wetenschap	science

Vragen bij tekst 1

1 Wat voor werk doen Arie en Marianne?
2 Maak een lijstje van andere namen van beroepen die je kent. Denk eraan: alle beroepen hebben het artikel 'de', omdat ze naar personen verwijzen.
3 Vinden ze hun baan leuk? Waarom (niet)?
4 Wat verwachten Arie en Marianne van hun baan en/of wat vinden ze positief aan hun huidige werk? (bijvoorbeeld: contact met mensen)
5 Wat is volgens jou de relatie tussen hen twee? Denk je dat ze goede vrienden zijn, of eerder collega's of oppervlakkige kennissen? Waarom denk je dat?

oppervlakkige kennissen	superficial acquaintances

Oefening 1

(a) Kijk naar deze lijst met aspecten die belangrijk kunnen zijn bij het selecteren van een job. Pik er 5 punten uit die voor jou belangrijk zijn en orden ze naar belangrijkheid. Pik ook het aspect uit dat voor jou het minst belangrijk is.

werkzekerheid doorgroeimogelijkheden groot bedrijf
salaris contact met mensen uitdagend werk plaatselijk
flexibele werkuren gevarieerd werk veel reizen
regelmatige werkuren veel onderweg zijn leuke collega's
thuis werken op een kantoor werken opleidingen
kinderopvang op werk sociale relevantie werken in
een wagen/auto van de zaak een team goede pensioenregeling
kleine organisatie veel verantwoordelijkheid prestige
weinig verantwoordelijkheid zelfstandig werken

doorgroeimogelijkheden	possibilities for growth within the company
het kantoor	the office
de kinderopvang	childcare
onderweg zijn	to be on the road
de pensioenregeling	pension scheme
uitdagend werk	challenging work
de verantwoordelijkheid	responsibility
de wagen	the car (more formal than **auto**)
de werkzekerheid	job security

(b) Bespreek je keuze met een of twee medestudenten. Bespreek ook waarom ze zo belangrijk en onbelangrijk voor je zijn.

(c) Schrijf een stukje van 70 woorden over jouw ideale baan. Gebruik de woorden en uitdrukkingen uit de vorige oefening. Begin je tekst met: In mijn ideale baan heb ik / ben ik / zijn er / kan ik, enz. Gebruik voegwoorden (conjunctions) om te nuanceren. Let goed op je zinsstructuren.

(d) If possible, re-distribute the texts among your fellow students and guess whose profile you are holding. You can take this opportunity to assist one another with grammar and structures, before handing in your text for correction.

Tekst 2 Maandagmorgen op de tram

Luister naar de volgende dialoog tussen Elke en Tom.

Elke (33) en Tom (40) werken allebei op de redactie van een lokale krant en komen elkaar op maandagmorgen tegen in de tram.

Elke Hé Tom, goeiemorgen! Hoe is 't?

Tom Ça va, hoe was 't weekend? Iets tofs gedaan?

Elke Ja, zaterdag zijn we met de kinderen naar Planckendael geweest en gisteren zijn we gezellig thuisgebleven. Het was Arno's verjaardag, dus we hebben pannenkoeken gebakken en ijsjes gegeten, heel knus allemaal. En jij?

Tom Tsja, niet zo gezellig vrees ik, ik heb eigenlijk het hele weekend aan dat rapport over de verbrandingsoven gewerkt. Wat een soep is dat, zeg. Heb jij daar onderzoek naar gedaan?

Elke Ja, tenminste, ik heb die eerste reportage gemaakt, toen dat jongetje kanker kreeg. Heel erg zielig allemaal. Toen bleek dat er iets niet in orde was met de vergunningen.

Tom Mmm, ja, het is nogal onduidelijk. Ik ben er nog wel even zoet mee. Vandaag ga ik alle contacten nog eens checken, want we mogen hier echt geen fouten maken.

Elke Nee, je hebt gelijk, succes ermee. Ik zit nog altijd op die zaak van schepen Willems, je weet wel, met die dure villa in Spanje. Het proces komt deze week voor. Wat had die man een lef zeg, hij had zelfs niet de moeite genomen iets te verbergen.

Tom Wat leven we toch in een schone wereld, hè! Zeg, heb je gehoord dat Philips, die verslaggeeft vanuit het parlement, er de brui aan geeft? Hij heeft zijn huis verkocht en gaat in Portugal wonen en als freelancer werken.

Key vocabulary

allemaal	all
de brui geven aan iets	to give something up
de kanker	cancer
knus	cosy
lef hebben	to have guts
onderzoek doen naar iets	to do research into something
Planckendael	Zoo, near Mechelen (Belgium)
de reportage	report for media
de schepen (Dutch: de wethouder)	alderman
schoon	beautiful (only in Flanders)
de soep	*here*: mess
tof	nice, 'cool' [more used in Flanders]
verbergen	to hide
de verbrandingsoven	incinerator
de vergunning	license
verslaggeven	to report
zielig	sad
zitten op iets	to be working on something
zoet zijn met iets	to be occupied with something for a while

N.B. The Flemish often use **op** when the Dutch would use **in**, so they go **op restaurant**, **op café** and they are **op de tram**.

Vragen bij tekst 2

1 Komen Elke en Tom uit Nederland of Vlaanderen? Maak een lijst van alle regionale elementen.

2 Wat organiseerde Elke voor de verjaardag van haar zoon Arno?

3 Wat heeft Tom in het weekend gedaan?

4 Welke 'schandalen' onderzoeken ze?

5 Zoek het woord 'soep' op in het woordenboek en kijk of je nog andere uitdrukkingen vindt.

6 Wat is volgens jou de relatie tussen Elke en Tom? Kennen ze elkaar goed? Zijn ze van dezelfde leeftijd? Hebben ze een gelijke status? Waarom denk je dat?

7 Tom en Elke noemen hun collega bij zijn achternaam; 'Philips'. Doe je dat ook in jouw land?

8 Zou je zelf graag journalist zijn? Waarom wel/niet? Wat zijn de voor- en nadelen van deze job volgens jou?

het nadeel	disadvantage
noemen	to call
de rang	rank
de uitdrukking	expression
de voor- en nadelen	the pros and cons
het voordeel	advantage

Cultuur

REGIONAL VARIATION AND MINORITY LANGUAGES

The previous dialogue was set in Antwerp, Flanders, which you could notice by the use of certain words and references. Although the official language in Flanders is Dutch and the written language is the same as in the Netherlands, you may find that what you hear on the street can sometimes be quite different. For example:

(a) use of personal pronouns **gij/ge** instead of **jij/je**, with its own verb form. For example:

Gij zijt zot zeker!
Are you crazy!

Gij werkt te hard.
You work too hard.

(b) Use of object pronoun **u** and possessive **uw** instead of **je/jou(w)** in an informal setting. For example:

Zeg, Jan, ik zal u morgen terugbellen.
I will call you back tomorrow.

Amai, Marianne, uw huis is echt heel schoon.
Your house is really very beautiful.

(c) Use of **-ke** instead of **-je** in some diminutives. For example:

een babyke, een glaske

(d) French influence on vocabulary. For example:

allez	come on	**een tas**	a cup
ça va	I'm fine	**madame**	Mrs
ça va?	everything all right?	**plezant**	nice, fun
merci	thank you		

Many words relating to food, car parts, etc.

Please note that these are not used throughout Flanders and are not normally used when writing. Many people speak dialects at home but speak standard Dutch at work or school. Some Flemings would like this informal speech to become an official language, but they are a minority.

In the Netherlands, **Fries** (in the Northern province of Friesland) and **Limburgs** (in the Southern province of Limburg) have gained official minority language status, and **Zeeuws** (in the South-Eastern province of Zeeland) is campaigning to gain this right as well. Linguists have argued that Zeeuws and Limburgs are dialects rather than separate languages and that granting them language status is a mistake. Fries on the other hand has a long tradition as an official minority language. In the language family tree, Fries is a sibling of English and a cousin of Dutch.

Oefening 2

Welke uitdrukking hoort bij welke definitie?

	Uitdrukking		*Definitie*
1	de brui geven aan iets	(a)	bezig zijn met iets
2	de reportage	(b)	het verslag
3	doorgroeimogelijkheden	(c)	oninteressant
4	flexibele werktijden	(d)	in slaap vallen
5	saai	(e)	hogerop kunnen in het bedrijf
6	suffen	(f)	voor een tijdje bezig zijn met iets
7	zitten op iets	(g)	zelf kiezen op welke uren je werkt
8	zoet zijn met iets	(h)	ophouden met iets

Oefening 3

Welk Vlaams woord betekent hetzelfde als welk Nederlands woord? Hier heb je een goed woordenboek voor nodig of een moedertaalspreker.

	Vlaams-Nederlands		*Noord-Nederlands*
1	het appelsiensap	(a)	de aardappel
2	de zak	(b)	de Eerste Kamer
3	de (muize)strontjes	(c)	de hagelslag
4	de confituur	(d)	de jam
5	de frieten	(e)	de jus
6	de Kamer	(f)	de patat
7	de mutualiteit	(g)	de Tweede Kamer
8	de patat	(h)	de ziekteverzekering
9	de saus	(i)	een pilsje
10	de Senaat	(j)	het kopje
11	de tas	(k)	de tas

12	een pintje	(l)	leuk
13	plezant	(m)	mooi
14	proper	(n)	schoon
15	schoon	(o)	het sinaasappelsap/jus d'orange

Oefening 4

1 Interview je medestudenten over hun weekend. Hebben ze gewerkt of zijn ze weg geweest? Vinden ze het normaal om te werken in het weekend?

2 Vorm een groepje en bespreek het volgende:

(a) Is een uitstap naar de dierentuin voor jou normaal met kinderen? (In België is dit heel populair. Gezinnen met kinderen hebben vaak een abonnement op de dierentuin, zodat ze zo vaak kunnen gaan als ze willen.)

(b) Eten jullie ook pannenkoeken op verjaardagen? Wat is een typische traktatie voor jonge kinderen?

het abonnement (op)	subscription (to)	**de traktatie**	treat

Oefening 5

Schrijf een dialoogje over een ontmoeting tussen jezelf en een vriend of collega's morgens in de tram. Waarover praten jullie? Je kan inspiratie putten uit je interviews van Oefening 4.

Structuren

ER AND DAAR

In Unit 5, we have dealt with three uses of **er**. To summarize:

(a) **er** when the sentence has an indefinite subject (e.g. *een* paard).

***Er* staat een paard in de gang.** [line of popular carnival song]

(b) **er** as reference to place.

Ik ben *er* nog nooit geweest.

(c) **er** with reference to number.

Hoeveel kinderen heb je? Ik heb er drie.

We are introducing a fourth use of **er** here:

Er in combination with a preposition

This is particularly important when using verbs with a fixed preposition.

Ik vraag de verkoper naar de prijs.
Ik vraag de verkoper *ernaar*. **(vragen *naar*)**

Succes met je examen.
Succes *ermee*. **(succes hebben *met*)**

Doe jij onderzoek naar die zaak?
Doe jij onderzoek *ernaar*? **(onderzoek doen *naar*)**
Doe jij *er* onderzoek *naar*?

Hij geeft de brui aan zijn werk.
Hij geeft de brui *eraan*. **(de brui geven *aan*)**
Hij geeft *er* de brui *aan*.

Ik stap op de Grote Markt uit de tram.
Op de Grote Markt stap ik *eruit*. **(stappen *uit*)**
Ik stap *er* op de Grote Markt *uit*.

The examples show that **er** + *the preposition can be split up*. This gives a more informal feeling, and is therefore particularly done when speaking. In this case **er** is positioned immediately to the right of the finite verb and the *preposition* moves to the end of the sentence.

Met changes to **mee** in combination with **er**:

Ik schrijf met een pen.
Ik schrijf *ermee*.

Naar changes into **naartoe** in combination with **er** when indicating direction:

Ik ga vanmiddag naar het feest.
Ik ga *er* vanmiddag *naartoe*.

Daar is the stressed form of **er**, and can be used for emphasis.

Rijd jij met een Toyota Carina?
Nee hoor, *daar* rijd ik niet *mee*!

Oefening 6

1 Beschrijf deze twee kantoren en gebruik **er is, er ligt/zit/staat/hangt**.

Bijvoorbeeld

Er liggen in dit kantoor veel papieren op de grond, maar daar ligt er niets.

2 In welke van deze twee kantoren zou je graag werken? Waarom?

Oefening 7

Geef antwoord op de vragen. Voor vragen 1 tot en met 7 gebruik je de informatie tussen haakjes. Voor vragen 8 tot en met 10 bedenk je zelf wat.

Bijvoorbeeld

Hoeveel kandidaten zijn er voor deze job? (5)
Er zijn er vijf.

1 Hoeveel vacatures heb je geselecteerd? (3)
2 Hoeveel stoelen heb je nodig voor die vergadering? (10)
3 Hoeveel mensen drinken er koffie en hoeveel thee? (6/4)

4 Hoeveel mensen komen er in aanmerking voor deze functie? (2)
5 Hoeveel jaarverslagen heb je afgedrukt? (25)
6 Hoeveel mensen heb je onder je? (60)
7 Hoeveel plaatsen zijn er nog vrij voor die cursus? (17)
8 Hoeveel jobs heb jij in je leven al gehad?
9 Hoeveel kopjes koffie/thee drink jij op een normale werkdag?
10 Hoeveel Nederlandse en Vlaamse mensen ken je?

in aanmerking komen voor	to be eligible for	**de vergadering**	meeting
het jaarverslag	annual report		

Oefening 8

Een van je medestudenten is op zoek naar werk. Jij werkt op een uitzendbureau en je maakt een profiel van hem/haar. Je interviewt hem/haar over zijn/haar professionele leven. Stel hem/haar de volgende vragen en verzin er nog twee bij. Je kunt ook door blijven vragen, zoals in het voorbeeld. Je medestudent probeert **er/daar** in de antwoorden te gebruiken. Draai daarna de rollen om.

Bijvoorbeeld

A Heb je ooit in een fabriek gewerkt?
B Ja, tien jaar geleden, als student, in een vleesfabriek. Ik heb **er** toen drie weken gewerkt.
A Vond je dat leuk?
B Nee, het was **er** erg vies en ik heb **er** ook maar heel kort gewerkt.

1 Ben je al eens naar een interimkantoor geweest?
2 Heb je altijd op kantoor gewerkt?
3 Heb je wel eens in Nederland of België gewerkt?
4 Wil je graag (nog) in Nederland of België werken?
5 Zou je graag thuis werken?
6 . . .

doorvragen	to keep on asking	**het interimkantoor (Flemish) = het uitzendbureau (the Netherlands)**	employment agency

Oefening 9

Geef antwoord op de volgende vragen. Volg het voorbeeld. Probeer een natuurlijk antwoord te geven, dus gebruik pronomina (pronouns) waar nodig.

Bijvoorbeeld

denken *aan*

Denk je aan die brief voor het ministerie? Ja, hoor, ik ______________
Ja hoor, ik denk eraan.

1 soliciteren *naar*
Heb je naar die functie gesoliciteerd? Nee, ______________

2 onderzoek doen *naar*
Doet hij onderzoek naar de relatie tussen de pil en borstkanker? Ja, hij ______________

3 praten *over*
Praat jij met je vrienden vaak over relaties? Oh nee, ______________ [nooit] [+emphasis]

4 antwoorden *op*
Heb jij al op die e-mail van de gemeente geantwoord? Nee, ______________ [nog niet]

5 houden *van*
Lust jij graag boterhammen met pindakaas? Oh ja, ______________ [+emphasis]

6 een hekel hebben *aan*
Ga jij mee schaatsen dit weekend met het team? Pff, nee, ______________ [+emphasis]

7 bezig zijn *met*
Werk je nog altijd aan dat dossier over de bouwfraude? Ja, ______________ [nog een paar weken]

8 gaan *over*
Gaat dat boek over time management? Ja, ______________ [deels]

9 afhangen *van*
Komt je partner morgenavond ook naar je afscheidsborrel? Misschien, dat ______________

10 het eens zijn *met*
Ben je het eens met de mening van je baas? Nee, ik ______________ [helemaal niet]

de afscheidsborrel	leaving/farewell drinks	**deels**	partly

Tekst 3 Een e-mail over een functioneringsgesprek

Arie in het callcenter schrijft naar zijn team om hen uit te nodigen voor de jaarlijkse functioneringsgesprekken. Hij doet zijn best om zijn team gerust te stellen. Lees zijn e-mail en beantwoord de vragen.

subject: functioneringsgesprek
datum: 3 februari 2004
van: arie.vandebril@callcenter.nl
aan: 'team'

Hoi allemaal,

Het is weer zover! Het jaarlijkse functioneringsgesprek komt eraan. Geen paniek, het gaat hier om een positieve kijk op jullie prestaties van het afgelopen jaar. We bekijken en bespreken jullie doelstellingen en je salaris uiteraard.

Zouden jullie me allemaal kunnen emailen wanneer het jullie het beste uitkomt? De gesprekken zijn volgende week dinsdag (10/4) en duren ongeveer 40 minuten. Ik zou graag van iedereen ten laatste maandag een kort verslagje willen hebben. Daarin zet je een samenvatting van je doelstellingen en eventueel enkele andere punten die je graag zou willen bespreken. Vergeet ook niet het evaluatieformulier in te vullen. Dit breng je op het gesprek mee.

Je hoeft helemaal niet zenuwachtig te zijn voor dit gesprek. We willen vooral kijken hoe we als team nog beter kunnen presteren. Het beste is om eventuele knelpunten zo snel mogelijk uit de weg te helpen. Als je hier nog vragen over hebt, spreek me gerust even aan.

Tot dinsdag!

Arie

Key vocabulary

afgelopen	past
bespreken	discuss
de doelstelling	objective
eventueel	possible
het functioneringsgesprek	staff review, appraisal
gerust	without any fear/problem
geruststellen	to reassure
het is weer zover	it's that time again
jaarlijks	annual
het knelpunt	sticking point
de prestatie	performance

uit de weg helpen	to get rid of	**uitkomen**	*here*: to suit
uiteraard	of course	**zenuwachtig**	nervous

Vragen bij tekst 3

1 Waarom schrijft Arie deze mail?
2 Wat wordt er op het gesprek besproken?
3 Wat moeten de collega's op voorhand doen?
4 Arie probeert zijn team gerust te stellen, waarom?
5 Wat is het effect van de uitroeptekens en de stijl van 'Het is weer zover!' en 'tot dinsdag!'?
6 Arie probeert heel positief te zijn. Kan je aanduiden in de tekst hoe hij dat doet?
7 De toon en stijl van de e-mail zijn informeel. Kan je hier voorbeelden van geven?
8 Hoe oud denk je dat Arie en zijn team zijn? Denk je dat er een sterke hierarchie is in dit bedrijf? Waarom (niet)?

op voorhand = van tevoren	in advance

Tekst 4

EEN E-MAIL VAN EEN KLANT

Dezelfde Arie Vandebril krijgt nu een e-mail van een van zijn klanten en hij reageert erop.

Kijk naar hoe de stijl verschilt van de vorige e-mail. De vragen zullen je helpen om dit te analyseren.

subject: levering DP2389A
datum: 29 januari 2004
van: erik.vermeer@baksteen.nl
aan: arie.vandebril@callcenter.nl
cc: 'baksteen account team'

Beste heer Vandebril,

Wij wachten sinds maandag 19/01/04 op de bovenvermelde levering van pcmcia cards aan onze vestiging te Vught. De verantwoordelijke daar probeerde reeds verscheidene malen tevergeefs contact op te nemen met uw team.

Deze producten waren vrij dringend en de leveringstermijn was 'gegarandeerd niet langer dan 15 dagen'. De bestelling is geplaatst eind december (22/12/03), dus dit heeft al wel erg lang geduurd.

Zou u eens willen nakijken wat er misgelopen is? U kunt me direct bereiken op mijn mobiele nummer 0646 098956.

Met vriendelijke groeten,

Erik Vermeer
Senior Executive IT Baksteen bvba

Key vocabulary

bereiken	to reach	**mislopen**	to go wrong
de bestelling	order	**nakijken**	to check
bovenvermeld	above mentioned	**tevergeefs**	to no avail
dringend	urgent	**de verantwoordelijke**	person responsible
de levering	delivery	**verscheidene**	several
de leveringstermijn	ETD, estimated time of delivery	**de vestiging**	branch

Vragen bij tekst 4a

1 Wat is er fout gelopen?
2 Is dit de eerste keer dat de klant het callcenter hierover contacteert?
3 Meneer Vermeer is kordaat, maar vriendelijk. Kan je hier voorbeelden van geven?

kordaat firm

EEN ANTWOORD PER E-MAIL AAN EEN KLANT

subject: re: levering DP2389A
datum: 29 januari 2004
van: arie.vandebril@callcenter.nl
aan: erik.vermeer@baksteen.nl
cc: 'baksteen account team'

Beste heer Vermeer,

Om te beginnen de allerbeste wensen voor het nieuwe jaar. Vervolgens onze excuses voor de late behandeling van uw bestelling. Er is een vertraging op alle leveringen van pcmcia cards deze maand, vanwege een brand bij onze producent in Taiwan. We hebben alle uitstaande bestellingen bij een andere producent geplaatst, maar hun leveringstermijn was drie weken.

Uw afdeling had hierover bericht moeten ontvangen, dus daar is blijkbaar iets misgelopen. Nogmaals onze excuses daarvoor. Dit zal niet meer gebeuren.

De nieuwe leveringsdatum voor DP2389A is 3 februari 2004. U kan het verloop van de bestelling on line volgen op www.callcenter.nl/orderingtool/html.

Neemt u gerust contact met me op als u nog vragen hebt.

Met vriendelijke groet,

Arie Vandebril
Teamleader pc parts Callcenter bvba

Key vocabulary

de afdeling	department	**de producent**	manufacturer
de behandeling	treatment	**uitstaand**	outstanding
blijkbaar	apparently	**vanwege**	due to
de brand	fire	**het verloop**	progress
ontvangen	receive	**de vertraging**	delay

Vragen bij tekst 4b

1 Wat is de reden voor de vertraging?

2 Hoe heeft Arie dit proberen op te lossen?

3 Wat is er nog misgelopen?

4 Duid aan in de tekst waar Arie zich verontschuldigt en een positief contact met zijn klant probeert te herstellen.

5 Neemt Arie persoonlijk de schuld op zich van de fout van zijn team?

herstellen	to repair	**de schuld op zich nemen**	to take the blame

Communicatie

ADDRESSING PEOPLE

There are different ways of addressing people, depending on your relationship with them and the aim of your communication.

In more formal *writing*, men are addressed as **heer** + surname and women as **mevrouw** + surname. No capitals are necessary for these titles.

Beste is a neutral way of addressing people. You would then finish the letter/e-mail with **met vriendelijke groet(en)** or the informal **groetjes**. A more formal way is to use **Geachte X** and to end with **Hoogachtend**. The latter is becoming increasingly less common in the everyday world of business, but is still widely used in official government communications, and legal and banking businesses, which tend to be more formal.

As is the case everywhere, *e-mail communication* tends to be less formal than written letters, as it is a medium in between the traditionally more informal spoken and rather formal written language.

Under the influence of the English-*speaking* world and the egalitarian principle, there is a tendency in the Netherlands – but less so in Belgium – to become very informal in the workplace. People use their first names and **je/jij**, rather than the more hierarchical **meneer/mevrouw** and **u**. So don't be surprised if you walk into a shop in the Netherlands and you are addressed with **je/jij**. Having said so, this is a tendency only and you might well come across situations and e-mails where you will be addressed with **u**. In Flanders, **u** would still be used in most cases where people don't know each other.

Oefening 10

Schrijf nu zelf twee e-mails (80 woorden elk), een voor je manager en een voor je klant, waarin je het onderstaande probleem behandelt, maar op een verschillende manier.

De situatie is als volgt:

Je werkt voor een online boekhandel. Dit is een klein bedrijfje met een klein, jong team werknemers en er is geen stricte hiërarchie. Een klant heeft twee exemplaren van een boek besteld, maar door een fout in het elektronisch bestelsysteem zijn er twintig exemplaren naar deze klant opgestuurd. Je moet je verontschuldigen tegenover de klant en hem/haar geruststellen dat hij/zij alleen voor de twee bestelde exemplaren moet betalen en dat jullie de andere achttien exemplaren kosteloos terug zullen ophalen. Het probleem is dat de leverancier de 18 boeken niet wil terugnemen en je bedrijf heeft normaal geen stock.

behandelen	to deal with, to treat	**de leverancier**	supplier
het exemplaar	copy	**terugnemen**	to take back
kosteloos	with no cost	**zich verontschuldigen**	to apologise

Communicatie

UITNODIGEN 1

The way you invite people will depend on what your relationship is with them, how well you know them, what the occasion is and so on. There are, as with most practical language functions, various set phrases to invite people and each of these carry slightly different undertones:

(a) direct way of phrasing an invitation:
Wil je vanavond bij me komen eten?
Kom je vanavond bij me eten?

(b) a more careful way of phrasing an invitation:
Zou je vanavond bij ons willen komen eten?
Heb je zin om vanavond bij me te komen eten?

(c) a formal way of inviting someone:
Je bent/wordt uitgenodigd voor mijn feestje volgende week zaterdag.
U bent/wordt vriendelijk uitgenodigd op de huwelijks-receptie van onze zoon Michael.

Even though there are some standard expressions to carry out a whole range of practical tasks, such as inviting someone, how you actually phrase something depends on what you want to achieve and who you are talking to. And even within certain contexts and expectations there are always various ways of using language to get a certain task done.

Oefening 11

Look again at Arie's e-mail on page 173. Even though Arie doesn't actually invite his staff explicitly for a staff review (it is taken for granted that they will attend one), he does invite them to suggest a time that would suit them best. Does he phrase this invitation in a direct manner?

Oefening 12

Maak zinnen waarin je iemand uitnodigt. Gebruik de informatie tussen haken. Er zijn altijd meerdere mogelijkheden. Probeer te variëren.

Bijvoorbeeld

vrienden (morgen–lunchen)	**Wil je morgen komen lunchen?**
baas–secretaresse (morgen–lunchen)	**Zou je morgen met me willen lunchen?** **Zullen we morgen samen lunchen?**

1 moeder – dochter (dit weekend – naar huis komen)
2 vrienden – lang niet gezien (volgende week – uit eten gaan)
3 collega's (dinsdag – naar de vergadering komen)
4 docent – student (voor de les – naar kantoor komen)
5 mede-student die je erg aardig vindt, maar je bent bang om afgewezen te worden (vanavond – wat gaan drinken)

afgewezen te worden to be rejected

Tekst 5 Uitnodigingskaartje

Look at the different invitations below, both for a leaving reception at work, and see what else the invitations 'do' beyond inviting people.

De uitnodiging hieronder is een **uitnodigingskaartje**, een geschreven uitnodiging op een kaart.

Geachte medewerkers en relaties van de Dienst Kinderopvang,

Per 1 juli a.s. zal de algemeen directeur, mevrouw Van Oorschot tot Sevenaer, afscheid nemen van de de Dienst Kinderopvang. Zij heeft een nieuwe functie aanvaard als directeur van de Dienst Emancipatiebeleid.

Vanaf de oprichting in 1993 is zij de drijvende kracht geweest achter de uitbreiding en professionalisering van de kinderopvang in Utrecht. Op 'zeer eigen' wijze heeft zij de medewerkers en relaties van onze organisatie weten te inspireren.

Wij stellen u graag in de gelegenheid om persoonlijk afscheid te nemen van mevrouw Van Oorschot tot Sevenaer.

De receptie wordt gehouden op donderdag 2 juli a.s. van 17.00–19.00 in:

De Prinsenkelder, Oudegracht 2, Utrecht

Key vocabulary

aanvaarden	accept	**in de gelegenheid stellen**	give someone the opportunity
afscheid nemen van	say goodbye to	**de medewerker**	employee
a.s. (aanstaande)	near, forthcoming	**de oprichting**	foundation
de dienst	service, department	**de relatie**	work relation
de drijvende kracht	driving force	**de uitbreiding**	expansion
de functie	position	**de wijze**	way, manner

Deze uitnodiging komt uit een interne nieuwsbrief voor werknemers.

> Afscheid van Hester van Voort
>
> Misschien weet nog niet iedereen het, maar Hester gaat ons verlaten. Zij heeft zich ruim twee jaar als manager van stadsdeel Zuid met veel enthousiasme ingezet voor Utrecht en haar stadsdeel in het bijzonder. Niemand is erg blij dat ze weggaat. Maar ja, zij gaat met haar gezin verhuizen naar Groningen en heeft daar een leuke nieuwe baan als . . . stadsdeelmanager.
>
> Geen afscheid zonder receptie. Iedereen is van harte welkom in buurthuis de Brug, Schrijversplantsoen 48, op 5 juli a.s. vanaf 5 uur.

Key vocabulary

in het bijzonder	in particular	**verlaten**	leave
de stadsdeelmanager	district manager	**zich inzetten voor**	devote/dedicate oneself to
ruim	more than, over		

Vragen bij tekst 5

1 Dit zijn twee uitnodigingen voor een afscheidsreceptie, maar ze zijn heel verschillend. Maak een lijst van de verschillen.

Uitnodiging mevrouw Van Oorschot tot Sevenaer	**Uitnodiging Hester van Voort**
een (formele) aanhef: geachte medewerkers en relaties	geen aanhef, alleen een titel

2 De tweede uitnodiging is een open uitnodiging voor alle medewerkers. Het staat in het medewerkersblaadje dat iedereen leest. Er is geen aanhef. Als je een aanhef zou schrijven, wat zou dan een goede aanhef zijn? Leg uit waarom.
3 De uitnodigingen verwijzen op een heel verschillende manier naar Mevrouw Van Oorschot tot Sevenaer en Hester van Voort. Hoe doet elke uitnodiging dat en wat is het effect ervan?
4 Wat zegt de tekst over de kwaliteiten van mevrouw Van Oorschot tot Sevenaer in relatie tot haar werk? Wat zegt de andere tekst over Hester en haar werk? Wat is het verschil?
5 Waarom denk je dat de twee uitnodigingen op deze verschillende manieren zijn geschreven? (denk aan de hiërarchische relatie tussen de genodigden en de vertrekkende collega in beide uitnodigingen).

Structuren

MORE SUBCLAUSES

Subclauses are linked to main clauses by subordinating conjunctions. These conjunctions express a relationship between the two clauses. Here are the most important types of relationship, plus some examples.

Time

voordat	**Ik schrijf een paar punten op *voordat* ik met de baas ga praten.**
wanneer	**Ik zal die brieven posten *wanneer* ik naar huis toe ga.**
terwijl	**Ik kan het eten klaarmaken *terwijl* de kinderen TV kijken.**
nadat	**Jan komt naar de vergadering *nadat* hij met zijn team overlegd heeft.**
sinds	***Sinds* ze ontslagen is, voelt ze zich futloos en depressief.**

Contrast

ondanks	***Ondanks* het feit dat het regent, gaan we toch fietsen.**
hoewel	***Hoewel* het niet altijd makkelijk is, moet je toch altijd je best blijven doen.**

Comparison

alsof	**Je moet in elk sollicitatiegesprek doen *alsof* het je droombaan is.**
zoals	**Probeer het te doen *zoals* hij het heeft gedaan.**

Condition

als	***Als* je een goed diploma hebt, kan het niet moeilijk zijn een baan te vinden.**
tenzij	**We kunnen niet internetten, *tenzij* je broer de PC heeft gerepareerd.**

Cause/reason

omdat	**Ik ben vroeg naar m'n werk gegaan, *omdat* ik vreselijk veel werk heb.**
zodat	**Je moet je heel positief opstellen, *zodat* je als optimist overkomt.**

Oefening 13

Combineer twee zinnen om een nieuwe zin te maken.

Ik ga vaak koffie halen	omdat er zo veel spanningen in het team zijn.
Ik krijg vaak hoofdpijn	wanneer ik me verveel op kantoor.
Ik wil van job veranderen	nu ik terug ben van vakantie.
Ik lees meestal de krant	als ik te veel koffie drink.
Ik voel me erg gestrest	terwijl mijn vriend(in) de afwas doet.

Oefening 14

Maak van twee zinnen een nieuwe zin. Gebruik de conjunctie tussen haakjes.

Bijvoorbeeld

Ik doe mijn baan niet graag. Mijn baas is heel aardig. (hoewel)
Ik doe mijn baan niet graag hoewel mijn baas heel aardig is.
Hoewel mijn baas heel aardig is, doe ik mijn baan niet graag.

1 Ik maak het eten klaar. Ik ben thuis. (wanneer)
2 Ik koop een nieuwe auto. Ik heb een nieuwe baan. (als)
3 Wij zijn gewoonlijk klaar met eten. Het nieuws begint. (voordat)
4 Arie leest de krant. Zijn vrouw strijkt de hemden. (terwijl)
5 Ik voel me veel beter. Ik ben met die nieuwe baan begonnen. (sinds)
6 We gaan aan tafel. Je vader komt thuis. (zodra)
7 Ik zal je bellen. Ik ben terug uit Amerika. (wanneer)
8 Ik heb veel meer tijd dan in Nederland. Ik (nu) woon in Engeland. Ik heb hier veel minder verplichtingen. (omdat)
9 Je gaat hier rechtdoor. Je ziet het politiekantoor aan je rechterkant. (totdat)
10 Jij was nog klein. Je verhuisde naar het noorden. (toen)

toen	when (+ past tense)	**zodra**	as soon as
totdat	until		

Oefening 15

1 Kies een conjunctie om twee zinnen aan elkaar te schrijven en gebruik de voegwoorden in de box. Er zijn meerdere opties. Maak minstens 5 zinnen. Je kunt met beide zinnen beginnen.

hoewel – omdat – zodat – terwijl – maar – want

Zij is heel mooi.	Zij is heel intelligent.
Zij heeft geen baan	Zij vindt geen geschikte baan.
Zij heeft geen diploma.	Zij is niet getrouwd.
Zij is heel aardig.	Zij heeft lang gestudeerd
Zij is heel bekwaam.	Zij heeft een schitterende carrière.

2 Bespreek je keuze met een medestudent. Heb je dezelfde combinaties?

Tekst 6 Brochure van de Vlaamse overheid

In deze brochure zet de Vlaamse regering een programma uiteen om werknemers aan te moedigen er iets bij te studeren en hun kansen op de arbeidsmarkt te vergroten.

aanmoedigen	to encourage	**uiteenzetten**	to outline
de arbeidsmarkt	labour market		

DE OPLEIDINGSCHEQUES VOOR WERKNEMERS – OVER JE OPLEIDING BEN JIJ DE BAAS

Werken aan je toekomst wordt veel goedkoper

Wie in onze maatschappij mee wil, schoolt zich bij met een opleiding. Maar de kostprijs van een opleiding kan hoog oplopen. De Vlaamse overheid past hier nu een mouw aan: met de opleidingscheques betaalt ze de helft van de kosten van jouw opleiding. Zo staan we 100% achter jouw keuze.

Voor wie zijn de cheques er?

Alle werknemers en ambtenaren die wonen in Vlaanderen kunnen van de cheques gebruik maken. Iedereen in het bedrijf, van de portier tot de algemeen directeur, kan een opleiding volgen. Maar ook als je bij een bakker, metselaar of notaris werkt, heb je recht op opleidingscheques.

17 miljoen euro zolang de voorraad strekt

De Vlaamse Overheid trekt hier een budget van ongeveer 17 miljoen euro voor uit. Vanaf 1 september kan je ze bestellen. Maar stel je beslissing om een opleiding te volgen niet te lang uit, want op is op.

naar: www.vdab.be

Key vocabulary

de ambtenaar	civil servant
de beslissing	the decision
een budget uittrekken voor	to budget for
ergens achter staan	to approve or support something
ergens een mouw aan passen	to find a way round something; *here*: to help you out, to find a solution
hoog oplopen	to rise high
meewillen	*here*: to want to be part of something
de metselaar	brick layer
de notaris	notary (a lawyer legally empowered to witness the signing of documents to make them valid)
op is op	if all is finished, it is finished (expression often used in sale adverts)
de opleiding	training
recht hebben op	to have a right to
uitstellen	to postpone
zich bijscholen	to take a training/refresher course
zolang de voorraad strekt	while stock lasts

Vragen bij tekst 6

1 Wat biedt de Vlaamse overheid aan?

2 Voor wie zijn de cheques bestemd?

3 Hoeveel betaalt de overheid?

4 Kijk naar de titel: welk contrast zie je? Waarom spreekt dit aan?

5 Hoe spreekt de overheid de lezer aan in paragraaf 1? En hoe spreekt de overheid over zichzelf? Zijn ze hier consequent in?

6 In wat voor context zie je normaal de uitdrukkingen 'zolang de voorraad strekt' en 'op is op' (paragraaf 3)? Waarom denk je dat ze hier worden gebruikt?

aanspreken (4) to appeal | **aanspreken** (5) to address

Tekst 7 Volg een cursus!

Lees het volgende artikel over het verhogen van je kansen op de arbeidsmarkt. Het komt uit een Nederlands tijdschrift en gaat over cursussen die je helpen je zelfvertrouwen te vergroten.

Volg een cursus!

Heb je het gevoel dat je op je werk niet helemaal uit de verf komt? Zeg je vaak maar 'ja' terwijl je eigenlijk 'nee' wil zeggen? Met een 'powercursus' leer je jezelf beter te profileren.

Ook een cursus persoonlijke effectiviteit valt onder de 'powercursusssen'. Hier leer je je eigen kwaliteiten en mogelijkheden beter kennen door kritisch naar jezelf te kijken. Martine geeft deze training bij Hofman & partners: 'Het is een soort groeitraining: de cursist en de organisatie komen aan bod, maar ook bijvoorbeeld de klanten. De deelnemer leert op verschillende niveaus naar die verschillende belangen te kijken. Zo'n training kan bevestigend werken, maar kan ook heel confronterend zijn. Soms blijkt dat mensen heel anders overkomen dan ze denken. Als je zelf vindt dat je goed opkomt voor je eigen belangen, kan het gebeuren dat een andere cursist zegt: "Ik vind juist dat ik met jou alle kanten op kan". Of iemand die denkt dat ze goed kan luisteren naar de mening van anderen, terwijl dat op de rest helemaal niet zo overkomt. Ik vind dat je met dit soort training investeert in je eigen professionaliteit. Naast de deskundigheid, zorgt een dergelijke training ervoor dat je als persoon beter overkomt en slagvaardiger bent.'

Key vocabulary

aan bod komen	to get a chance
alle kanten opkunnen met iemand	to be able to make this person do anything
bevestigend	affirmative
confronterend	confrontational
de deelnemer	participant
deskundigheid = professionaliteit	expertise/ professionalism
eigen	own
het niveau	level
overkomen	to come across
slagvaardig	decisive/on the ball
uit de verf komen	live up to one's promise
voor je belangen opkomen	to stand up for one's interests
het zelfvertrouwen	confidence
zich profileren	to create a distinct profile of oneself
zorgen voor	to take care of

Vragen bij tekst 7

1 Wat is het doel van de 'powercursussen'?
2 Wat leer je door 'kritisch naar jezelf te kijken'?
3 Hoe ervaren de cursisten vaak deze training?
4 Kan je voorbeelden geven van hoe mensen soms anders overkomen dan ze denken?
5 Hoe kan zo'n cursus, volgens het artikel, het leven positief beïnvloeden?
6 Deze paragraaf is grotendeels een citaat van Martine, de docent bij Hofman & partners. Denk je dat de schrijvers van dit artikel kritisch staan tegenover dit soort cursussen?
7 Voor welk publiek is de tekst geschreven denk je? Leg uit.

Oefening 16

Vul één van de volgende woorden of uitdrukkingen in, in de correcte vorm.

achter iets staan **uit de verf komen**
er een mouw aan passen **op is op**
zolang de voorraad strekt **aan bod komen**
voor de belangen opkomen van **zich profileren** **overkomen**

[advertentie in de krant]

TOTALE UITVERKOOP
ALLES MOET WEG
ALLE SPORTSCHOENEN SLECHTS €10*

(1) ________________________

(2) * ________________

[op een vergadering]

manager	Bart is twee weken op vakantie en Corrie gaat vanaf volgende week met zwangerschapsverlof.
werknemer	Oei, en er is zoveel werk!
manager	Dat weet ik, maar we krijgen een extra administratieve hulp en ik zal ook meehelpen. Kortom, we (3) ________________ .

[in een brochure]	Amnesty International (4) ______________________ gevangenen wereldwijd. Ze voeren campagne tegen martelpraktijken en onmenselijke omstandigheden.
[in krantenartikel]	Grote kledingmerken (5) ______________________ graag als milieuvriendelijk en ethish, maar bij veel kritische consumenten (6) ______________________ als geldwolven die over lijken gaan.
[sollicitant op gesprek]	Ik denk dat mijn talenten in deze baan sterk (7) ______________________ . Het profiel staat me op het lijf geschreven.
[ouders tegen vrienden]	Wij (8) ______________________ de beslissing van onze zoon. Als hij een jaar wil gaan reizen voor zijn studie is dat prima. Je kinderen moeten de kans krijgen te doen waar ze in geloven. Daar zullen ze je altijd dankbaar voor zijn.
[in evaluatiegesprek]	Ik heb het gevoel dat mijn agendapunten nooit (9) ______________________ . Ik doe altijd mijn best om discussiepunten aan te brengen, maar niemand schijnt te luisteren.

agendapunten	discussion points for a meeting
bewust	conscious
campagne voeren	to campaign
dankbaar	grateful
ethisch	ethical
geldwolven die over lijken gaan	merciless money-grubbers
gevangenen	prisoners
kortom	in short
martelpraktijken	torture
mileuvriendelijk	environmentally friendly
onmenselijke omstandigheden	inhuman circumstances
op het lijf geschreven staan	to be made/cut out for something
schijnen	to seem
wereldwijd	worldwide

Oefening 17

Verzin zelf extra informatie om de volgende zinnen af te maken. Gebruik de uitdrukking tussen haakjes en let goed op de structuur van je zinnen.

Bijvoorbeeld

Het is niet altijd gemakkelijk, maar we ______________ [achter iets staan]
maar we staan achter de keuze die we gemaakt hebben.

1 Ik ga een cursus volgen zodat ik ______________ [uit de verf komen]
2 Ik vind het heel goed dat Amnesty International ______________ [opkomen voor]
3 Er zijn veel problemen met leveringen deze week maar we ______________ [een mouw passen aan]
4 Arie heeft een voorstel en hij vroeg me of ik ______________ [het ermee eens zijn]
5 We zitten al over ons budget, dus de kosten ______________ [hoog oplopen]
6 Ik vind dat een organisatie als Greenpeace ______________ [zich profileren als]
7 Je moet die subsidie aanvragen want je ______________ [recht hebben op]

Communicatie

COMPLIMENT

It is good to know how to phrase a compliment. Here are some examples:

Wat zie je er mooi uit!	You look pretty!
Je ziet er goed uit!	You're looking well!
Leuke jurk!	Nice dress!
Goh, dat kan jij goed!	Wow, you're good at that!
Goh, wat kan jij dat goed!	Wow, you're good at that!
Dat heb je heel goed gedaan.	You've done that very well.
Dat is een heel mooie tas die je daar hebt!	That is a very nice bag you've got there!

KRITIEK

It is equally important or even more so to be able to offer criticism in an acceptable manner. Bear in mind that the Dutch are quite direct and will voice their criticism quite openly. Don't take it personally or think that they are being rude.

Dat lijkt me geen goed idee.
I don't think that's a good idea.

Dat is onzin!
That's nonsense!

Dat lijkt nergens op.
That looks terrible.

Je lijkt wel zwanger in die jurk.
You look pregnant in that dress.

Je hebt wel veel komma's in je tekst.
You do have quite a lot of commas in your text.

Jij komt altijd te laat!
You're always late!

You can offer criticism in the shape of advice, which sounds less harsh. Phrasing things positively also makes a difference.

Dat zou ik niet doen, als ik jou was.
I wouldn't do that, if I were you.

Ik zou het anders doen als ik jou was.
I would do it differently if I were you.

Je kan ook minder bijzinnen gebruiken.
You could use less subclauses.

Je kan ook meer hoofdzinnen gebruiken.
You could use more main clauses.

Dat lijkt me een beetje snel.
That seems a bit quick to me.

Misschien moet het wat langzamer.
Maybe it has to be a bit slower.

Oefening 18

Maak complimentjes. Volg het voorbeeld en creëer mini-dialoogjes met een medestudent. Verzin zelf nog een compliment erbij voor je medestudent.

Bijvoorbeeld

(hippe schoenen)	A	**Wat heb je hippe schoenen! Waar komen die vandaan?**
	B	**Oh, ik heb ze bij V&D gekocht, niet duur!**

1 (goede rapporten schrijven)
2 (mooi tekenen)
3 (chique leren tas)
4 (efficiënt organiseren)
5 (. . .)

Oefening 19

Je bent manager en je schrijft een rapport over het functioneringsgesprek van een van de medewerkers. Herschrijf de volgende kritiek als advies zodat het vriendelijker klinkt.

Example

Wat ben jij een slechte organisator.
Je kan bijvoorbeeld je planning op papier zetten. Dat helpt om je werk te organiseren.

1 Gebruik minder stopwoorden.
2 Je verspilt te veel tijd.
3 Je werkt te traag.
4 Wat ben je toch een doemdenker!
5 Je bent erg passief.

de doemdenker	doom-monger/defeatist	**verspillen**	to waste
het stopwoord	stopgap/filler		

Oefening 20

Bespreek de volgende punten in groepjes.

Denk je dat het initiatief van de Vlaamse overheid een succes wordt? Waarom denk je dat ze graag willen dat mensen meer leren en studeren? Denk je dat de 'powercursussen' handig zijn voor iemand in zijn/haar dagelijkse werk? Heb je zelf weleens een cursus gevolgd die te maken had met je werk? Was dat een positieve ervaring?

Oefening 21: Schrijfoefening

Kijk op http://cursus.pagina.nl/ en zoek naar een cursus die interessant voor jou zou zijn. Schrijf een e-mail van 100 woorden aan je baas en zeg:

(a) welke cursus je wilt volgen;
(b) waarom;
(c) waarom dat goed is voor de zaak.

Vraag dan om toestemming om op die cursus te gaan.

Tekst 8 Banen in de krant

Lees de volgende twee vacatures en beantwoord de vragen over de verschillen. De eerste vacature komt uit België en is voor een hogere functie, de tweede, op pagina 193, komt uit Nederland en is voor een arbeider.

TEKST 8A

Vacature 1 (Vlaanderen)
Office Manager Uitzendkantoor

Functieomschrijving

U bent verantwoordelijk voor het volledige beheer en het rendement van uw kantoor. Door middel van klantenwerving en klantenopvolging zorgt u voor de systematische groei van uw kantoor. U speelt een cruciale rol in de motivatie, coaching en groei van uw medewerkers. Als volwaardige HR-adviseur evalueert u samen met uw klanten hun behoeften en biedt u steeds de juiste oplossing aan. Zo bouwt u een sterke langetermijnrelatie op.

Profielomschrijving

U bent minstens een gegradueerde met een sterke commerciële gedrevenheid. U beheerst de beide landstalen perfect – Een sterke ervaring in een gelijkaardige sector is noodzakelijk. U kunt goed organiseren en verschillende projecten in goede banen leiden. U weet als people manager een tiental medewerkers te coachen en te begeleiden. U beschikt over een flinke dosis energie en doorzettingsvermogen.

Aanbod

Wij bieden u uitdagende functies in een dynamisch en groeiend bedrijf. Wij investeren in onze werknemers door permanente opleiding en begeleiding. U kunt rekenen op een motiverend salaris aangevuld met extralegale voordelen. De Office Manager beschikt over een auto en een GSM.

Key vocabulary

aanbieden	to offer
het aanbod	offer
aanvullen	to supplement
begeleiden	to guide, to counsel
het beheer	management
beheersen	to master
de behoefte	need
beschikken	to have at one's disposal
het doorzettingsvermogen	perseverance
extralegale voordelen [*Vlaams*]	additional benefits to your salary, such as a car/computer/phone
de gegradueerde	graduate
de GSM = de mobiel [*Vlaams*]	mobile phone
in goede banen leiden	steer in the right direction
de klantenopvolging	following up customers
de klantenwerving	recruiting new customers
de langetermijnrelatie	long-term relationship
minstens	at least
noodzakelijk	necessary
de omschrijving	description
het rendement	return
volwaardig	able

Oefening 22

Maak een lijst met verantwoordelijkheden van de functie, eisen aan de kandidaat en de arbeidsomstandigheden (zoals 'extralegale voordelen'). Vul de tabel in.

Verantwoordelijkheden	*Eisen*	*Arbeidsomstandigheden*

arbeidsomstandigheden working conditions
de eis, eisen demand, demands
verantwoordelijkheden responsibilities

Vragen bij tekst 8a

1 Maak een lijstje van de woorden en zinnen in de tekst die een positief en een gewichtig beeld geven van de baan.

Positief	*Gewichtig*
uitdagende functie	U bent verantwoordelijk voor het volledige beheer.

2 Wordt deze baan goed betaald? Waarom denk je dat?

3 Zijn er doorgroeimogelijkheden? Hoe weet je dat?

4 De tekst is vrij statisch omdat er veel substantieven (nouns) gebruikt zijn. Onderstreep ze allemaal.

5 Als je naar deze lijst substantieven in de tekst kijkt, vind je ze dan makkelijk of moeilijk, informeel of formeel, en wat is hiervan het effect op de tekst?

gewichtig weighty, important

TEKST 8B

Vacature 2 (Nederland)
Energieke Vakman voor Bloembollensector

Functie-eisen
Hij dient te beschikken over goede contactuele eigenschappen. Hij moet goed kunnen functioneren binnen een klein team. Ervaring in de bloembollensector is een pre. Binnen de kwekerij zal hij moeten helpen bij het rooien, het planten etc. Binnen de export zal hij zorg dragen voor het exportklaarmaken van bloembollen.

Arbeidsvoorwaarden
Goede salariëring overeenkomstig het functieniveau, uitstekende werksfeer, afwisselend werk.

Key vocabulary

afwisselend = gevarieerd	varied	**de kwekerij**	nursery (garden)
de arbeidsvoorwaarde	term of employment	**overeenkomstig**	according to
de bloembollensector	the bulb sector	**de pre**	advantage
de eigenschap	characteristic	**rooien**	dig up
de eis	demand	**de vakman**	skilled worker
klaarmaken	to prepare	**zorg dragen voor**	to take care of

Vragen bij tekst 8b

1 Onderstreep de woorden in de tekst die een positief beeld geven van de baan. Vergelijk dit met de eerste advertentie. Wat is het verschil?

2 Wat is de taak van de sollicitant volgens de zin: 'Hij zal zorg dragen voor het exportklaarmaken van bloembollen'?

3 Wordt deze baan goed betaald? Waarom denk je dat?

4 Zijn er doorgroeimogelijkheden? Waarom denk je dat?

5 De sollicitant wordt hier niet rechtstreeks aangesproken zoals in de vorige advertentie. Wat is het effect?

6 Gebruikt deze tekst even veel substantieven als de vorige advertentie? Wat is het effect?

9 Telefoongesprek

Luister naar het telefoongesprek tussen een sollicitant en het bloembollenbedrijf van de laatste advertentie en beantwoord de vragen. Luister enkele keren voordat je de tekst gaat lezen om je antwoorden te controleren.

Linda	Goeiemorgen, Bloembollen n.v., met Linda.
Jan	Goeiemorgen mevrouw, u spreekt met Jan Karnemelk. Ik bel in verband met die baan voor een vakman. Is die nog vrij?
Linda	Ja hoor. Hebt u ervaring in de sector?
Jan	Ja, ik werk al drie jaar in deze sector, maar ben recent verhuisd en zoek nu werk in deze regio. Weet u ook of ik de baan deeltijds kan doen?
Linda	Dat is niet echt de bedoeling, maar we kunnen dat wel bekijken. Het hangt een beetje van de andere kandidaten af. Zou u ons uw CV willen doorsturen of doorfaxen? Dan bellen we u zo snel mogelijk terug om een afspraak te maken voor een sollicitatiegesprek.
Jan	Dat is goed. Ik stuur mijn CV vanmiddag op. Dank u wel, mevrouw.
Linda	Tot uw dienst. Dag.

Vragen bij tekst 9

1 Waarom solliciteert Jan naar deze baan?
2 Kan hij ook deeltijds werken?
3 Hoe introduceren Linda en Jan zich en hoe spreken ze elkaar aan?

Oefening 23

Schrijf nu samen met een andere student een dialoogje over iemand die belt om meer informatie over de eerste vacature. Denk na over de vragen die deze persoon kan stellen. Zou het taalgebruik in dit gesprek hetzelfde zijn als in het telefoongesprek hierboven? Speel de dialoog voor de klas.

Structuren

WORD ORDER IN MAIN AND SUBCLAUSES – VERBS

Main clauses

	finite verb		*non-finite verb(s)*
with one verb			
Ik	**vertrek**	**vanavond.**	
Vanavond	**vertrek**	**ik.**	
Wanneer	**vertrek**	**je?**	

with two verbs

Ik	**moet**	**om 8 uur**	**zeker**	**vertrekken.**
Ik	**heb**	**gisteren**	**de kaartjes**	**gekocht.**

with three verbs

Wanneer	**zou**	**je**	**me**	**kunnen**	**helpen?**
Ik	**ben**	**gisteren**	**om 8 uur**	**gaan**	**slapen.**
Hij	**zou**	**de kaartjes**	**gisteren**	**hebben**	**gekocht.**
Hij	**zou**	**de kaartjes**	**gisteren**	**gekocht**	**hebben.**

Subclauses

main clause	*subclause*			
	conjunction	*subject*	*rest*	*verb cluster*
Ik ben moe	**omdat**	**ik**	**vannacht niet**	**geslapen heb.**
Ik ben moe	**omdat**	**ik**	**vannacht niet**	**heb geslapen.**
Ik ben moe	**omdat**	**ik**	**te laat**	**ben gaan slapen.**

TIME/MANNER/PLACE

Another important matter in sentence structure is the order of the adverbials, which is different from English. Have a look at the examples below.

		time	*manner*	*place*	
Ik	**ga**	**straks**	**nog snel**	**naar de Aldi.**	
We	**vertrekken**	**morgen**	**met de auto**	**naar Frankrijk.**	
Sandra	**wil**	**om 8 uur**		**in de kerk**	**zijn.**

Oefening 24

Maak correcte zinnen met deze woorden, zoals in het voorbeeld.

Bijvoorbeeld

vanavond / naar de film / wij / willen / gaan / .
Wij willen vanavond naar de film gaan.

1 straks / jullie / kopen / Zouden / willen / brood / ?
2 heb / een mooie film / gezien / ik / Gisterenavond / op de televisie / .

3 volgende week / jullie / Vliegen / ook / naar Amsterdam / ?
4 Wij / de test / niet zo moeilijk / vonden / **omdat** / hadden / goed / gestudeerd / we / .
5 Kan / bellen / me / je / **zodra** / een antwoord / hebt / je / ?
6 Het / is / leuk / **als** / je / geeft / zomaar / iemand / een bloemetje / .
7 vertelde / me / Hij / **dat** / vol spanning / heeft / hij / in dat boek / gelezen / de hele nacht / .
8 Ik / denk / **dat** / thuis / vanavond / hij / zal / heel moe / komen / .
9 **Hoewel** / ik / was / niet boos / , / was / toch / erg / ik / teleurgesteld / .
10 **Wanneer** / mijn baas / stuurt / een e-mail /, / er / staan / in / spelfouten / altijd / .

Oefening 25

Maak de volgende zinnen af.

1 Ik ga terug studeren als ______________
2 Ik verander van baan wanneer ______________
3 Ik neem ontslag want ______________
4 Ik ben misschien student, maar ______________
5 Ik studeer elke dag Nederlands, tenzij ______________
6 Ik studeer Nederlands omdat ______________
7 Hoewel ik weinig tijd heb, ______________
8 Sinds ik in [woonplaats] woon, ______________
9 Terwijl jullie de oefening maken, ______________
10 Ik herlees elke week alle hoofdstukken, zodat ______________

Tekst 10 Persoonlijkheidstest

TEKST 10a

Bekijk de volgende lijst met eigenschappen. Kies in elke rij, uit kolom A, B of C, het woord dat het beste bij je past. Als je al die woorden op een rijtje zet, krijg je een profiel van jezelf.

A	B	C
veranderlijk	zelfbewust	bedreven
saboteren	trotseren	afwegen
timide	solide	rationeel
wantrouwig	duidelijk	onberispelijk
speculatief	onveranderlijk	fatsoenlijk
controversieel	robuust	respectabel

rusteloos	zelfverzekerd	gepast
vreedzaam	krachtig	ervaren
gejaagd	gedecideerd	netjes
grillig	onverschrokken	onpartijdig
reactief	flexibel	precies

Key vocabulary

afwegen	to weigh up
bedreven	skilled
fatsoenlijk	decent
gejaagd	stressed
gepast	appropriate
grillig	whimsical
krachtig	powerful
onberispelijk	impeccable
onpartijdig	impartial
onverschrokken	fearless
trotseren	to defy, to stand up (to)
vreedzaam	peaceful
wantrouwig	suspicious
zelfbewust	self conscious
zelfverzekerd	confident

Vragen bij tekst 10a

1 Zitten je antwoorden vooral in kolom A, B of C?
2 Beschrijf kort het type van personen uit kolom A, B en C.
3 Geeft de test een accuraat beeld van jezelf?
4 Lees nu de beschrijving van de verschillende types hieronder.

TEKST 10B

vooral A	vooral B	type C / mix van A+B
Een twijfelende persoonlijkheid	Extreem sterke persoonlijkheid	Een gebalanceerde persoonlijkheid
Kernwoorden: besluiteloos, aarzelend	Kernwoorden: onbuigzaam, ambitieus, assertief	Kernwoorden: attent, tolerant, aardig
Je bent iemand die twijfelt aan zijn/haar capaciteiten, die wat onzeker in het leven staat. Misschien ben je wel tevreden met je persoonlijke situatie, maar het kan ook betekenen dat je er niet uithaalt wat er in zit. Misschien moet je ambitieuzer zijn. Besef dat iedereen unieke talenten en mogelijkheden heeft.	Je bent iemand met een extreem sterke persoonlijkheid. Iemand die heel goed weet wat hij/zij wilt. Je zal niet snel rusten voordat je je doel hebt bereikt. De kans op succes is bij jou heel groot. Maar de kans is ook groot dat je gefrustreerd raakt als je je doel niet bereikt.	Je bent iemand die zowel opkomt voor zijn of haar eigen belang, als dat van anderen. Waarschijnlijk heb je geen moeite om anderen te helpen met het bereiken van hun doelen. Je heb ook oog voor je eigen doelstellingen. Je bent een goede teamspeler, weet wat je wil en kan goed omgaan met voor- en tegenspoed.

aardig	nice	**het kernwoord**	keyword
aarzelen	to hesitate	**onbuigzaam**	uncompromising
attent	considerate	**raken**	*here*: to get
bereiken	to reach	**twijfelen**	to doubt
beseffen	to realise	**uithalen**	to take out
het doel	goal, aim	**voor- en tegenspoed**	ups and downs
de doelstelling	objective	**waarschijnlijk**	probably

Vragen bij tekst 10b

1 Welk type is het meest positieve volgens de schrijver? Kan je voorbeelden geven van woorden die dit illustreren?

2 Welk type vindt de schrijver het meest negatieve? Illustreer dat aan de hand van de tekst.

Oefening 26

Bespreek in groepjes wat volgens jullie de ideale eigenschappen zijn voor de volgende banen.

1 een docent

2 een verkoper van computers

3 een verkoper van cosmetica

4 een verpleegster

5 een chirurg

6 een secretaresse

7 een diplomaat

8 een huisvrouw en moeder

9 een president

Oefening 27

1 Kijk naar Type A. De beschrijving van dit type persoon is vrij negatief. Maak een nieuwe beschrijving in 50 woorden van dit type persoon die de positieve kanten van dit type beschrijft.

2 Geef een nieuwe beschrijving in 50 woorden voor Type B, die de negatieve kanten van deze persoonlijkheid benadrukt.

Tekst 11 Test je carrièrevaardigheden

De volgende tekst is een vraag uit een carrièretest gericht op 'de professionele carrièregerichte werknemer'.

Test je carrièrevaardigheden

Vraag 1:
Je zit in een vergadering. Er is een probleem in je team doordat er een collega ziek is. De directeur zit hiermee in haar maag. Zij heeft het te druk om zijn werk te doen, net als de andere aanwezigen op de vergadering. Toch vraagt ze wie het kan overnemen om zo een belangrijke deadline te halen. Wat doe je?

(a) Je roept hoorbaar dat je dit weekeinde wel zal werken, omdat een afspraak met vrienden niet doorgaat.
(b) Je vindt dat de directeur zit te zeuren en je roept dat zij moet zorgen voor genoeg mensen, zodat er een einde komt aan de ziekmakende werkdruk.
(c) Je gaat druk zitten bladeren in je agenda, alsof je aan het zoeken bent naar een gaatje. Tegelijkertijd probeer je duidelijk uit te stralen dat het niet zal lukken.
(d) Je zegt dat dit typisch past in het pakket van collega X en je stelt voor om het werk aan hem/haar te geven.

Key vocabulary

de aanwezige	person present
bladeren	to leaf through
doorgaan	to take place
hoorbaar	audible
in je maag zitten met iets	be troubled by something
lukken	*here*: to manage, to work
naar een gaatje zoeken	see if you can fit it in
net als	just like
uitstralen	to radiate
de vergadering	the meeting
de werkdruk	pressure of work
zeuren	to nag
ziekmakend	sickening

Vragen bij tekst 11

1 Welk antwoord zou jij geven?
2 Welk antwoord is het eerlijkste?
3 Welk antwoord is het minst eerlijk?
4 Welk antwoord denk je dat de schrijver van de tekst het beste vindt? Waarom?
5 Aan welk taalgebruik in de tekst kun je zien dat de tekst is geschreven voor relatief jonge mensen?
6 Welke mentaliteit over werk en carrière spreekt uit het antwoord?

Lees het commentaar bij de antwoorden.

> Met antwoord (b) heeft u natuurlijk gelijk, maar maakt u zeker geen goede indruk. Bij antwoord (d) is het dom om uw collega een goede kans te geven, maar nog altijd beter dan uw directeur voor zeurkous uit te maken. Als u het echt niet zelf wilt doen is (c) natuurlijk de goede oplossing, maar de echt ambitieuze medewerker laat zich deze kans niet ontnemen en geeft antwoord (a).

ontnemen	to take away	**uitmaken**	to call someone names

Oefening 28

Ga naar www.123test.nl. Hier vind je testen over werk en beroepskeuze. Surf rond de site en probeer een test te doen. Maak notities van je ervaring en opmerkingen en breng die mee naar de klas. (Wil je meer algemene persoonlijkheidstesten, dan kan je die vinden via www.test.pagina.nl.)

Oefening 29: Groepsdiscussie

Vind je dit soort tests handig?
Denk je dat ze je een goed beeld van jezelf kunnen geven?
Vind je dat sowieso belangrijk?

Structuren

RELATIVE CLAUSES

Relative clauses give more information about a person or a thing; the antecedent. In the following example, **iemand** is the antecedent and the relative clause is underlined. Usually, the antecedent is followed immediately by the relative clause. For example:

Wij zoeken *iemand* <u>die flexibel en enthousiast is.</u>

Die/dat

Relative clauses are structured like a subclause, with the verb moving to the end of the clause. They are introduced by the **relative pronoun**, **die** or **dat**. If the antecedent is a **de**-word you use **die**, if the antecedent is a **het**-word you use **dat**. For example:

het team: **Wij hebben een *team* <u>*dat* schitterend samenwerkt.</u>**

de mensen: **Wij zoeken nog *mensen* <u>*die* aan ons project willen meewerken.</u>**

Wie/wat

If there is no clear antecedent, if it is a superlative, **alles/(n)iets**, or if the antecedent is a whole sentence you use the relative pronoun **wie** for people and **wat** for things. For example:

Het *minste* wat we kunnen doen, is een kaartje sturen.
***Alles* wat hij vertelt, is gebaseerd op leugens.**

Wie geïnteresseerd is, kan contact opnemen met de manager.
***Hij is niet de favoriet van de directie*, wat algemeen bekend is.**

Objects and people

When a relative clause is used with a preposition, **waar** + preposition is used if you're referring to objects, and preposition + **wie** if you're referring to people. For example:

***De stoel* waarop u momenteel zit, was ooit het eigendom van Elvis Presley.**

***De stoel* waar u momenteel op zit, was ooit het eigendom van Elvis Presley.**

***De vriend* aan wie ik dat boek heb uitgeleend, is nu verhuisd.**

Oefening 30

Vul **die** of **dat** in.

1 De jongen _______ op deze foto naast mij staat, is mijn broer.
2 Ik heb een persoon nodig _______ zich 100% voor zijn baan wil geven.
3 Dat meisje is iemand _______ heel goed een team kan leiden.
4 Ik kreeg gisteren het kaartje _______ je me uit Corsica had opgestuurd.
5 Het schilderij _______ daar aan de muur hangt, heeft je grootvader geschilderd.
6 Het is een voorstel _______ nog verder moet uitgewerkt worden.
7 Ze sturen me vandaag nog het contract op _______ ik dan moet tekenen en terugsturen.
8 Ik heb een baan gevonden _______ me op het lijf geschreven staat.
9 Een van mijn collega's, _______ daar al jaren werkt, heeft me dat verteld.
10 Zij heeft een maandsalaris, _______ ik niet eens op een jaar verdien.

Oefening 31

Vul **wie** of **wat** in.

1 Het meeste _______ je kan krijgen is 100 punten
2 _______ meer weet over de overval, moet de politie bellen.
3 _______ ik maar niet begrijp, is hoe wreed mensen kunnen zijn.

4 Alles ______ je op het nieuws hoort, is beïnvloed door de veiligheidsdiensten.
5 Zij heeft een relatie met de buurman, ______ de hele straat weet.
6 Wij moeten weten ______ het slachtoffer voor het laatst gezien heeft.
7 ______ we nog moeten kopen staat op het lijstje.
8 Iets ______ we niet mogen vergeten, zijn de bloemen voor de organisatoren.
9 De kleuren op de brochures zijn niet zo mooi, ______ me eigenlijk wel stoort.
10 Ik vraag me soms af ______ al die dure spullen koopt.

Oefening 32

Schrijf de zinnen aan elkaar. Maak telkens 2 zinnen, zoals in het voorbeeld.

Bijvoorbeeld

Ik zit op een stoel. De stoel is zwart.
De stoel waarop ik zit, is zwart.
De stoel waar ik op zit, is zwart.

1 De factuur zit in een envelop. De envelop ligt op de vensterbank.
2 Ik schrijf met een pen. De pen heb ik gekregen van een klant.
3 Ik heb een pen van een klant gekregen. Die klant is nu failliet.
4 Ik verhuis naar een andere afdeling. Die andere afdeling is heel groot.
5 Ik zoek naar een boek. Dat boek is nergens te vinden.
6 Hans komt uit een dorp. Dat dorp is heel bekend om zijn kazen.
7 Ik protesteer tegen de oorlog. Die oorlog is onwettig.
8 Ik stem voor een vrouw. Die vrouw kent haar dossiers.
9 Wij rijden langs een gebouw. Het gebouw is ontworpen door Rietveld.
10 De schrijver gaat schuil achter een pseudoniem. Het pseudoniem is een anagram van zijn echte naam.

Oefening 33

Geef meer informatie over het cursieve zinsdeel, zoals in het voorbeeld.

Bijvoorbeeld

Ik kijk naar *een programma*.
Het programma waarnaar ik kijk, is interessant.

1 Ik heb een hekel aan *iets*.
2 Ik werk voor *het bedrijf*.
3 Ik soliciteer naar *de baan*.
4 Ik ben vaak bezig met *iets*.
5 Ik hou echt van *een stad*.

Oefening 34

Schrijf twee definities van 30 woorden: een van een object en een van een persoon. Noem het object of de persoon niet en gebruik relatieve bijzinnen. Deze definities lees je voor voor je medestudenten. Zij moeten raden over wat of wie het gaat.

Example

een ding
Het is iets *waarmee* je mensen pijn kan doen, maar *wat* ook heel nuttig kan zijn. Het is iets *wat* je meestal in de keuken vindt en *waar* je vlees of brood *mee* kan snijden.

Een mes!

een persoon
Het is iemand *voor wie* veel Nederlanders respect hebben en *op wie* ook veel Nederlanders gestemd hebben. Het is iemand *die* een belangrijke politieke rol heeft gespeeld en *die* op laffe wijze vermoord is. Het is iemand *over wie* sommige mensen zeggen dat hij een racist was.

Nederlands politicus Pim Fortuyn!

Talking about people

You have already learned many different structures, communicative tools and strategies to talk about people. Relative clauses are another useful tool when describing people's personalities, likes, dislikes, skills, etc.

Oefening 35

Werk in paren. Een van jullie gebruikt tabel A, de ander gebruikt tabel B. Vraag aan elkaar informatie over de verschillende personen. Gebruik verschillende structuren die je geleerd hebt om personen te beschrijven, inclusief relatieve bijzinnen.

Bijvoorbeeld

A Waarin is Mario geïnteresseerd?

B Hij heeft interesse voor moderne kunst en lezen. Waar is hij goed in?

A Hij kan goed schrijven en luisteren. Waar heeft hij een hekel aan?

B Aan hemden strijken en administratieve taken.

A	*Interesse*	*houdt van*	*kan goed*	*hekel aan*
Mario			schrijven, luisteren	
Karel	sport, doe-het-zelven			afwassen, op kantoor zitten
Gemma		wandelen in de natuur, klassieke muziek	teksten structureren, analyseren	chaos, luidruchtige mensen
je partner				

B	*Interesse*	*houdt van*	*kan goed*	*hekel aan*
Mario	moderne kunst, lezen	lekker eten, gezelligheid, uitgaan		hemden strijken, administratieve taken
Karel		TV kijken, naar de kroeg gaan	met mensen omgaan, delegeren	
Gemma	paardrijden, geschiedenis			
je partner				

Oefening 36

Je partner uit de vorige oefening is pas bij jouw bedrijf komen werken. Je moet een stukje van 200 woorden schrijven voor het bedrijfskrantje om hem/haar voor te stellen aan het bedrijf. Gebruik de informatie uit de vorige oefening en vraag zo nodig om extra informatie.

A closer look

'OP DE HEI ZITTEN'

Lees de volgende definitie van 'op de hei zitten' van www.floor.nl, een website met informatie over management.

'Op de hei zitten'

Met de hele afdeling of het management een paar dagen in een conferentieoord zitten, bijvoorbeeld om te focussen op de corporate strategy, kwaliteit of resultaatgericht werken. Partners van grote kantoren gaan echter in retraite om zich te bezinnen op de strategische visie voor de komende jaren.

Key vocabulary

de afdeling	department	**resultaatgericht werken**	working in result-oriented fashion
het conferentieoord	conference venue	**zich bezinnen over**	to reflect upon, to contemplate
echter	however		
de hei	heath(land), moorland		
in retraite gaan	go into retreat		

Vragen bij A closer look *(a)*

1 Welke beelden komen in je hoofd bij het woord 'hei'?

2 Verwacht je een woord zoals 'hei' en de beelden die het oproept in een tekst over werk en management? Waarom denk je dat dit concept is gebruikt?

3 Denk je dat de schrijver kritisch is over het fenomeen 'op de hei zitten'? Waarom wel/niet?

WEI-GEVOEL

The following text is an extract from Youp Van 't Hek's weekly column in the Dutch daily newspaper *NRC Handelsblad*. He presents a more ironic view of modern management and 'op de hei zitten'. This is a rather difficult text at this stage, so don't try to understand every word. Use the reading strategies you have learnt earlier. Read through the text several times to get a general idea. Then discuss this with your fellow students before going into more detail and answering the questions. Afterwards, you can listen to the recording and try to copy the intonation whilst reading yourself.

Wei-gevoel

Een wildvreemde jongen vertelde mij dat hij in een congrescentrum met het hele bedrijf alle namen van de werknemers had gezongen. Er was een melodie gemaakt, er verscheen een heuse dirigent, via de overheadprojector kwamen de namen op een scherm en voor hij het wist, stond de hele zaal uit volle borst te zingen. Sappig detail: alle mensen kregen een petje op en de lolbroeken droegen dat petje achterstevoren! Toen ze na de pauze terugkwamen was de motivatietrainer zogenaamd boos dat iedereen weer op zijn oude plek was gaan zitten. Dat was te voorspelbaar gedrag. Waarom ze dat deden? De jongen antwoordde dat zijn trui op de stoel lag en dat zijn tas daar nog stond. Het leek hem redelijk raar om bij een ander zijn tas te gaan zitten! Dat leek hem zelfs onbeschoft. Hier had de boerenkoolpsycholoog uiteraard geen antwoord op.

[. . .]

Als ik directeur van zo'n bedrijf was, zou ik zo'n gebakken luchtverkoper zeker inhuren en hem vragen om iets heel vernederends te bedenken. Daarna zou ik achterin de zaal plaatsnemen en iedereen die er aan meedeed op staande voet ontslaan wegens gebrek aan persoonlijkheid. Dom kuddegedrag. Wei-gevoel dus. Oprotten en nooit meer terugkomen. Waarom doen mensen mee? Waarom zo'n lage schaamtedrempel? Meeklappen is toch iets voor analfabeten op een schlagerfestival? Wie legt mij dit een keer uit? Zelf heb ik ook een klein bedrijf en ik heb geen seconde moeite om mijn personeel te motiveren. We hebben een oergezonde deal: Zij werken en ik betaal ze. Als ik ze zou vragen om voor het groepsgevoel in de Ardennen aan een den te gaan hangen, zouden ze collectief ontslag nemen. En terecht.

Youp Van 't Hek (NRC 18-11-2000)

Key vocabulary

achterstevoren	the wrong way round
de analfabeet	illiterate person
de boerenkool	kale (kind of cabbage; *connotation*: banal, common, stupid)
de den	pine tree
gebakken lucht	hot air
gebrek aan	lack of
heus	real, actual
inhuren	to hire
de kudde	herd
de lolbroek	clown, joker
meeklappen	to clap along
onbeschoft	rude
ontslaan	to dismiss
ontslag nemen	to resign
oprotten	bugger off
de pet	cap
raar	strange
de schaamtedrempel	threshold of shame
het scherm	screen
op staande voet	immediately
terecht	rightly so
uit volle borst	at the top of one's voice
uiteraard	obviously
vernederend	humiliating
verschijnen	to appear
voorspelbaar	predictable
wegens	because of
de wei	field, meadow
wildvreemd	perfectly strange
zelfs	even
zogenaamd	so-called

Vragen bij A closer look *(b)*

1 Maak een lijstje van de woorden die Youp gebruikt om de organisatoren van deze evenementen te beschrijven. Voorbeeld: een heuse dirigent, de motivatietrainer.

2 Welke woorden in paragraaf 2 beschrijven het gedrag van de werknemers? Maak nog van een lijstje.

3 Denk je dat de woorden die je in 1 en 2 hebt gevonden grappig bedoeld zijn?

4 In de laatste paar regels beschrijft Van 't Hek zijn eigen bedrijf. Hij zegt over zichzelf en zijn medewerkers: 'We hebben een oergezonde deal'. Wat vindt hij ongezond?

5 Ben je het met Van 't Hek eens?

6 Het is de taak van een columnist als Van 't Hek om mensen tegen de schenen te schoppen. Hoe doet hij dat hier met zijn taalgebruik? Geef voorbeelden uit de tekst.

7 Lees je graag columns (in je eigen taal)? Waarom wel/niet?

tegen de schenen schoppen to step on (someone's) toes

Je kan de columns van Youp Van 't Hek en andere columnisten lezen op de website van het NRC Handelsblad: http://www.nrc.nl/columns/index.html

Unit 7
Open gordijnen

This unit focuses on talking about the communities where people live or have lived, and the relationships they have with the people around them, particularly their immediate neighbours. We will also look at how people talk about their lifestyle. Furthermore, we will look at how language use affects objectivity and subjectivity.

TOPICS

- Where you live and relationships with neighbours (now and in the past)
- Dutch homes and living arrangements
- Objectivity and subjectivity in language use
- **Gezellig**
- Personal relationships
- Work: conditions and pay
- Dieting

FUNCTIONS

- Talking about lifestyles
- Talking about relationships
- Talking about hobbies and leisure activities
- Using subjective language to express an opinion or make descriptions
- Saying what you would do if . . .
- Saying what you had intended to do
- Talking about rumours
- Talking about health and dieting
- To recognise underlying ideas in a text
- To talk about the role of work in people's private lives

GRAMMAR

- Imperfect
- Differences in use between imperfect and present perfect
- **Met z'n** . . .
- Past perfect
- **Zou**: (conditional; in polite questions; uncertain information; hypothetical past)
- Infinitives
- **Om** + **te** + infinitive

Tekst 1 Misha over de buurt waar ze woont

Listen to Misha a few times without reading along. Then answer the recorded questions in **Oefening 1,** and then study what Misha says more closely by reading the text and answering the questions in **Oefening 2.**

Ik woon in een echte volksbuurt midden in het centrum van de stad. Ik heb m'n huis gevonden via een vriendin. Die vriendin woonde hier in de buurt en wist dat 't echtpaar dat hier woonde naar 'n bejaardentehuis ging. Ik heb direct bij de woningbouwvereniging aan de bel getrokken. Ik mocht er direct in want ik stond al een aantal jaren op de wachtlijst.

Ik ben nu bijna drie jaar geleden verhuisd, en het bevalt me hier prima. Hiervoor woonde ik in een flat in een nieuwbouwwijk, dat was totaal anders. Ik had bijna geen contact met de buren, sociale controle bestond er niet. Iedereen leefde gewoon langs elkaar heen. Dat was erg onpersoonlijk, en ik voelde me er dan ook eenzaam.

Hier kent iedereen elkaar, en we hebben in de straat veel contact onderling. Wat dat betreft, vind ik het hier veel prettiger wonen, want het geeft me een gevoel van geborgenheid, ik hoor hier thuis. Mensen groeten elkaar op straat, je stopt vaak om een babbeltje te maken. Zelfs de winkeliers kennen je hier, en dat is erg gezellig.

Key vocabulary

aan de bel trekken	to draw someone's attention to something
een babbeltje	chat
het bejaardentehuis	old people's home
eenzaam	lonely
de geborgenheid	security/safety
het bevalt me	I like it
langs elkaar heen leven	live near each other without making contact
de nieuwbouw	new(ly) built house(s)
onderling	amongst ourselves
thuishoren	to belong somewhere
de volksbuurt	working class neighbourhood
de winkelier	shopkeeper
de woningbouw-vereniging	housing corporation

Oefening 1: Luistervragen

1 Hoe lang woont Misha al in haar huis?
2 In wat voor woning woonde Misha hiervoor?
3 In wat voor buurt was dat?
4 Vindt Misha de buurt waar ze nu woont prettig?
5 Als je luistert naar het accent van Misha, denk je dan dat ze uit Nederland komt of uit Vlaanderen?

Oefening 2

1 Leg in je eigen woorden uit hoe Misha haar huidige woning heeft gevonden.
2 Wat vindt Misha prettig aan de wijk waar ze nu woont?
3 Wat zijn volgens jou de voor- en nadelen van wonen in een nieuwbouwwijk?
4 Wat zijn volgens jou de voor- en nadelen van wonen in een oudere buurt of een volksbuurt?

Oefening 3

Maak een lijst van dingen die je positief vindt aan de plek waar je woont. Begin je zinnen met: **Ik voel me er thuis omdat . . .**

Bijvoorbeeld

Ik voel me er thuis omdat iedereen elkaar kent.
Ik voel me er thuis omdat er veel sociale controle is.

Oefening 4

Maak een lijst van dingen die je negatief vindt aan de plek waar je woont. Begin met: **Ik voel me er niet thuis omdat . . .**

Bijvoorbeeld

Ik voel me er niet thuis omdat er weinig sociale controle is.
Ik voel me er niet thuis omdat er veel geluidsoverlast is. (noise pollution)

Oefening 5

Gebruik de lijsten uit de vorige twee oefeningen om te oefenen met de structuur: **Wat dat betreft, vind ik het . . .**

Maak hele zinnen. Geef positieve en negatieve beschrijvingen van waar je woont. Zeg dan wat jij ervan vindt.

Bijvoorbeeld

Waar ik woon, kent iedereen elkaar. Wat dat betreft vind ik het er prettig wonen.
Waar ik woon, is veel geluidsoverlast. Wat dat betreft vind ik het er niet prettig wonen.

Structuren

TALKING ABOUT THE PAST: THE IMPERFECT

When Misha describes where she lives now, she uses the present tense:

Ik *woon* in een echte volksbuurt.

When describing where she used to live, she uses a past tense, the imperfect. Look at the following examples of the imperfect tense:

Ik *woonde* in een nieuwbouwwijk.
Iedereen *leefde* gewoon langs elkaar heen.

Dat *was* erg onpersoonlijk.
Ik *voelde* me er eenzaam.

Wij *voelden* ons vanaf het begin thuis in deze buurt.
Ik *werkte* meer dan 50 uur per week.
Wij *werkten* nooit meer dan 7 uur per dag.

Woonde, leefde, voelde(n), werkte(n) are imperfect forms of regular verbs. Try and establish a pattern for forming the imperfect of regular verbs by filling in the table below.

	imperfect, singular *(**ik, jij, u, hij, zij**)*	*imperfect, plural* *(**wij, jullie, zij**)*
voelen	stem + ______________	stem + ______________
werken	stem + ______________	stem + ______________

Which ending to use in the imperfect tense depends on the last letter of the stem. Fill in the table to establish a rule.

stem of the verb ends in	*ending for the imperfect singular*	*ending for the imperfect plural*
s, **f**, **t**, **k**, **ch**, **p** (soft ketchup)	______________	______________
not **s**, **f**, **t**, **k**, **ch**, **p** (soft ketchup)	______________	______________

Irregular verbs don't form the imperfect according to a specific pattern. Examples are:

Ik *had* bijna geen contact met de buren.
Sociale controle *bestond* er niet.

At the back of this book you will find a list with irregular verbs with their imperfect forms.

Oefening 6

Jamie kwam gisteren te laat op zijn werk. Zet de werkwoorden tussen haakjes in de *imperfect tense* om te vertellen wat er is gebeurd.

1 Ik (gaan) gisteren om half acht van huis naar mijn werk.
2 Mijn auto (willen) niet starten.
3 Ik (besluiten) om met de trein te gaan.
4 Ik (moeten) eerst een kwartier lopen naar het station.
5 Toen ik op het station (komen), (zijn) er problemen met de treinen vanwege een stroomstoring.
6 Na drie kwartier wachten, (komen) er een bus van de spoorwegen.
7 Er (zijn) te veel mensen, dus ik (kunnen) de bus niet in.
8 Ik (moeten) op de tweede bus wachten, die een halfuur later (komen).

9 De busreis (duren) door alle files een uur.
10 Op het station (moeten) ik in een lange rij wachten op een taxi.
11 Uiteindelijk (zijn) ik twee uur te laat op m'n werk.

de file	traffic jam	**de stroomstoring**	power failure
de spoorwegen	rail company		

Oefening 7

Zet de werkwoorden tussen haakjes in de *imperfect tense*.

Toen ik klein (zijn) _____________ , (wonen) _____________ ik in Zaltbommel. We (hebben) _____________ een huis met een grote tuin, dus ik en mijn broertje (kunnen) _____________ heerlijk buitenspelen. We (spelen) _____________ vaak met kinderen uit de buurt. We (voetballen) _____________ , (knikkeren) _____________ , (verstoppertje spelen) _____________ , en 's winters (schaatsen) _____________ we. In de zomer (gaan) _____________ we meestal een paar weken naar de kust. M'n ouders (huren) _____________ dan een huisje aan het strand in Zeeland. Dat vonden we fantastisch – we (gaan) _____________ dan elke dag in zee zwemmen.

knikkeren	play marbles	**verstoppertje spelen**	play hide-and-seek
de kust	coast		

Oefening 8

In de volgende teksten praten kinderen over de dingen die ze doen. Zoek moeilijke woorden op in een woordenboek. Herschrijf dan alle teksten in de *imperfect tense*, alsof de kinderen nu volwassen zijn en over hun jeugd praten.

Jules
Ik speel thuis het meeste met mijn Lego, maar ik speel ook graag met mijn computerspelletjes. In de zomer ga ik graag zwemmen. We gaan ook vaak naar het strand, dat vind ik echt te gek.

Hakim
Als ik uit school thuiskom, moet ik natuurlijk eerst mijn huiswerk maken, maar daarna mag ik buitenspelen. Ik voetbal vaak met mijn vrienden op straat. Ik zit ook op een voetbalclub. Dinsdags train ik, en in het weekend moet ik een wedstrijd spelen met mijn elftal.

Rowenna
Mijn vriendinnen en ik bellen 's middags vaak heel lang. We kletsen lekker met elkaar als we uit school thuiskomen. Meestal drink ik wel eerst een kopje thee met mijn moeder, dat vind ik ook heel gezellig.

Petra
Woensdagavond moet ik turnen en op donderdag heb ik gitaarles. Ik moet ook vaak oefenen want ik zit in een band. 's Avonds kijk ik graag tv. Het liefst kijk ik naar soaps, de Nederlandse en de buitenlandse, ik zie ze allemaal graag.

kletsen	to chat	**turnen**	to do gymnastics

Oefening 9

Mariska woont alleen. Ze heeft 's nachts de politie gebeld omdat ze denkt dat iemand wilde inbreken. De politie wil weten wat er is gebeurd. Hieronder zie je Mariska's verhaal in de *present tense*. Herschrijf alles in de *imperfect tense*.

Ik kom om kwart over tien thuis. Ik deactiveer het alarm en loop naar de keuken. Ik geef de kat te eten en ga naar bed. Rond een uur of één hoor ik een geluid. Ik denk dat het de kat is, maar die slaapt op de stoel naast mijn bed. Toen hoor ik weer een geluid, uit de keuken. Iemand doet de buitendeur open. Ik zeg hard 'Wie is daar?'. Ik hoor niets. Doodsbang bel ik direct de politie op mijn mobiel. Daarna roep ik nogmaals. Ik ga kijken in de keuken, maar er is niemand. Er is ook niets weg.

Communicatie

TALKING ABOUT THE PAST: USING THE IMPERFECT AND THE PRESENT PERFECT

(a) Use the imperfect tense to describe habits and/or regular events from the past.

Iedereen *leefde* langs elkaar heen.
Er *was* geen contact tussen de buren.
We *gingen* elk jaar op vakantie naar Frankrijk.

(b) When describing events from the past, introduce them (and sometimes round them off) in the present perfect tense, but give all other information in the imperfect.

Ik *heb* mijn huis *gevonden* via een vriendin.	(present perfect)
Die vriendin *woonde* in de buurt.	(imperfect)
Ik *kende* haar al vier jaar.	(imperfect)
Zij *vertelde* me dat . . .	(imperfect)

(c) Dramatic involvement. Choosing between the perfect and imperfect is usually not a case of right or wrong. Often, either can be used. The imperfect gives a feeling of involvement and drama; the present perfect creates a feeling of distance.

Ik ben in Griekenland op vakantie geweest, is an observation you might make as if you were running off a list (*The year before I went to France, two years ago Mexico*).

Ik was in Griekenland op vakantie, gives a sense of drama, you picture yourself there. It feels like it's part of a story – you expect more information to follow, as if you're saying: *Picture this. I was on holiday in Greece when . . .*

Oefening 10: Discussion about the imperfect and present perfect tenses

Look at the following excerpts from Text 1. For each excerpt, discuss which tenses are used, and whether Misha uses the perfect and imperfect tenses in the same way as described above.

1 Misha describes how she found her house.

Ik heb m'n huis gevonden via een vriendin. Die vriendin woonde hier in de buurt en wist dat 't echtpaar dat hier woonde naar 'n bejaardentehuis ging. Ik heb direct bij de woningbouwvereniging aan de bel getrokken.

2 Misha describes where she lived before.

Ik ben nu bijna drie jaar geleden verhuisd, en het bevalt me hier prima. Hiervoor woonde ik in een flat in een nieuwbouwwijk, dat was totaal anders. Ik had bijna geen contact met de buren, sociale controle bestond er niet. Iedereen leefde gewoon langs elkaar heen. Dat was erg onpersoonlijk, en ik voelde me er dan ook eenzaam.

Oefening 11

Hieronder staan drie korte krantenartikels. Zet de werkwoorden tussen haakjes in de juiste tijd.

1

IN DE IRAKEZE stad Basra (doden) opstandelingen gisteren drie Amerikaanse soldaten. De soldaten (zijn) op patrouille door de stad. De terroristen (vuren) op de patrouillewagen vanuit een auto die de andere richting op (rijden). Een tweede Amerikaanse patrouillewagen (achtervolgen) de auto. Twee Irakezen (raken) gewond. In totaal de Amerikanen (arresteren) vijf terroristen.

2

EEN 71-jarige man uit Hilvarenbeek (omkomen) maandagmiddag bij een verkeersongeval. De bejaarde man (geven) zijn vrouw aanwijzingen bij het achteruitrijden met de auto. Ze (rijden) over hem heen. Volgens de politie (geven) de vrouw gas in plaats van te remmen toen haar man achter de auto (staan). Hij (raken) gewond aan beide benen en (overlijden) later in het ziekenhuis.

3 **IN WEESP** (woeden) in de nacht van woensdag op donderdag een zeer grote brand bij het bedrijf Van Larens. Niemand (raken) gewond en er (komen) geen gevaarlijke stoffen vrij. Het vuur (ontstaan) rond 1.15 uur aan de Lakenstraat in de buurt van de snelweg A4. Dankzij de inzet van honderd brandweerlieden (zijn) de brand onder controle rond 04.30 uur. De politie (houden) er rekening mee dat de brand is aangestoken. De omvang van de schade (zijn) donderdagochtend nog niet bekend. De productie (niet stilliggen) volgens een woordvoerder van het bedrijf.

Key vocabulary

de aanwijzing	instruction
achtervolgen	chase
bejaard	old/senior citizen
de brandweer	fire brigade
een brand woedt	a fire rages
gas geven	to accelerate
gevaarlijke stoffen	dangerous substances (*here*: chemicals)
gewond raken	get injured
de inzet	efforts
is aangestoken	has been lit
lieden	people (not used much on its own)
omkomen	to be killed
de omvang	dimension
op patrouille	on patrol
de opstandeling	rebel
overlijden	to die
rekening houden met	take into account
remmen	to brake
de schade	damage
de snelweg	motorway/freeway
stilliggen	be closed down
de tijd	tense
het verkeersongeval	traffic accident
vrijkomen	to be released

Oefening 12

Think of a (preferably funny or curious) incident which happened to you in the past few days, and write it down in approx. 60–100 words. Pay particular attention to your use of the present perfect and the imperfect tenses.

Example

Verleden week ben ik een oude schoolvriend tegengekomen. Ik moest naar een van onze klanten voor een vergadering. Toen ik voor het kantoor van de klant uit de taxi stapte, stond hij op een taxi te wachten. We hadden elkaar al bijna twintig jaar niet meer gezien, dus het was een flinke verrassing. We zijn 's avonds samen uit eten gegaan.

Cultuur

WONEN

Leestekst

Buitenlanders blijven er zich over verbazen, die open gordijnen. In andere landen zit 's avonds alles potdicht, maar in Nederland kun je als het donker is, gewoon door het raam kijken om te zien hoe iedereen woont. Waarom we ons zo open en bloot laten bekijken is moeilijk te zeggen.

Eind jaren vijftig zagen de huiskamers van een doorsneegezin er bijna allemaal hetzelfde uit: de tafel in het midden, een zithoek rond een salontafel met een perzisch tapijtje, een rond kanten kleedje en een thee- of koffieservies erop, langs de muur een dressoir, een radio op een apart tafeltje en natuurlijk voor het raam wat sanseveria's.

Tegenwoordig zouden we zo'n interieur kleinburgerlijk noemen, maar toen was men er erg tevreden mee. Daar was alle reden toe. Nooit eerder had de gemiddelde Nederlander zo veel wooncomfort gekend. In de 19de eeuw hokten honderdduizenden arbeidersgezinnen samen in eenkamerwoningen in overvolle steden. Deze vuiligheid en armoede, en de daarmee gepaard gaande dronkenschap, ruzies en zedeloosheid baarden de gegoede burgerij grote zorgen. Want stel je voor dat deze grauwe massa in verzet zou komen.

Er was maar één oplossing, het volk opvoeden. Eind 19de eeuw begon de burgerij, in nauwe samenwerking met de overheid, een groot beschavingsoffensief. De arbeidersman moest leren thuis te zitten in plaats van in het café zijn karig loon te verbrassen, de arbeidersvrouw moest leren goed en voedzaam te koken en haar woning huiselijk, gezellig en knus in te richten, zodat haar man en kinderen geen reden meer hadden op straat rond te hangen.

In een halve eeuw tijd leerde de Nederlander netjes, schoon en fris te wonen. Warmte, gezelligheid en huiselijkheid werd de norm. Maar toen kwamen de jaren zestig. Burgerlijkheid werd een vies woord. Feministen maakten bezwaar dat de vrouw altijd maar thuis als huisvrouw moest blijven. Iedereen wilde zich individueel kunnen ontplooien.

Het ideaal werd ieder een eigen kamer, een eigen televisie en een eigen telefoon, en natuurlijk een op maat ingericht huis. Wonen is iets emotioneels geworden. Wonen is leven en genieten. De huiselijkheid is gebleven, maar tegenwoordig vullen we die zelf in. Daar doen we niet geheimzinnig over. Anderen mogen best zien hoe gezellig het bij ons thuis is.

naar: www.20eeuwennederland.nl

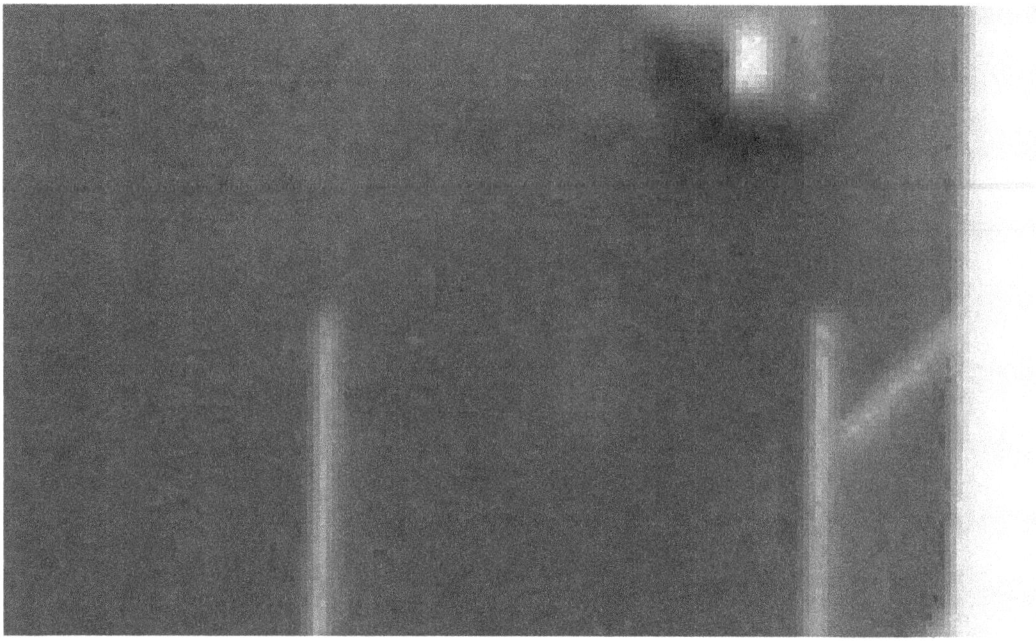

Key vocabulary

de armoede	poverty	**knus**	cosy/friendly
de beschaving	civilisation	**ontplooien**	develop (emotionally)
het bezwaar	complaint	**op maat**	on demand
daar . . . toe	for this	**open en bloot**	openly
de daarmee gepaard gaande	the accompanying	**de overheid**	(local) government
		overvol	completely full
doorsnee-	average	**perzisch tapijtje**	thick, carpet-like table cloth
het dressoir	sideboard		
de gegoede burgerij	bourgeoisie	**potdicht**	shut tight
genieten	enjoy	**samenhokken**	live together in cramped conditions
de grauwe massa	the masses		
de huisvrouw	housewife	**stel je voor**	imagine
in verzet komen	to rebel	**verbrassen**	squander away/waste
de inslag	streak, characteristic	**voedzaam**	nutritious(ly)
kanten	made of lace	**de vuiligheid**	dirt
het karig loon	meagre wages/pay	**de zedeloosheid**	immorality
kleinburgerlijk	lower middle class/ parochial	**de zithoek**	seating area
		zorgen baren	cause concern

Oefening 13

Onderstreep in de tekst alle werkwoorden in de *imperfect tense*. Zoek dan de infinitieven bij deze vormen van de *imperfect tense*.

Oefening 14: Vragen

1 De tekst beschrijft hoe Nederlanders woonden in drie periodes. Welke periodes?

2 Beschrijf in het kort hoe de Nederlanders in die periodes woonden.

3 Wie waren verantwoordelijk voor de veranderingen van de eerste naar de tweede periode?

4 Wie waren verantwoordelijk voor de veranderingen van de tweede naar de derde periode?

5 De tekst beschrijft de veranderingen na de 19de eeuw als volgt:

- er was maar één oplossing
- het volk opvoeden
- het volk vertrouwd maken met huiselijkheid, netheid, zedelijkheid, verantwoordelijkheidsbesef
- een beschavingsoffensief
- de arbeidersman moest leren thuis te zitten
- de arbeidersvrouw moest leren goed en voedzaam te koken
- op straat rondhangen

Als je naar dit taalgebruik kijkt, denk je dan dat de schrijver meer sympathie heeft voor de burgerij die de arbeiders wil veranderen, of voor de arbeiders zelf? Waarom?

6 Zie je in alinea drie ook taalgebruik waaruit je deze conclusie kunt trekken?

7 Denk je dat deze beschrijving over wonen in Nederland objectief is?

8 Herken je de huidige ideeën over wonen uit de laatste paragraaf ook in jouw land?

Oefening 15

'Wonen is iets emotioneels geworden. Wonen is leven en genieten.'

In Nederland zijn woonprogramma's op televisie erg populair. Probeer op het internet informatie over Nederlandse woonprogramma's te vinden (bijvoorbeeld op www.tvgids.nl). In welke woorden spreekt men over huizen en wonen (**gezellig**? **chique**? **ruim**? **knus**? etc.). Wat zeggen deze woorden over Nederlanders en wonen?

Oefening 16

Bespreek in groepjes wat je van woonprogramma's op televisie vindt. Bevorderen ze bijvoorbeeld individualiteit, een ideaal dat mensen tegenwoordig hoog in 't vaandel dragen, of juist niet?

hoog in 't vaandel dragen/hebben	feel very strongly about something

Oefening 17

Schrijf een korte tekst van 100–150 woorden over de ontwikkelingen van wonen in je geboorteland. Beschrijf eerst hoe een doorsneegezin vroeger woonde, en beschrijf daarna hoe de idealen zijn veranderd.

Cultuur

GEZELLIG

You will find that **gezellig** is an important concept to the Dutch. **Gezellig** means enjoyable, pleasant, sociable, cosy, entertaining and many other things. **Gezellig** usually refers to people having a good time in each other's company. About a party you might ask the following day:

Was het gezellig?

The answer could be

Ja, het was heel gezellig / Nee, het was niet echt gezellig.

To the Dutch **gezellig** often carries connotations of people coming together in a certain snug, cosy homeliness. An important example of **gezellig** in this context is the tradition of having morning coffee with family or friends. A **kopje koffie** (note that the diminutive **kopje** indicates 'gezellig') in the morning, enjoyed in pleasant, sociable company is considered an important **gezellig** ritual.

VERJAARDAGEN

Verjaardagen (birthdays) are also considered important **gezellig** occasions (see Unit 4). Traditionally, Dutch birthdays are celebrated in the home amongst the immediate family, with relatively few friends and acquaintances amongst the invited (although this is changing). The ritualised traditional aspects of Dutch birthdays emphasize **gezellig**, from everyone shaking hands upon arrival and often kissing each other three times (everyone knows each other), all the guests sitting in a big circle (everyone is included), the compulsory **kopje koffie met gebak** (cake), followed by (alcoholic) drinks and nibbles, to everyone shaking hands and kissing again at the end of the evening.

When such homeliness is absent from an occasion or celebration, for instance a group of young people visiting 'a rave' in a nightclub, the Dutch use **gezellig** less often to describe the event. Alternatives could be:

Het was hartstikke leuk. **Het was te gek.** **Het was top.**

Tekst 2 Buren

Listen to the recordings a few times without reading along. Then listen to the questions and answer them. Next study the dialogue more closely by reading along and looking up difficult words.

Giovanni

Martine en ik kunnen het heel goed vinden met onze buren, Mart en Siem. Wij woonden al in ons huis toen de jongens naast ons kwamen wonen. We waren blij dat we buren kregen van onze leeftijd. We doen veel voor elkaar: we halen soms boodschappen, en nemen de post aan, we passen op elkaars poes tijdens de vakanties, en één keer in de maand eten we bij elkaar. Het is fijn om buren te hebben die je kunt vertrouwen. Mart en Siem zijn ook leuke, sociale jongens, we gaan regelmatig stappen met z'n vieren, dat is erg gezellig.

Charlotte

Het klikte direct met Hennie en Sao. Op de dag van m'n verhuizing kwamen ze 's avonds langs met een fles champagne, en toen was het meteen goed. We hebben een bijzondere band opgebouwd; we zijn buren én vrienden. Daarvoor had ik bij buren altijd het gevoel: fijn dat ze er zijn, maar we hoeven de deur niet bij elkaar plat te lopen. Bij Hennie en Sao is dat anders. Ze zijn vreselijk aardig en ik kan altijd bij ze aankloppen. Ik heb na mijn scheiding een moeilijke periode gehad, maar met hun steun heb ik me erdoor geslagen. Ze zijn zo warm en oprecht. Ze stonden altijd voor me klaar. Ze hebben echt met me meegeleefd. Als ik het niet meer zag zitten, kon ik altijd even bij ze langs. Het is een stel uit duizenden – betere buren kan ik me niet wensen.

Key vocabulary

bij iemand aankloppen	to knock on someone's door
de deur plat lopen	always be knocking on someone's door
iets niet meer zien zitten	not able to see your way out
ik heb me erdoor geslagen	I got through it
klikken	to hit it off
meeleven	empathise
met z'n vieren	the four of us
oprecht	sincere
uit duizenden	one in a thousand
voor iemand klaarstaan	be there for someone

Oefening 18: Luistervragen

1 Wonen Giovanni en Martine langer of korter in hun huis dan Mart en Siem?
2 Waarom waren Giovanni en Martine blij met hun nieuwe buren?
3 Wat doen Giovanni en z'n vrouw, en Mart en Siem voor elkaar?

4 Woont Charlotte langer of korter in haar huis dan Hennie en Sao?
5 Wat was de oorzaak van Charlottes moeilijke periode?
6 Hoe hebben Hennie en Sao Charlotte geholpen?

Oefening 19: In paren

Bespreek je relatie met een of meer van je buren. Gebruik zoveel mogelijk uitdrukkingen uit de dialogen. Schrijf na de discussie in paren een kort stukje van 60–70 woorden over een van je relaties met de buren voor de buurtkrant.

Structuren

MET Z'N

This structure is used to indicate how many people were present at a gathering. In the dialogue above, Giovanni says:

We gaan regelmatig stappen *met z'n vieren*.

By adding **-en** to a number, you can refer to any number of people in this way. Note that the spelling rules apply:

We waren gisterenavond *met z'n drieën*.
Ze willen *met z'n zessen* op vakantie.

You will also come across: **met z'n allen** (all of us).

We zijn *met z'n allen* naar een nachtclub gegaan.

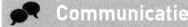

Communicatie

SUBJECTIEF

As you know, language which expresses a personal opinion, rather than an objective fact, is called subjective. In describing a painting, **mooi** is a subjective statement, **vierkant** an objective statement. People often use subjective language, particularly when discussing personal matters. The Dutch too. In fact, you might find the Dutch eager and quick to express their personal opinion. Belgians are generally thought much less forward in expressing their opinions.

Oefening 20

Lees de volgende beschrijvingen van geurtjes voor mannen en vrouwen met veel subjectieve vocabulaire. Beantwoord de vragen.

Zwoel, zoet of zacht?

geur 1: Warm en exotisch, met een vleugje leer.
geur 2: Heeft een zachte, kruidige geur.
geur 3: Mysterieus en verleidelijk met een bloemig tintje.
geur 4: Opwekkend en fris.
geur 5: Ultravrouwelijk, met een mix van frisse en warme tonen.
geur 6: Mannelijk, fris en sportief.
geur 7: Eerst fruitig, maar met een zwoele, warme ondertoon.
geur 8: Donker en sensueel.
geur 9: Zo fris, daar word je vrolijk van.
geur 10: Spannend en sexy.
geur 11: Een sterke, opvallende, kruidige geur.
geur 12: Heel elegant en chic.

naar: Flair, Nr. 5, 23 jan. t/m 1 feb. 2004, pp. 40–41

1 Zijn deze beschrijvingen allemaal compleet subjectief, of gedeeltelijk ook objectief? Welke woorden zijn minder subjectief?

2 Gebruik jij zelf parfum of eau de toilette? Beschrijf de geur die jij het lekkerst vindt.

3 Welke geuren (uit het lijstje hierboven) zijn voor mannen en welke voor vrouwen, denk je? Waarom?

het geurtje fragrance

Oefening 21

Beschrijf de volgende personen/zaken alsof het geuren zijn.

1 je lievelingsdrank
2 je favoriete acteur/actrice
3 je beste vriend(in)
4 koningin Beatrix
5 jezelf
6 België of Nederland
7 je eigen land
8 je werk en/of studie

Oefening 22

Geef nu een zo objectief mogelijke beschrijving van de personen en zaken in de vorige oefening.

Oefening 23

Maak negatieve beschrijvingen (niet per se als geur) van de volgende personen en zaken. Je mag zo subjectief zijn als je wilt. Gebruik een woordenboek om woorden op te zoeken.

1 Openbaar vervoer
2 Je minst favoriete film
3 Je minst favoriete acteur of actrice
4 De vervelendste vakantie die je ooit hebt gehad
5 Het weer in Nederland en België

Tekst 3 Myra's dagboek

ZATERDAG

Ik zou vanmiddag met Lieke gaan winkelen, maar daar is niets van gekomen. We hadden de afspraak al een tijdje geleden gemaakt, maar we zouden nog bellen om een tijdstip af te spreken. Ik had al een paar dagen niets van haar gehoord, dus ik besloot haar vanochtend te bellen.

De telefoon ging wel tien keer over. Geen gehoor. Ik zou net ophangen toen Shalom opnam. Hij was erg kortaf, en zei dat Lieke er niet was, ze logeerde een paar dagen bij haar moeder. Hij zei dat hij te laat was voor z'n werk, en brak ons gesprek snel af. Het voelde een beetje vreemd, alsof er iets mis was. Het was bijna onbeschoft zo snel als hij ophing. Gelukkig had ik 't nummer van Liekes moeder, dus ik kon haar direct bellen.

Ze barstte direct in tranen uit: 'Hij heeft me bedrogen. Hij is vreemdgegaan met een collega'.

'Ik stond paf. Dat kon ik me gewoon niet voorstellen van Shalom. Daar was hij 't type niet voor. Ik zou donderdagavond gaan eten met Francisca, maar die kon op 't laatste moment niet. Ik dus maar naar huis. Normaal had ik gebeld, maar de batterij van m'n mobieltje was leeg, dus Sholom wist van niets. Ik wist dat hij thuis zou zijn, want hij zou z'n belastingaangifte invullen. Toen ik thuiskwam, stond er een vreemde auto op 't pad. Het bleek de auto van die collega; ze had Sholom een lift gegeven. Ze stonden in de keuken te zoenen'.

Ik dacht direct: 'Hoe zou ik reageren in zo'n situatie, als Chef met 'n ander stond te zoenen? Zou ik kwaad worden? Zou ik beginnen te schreeuwen, zou ik ze uitschelden? Of zou ik gewoon in tranen uitbarsten?'

Key vocabulary

afbreken	to break off
de belastingaangifte	tax declaration
blijken	prove to be
het dagboek	diary
er was iets mis	something was wrong
geen gehoor	no answer
iemand bedriegen	to cheat on someone
in tranen uitbarsten	to burst into tears
kortaf	curt, short
logeren	stay/sleep over
net	just
onbeschoft	rude
opnemen	to answer (phone)
overgaan	to ring (telephone)
paf staan	to be flabbergasted
het tijdstip	time (of meeting)
uitschelden	call names
van niets weten	to know nothing of it
vreemdgaan	to have an affair
zoenen	kiss

Oefening 24

1 Waarom belt Myra Lieke?

2 Waar is Lieke volgens Shalom?

3 Waarom vindt Myra Shalom onbeschoft aan de telefoon?

4 Hoe komt Lieke erachter dat Shalom een affaire heeft?

erachter komen to find out

Oefening 25

1 De meeste mensen schrijven in hun dagboek op een hele informele manier. Wat maakt deze tekst van Myra informeel? (bijvoorbeeld welke woorden of structuren?)

2 Herschrijf deze tekst op een zakelijke, objectieve manier.

Structuren

TALKING ABOUT THE PAST: THE PAST PERFECT

The past perfect is formed much like the present perfect. Here are some examples from the text:

We *hadden* de afspraak een tijdje geleden *gemaakt*.
Ik *had* al een paar dagen niets *gehoord*.
Ze *had* Shalom een lift *gegeven*.

The past perfect has two uses. Firstly, to make clear that one thing took place before another in the past:

Ik *had* Lieke net *gebeld* toen ze op de deur klopte.
We *waren* al *vertrokken*, toen het begon te regenen.

Secondly, you use the past perfect to fantasize about a past which didn't happen. (Note that **zou** can be used here also.)

Als ik harder *had gewerkt*, *was* ik voor m'n examen *geslaagd*.

Oefening 26

Combineer de volgende zinnen, zodat het ene voor het andere gebeurde.

Bijvoorbeeld

Ik waste net af. Roland bood aan om te helpen.
Ik had net afgewassen toen Roland aanbood om te helpen.

1 Ik viel net in slaap. Ik hoorde buiten een geluid.
2 Ik maakte al een afspraak met Ben. Henri en Jacqueline vroegen of ik kwam eten.
3 Het vliegtuig vertrok al. Chris kwam op het vliegveld aan.
4 Jonah maakte het avondeten al klaar. Ik kwam thuis.
5 Marina hoorde nog nooit van Fellini. Tjeerd nam haar mee naar *La Dolce Vita*.
6 Dave richtte zijn nieuwe huis nog niet helemaal in. Hij verhuisde verleden maand.

inrichten to furnish

Oefening 27

Je werkt aan een belangrijk project. Jij en je collega's zijn veel problemen tegengekomen. Jullie bespreken wat jullie anders hadden kunnen doen.
Maak zinnen met **als** en **dan**. Gebruik de gegeven informatie.

Bijvoorbeeld

de planning beter volgen – op tijd klaar zijn
Als we de planning beter hadden gevolgd, dan waren we op tijd klaar geweest.

1 problemen eerder melden – minder tijd verliezen
2 een duidelijkere rolverdeling hebben – efficiënter werken
3 vaker vergaderen – de communicatie beter zijn
4 een realistischere deadline afspreken – een beter product leveren
5 meer mensen hebben – sneller werken
6 een gedetailleerdere begroting maken – de kosten in de hand houden
7 duidelijkere doelstellingen formuleren – gerichter werken

de doelstelling	aim	**in de hand houden**	to keep in check

ZOU

In the text above you come across **zou** a number of times. Often in the text, **zou** is used to indicate that Myra (or others) had made plans to do something:

Ik zou met Lieke gaan winkelen.
I was going to go shopping with Lieke.

We zouden nog bellen.
We had planned to give each other a call.

However, as you have seen in Unit 2, **zou** has various different uses, like asking polite questions and giving polite advice. **Zou** is also used in conditional sentences:

Als ik de loterij won, (dan) *zou* ik een nieuwe laptop *kopen*.
If I won the lottery, (then) I would buy a new laptop.

The **zou**-clause can also be replaced by the imperfect:

Als ik de loterij won, *kocht* ik een nieuwe laptop.

Furthermore, zou is also used to report uncertain information or information which you have heard from others, and about which you are not sure:

Pedro *zou* gisteren tot 11 uur 's avonds *hebben gewerkt*.
Pedro is supposed to have worked until 11 last night.

Note that auxiliary (**hebben/zijn**) and modal verbs appear in their infinitive form after **zou**.

Look up other uses of **zou** in Unit 2 and then do the following exercises.

Oefening 28

Je hebt een week vrij gehad. Je had plannen om allerlei dingen te doen, maar je hebt niet veel gedaan. Maak een lijst van de dingen die je had willen doen. Gebruik de gegeven informatie.

Bijvoorbeeld

veel Nederlandse woordjes leren
Ik zou veel Nederlandse woordjes leren.

1 mijn bankafschriften in een map ordenen
2 mijn lidmaatschap van de boekenclub opzeggen
3 de vakantiefoto's van vijf jaar geleden in een album plakken
4 een afspraak maken met de tandarts
5 de keuken een goeie beurt geven
6 alle oude e-mails van m'n computer wissen
7 in de tuin al het onkruid wieden
8 mijn CD's op alfabetische volgorde zetten

het bankafschrift	bank statement	**de map**	folder
een afspraak maken	make an appointment	**het onkruid**	weeds
		opzeggen	cancel
een goede beurt geven	give a good clean	**plakken**	stick
		de tandarts	dentist
het lidmaatschap	membership	**wissen**	delete

Oefening 29

In de situatie uit **Oefening 28** kun je ook de *past perfect* gebruiken. Gebruik de informatie uit **Oefening 28** en maak een lijst met dingen die je had gedaan als je meer tijd had gehad. Begin met: **Als ik meer tijd had gehad . . .**

Bijvoorbeeld

veel Nederlandse woordjes leren
Als ik meer tijd had gehad, had ik veel Nederlandse woordjes geleerd.

Oefening 30

Maak de volgende zinnen af met: **zou ik**

1 Als ik president van Amerika was, zou ik ______

2 Als ik niet hoefde te werken, zou ik ______

3 Als ik kon wonen waar ik wilde, zou ik ______

4 Als ik in Nederland woonde, zou ik ______

5 Als ik een miljoen mocht schenken aan 'n organisatie, zou ik ______

schenken	donate

Oefening 31

1 Onderstreep in deze tekst alle zinnen met **zou**. Zoek moeilijke woorden op in een woordenboek.

Als ik minister-president van Nederland was, zou ik het belastingstelsel drastisch veranderen. Ik zou het inkomensverschil tussen arm en rijk willen verkleinen. Om iedereen gelijke kansen te geven in het leven zou ik de kindersubsidie voor minima verhogen en de kosten van het onderwijs voor ouders verlagen.

Als ik minister-president was, zou ik ook de Nederlandse houding ten opzichte van Europa herzien en zorgen dat de dames en heren in Brussel niet eenzijdig belangrijke beslissingen voor Nederland kunnen nemen. Ik zou ook sceptischer willen zijn tegenover de grootmacht Amerika. Nederland loopt als een schaap achter de supermacht aan. Daar zou ik verandering in brengen. Nederland is van de Nederlanders, en wij hebben een eigen mening. Die mening zou ik duidelijk laten horen.

Key vocabulary

eenzijdig	one-sided
gelijke kansen geven	give equal opportunities
de grootmacht	world power
de houding	attitude
het inkomensverschil	difference/gap in income
de kindersubsidie	child benefit
de mening	opinion
de minima	people on low income

2 Herschrijf de eerste zin van elke alinea. Vervang **zou** door de *imperfect*.

Oefening 32: Groepsdiscussie

Wat zou jij veranderen als je de regeringsleider was van jouw land?

Oefening 33

Er zijn geruchten op je werk dat er grote veranderingen komen. Maak de informatie hieronder minder definitief door het te rapporteren als een gerucht, door middel van **zou/zouden**.

Bijvoorbeeld

Ze sluiten de kantine.
Ze zouden de kantine sluiten.

1 Ze willen 35 man ontslaan.
2 Iedereen krijgt minder vakantiedagen.
3 Ze gaan korten op de reisvergoedingen.
4 We krijgen aan het einde van het jaar geen bonus.
5 Werknemers moeten weer veertig uur per week gaan werken.
6 Iedereen moet opnieuw naar zijn eigen baan solliciteren.
7 Het bedrijf heeft miljoenen verlies geleden.
8 De president-directeur gaat volgende week de plannen presenteren.

het gerucht	rumour	**de reisvergoeding**	travel expense
korten	cut back	**solliciteren**	apply for a job

Cultuur

WERKEN, VAKANTIE, SALARIS

Most people in the Netherlands and Belgium have 23 or 24 holidays per year. Often, these are supplemented by **arbeidsduurverkorting** (formerly called **arbeidstijdverkorting**), whereby employees in full-time employment work fewer hours each week (often 36 or 38 instead of 40 hours). Some employees end up with as many as 40 days off annually. **Arbeidsduurverkorting** was introduced to create more jobs. Due to an ageing population, amongst other factors, **arbeidsduurverkorting** is being phased out in many industries.

Employees over the age of 35 usually receive additional **leeftijdsdagen**: additional holidays given for reaching a certain age, from one holiday upon reaching the age of 35 to three or four days around the age of 50.

Just before the summer holidays employees receive **vakantiegeld**: a financial supplement, meant to finance people's summer holidays. **Vakantiegeld** is usually a percentage of your annual **salaris**. Most people get around 8%.

Companies which have done particularly well in a given year may also decide to give their employees an additional month's salary: **een dertiende maand** (literally: 'thirteenth month') as a token of their appreciation.

Tekst 4 Lijnen

De zomer komt eraan en je wilt afvallen, maar het loopt steeds op niets uit. De pondjes vliegen er altijd weer aan. Maar het kan wél, met onze hulp. Wij geven je tips.

Tip 1: Eet met mate

Als je wilt afvallen, is het beter om niet echt te gaan diëten, maar om gezond te eten. Eet niet te veel, niet te vet en niet te zoet. Je hebt dan minder honger tijdens het lijnen, waardoor je het veel langer kunt volhouden.

Tip 2: Blijf realistisch

Je moet niet proberen direct 20 kilo af te vallen. Te snel afvallen is niet gezond, en het is frustrerend als je streefgewicht nog ver in de toekomst ligt. Kies een realistisch streefgewicht dat je binnen een maand kunt halen. Daarna kun je altijd weer een nieuw streefgewicht kiezen.

Tip 3: Lekker sporten

Ga lekker sporten met een groep vriendinnen. Je kunt elkaar dan motiveren, en omdat je je fitter voelt, heb je ook meer zin om gezond bezig te blijven. Bovendien voel je je door sport mentaal sterk, en het is hartstikke gezellig!

Tip 4: Blijf eten

Je moet tijdens het lijnen altijd blijven eten, anders werkt je stofwisseling niet optimaal. Als je stofwisseling niet optimaal werkt, verbrand je lichaam minder vet dan normaal. Als je dan stopt met je dieet, kom je extra snel weer aan – het zogenaamde jojo-effect.

Key vocabulary

aankomen	gain weight
afvallen	lose weight
halen	reach
lijnen	to slim, to be on a diet
de stofwisseling	metabolism
het streefgewicht	target weight

Oefening 34: Bespreek in paren

Wat is volgens jou de achterliggende gedachte achter deze manier van afslanken?

Oefening 35

Beantwoord de vragen.

1 Is zwaarlijvigheid een groot probleem in jouw land?

2 Waarom wordt zwaarlijvigheid in veel landen gezien als een nationaal probleem? Met andere woorden, waarom is het niet alleen iets persoonlijks?

3 Wat zijn volgens jou de belangrijkste oorzaken van zwaarlijvigheid?

4 Kun je praktische oplossingen bedenken om het probleem aan te pakken?

zwaarlijvigheid obesity

Oefening 36

Bespreek in paren je eetgewoontes. Wat eet je bijvoorbeeld 's ochtends voor ontbijt, en eet je bewust gezond, of let je daar niet op? Zou je er meer op willen letten?

Structuren

INFINITIVES

We have seen that certain verbs, like modal verbs, are followed by another verb in the infinitive.

Ik ga met een vriendin *tennissen.*
I'm going to play tennis with a girlfriend.

We blijven laat *werken.*
We're staying to work late.

When another verb is added to these patterns (like another modal, or an auxiliary), all verbs at the end of the sentence are infinitives.

Ik ga met een vriendin *tennissen.*
I'm going to play tennis with a girlfriend.

Ik moet met een vriendin *gaan tennissen.*
I should go and play tennis with a girlfriend.

Ik ben met een vriendin *gaan tennissen.*
I went to play tennis with a girlfriend.

We blijven laat *werken.*
We're staying to work late.

We willen laat *blijven werken*.
We want to stay late to work.

We zijn laat *blijven werken*.
We stayed to work late.

We weigeren laat *te blijven werken*.
We refuse to stay to work late.

The same thing happens when another verb is added to the pattern **om** + **te** + infinitive.

Om dat *te zeggen*, moet je gek zijn.
In order to say that you must be crazy.

Om dat *te kunnen zeggen*, moet je eerst onderzoek doen.
In order to be able to say that, you have to investigate/research it first.

Oefening 37

Brian wil afvallen en gezonder gaan eten. Gebruik onderstaande informatie en maak een lijst van zijn doelen. Begin elke zin met: **Brian wil**

Bijvoorbeeld

Brian: ik ga minder koffie drinken.
Brian wil minder koffie (gaan) drinken.

Brian:

1 Ik ga minder vet eten.
2 Ik ga proberen vier kilo af te vallen.
3 Ik ga twee keer per week zwemmen.
4 Ik ga genoeg blijven eten.
5 Ik kan af en toe snoepen.
6 Ik ga geen honger hoeven (te) lijden.
7 Ik ga op weekdagen proberen niet te drinken.
8 Ik ga thee leren drinken zonder suiker.

het doel	goal

Oefening 38

Je hebt een lange lijst met activiteiten voor het weekend (zie hieronder). Presenteer je suggesties aan je partner door zinnen te maken met:

Ik wil met je
We kunnen
Als je wilt, kunnen we
(NB: andere zinnen mogen ook.)

Bijvoorbeeld

We gaan een eind fietsen.
Ik wil een eind met je gaan fietsen.
We kunnen een eind gaan fietsen.
Als je wilt, kunnen we een eind gaan fietsen.

1 We gaan mijn ouders bezoeken.
2 We gaan langs het strand wandelen.
3 We laten zondag de kinderen de auto wassen.
4 We gaan zaterdagochtend het huis schoonmaken.
5 We proberen zaterdagmiddag een vakantie te boeken.
6 We blijven zaterdagavond thuis TV kijken.

A closer look

WAAROM WERK IK EIGENLIJK?

'Waarom werk je eigenlijk?' vroeg ik laatst aan een vriendin. Ze had me uitgebreid verteld hoeveel moeite het haar elke dag kost om uit bed te komen, in de auto te stappen en naar haar werkplek te rijden. Ze houdt geen tijd meer over voor sociale contacten of hobby's. Ze is 's avonds zo moe dat ze ook amper meer vriendelijk kan zijn tegen haar vriend. Ze hebben dan ook veel ruzie de laatste tijd.

Ze kijkt me aan of ze het in Keulen hoort donderen. 'Moet ik dan thuis gaan zitten nietsdoen?' vraagt ze. 'Dat zeg ik niet,' zeg ik, 'maar ik vraag wel waarom je werkt.' Ze denkt even na. 'Een mens moet toch werken?' zegt ze na een poosje. En even later: 'Ik heb die hele rotstudie toch niet gedaan om er nu niets mee te doen?' 'Je hoeft er ook niet niets mee te doen, maar moet je er per se mee doen wat je er nu mee doet?' vraag ik haar een beetje gemeen. Dan begint ze te vertellen hoe het bij haar thuis vroeger ging. Haar ouders, met name haar vader, stond erop dat je afmaakte waar je aan begon. Anders was je een slappeling, of erger nog: dom.

'Ik ben eigenlijk steeds bezig geweest om te bewijzen dat ik niet slap en dom was,' zegt ze. 'Ik loop me nu het vuur uit de sloffen in een baan die ik eigenlijk helemaal niet leuk vind. Het interesseert me eigenlijk niet voldoende . . . Ik zou veel liever die halve baan hebben die afgelopen weekend in de krant stond, en dan wat meer sporten en schrijven.'

Waarom werken mensen? Om brood op de plank te hebben. Omdat het een roeping is. Omdat het een mooie manier tot zelfontplooiing is. Dit zijn de redenen die vaak genoemd worden. Mensen met een (dreigende) burnout hebben vaak nog een ander verhaal. Werk heeft vaak ook te maken met iets goed willen maken of iets bewijzen aan belangrijke figuren van vroeger, vaak de ouders. Ze verwarren wat ze doen met wie ze zijn. En doen daarom vaak niet wat ze eigenlijk zouden willen, wie ze eigenlijk zouden willen zijn. Vaak weten ze dat niet eens, of niet meer. Op een gegeven moment duikt in het burnoutproces de vraag op: hoe nu verder? Deze vraag kan een mooi begin zijn om je eigen weg in werk te gaan ontdekken. Je kunt het hierover hebben met mensen uit je omgeving die je vertrouwt, maar natuurlijk ook met een eventuele therapeut.

Key vocabulary

amper	hardly
bewijzen	to prove
brood op de plank hebben	make a living
doorzetten	persevere
dreigende	threatening
erop staan	insist
gemeen	nasty, mean
geschikt	right
heeft te maken met	has to do with
het in Keulen horen donderen	be stunned, flabbergasted
het vuur uit de sloffen lopen	wear oneself out
merken	to notice
per se	necessarily, at any price
de roeping	a calling
de rotstudie	damned studies
de slappeling	weakling
uitgebreid	extensively
verwarren	to confuse
de vraag duikt op	the question arises
de zelfontplooiing	self-fulfilment

Oefening 39: vragen

1 Waarom heeft de vriendin van de schrijver haar huidige baan genomen?
2 Wat voor werk zou ze liever doen?
3 Welke (subjectieve) woorden of uitdrukkingen gebruikt de schrijver om over werk te praten?
4 Wat vindt de schrijver belangrijker, werk of persoonlijk geluk?
5 Waarom doen sommige mensen werk dat ze niet echt willen doen, volgens de schrijver?
6 Denkt de vriendin van de schrijver hetzelfde over werk aan het einde van de column als aan het begin?
7 Waarom vindt de schrijver het belangrijk om de vraag te stellen 'Waarom werk ik eigenlijk?'

8 Uit wat voor soort publicatie denk je dat de tekst komt? Wie zijn de lezers van deze publicatie? Waarom denk je dat? Wijs aan in de tekst.

Oefening 40: Discussiepunten

1 Vind je het belangrijk om in je werk persoonlijk geluk na te streven?
2 Kan het nastreven van zelfontplooiing in je carrière problemen veroorzaken? Zo ja, welke?
3 Is het altijd realistisch en/of praktisch om werk te zoeken dat je leuk vindt? Licht toe.
4 Vind je zelf dat je werk of studie je privéleven positief of negatief beïnvloedt? Op wat voor manier(en)?

Unit 8
Ik doe wat ik wil

This unit takes the issue of identity and language use into such areas as talking about immigration, integration and individualism. We delve below the surface to look at implicit messages people leave in their writing about, for instance, the identity of an organisation or their ideas about male and female relations. You will also learn how to structure texts and how to make stylistically effective descriptions depending on what you want to achieve with your messages.

TOPICS

- Immigration
- Integration
- Individualism
- Cultural symbols
- Fatherhood
- Colours
- Identity
- Male and female identity
- Signalling words and markers

FUNCTIONS

- Debates and discussions
- Ways of voicing an opinion
- Stating contrasts between then and now
- Talking about travelling and holidays
- Describing things
- Writing cohesively
- Style in writing: adding more zest and colour
- Rhyme and rhythm

GRAMMAR

- **Hoeven–moeten–mogen**
- Reflexive verbs and reflexive pronouns
- Separable reflexive verbs
- Past participle as adjective
- Present participle
- Word order: adverbs and subordinating conjunctions

Tekst 1 Het dragen van hoofddoekjes

EEN DEBAT OP SCHOOL OVER DE VRAAG OF HET DRAGEN VAN HOOFDDOEKJES MOET WORDEN VERBODEN

Theo: Als allochtonen in Nederland willen wonen dan moeten ze zich aanpassen aan de regels en zich gedragen zoals Nederlanders. En het dragen van een hoofddoek hoort gewoon niet bij de Nederlandse gewoontes. Dus als vrouwen een hoofddoek dragen zeggen ze eigenlijk: ik wil niet bij jullie horen. Ik wil geen Nederlander worden.

Ciska: Sorry hoor, maar dat is klinkklare nonsens! Ten eerste dragen vrouwen geen hoofddoek om zich te onderscheiden van Nederlanders, maar omdat het bij hun geloof hoort. Ten tweede willen de meeste immigranten wel degelijk integreren en bij de Nederlanders horen, maar dan wel met behoud van hun eigen respect en identiteit.

Amina: Ik wil even iets rechtzetten over het dragen van een hoofddoekje. Mensen zegggen vaak dat het dragen van een hoofddoek een teken van onderdrukking van vrouwen is. Maar als moslima *hoef* ik geen hoofdoek te dragen, maar ik *mag* een hoofdoek dragen. Het hoeft echt niet. Ik wil het zelf. En trouwens, je kunt toch best een goede moslim zijn en tegelijkertijd een goed geïntegreerd persoon?

Tobi: Je integreren in een ander land heeft toch niks met een hoofddoek te maken? Integreren betekent jezelf ontplooien en het ontwikkelen van persoonlijke eigenschappen, zoals flexibel zijn, anderen kunnen respecteren, zelfverzekerd zijn. Zo'n hoofdoek op zich betekent toch niets? Het gaat erom hoe je je gedraagt.

Ali: Je hebt gelijk dat jezelf ontwikkelen ook te maken heeft met persoonlijke eigenschappen. Maar je kunt cultuur echt niet los zien van hoe mensen zich gedragen. Je cultuur en achtergrond bepalen voor een groot gedeelte wat je belangrijk vindt. Bovendien betekenen hoofddoekjes wel degelijk wat. Het is een symbool. Net zo goed als de kleur oranje voor Nederlanders iets betekent, maar voor buitenlanders weer niks.

Key vocabulary

de achtergrond	background
de allochtoon	immigrant (normally used for non-western immigrants only)
bepalen	to determine
betekenen	to mean
dragen	to wear
dus	so
de eigenschap	characteristic
de gewoonte	convention, habit
het gaat erom	it is about/ the main thing is
het hoofddoekje	headscarf
horen bij	to belong to
iets (niet) los zien van	(not) seeing something separate from
iets rechtzetten	to put something right, to explain something
klinkklare nonsens	absolute/complete nonsense
met behoud van	keeping
de onderdrukking	oppression
ontwikkelen	to develop
op zich	in itself
de regel	rule
te maken hebben met	to do with
tegelijkertijd	at the same time
het teken	sign
trouwens	besides
wel degelijk	definitely (used to indicate a strong contrast)
zelfverzekerd	self-assured, confident
zich aanpassen (aan)	to adapt (to), to integrate
zich gedragen	to behave
zich onderscheiden van	to distinguish oneself from
zich ontplooien	to develop one's potential

Oefening 1

Luister naar het debat. Schrijf in het kort op wat de visie is van de verschillende personen in dit debat. De eerste is al gedaan.

1 Theo — Theo vindt dat allochtonen zich moeten aanpassen aan de Nederlandse gewoontes en daarom geen hoofddoekjes mogen dragen.

2 Ciska ______________________________

3 Amina ______________________________

4 Tobi ______________________________

5 Ali ______________________________

Oefening 2

Speel dit debat na en probeer zo authentiek mogelijk te klinken.

Vragen bij tekst 1

Beantwoord de onderstaande vragen in het Nederlands.

1 Waarom vindt Theo dat vrouwen en meisjes geen hoofddoekje mogen dragen?
2 Welke uitdrukking gebruikt Ciska om te laten zien dat ze het helemaal niet eens is met Theo?
3 Waarom dragen vrouwen een hoofddoekje volgens Ciska?
4 En waarom vinden volgens haar sommige Nederlanders het dragen van een hoofddoekje niet goed?
5 Wat bedoelt Amina als ze zegt dat zij een hoofddoekje *mag* dragen?
6 Hoe definieert Tobi integratie in een ander land?
7 Ali is het gedeeltelijk eens met Tobi. Waar is hij het mee eens?
8 En met welk punt is Ali het niet eens met Tobi?

definiëren	to define	**gedeeltelijk**	partly

Oefening 3

Vul de gaten in de tekst in. Maak gebruik van de onderstaande woorden. Denk erom dat je de vorm en de plaats van de werkwoorden soms moet aanpassen.

op zich   los zien van   onderdrukking   zich gedragen
respect   bepalen   gewoontes   regels
te maken hebben met   zich aanpassen   betekenen
dragen   trouwens   wel degelijk

Yvette Mensen zeggen steeds dat buitenlanders 1) _______ moeten 1) _______ aan de Nederlandse 2) _______ , maar als diezelfde mensen op vakantie gaan naar Marokko dan passen zij zich toch ook niet aan? Zij 3) _______ gewoon bikini's en korte broeken en drinken alcohol. Op die manier toon je geen 4) _______ voor de cultuur van de ander.

Marjolein Ik vind dat iedereen moet kunnen leven zoals ze dat zelf willen. En als dat 5) _______ dat ze een korte broek dragen in Marokko dan is dat prima, volgens mij. 6) _______ , ik vind het een teken van 7) _______ als vrouwen geen korte broek mogen dragen.

Yvette Nee, sorry hoor. Ik vind dat je 8) ______ rekening moet houden met de cultuur van andere mensen. Een bikini of een korte broek dragen is 9) ____________ niet erg. Maar je kunt het niet 10) __________________ de context. Op het strand in een toeristische badplaats is het OK. In een park in het midden van Marrakech niet. De context 11) ______ wat wel of niet kan.

Marjolein OK, dat ben ik wel met je eens. Toch vind ik dat het belangrijker is hoe mensen 12) ____________ Je moet anderen respecteren door je aan de 13) ______ te houden en dat 14) ______ volgens mij niks 14) __________________ wat voor kleren je wel of niet draagt.

rekening houden met taking account of

Cultuur

IMMIGRATIE EN INTEGRATIE

Since the 1950s there has been a steady stream of immigrants to the Netherlands and Flanders. In the Netherlands immigrants came initially from Indonesia (after it gained independence), Italy and Spain. In the 1960s people from Morocco and Turkey, and to a lesser extent Italy and Spain, **gastarbeiders** (guest workers), were invited to come to the Netherlands to provide cheap labour. In the seventies, this stream of immigrants was joined by people from Surinam, an ex-colony of the Netherlands.

The question of integration wasn't raised in a serious and consistent way until the early 1990s. The government had not developed a policy of integration for the guestworkers as they were expected to return to their countries after some years of work. The immigrant stream from Indonesia and Surinam was only temporary and people from these countries settled and integrated into Dutch society. The immigration from Turkey and particularly Morocco, on the other hand, continued as part of the policy of family reunification.

Whilst many people from immigrant communities have integrated and settled fully into Dutch society, the continuing growth of some immigrant communities has led some people to call for stronger demands on immigrants to integrate, or even to assimilate.

The original laissez-faire attitude, seen by some as typical Dutch tolerance, by others as just not caring, has now been substituted by an increasingly less tolerant approach and an anti-immigration stance.

The demand for **inburgering** 'integration' applies particularly to non-western immigrants. Immigrants from western countries are generally not confronted with the same demand for learning the language and the mores of the country.

The phases of immigration to Flanders are roughly similar to those of the Netherlands: immigrants from Morocco and Turkey followed those from Italy, Spain and Greece. It is remarkable, however, that Belgium does not have a big influx of immigrants from its former colony Zaïre. Belgium has never encouraged inhabitants of the colonies to move to Belgium.

For more information on the **inburgeringsprogramma's** in the Netherlands go to www.postbus51.nl and type in **inburgering** as a search term.

AUTOCHTOON EN ALLOCHTOON

Immigrants are variously described as **allochtoon**, often contrasted with **autochtoon**, the native Dutch. Other terms which are used are **nieuwkomer**, **immigrant**, or **buitenlander**. The term **gastarbeider** isn't used any more. As these terms all cover a large group of very different people, you should be wary of using them. It would be better to refer to specific people by their nationality, although note that many people have the Dutch nationality as well. It would be more accurate then to refer to people as Dutch or Dutch with a different background, say, a **Marokkaanse Nederlander** or a **Nederlander van Marokkaanse/Turkse/Somalische afkomst**.

CULTUUR EN ACHTERGROND

In the discussion at the start of this unit Tobi and Ali present very different views. Tobi seems to deny that there is such a thing as culture: he defines integration in purely individual and personal terms. Despite his denial of the importance of cultural background, he unwittingly reveals his own Dutch cultural bias by seeing values as self-development and being self-confident as very important. Ali's view on the other hand is more in line with the one held by anthropologists: your behaviour and your ideas are determined to a large extent by your previous social and cultural experiences.

ORANJE

Orange has become the national colour of the Netherlands. Despite the fact that using orange has royal and political origins, for most Dutch people orange is mainly associated with the national colour of sporting teams, notably the Dutch football team. It creates a superficial sense of national identity and tends to have celebratory rather than nationalistic overtones. During European and World Cup Football, orange is the name of the game, and people decorate cafés, shops and sometimes even their houses in orange. Many retailers also cash in on the 'orange mania' creating specially orange coloured products for the occasion, whether these are ready-made puddings, sweets or simply balloons. The only other time that people sport orange is on the 30th of April, **Koninginnedag**, literally 'Queen's Day', a bank holiday when most big cities have a **vrijmarkt** where people are allowed to sell goods, unwanted clothes or any other unwanted items, on certain streets.

Oefening 4

In het debat werden de hoofddoek en de kleur oranje culturele symbolen genoemd. Bedenk zelf een aantal voorbeelden van dingen die culturele betekenis hebben in je eigen of in een andere cultuur. Denk bijvoorbeeld aan manieren van groeten, eetgewoontes en geloofssymbolen.

Oefening 5

Hou nu zelf een debat met je groep. Bereid het debat voor door een aantal meningen op te schrijven. Bedenk ook hoe anderen op die meningen zouden kunnen reageren, en met welke tegenargumenten je dan zelf zou kunnen komen. Gebruik een woordenboek bij de voorbereiding.

Je kunt de volgende beweringen gebruiken voor je debat:

- Als je in een ander land gaat wonen moet je je volkomen aanpassen aan de conventies van dat land.
- Als vrouwen een hoofddoek dragen zeggen ze eigenlijk: ik wil niet bij jullie horen.
- Integreren heeft niks met hoofddoekjes en uiterlijkheden te maken. Het gaat om zelfontplooiing en gedrag zoals anderen respecteren.
- Je achtergrond en cultuur bepalen hoe je denkt en hoe je je gedraagt en welke betekenis je aan bepaalde symbolen hecht.

de bewering	statement	**uiterlijkheden**	appearances

Oefening 6

Bespreek in een klein groepje wat **integreren** volgens jou betekent. Schrijf je definitie dan op. Begin met: Integratie betekent volgens mij dat . . .

Doe nu hetzelfde voor **jezelf ontplooien**. Begin met: Jezelf ontplooien betekent volgens mij dat . . .

Structuren

HOEVEN – MOGEN

Niet hoeven is often contrasted with **moeten**:

***Moet* jij dit nog afmaken?**
Nee, dat hoef ik niet te doen, dat doet mijn collega wel.

But as you can see from the debate above, people sometimes contrast (**niet**) **hoeven** with **mogen**:

Ik *hoef* geen hoofddoekje te dragen. Ik *mag* een hoofddoekje dragen.
Ik *hoef niet* elke zondag naar de kerk. Ik *mag* elke zondag naar de kerk.

Oefening 7

Vul de correcte vorm in van het werkwoord **hoeven**, **moeten** of **mogen**.

1 Jantien denkt dat ze van haar werkgever na de geboorte van haar tweede kind weer snel _______ gaan werken. Maar volgens mij _______ dat helemaal niet.

2 Moet je elke dag trainen?
Nee, ik _______ niet elke dag te trainen, maar ik _______ wel elke dag gebruik maken van de faciliteiten als ik dat wil.

3 Veel mensen denken dat je elke dag vijf keer _______ bidden als je moslim bent. Maar dat _______ niet per se, als je dat niet wilt of niet kunt doen.

4 We hebben de taken goed verdeeld, vind ik. Als een van ons kookt, _______ hij/zij niet af te wassen. Dat _______ de ander dan doen.

5 Mama, _______ ik zaterdag naar het verjaardagsfeestje van Jeroen?
Ja, natuurlijk _______ je dat, lieverd. Maar eerst _______ je je kamer opruimen.

REFLEXIVE VERBS

These are verbs which need an extra pronoun to refer back to the subject, as in for example **zich aanpassen** 'adapting oneself'. Note that in English, you don't normally have to add the pronoun myself, himself, etc., but you must do this in Dutch.

zich aanpassen aan	to adapt (oneself) to; to integrate in
zich voelen	to feel (in oneself)
zich ontplooien	to develop one's potential
zich ontwikkelen	to develop (oneself)
zich gedragen	to behave oneself
zich schamen	to be ashamed/embarrassed
zich bemoeien met	to interfere with
zich veroorloven	to afford
zich vervelen	to be bored
zich verontschuldigen	to apologise
zich ergeren aan	to be irritated/annoyed by
zich concentreren	to concentrate
zich interesseren in/voor	to be interested in
zich onderscheiden van	to distinguish oneself from

Reflexive pronouns

Ik pas	***me***	**aan aan jou.**
Jij voelt	***je***	**toch wel goed?**
U past	***zich***	**altijd aan bij bij anderen.**
Hij/zij ontplooit	***zich***	**tot een fantastische docent.**
Het ontwikkelt	***zich***	**tot een groter probleem dan ik eerst dacht.**
Wij schamen	***ons***	**dood voor die blunder.**
Jullie gedragen	***je***	**als kinderen.**
Zij bemoeien	***zich***	**overal mee.**

Examples:
Wij beginnen *ons* steeds meer *voor* politiek te *interesseren*.
Vera *ergert zich* nogal *aan* herrie.
Jaap doet het niet zo goed op school, maar dat is volgens mij omdat hij *zich* niet goed kan *concentreren*.

Verbs which can be reflexive and non-reflexive

Some verbs can be used both in a reflexive (referring back to the subject) and a non-reflexive way:

zich ontwikkelen refers to the subject, e.g. oneself or itself:

> **Hij begint *zich* tot een goed kunstenaar te *ontwikkelen*.**
> **Het voetbalelftal heeft *zich ontwikkeld* tot een team van wereldformaat.**

ontwikkelen refers to an object

> **Hij *ontwikkelt* zijn taalgevoel door veel te lezen.**
> **Ik laat mijn filmpjes gewoon bij Fotoshop *ontwikkelen*.**

Other examples:

(zich) wassen	**(zich) verbazen**	**(zich) scheren**
(zich) vervelen	**(zich) amuseren**	**(zich) aankleden**

Expressions with reflexive verbs which are separable

zich iets aantrekken van to let something worry you/ to be upset by something

> **Ik *trek me* kritiek nogal *aan*.**

zich uitdrukken to express (yourself)

> **Ik *druk me* redelijk *uit* in het Nederlands, dacht ik.**

zich aankleden to dress

> **Hij loopt de hele ochtend in zijn badjas rond en *kleedt zich* pas om een uur of twaalf *aan*.**

de badjas dressing robe

Oefening 8

Vul het correcte reflexieve pronomen in.

1 Ik mag dan wel lijnen, maar ik kan ______ zo af en toe wel een extra biertje veroorloven.
2 Farid heeft net een nieuwe baan, maar hij verveelt ______ daar te pletter.
3 Wij hebben ______ als beesten gedragen op Hugo's feestje. Ik vind dat we hem even moeten bellen om ______ te verontschuldigen.

4 Ik heb zo'n hekel aan mannen die ______ niet scheren. Het staat zo slordig.
5 Jullie vervelen ______ toch niet? Jullie zijn zo stil.
6 Mijn ouders bemoeien ______ steeds met mijn zaken. Ik ben verdomme al twintig.
7 Voelt u ______ wel goed? U ziet er een beetje pips uit.

een hekel hebben aan	to dislike	**verdomme**	damn it
er pips uit zien	to look a bit pale	**zich te pletter vervelen**	to be bored stiff
slordig staan	it looks messy/unkept		

Oefening 9

Luc en Floor houden van regelmaat. Ze staan altijd op precies dezelfde tijd op. Floor moet dan ook hun dochtertje Dionne uit bed halen. Beschrijf nu in korte zinnen wat Luc

en Floor doen en hoe laat.

Luc	*tijd*	*Floor*	
zich wassen	07.00	zichzelf wassen	06.30
zich scheren	07.10	zichzelf aankleden	06.45
zich aankleden	07.20	Dionne wassen	07.00
		Dionne aankleden	07.10

Bijvoorbeeld

Luc wast zich om zeven uur. *Or:* **Om zeven uur wast Luc zich.**

Oefening 10

Werk met z'n tweeën en stel elkaar de volgende vragen. Antwoord met volle zinnen.

1 Waar erger jij je aan?
2 Vind je het moeilijk je te concentreren op de les?
3 Hoe voel je je als iemand je kritiek geeft?
4 In wat voor situaties verveel je je?
5 Waar interesseer je je in/voor?

Oefening 11

Stel elkaar dezelfde vragen als bij de vorige oefening, maar doe het formeler.

Bijvoorbeeld

Waar ergert u zich aan?

Oefening 12

Werk in kleine groepjes en stel elkaar vragen zodat je het schema hieronder kan invullen. Probeer overeenkomsten te vinden met een of meer van je medestudenten, zodat je ook de kolom van **jullie** en **wij** kan invullen.

	ik	**jullie**	**de docent(e) of een vriend/in**	**wij**
zich ergeren aan				
zich interesseren voor/in				
zich verbazen over				
zich schamen voor				

het schema table

Oefening 13

Werk weer met z'n tweeën, en stel elkaar dezelfde vragen als in **Oefening 10**, maar geef nu een uitgebreider antwoord daarop.

Bijvoorbeeld

Ik vind het moeilijk me te concentreren als we grammatica bespreken, maar ik vind het makkelijk als we een debat hebben.

Oefening 14

Schrijf nu een kort stukje van ongeveer 100 à 150 woorden voor een studentenblad of een personeelsblad waarin je je partner (of een gefingeerd persoon) beschrijft. Je richt je vooral op de dingen waarvoor hij/zij zich schaamt en waaraan hij/zij zich ergert enz., gebaseerd op de vorige oefening.

Communicatie

WAYS OF VOICING AN OPINION

Sorry hoor, maar dat is klinkklare nonsens!
Sorry, but that's absolute nonsense!

Ik geloof echt niet dat . . .
I really don't believe that . . .

Ik wil even iets rechtzetten over . . .
I just want to rectify something about . . .
I just want to put right a certain misconception . . .

Het gaat erom . . .
The thing is . . .

Je hebt gelijk dat . . .
You are right that . . .

Ik ben het met je eens dat . . .
I agree with you that . . .

Ik ben het niet met je eens dat . . .
I don't agree with you that . . .

Ik wil even dit zeggen: . . .
I just want to say this: . . .

SIGNAALWOORDEN 'MARKERS'

Structuring points and information

ten eerste, ten tweede, ten derde, ten slotte
first(ly), second(ly), third(ly), finally

verder	**ook**	**tevens**
further(more)	also	also (fairly formal)

Indicating there is an extra argument

bovendien	**daar komt bij dat**	**trouwens**
moreover	in addition	besides

Indicating that the following conclusion is derived from the previous statement

dus	**kortom**
so	so (used mainly in writing)

Contrasting information

tegelijkertijd	**hoewel**	
at the same time	although, even though	
aan de ene kant	**aan de andere kant**	**daarentegen**
on the one hand	on the other hand	on the other hand
niettemin	**toch**	
nevertheless	nevertheless, however	

Qualifying information

althans, dat vind ik	**volgens**
at least, that's my opinion	according to

tenminste, dat stond in de krant / was op het nieuws
at least, that was in the newspaper/on the news

Giving reasons

daardoor	**daarom**	**omdat**	**de reden daarvoor**
because of that	because of that, therefore	because	the reason for that

WORD ORDER – ADVERBS

When the signalling word is an adverb, as most of the words and expressions above are, then inversion occurs, when the adverb is used at the start of a sentence. The verb remains in second place:

Tevens is het druggebruik afgenomen.
Toch geloven veel mensen hem niet.

Exceptions are the words, **tenminste**, **althans**, **trouwens**, **kortom**. These words, when used at the start of the sentence, are followed by a comma and a normal main clause:

Trouwens, dat is laatst nog door de minister-president gezegd.
Kortom, het was een geslaagd programma.

When subordinating conjunctions are used as structuring words: e.g. **hoewel**, **omdat**, **daar komt bij dat**, they form the start of a sub clause and therefore the verb will go to the last verb position in the sentence:

Omdat dit nu eenmaal de beste oplossing is.
Men vond het programma over het algemeen geslaagd, hoewel er ook enkele negatieve opmerkingen waren.

Oefening 15

Vul telkens een van de onderstaande signaalwoorden in, zodat de tekst logisch is en vlot loopt.

althans tenminste volgens
aan de ene kant aan de andere kant

1 We moeten onze tolerantie beschermen zonder zelf intolerant te worden, ______ dat zei iemand op het nieuws en ik vond dat wel een mooie uitspraak.
2 Nederland is een van de meest economisch succesvolle landen in de wereld, ______ dat stond in een blaadje van het ministerie.
3 ______ de directeur van dat bedrijf heeft het nieuwe beleid een behoorlijke winst opgeleverd.
4 Hij zegt dat hij ziek is, maar ______ mij heeft hij gewoon een baaldag.
5 Ik weet niet wat ik van het voorstel dat het collegegeld omhoog gaat moet denken. ______ moet iedereen gratis kunnen studeren, maar ______ is het ook niet goed als de universiteiten niet genoeg geld hebben.

de baaldag	a sickie	**de uitspraak**	statement
opleveren	to gain	**de winst**	profit

Oefening 16

Vul telkens een van de onderstaande signaalwoorden in, zodat de tekst logisch is en vlot loopt.

daar komt nog bij dat **verder**
niettemin **ook** **toch** **hoewel** **bovendien**
daarom **daarentegen**

Vaderschap

Tegenwoordig is het vaderschap 'in'. Er zijn veel 'vaderboeken' op de markt en er is zelfs een vaderwebsite www.ikvader.nl. 1 ______ is er een vaderscheurkalender. 2 ______ besteedt de pers veel aandacht aan zorgende vaders.

3 ______ de overheid in een nieuwe campagne de discussie over de verdeling van zorgtaken thuis op gang wil brengen.

4 ______ is deze campagne niet zo vooruitstrevend als het lijkt. De toon van de campagne is namelijk heel voorzichtig. 5 ______ krijgen vrouwen de schuld van het kleine aandeel van mannen in zorgtaken. Er wordt zelfs gesproken van 'moedermaffia' en de vrouw als 'monsterlijke zeurmachine'. 6 ______ zouden mannen geen zin hebben om te zorgen.

Dus, 7 ______ het lijkt alsof de zorgende man nu realiteit is geworden, is er 8 ______ weinig veranderd. De vrouw blijft zorgen en krijgt de schuld, mannen die zorgen worden 9 ______ als helden gezien.

Gebaseerd op een lezersbrief in *Opzij* november 2003

Key vocabulary

aandacht besteden aan	give attention to
het aandeel	part
de campagne	campaign
een discussie op gang brengen	to start a discussion
de held	hero
'in' zijn	to be popular/trendy
lijken	to seem
namelijk	as it happens/the fact is
de overheid	government
de pers	press
de scheurkalender	block-calendar, tear-off calendar
de schuld krijgen van	to be blamed for
tegenwoordig	these days, nowadays
het vaderschap	fatherhood
vooruitstrevend	progressive
voorzichtig	careful
zelfs	even
zeuren	to moan, nag
zorgen, zorgende vaders	to care, fathers who take on a caring role

Oefening 17

Lees de onderstaande tekst over een rapport over integratie. Vul structuurwoorden en/of uitdrukkingen in zodat de tekst logisch is en vlot loopt.

De conclusie van het rapport '*Bruggen bouwen*' dat de integratie van allochtonen geheel of gedeeltelijk is geslaagd, heeft veel kritiek gekregen. Vooral de rechtse politici zagen liever formuleringen als: 'de integratie is mislukt' en 'een harde aanpak is noodzakelijk'.

1 Het rapport geeft ______ aanbevelingen wat betreft het verbeteren van integratie. Deze zijn o.a.:

2 ______ moeten wijken met veel allochtonen en wijken met weinig allochtonen gemengd worden.

3 ______ moeten gemengde scholen meer subsidie krijgen en niet de scholen met veel allochtonen.

4 ______ moeten allochtone kinderen op jonge leeftijd de Nederlandse taal leren.

5 ______ moeten de waarden van de Nederlandse samenleving en de Nederlandse geschiedenis meer aandacht krijgen.

6 ______ is de conclusie van het rapport niet onjuist. Want over de afgelopen jaren hebben Turken en Marokkanen hun positie qua scholing en arbeidsparticipatie elk jaar verbeterd.

7 ______ , er is geen enkele reden om aan te nemen dat de immigratie is mislukt.

Key vocabulary

de aanbeveling	recommendation	**is geslaagd**	has been successful
aannemen	to accept	**is mislukt**	has failed
de afgelopen jaren	the past years	**de kritiek**	criticism
de arbeids-participatie	levels of employment	**noodzakelijk**	necessary
		onjuist	incorrect
bruggen bouwen	to build bridges	**qua**	in terms of
geheel of gedeeltelijk	completely or partially	**de scholing**	education
gemengd	mixed	**de wijk**	district, area
de harde aanpak	tough measures		

Oefening 18: Discussie

Gebruik óf de tekst over het vaderschap óf de tekst over het rapport *Bruggen bouwen* als basis voor een debat of een discussie. Als je meer informatie wilt over de beide onderwerpen, kun je kijken op de website: www.ikvader.nl, of je kunt zoeken onder de zoektermen *Commissie Blok*, *integratiebeleid*.

Bedenk voordat je het debat of discussie begint, welke vragen je wilt stellen, wat je argumenten zijn, en wat de tegenargumenten zouden kunnen zijn. Denk je ook dat het vaderschap 'in' is? Voorbeeldvragen:

- Wanneer ben je een zorgende vader? Welke taken moet je bijvoorbeeld op je nemen?
- Vind jij ook dat moeders vaak negatief gerepresenteerd worden in de media, terwijl mannen die zo af en toe hun kind naar school brengen als helden worden gezien?
- Is het belangrijk dat de zorgtaken door de vader en moeder worden gedeeld en waarom?
- Is de integratie redelijk geslaagd in jouw land?
- Bespreek de aanbevelingen van het rapport een voor een. Vind je dat dit goede maatregelen zijn om de integratie te verbeteren? Waarom wel/niet?

Oefening 19

Schrijf nu een reactie op een van de teksten. Gebruik signaalwoorden om de tekst zo duidelijk mogelijk te structureren. Denk om de woordvolgorde.

Tekst 2 Fatsoen

Luister naar de tekst en beantwoord de luistervragen. Lees daarna de tekst en beantwoord de begripsvragen.

Fatsoen

Mijn moeder mocht vroeger haar sokjes niet uit van mijn oma, dat gaf maar aanstoot. Daar lachen wij heden ten dage om, die rare, preutse mensen van vroeger. Nee, dan wijzelf: vrijgevochten en assertief lopen we met diepe decolletés voor en achter. Niemand vertelt ons wat wel en niet mag, dat bepalen we lekker allemaal zelf.

We willen ons associëren met de echt lekkere chicks, de sekspoezen. En wat is nou het allermooiste: nog niet zo lang geleden werden deze vrouwen gezien als domme blondjes, vandaag de dag lees je dat het juist zeer zelfbewuste vrouwen zijn, die op een vanzelfsprekende manier met hun seksualiteit omgaan en kracht uitstralen. Eigenlijk zijn het feministes *pur sang*. Ze hebben zelfs, en nou komt het, een Boodschap. Welke precies is niet echt duidelijk in woorden te vatten, maar we voelen allemaal wel dat het een krachtige boodschap is. Dus het is zaak dat de toekomstige generatie doorgaat met zoveel mogelijk vlees te laten zien, daarmee de boodschap uitseinend: ik doe wat ik wil en ik heb maling aan wat anderen daar van denken. Individualisme is in, fatsoen is uit.

Gebaseerd op een tekst uit de rubriek Moordkuil in *Opzij*, september 2003

Key vocabulary

aanstoot geven	to cause offence	**raar**	weird, strange
de boodschap	message	**de sekspoes**	sex kitten
doorgaan met	to continue	**toekomstig**	future
het fatsoen	decency	**uitseinen**	to signal (to the world)
heden ten dage	these days	**uitstralen**	radiate
de kracht	strength	**vandaag de dag**	nowadays
maling hebben aan	not giving a damn	**vatten**	to capture
mocht haar sokjes niet uit	was not allowed to take her socks off	**het vlees**	flesh
preuts	prudish	**vrijgevochten**	liberated
		zelfbewust	self-assured

Luistervragen bij tekst 2

1 Waar lachen we heden ten dage om?
2 Wat voor kleren dragen wij vrouwen tegenwoordig, volgens dit stukje?
3 Worden sekspoezen tegenwoordig gezien als domme blondjes of als assertieve, zelfbewuste vrouwen?

Begripsvragen bij tekst 2

1 Maak een lijstje met de verschillen die de schrijfster noemt tussen nu en vroeger.

Begin met: Vroeger mochten meisjes hun sokjes niet uit.
Heden ten dage/vandaag de dag . . .

2 In dit stukje zegt de schrijfster: dat bepalen we lekker allemaal zelf. Geeft het woord 'lekker' hier aan dat de schrijfster het goed vindt dat we zelf kunnen bepalen wat wel en niet mag?

3 Welke vrouwen zijn eigenlijk feministes *pur sang* volgens de media en waarom?

4 Wat is de Boodschap van deze 'feministes' volgens de schrijfster?

5 De schrijfster geeft in de laatste regels een tegenovergestelde interpretatie van 'de boodschap'. Welke interpretatie is dat?

6 Vindt de schrijfster het een goede zaak dat vrouwen tegenwoordig zoveel bloot laten zien? Waarom denk je dat?

7 En vindt zij het een goede zaak dat individualisme in is? Waarom denk je dat? Leg uit aan de hand van de uitdrukkingen die ze gebruikt.

Oefening 20

Bespreek verschillen in moraal van vroeger en nu. Schrijf die op en maak gebruik van het patroon:

Vroeger . . ., heden ten dage/tegenwoordig/nu/vandaag de dag . . .

Voorbeeld

Vroeger mochten getrouwde vrouwen niet werken, tegenwoordig moeten getrouwde vrouwen vaak werken.

Vroeger waren mensen beleefd tegen elkaar: je zei zelfs gedag tegen vreemden, heden ten dage groet niemand elkaar meer op straat.

Oefening 21

Wat mocht jij (of mochten jouw ouders) vroeger niet, wat kinderen tegenwoordig wel mogen? Bespreek met je partner en schrijf de zinnen op.

Voorbeeld

Ik mocht vroeger niet naar popmuziek luisteren op de radio. Tegenwoordig hebben kinderen vaak hun eigen stereo op hun kamer.

Oefening 22

Wat moest jij (of moesten jouw ouders) vroeger wat kinderen tegenwoordig niet meer hoeven? Bespreek met je partner en schrijf de zinnen op.

Voorbeeld

Ik moest vroeger altijd helpen met de afwas. Vandaag de dag moet je kinderen betalen om de afwas te doen.

Mijn ouders moesten vroeger een uur naar school lopen. Tegenwoordig nemen kinderen de bus.

Oefening 23

Bespreek de volgende vragen over de tekst in kleine groepjes:

1 Ben je het eens met de schrijfster dat bloot tonen als vooruitstrevend en assertief wordt gezien?
2 Vind je het goed dat mensen tegenwoordig veel bloot laten zien? Waarom wel/niet?
3 Vind je het een goede zaak dat individualisme in is? Waarom wel/niet?

bloot tonen to show bare/naked bits

Cultuur

OPZIJ

Opzij is a popular monthly feminist publication. Their website is www.opzij.nl.

INDIVIDUALISME

Just as in many other Western cultures, there has been a strong tendency in the Netherlands to move towards an appreciation of individualism. Many people, however, see in this move a 'free for all' attitude which seems to promote a selfish attitude to society. In the next unit the topic of **waarden en normen** 'values and norms' will be discussed in greater detail.

Oefening 24

Schrijf nu een reactie voor de rubriek 'Moordkuil van Opzij' waarin je aangeeft of je het wel of niet eens bent met de schrijfster en waarom.

Tekst 3

In de onderstaande tekst beschrijft de schrijver de identiteit van *Anders Reizen*, www.andersreizen.nl, een reismagazine met reistips en praktische informatie over bestemmingen voor en door de avontuurlijke reiziger.

Anders Reizen is een site voor de reiziger die meer zoekt dan zon, zee en strand. Dat kan de *couleur locale* zijn, de natuur, de cultuur . . . noem maar op wat voor eigens een land, streek of stad kan hebben dat deze tot een interessante reisbestemming maakt.

We zijn allergisch voor de uitingen van het massatoerisme. We hebben een hekel aan de egaliseermachine van de toeristenindustrie, die al menige kuststreek met unieke vissersdorpjes hebben gedegradeerd tot een volstrekt inwisselbare vakantiebestemming, waar de lokale keuken is vervangen door MacDonalds en Patatje van Adje.

Wij houden juist van de verscheidenheid, de culturele rijkdom, het bijzondere dat andere landen en volken te bieden hebben: de eigen keuken, de eigen bouwstijl, de eigen zeden en gewoonten, het typerende landschap dat nog niet is omgetoverd tot een park vol golfbanen, zwemparadijzen, hotelflats en bungalowcomplexen.

We kiezen bovendien bewust voor vormen van toerisme waarbij natuur en cultuur worden gerespecteerd. Niet uit idealisme maar uit welgemeend eigenbelang: zodat we ook in de toekomst nog leuke bestemmingen kunnen blijven bezoeken.

Key vocabulary

allergisch zijn voor	to be allergic to
de bestemming	destination
bewust	consciously
bieden	to offer
de bouwstijl	architectural style
delen	to share
het eigenbelang	self-interest
de golfbaan	golf course
inwisselbaar	interchangeable
de kuststreek	coastal region
landen en volken	countries and (its/their) people
het landschap	landscape, scenery
menige	many
omtoveren	to change (as if by magic)
de streek	region
de verscheidenheid	diversity
vervangen	to substitute
het vissersdorpje	fishing village
volstrekt	completely
welgemeend	well-intentioned
de zeden en gewoonten	customs and traditions
het zwemparadijs	swimming paradise

Vragen bij tekst 3

1 Wat willen de websitebezoekers waar Anders Reizen zich op richt van hun vakantie?
2 Waar hebben ze een hekel aan?
3 En waar houden ze van?
4 Waarom respecteren de websitebezoekers van Anders Reizen de natuur en cultuur van de landen waar zij naartoe gaan?
5 Wat denk je dat de schrijver bedoelt met 'leuke' bestemmingen? Wat voor bestemmingen zijn dat precies? Voor wie zijn die plaatsen 'leuk? Voor de toeristen of voor de bewoners?
6 Het reizen naar bestemmingen die nog niet ontdekt zijn door het massatoerisme, betekent dat die bestemmingen open komen te staan voor een grotere stroom toerisme. Wat voor problemen kan dat met zich meebrengen denk je?

Oefening 25

Je stelt een databank samen van publicaties die informatie geven over toeristische bestemmingen. De databank is bedoeld voor toeristen zodat ze kunnen zien bij welke publikaties of websites ze de informatie kunnen vinden die hen het meeste aanspreekt. Schrijf nu een kort stukje van ongeveer 100 à 150 woorden voor de databank over 'Anders Reizen' waarin je zo helder mogelijk de visie van de reismagazine weergeeft.

aanspreken	to appeal to	**de databank**	database

Oefening 26

Bespreek in kleine groepjes of je denkt dat de identiteit van de organisatie 'Anders Reizen' iets te maken heeft met de trend van individualisme en zo ja, op wat voor manier? Hoe individualistisch is het denk je, om naar 'leuke' bestemmingen te gaan? Denk je dat de uitdrukking 'collectief individualisme' hierop van toepassing kan zijn? Leg uit.

op van toepassing zijn be applicable to

Cultuur

REIZEN

When the summer comes the Dutch leave their country en masse. Travelling, particularly to foreign destinations, is very popular in the Netherlands, frequently for at least two, more often for three weeks or more. To ensure that the annual trek abroad does not clog up the roads completely, the government has ensured that the dates for the school summer holidays are spread over the country in three regions. There is only an overlap of approximately two weeks where all school children in the country are on holiday.

France remains an ever popular destination for many people, but more and more people go to 'exotic' destinations. Trips in **eigen land** are generally limited to short breaks.

Camping is an all-time favourite, especially for families, but equally renting a **bungalow**, or **vakantiehuisje** in a holiday park, particularly in the Netherlands itself, is also popular.

PATATJE VAN ADJE

Chips, or fries, remain the mainstay of Dutch fast food. **Patatje van Adje** is a name for a snack bar, because of the rhyme and because **Adje** (partly because of the use of the diminutive) is a Dutch name with working class overtones. Similarly a chain of sandwich bars is called **Broodje van Kootje**.

COULEUR LOCALE

Dutch has been influenced by different languages through contacts with countries throughout the world. There are a number of French words in the Dutch language for instance, harking back to the occupation by Napoleon of the Low Countries. The largest number of foreign words, however, have entered the Dutch language from English in the past few decades. And, despite the fact that some people see this as a threat to the Dutch language, the adoption of foreign words shows no signs of halting, particularly amongst young people.

Oefening 27

Bespreek met je partner wat je lievelingsvakantie is. Stel de volgende vragen aan elkaar. Je kunt in je antwoorden gebruik maken van de woordenlijst hieronder.

1 Wat wil je van je vakantie?

2 Waar heb je een hekel aan wat betreft toerisme en vakanties?

3 Wat doe je het liefst als je op vakantie bent?

4 Wat wil je het liefst eten als je op vakantie gaat? De keuken van het land of streek, of wil je het liefst hetzelfde soort voedsel eten als thuis?

Extra woordenschat

ontspannen	**relaxen**	**zonnebaden**
zwemmen	**wijn drinken**	**genieten van de zonsondergang**
avontuur	**nieuwe mensen ontmoeten**	**andere culturen zien**
strand	**wandelen**	**bergbeklimmen**
watersport	**surfen**	
musea bezoeken	**in de file staan**	

gezellig met je gezin/met vrienden/met je familie bij elkaar zijn

Key vocabulary

bergbeklimmen	to do mountaineering	**nieuwe mensen ontmoeten**	to meet new people
de file	traffic jam	**ontspannen**	to relax
genieten van	to enjoy	**het strand**	beach
gezellig met je gezin bij elkaar zijn	to have a nice time with your family	**zonnebaden**	to sunbathe

Oefening 28

Je bent zelf op een avontuurlijke vakantie geweest. Geef hier een korte mondelinge presentatie aan je medestudenten. Je kunt iets vertellen over een reis die je zelf hebt gemaakt, of je kunt inspiratie halen uit een van de **reisverslagen** op de website van 'Anders Reizen'. Je kunt eventueel ook op de websites kijken van bedrijven die dit soort vakanties organiseren. Zoek onder de termen **reizen**, **avontuur**, **cultuur** en/of **trekken**. Je kunt ook contact opnemen met een van die **reisorganisaties** en vragen of ze je een brochure kunnen sturen. (In dat geval vraag je docent om je te helpen een e-mail te schrijven.) Denk erom dat je je presentatie logisch en duidelijk structureert.

Tekst 4

Luister eerst naar de tekst en beantwoord de luistervragen.

Griekenland

Wat is het dat me steeds weer terug doet keren naar Griekenland? Wat het níet is kan ik zo vertellen: de overvolle stranden van Kreta en Corfu waar de Nederlandse en Engelse toeristen zich 's morgens al vol laten lopen met Heineken of John Smiths' en zich 's middags vol vreten aan kroketten of *fish and chips.*

Nee, wat me terug doet keren zijn de talloze kleine eilandjes, elk met een handvol dorpjes, waar je ondanks de toeristen toch nog het echte Griekse leven kan proeven.

Neem nou Santorini, of Thira, zoals de eilanders het zelf noemen. Ontstaan uit een kataclysmische vulkanische ontploffing, lijkt het alsof het kleurrijke eiland elke dag opnieuw uit de zwarte nacht ontploft. Voor mijn ogen, gewend aan een regenboog van grijs, is de intensiteit van de kleuren bijna ademberovend: de warme gloed van turkoois tegen puur, diep blauw; sprankelend, verblindend wit tegen felroze, oranje en paars.

Je loopt door nauwe witte straatjes in kleine witte dorpjes die zich aan de steile zwarte rotsen vastklemmen. Hier kom je een wit kerkje tegen met een glanzend turkooizen koepel en de in het zwart geklede oude vrouwtjes die even in de koele schaduw rusten. En iets verderop vind je een felgeel geschilderde binnenplaats overdekt met roze en oranje bougainvilla waaronder een tafel, stoel en fles rosé op je zitten te wachten.

Overal zie je die witte dorpjes tegen de felle Grieks-blauwe zee die tegen je blijft fluisteren om een verkoelende duik te nemen. En als je eindelijk op het zwarte, bijna grindachtige zand ligt, kijk je tegen een lucht die zo diep blauw is, dat je bijna bang bent erin te verdrinken.

naar: Helen Stanbridge

Key vocabulary

ademberovend	breathtaking
de binnenplaats	courtyard
een duik nemen	to go swimming (*literally*: to take a dive)
fel	bright
fluisteren	to whisper
gewend aan	to be used to
glanzend	shining
de gloed	glow
grindachtig	shingle (like gravel)
de kerk	church
koel	cool
de kroket	fast food snack: croquette filled with meat ragout
de lucht	sky
nauw	narrow
ondanks	despite
de ontploffing	eruption, explosion
ontstaan uit	its origins came from
overdekt	covered
overvol	overfull, packed
sprankelend	sparkling
steil	steep
talloze	countless
vastklemmen	to hold on tight/ to clamp
verblindend	blinding
verdrinken	to drown
zich vol laten lopen	to get drunk
zich vol vreten	to stuff your self

Luistervragen bij tekst 4

1 Wat vindt de schijfster niet leuk aan Griekenland?

2 Naar welke plekken in Griekenland gaat ze vaak terug?

3 Waarom is de intensiteit van kleuren zo ademberovend voor de schijfster?

4 Welke kleur kleding dragen de oude vrouwtjes, die ze in de schaduw tegenkomt?

5 Welke kleur heeft het strand?

Tekst 5

Luister eerst naar de tekst en beantwoord de luistervragen.

Brazilië: dé hotspot

Waarom ga, nee móet je ernaartoe?

Brazilië is carnaval, capoeira en caipirinha. Samba en stranden. Billen, bikini's en beach volleybal, warme nachten en wilde seks. De Brazilianen houden van het leven en laten dat graag merken.

Stuk voor stuk zijn de stranden hier een equivalent voor het aardse paradijs. Schommelen in de hangmat, dobberen in het zwembad, verse kokosnoot drinken en zwemmen tussen de dolfijnen, die permanent in de baai 'wonen'. Mooier bestaat niet.

gebaseerd op: *One*, februari 2004: fragmenten uit artikel: 'Reis naar het vakantieparadijs'

Luistervragen bij tekst 5

1 Hoe laten de Brazilianen zien dat ze van het leven houden?

2 Wat drinkt de schrijfster?

Begripsvragen bij tekst 4 en 5

Beantwoord de vragen, voor zover mogelijk, in het Nederlands.

1 Which words and phrases particularly show the distaste the author of tekst 4 feels for the aspects of Greece she doesn't like?
2 The author is very much appealing to our senses in her description of what she does like. She even uses these senses explicitly: **voor mijn ogen** and **proeven**. She mainly uses visual imagery to paint a picture for us. List all the words that contribute to the visual imagery.
3 To what other senses does she appeal? List these words.
4 The author in tekst 5 also makes use of 'sensuous words'. List the words that appeal to the various senses. To which senses does she mainly refer? Why do you think that might be?
5 This author also makes use of another strategy of creating a tempting description: rhythm and rhyme. Which words does she pair into groups to create this effect? Do you notice a rhythm between the groups?
6 Who do you think the readers of tekst 5 might be? What makes you think that?
7 What is the significance of the title of the text about Brazil? What does it suggest about individualism or collectivism in choosing a holiday destination?

Communicatie

ADDING ZEST

Rhyme and rhythm

Using groups of three is a favourite rhetorical tool for politicians and other public speakers as well as writers to enhance the point they are making. An example is the 'education, education, education' statement made by a British politician in a recent election campaign to convince the public that he really meant business. Equally rhyme (or in the examples below, alliteration) is an effective way of capturing your readers or listeners.

billen, bikini's en beach volleybal

warme nachten en wilde sex

Colours

One way of making descriptions more visual and intense is by adding extra words to the colours:

licht	**lichtroze**
fel	**felgeel**
donker	**donkerpaars**
diep	**diepblauw**
zacht	**zachtbruin**
hard	**hardgroen**
warm	**warmgrijs**

Some words are related to particular colours only:

strakblauw
gitzwart
spierwit
lijkbleek

Voorbeeld

Ik hou van contrasterende kleuren: een hard felgroen kussen tegen een donkerblauwe bank; een dieppaars dekbed tegen een zachtblauwe muur of een donkere warmgrijze onweerslucht tegen een veld van felgeel koolzaad.

de bank	sofa
het dekbed	duvet
het koolzaad	rape seed
het kussen	pillow

Adjectives (and adverbs): part of verb

Past participles can also be used as an adjective:

in het zwart *geklede* vrouwtjes	the past participle of *kleden*
een felgeel *geschilderde* binnenplaats	the past participle of *schilderen*

Present participles can also be used as an adjective or adverb. You form the present participle by placing a **d** after the infinitive form of the verb:

sprankelend, verblindend wit

Frequently a present participle gives the same information as a relative clause or a subclause, but it can be more aesthetic stylistically. The writers in the texts above made use of the present participle to create a stylistically attractive and a flowing text.

Compare:

sprankelend, verblindend wit	**het wit dat sprankelt en verblindt**
glanzend satijn	**het satijn dat glanst**
een verkoelende duik	**de duik die verkoelt**
ademberovende kleuren	**de kleuren die de adem beroven**
schommelend en dromend lig ik in mijn hangmat	**ik lig in mijn hangmat terwijl ik schommel en droom**

Oefening 30

Beschrijf de onderstaande dingen en mensen en maak gebruik van strategieën, zoals: groepjes van drie of twee, ritme en rijm.

Bijvoorbeeld

Your Dutch class	**Onze Nederlandse klas is vrolijk, vreemd en vrij.**
or:	**Klein en knus, progressief en pro-actief.**

1 Nederland en/of België
2 jouw land en/of stad
3 de regering
4 jouw huis of tuin
5 een film (of een boek) die je mooi vindt (of juist niet)
6 iemand die je bewondert

Oefening 31

Zoek thuis twee foto's of illustraties uit een tijdschrift op van iets dat je mooi vindt (een bepaald object, landschap of schilderij) en beschrijf dat alleen door de kleuren te noemen. Hang alle foto's op het bord of leg op tafel. Lees je beschrijvingen voor terwijl de rest van de groep raadt om welke foto het gaat.

Oefening 32

Herschrijf de onderstaande zinnen volgens het voorbeeld. Gebruik het tegenwoordig deelwoord (present participle).

Voorbeeld

Je ziet steeds vaker mensen op straat die bedelen.
Je ziet steeds vaker bedelende mensen op straat.

1 's Zomers drink ik liever een glas water dat verfrist dan zoete limonade.

2 Samuel heeft een parkiet die zingt.

3 Ik hou van Engeland: de smalle weggetjes, de heuvels die glooien en de slaperige dorpjes.

5 Ik hou juist van Nederland: de groene weiden, de vergezichten en de mensen die fietsen.

6 Bert heeft een boek geschreven dat gerucht maakt.

7 Haar haar dat glanst waaide zachtjes in de wind.

8 Ik geniet altijd van een fietstochtje door de bollenvelden, ik vind het heerlijk als ik langs een veld rij van hyacinten die zo zoet ruiken.

9 Ik vind schilderijtjes van meisjes die huilen zo kitsch.

10 Ja, dat ben ik met je eens. Ik zie ook liever een schilderij van jongetjes die vechten.

de bollenvelden	bulb fields	**vechten**	to fight
gerucht maken	controversial	**de vergezichten**	panoramas

Oefening 33

The literary text below compares a small mountain stream to a child. The original text used many present participles. Reconstruct the original text by replacing the underlined words with a present participle to make adjectives.

> **Een land van bergen en water dat snel stroomt. Aan de bergkant, tussen 't bos, een kleine weide. Een klein beekje dat vlug aanloopt, dat glinstert onder 't gras, dat links en rechts springt, in 't zoeken, zoeken van de laagte – en dat gestadig murmelt, tevreden als een kind dat wandelt en bloemen zoekt.**
>
> naar: Frederik van Eeden

gestadig	steady	**murmelen**	to murmer
glinsteren	to shine, shimmer	**stromen**	to stream
de kloof	ravine	**de weide**	meadow

Oefening 34

Zoek foto's op van Nederland of Vlaanderen of een andere plaats. Je kunt ansichtkaarten gebruiken of foto's van het internet. Beschrijf deze op een zodanige manier dat als je je beschrijving voorleest, je luisteraars een duidelijk beeld krijgen. Gebruik de verschillende technieken die je geleerd hebt (zintuigen, rijm, ritme, kleurwoorden en tegenwoordig deelwoord).

Oefening 35

Schrijf een artikeltje voor een reisbrochure voor Nederlanders over jouw land of regio. Beschrijf het zo aantrekkelijk mogelijk. Bedenk eerst hoe je het gaat aanpakken. Hoe kun je je lezer verleiden om naar jouw land/regio/stad te komen. Maak gebruik van adjectieven die een beroep doen op de zintuigen. Hoe voelt het, wat zie je, wat hoor je, wat proef je? Maak ook gebruik van ritme en rijm.

een beroep doen op de zintuigen	to appeal to the senses	**verleiden**	to tempt

A closer look

The text below uses definitions of male and female identity to set out (from a male perspective) what the problems are with ambitious women.

CARRIÈREVROUWEN – HELP!

Elke man kent dit wel: Je wil gewoon een avondje uit, een vrouw een beetje verwennen met een dineetje, wat aandacht en wat humor. Maar waar je ook over praat, zij weet het altijd beter, en het lijkt alsof ze er plezier in heeft je te kwetsen. 'Wij vrouwen zijn veel flitsender dan mannen', klinkt het regelmatig uit haar mond, of 'intelligenter', of 'we hebben meer sociale en emotionele vaardigheden'. Het is net alsof elk gesprek op een wedstrijdje moet uitdraaien.

Maar wat doe je als je verstrikt raakt in een relatie met zo'n vrouw die een houding van superioriteit aanneemt en mannen minacht? Volgens psychologe Hardman moet je eerst kijken naar wat deze vrouwen motiveert. Vooral hogeropgeleide vrouwen hebben dit probleem, zegt ze. Natuurlijk kun je niet alles in de schoenen schuiven van de jeugdervaringen, maar toch spelen deze meestal een heel belangrijke rol. In de tijd waarin deze vrouwen opgroeiden werd de vaderrol vaak nog traditioneel ingevuld. Dus: hij was er vaak niet en had weinig tijd voor zijn dochters. En om die afwezigheid en het gebrek aan aandacht van de vader te compenseren, begonnen deze vrouwen vaak zelf een mannelijke identiteit op te bouwen door het leveren van prestaties. Op die manier hoopten ze de goedkeuring van hun vaders te krijgen.

Kijk, zegt Hardman, in een goede relatie wissel je je houding vaak: soms ben jij de sterke en je partner de zwakke persoon, soms is dat net andersom. Maar deze vrouwen moeten leren om hun eigen zwakheid en afhankelijkheid toe te laten.

Therapie kan daar bij helpen. Vaak zitten vrouwen in zo'n vast patroon, dat ze bij elk gesprek proberen de partner beter af te zijn.

Maar mannen zullen ook zelf hun gedrag moeten aanpassen. Ze moeten duidelijker zeggen wat ze wel en niet leuk vinden aan hun partner. Mannen zijn soms geneigd zich terug te trekken als de vrouw teveel van hen verlangt. Je moet samen uitvechten wat wel en niet goed aanvoelt in je relatie door erover te praten. Maar het belangrijkste advies is toch wel: blijf bij jezelf!

gebaseerd op een artikel in *Men's Health*, november 1999

Key vocabulary

de aandacht	attention
aanvoelen	to feel, to sense
afhankelijk	dependent
de afwezigheid	absence
beter af zijn	to be better off
blijf bij jezelf	stay true to yourself
het dineetje	dinner
flitsend	flashy
geneigd zijn	to tend to
de goedkeuring	approval
hogeropgeleid	well-educated (usually refers to having a university or college education)
de houding	attitude
in de schoenen schuiven van	to blame on
kwetsen	to hurt (someone)
minachten	to look down upon
prestaties leveren	to achieve
de psychologe	female psychologist (male: **psycholoog**)
regelmatig	regularly
terugtrekken	to withdraw
toelaten	to allow
uitdraaien op	end in
de vaardigheid	skill
vast	fixed
verlangen van (iemand)	to desire/expect of (someone)

verstrikt raken in	to get ensnared in	**wisselen**	to change/swap
verwennen	to spoil	**zwak**	weak
de wedstrijd	match		

Vragen bij A closer look

Antwoord in het Nederlands. Wees zo expliciet mogelijk.

1 Welk probleem heeft de schrijver vaak als hij een avondje uitgaat met een vrouw?
2 Welk soort vrouwen nemen volgens de psychologe Hardman vaak een houding van superioriteit aan tegenover mannen?
3 En hoe komt het volgens haar dat vrouwen dit probleem hebben?
4 Hoe definieert Hardman een goede relatie?
5 Welke oplossing biedt Hardman voor het probleem?

De volgende vragen gaan dieper in op de tekst en op de ideeën die achter de tekst zitten.

6 De mannelijke schrijver laat vooral de psychologe aan het woord over het 'probleem'. Waarom doet hij dat denk je?
7 Lees de eerste zin nog een keer. Wat verwacht de schrijver denk je als hij een avondje uitgaat met een vrouw? Suggereren de woorden 'verwennen met een dineetje, wat aandacht en humor' dat hij een gelijkwaardige relatie en een goede discussie verwacht? Leg je antwoord uit.
8 Wat ziet de schrijver als karakteristiek van een mannelijke identiteit? En wat impliceert hij dat vrouwelijke karakteristieken zijn? Vul de kolommen in.

Mannelijke karakteristiek	Vrouwelijke karakteristieken

9 De schrijver geeft de indruk een genuanceerd argument te geven. Hoe komt het dat je als lezer deze indruk krijgt?
10 Wat is het advies dat vrouwen krijgen in dit stuk? En het advies dat mannen krijgen? Wie moet zich meer aanpassen aan de wensen van de partner?
11 Is er een conflict in het advies dat je samen je relatieproblemen moet uitvechten door er over te praten en het advies: blijf bij jezelf? Leg uit.

aan het woord laten	to allow someone to speak (*here*: to speak with the voice of)	**de indruk**	impression
genuanceerd	balanced	**ten opzichte van**	in relation to
		verwachten	to expect
		de wens	wish

Oefening 36

Schrijf nu een brief naar de redactie van het tijdschrift waarin bovenstaande tekst stond en beschrijf de kwestie van relatieproblemen vanuit het perspectief van de vrouw. Reageer zoveel mogelijk op de 'problemen' die in het stukje werden beschreven. Geef de indruk dat je zo genuanceerd mogelijk bent.

Unit 9
Typisch Nederlands?

In this unit we will focus on discussions of national identity and what the Dutch themselves and others consider to be'typically Dutch'. We look at the problems of talking about national identity, and whether there is such a thing at all. We look at some historical issues which are considered to have shaped the Netherlands and we will look at how different newspapers represent events from different perspectives. In addition you will learn more strategies for writing.

TOPICS

- Dutch stereotypes
- Topics relating to Dutch history and society (monarchy, Delta Project, Golden Age, slave trade, Indonesia, pillarisation)
- **Sinterklaas**
- Popular Dutch music
- National identity: does it exist?
- Different representations in the media

FUNCTIONS

- Stating your attitude or views
- Saying you can't think of anything
- Talking about national identity
- Talking about feelings
- Writing cohesively and coherently
- Stating views in a direct manner
- Stating views in a more careful and balanced manner
- Writing from a reader's perspective
- Writing: a polemical style
- Writing for different contexts and audiences
- Writing a project
- Comparing different representations in the media

GRAMMAR

- Verbs with **te** + infinitive
- Verbs with an infinitive, but without **te**
- Cohesion
- Passive voice: form and use

Tekst 1 Hoe zien Nederlanders zichzelf?

Als introductie voor een televisieprogramma over Nederland, worden de volgende korte vraaggesprekjes getoond. Luister naar de dialoogjes en beantwoord de vragen in **Oefening 1**.

Ineke, 58 jaar

journaliste Wat betekent het voor u om Nederlands te zijn?

Ineke Tja, dat is geen makkelijke vraag . . . geschiedenis is belangrijk, natuurlijk. Dat draag je mee. De Gouden Eeuw, bijvoorbeeld . . . De handel en cultuur uit die tijd . . . Maar ja, daar horen helaas ook minder mooie dingen bij, zoals de slavenhandel. Dat hoort ook bij ons.

journaliste Waar denkt u aan als u aan Nederland denkt?

Ineke Water. Een land van dijken, vroeger molens en stoomgemalen. En vooral de Deltawerken. Ja, daar ben ik echt trots op.

En ja, de Nederlandse vlag, natuurlijk. Als ik die zie, dan ontroert het me. Het geeft me een nationaal gevoel.

Fred, 49 jaar

Fred Nou we zijn tolerant en progressief. Denk maar aan abortus en het homohuwelijk. Die tolerantie tonen we ook ten opzichte van buitenlanders . . . hoewel dat minder wordt.

Ehhh, tja . . . verder . . . het koningshuis hoort ook bij het Nederlander zijn. Ik moet eerlijk zeggen dat ik daar zelf wel wat ambivalent tegenover sta, maar toch . . . als het puntje bij paaltje komt, is het toch wel belangrijk.

En verder speelt sport denk ik een belangrijke rol in ons nationale gevoel . . . Dat geldt vooral voor voetbal uiteraard, maar ook de nationale gekte bij schaatsen, vooral de elfstedentocht.

Irene, 35 jaar

journaliste Wat betekent Nederland voor je?

Irene Nederland is mijn thuis. En thuis is veiligheid, regen, wind en wolken, drop, hagelslag en hééééél vééééł regels. Verder zijn Nederlanders verschrikkelijk ontevreden zeurpieten terwijl we eigenlijk niks te klagen hebben.

Sylt, 18 jaar

Sylt Nederland bestaat eigenlijk niet. Het is een grote mengelmoes en dat maakt het dat er geen Nederlandse cultuur meer is. Misschien is dat juist wel Nederlands. En verder is het hier niet zo stipt. Er zijn weinig afspraken of regels.

journaliste Is er iets waarvan je zegt: ja dat is nou typisch Nederlands?

Sylt . . . Nee, ik kom nergens op . . . Of nou ja, Sinterklaas misschien.

Django, 17 jaar

Django Het zegt mij echt niets Nederlander te zijn. Ik zou net zo goed ergens anders geboren kunnen zijn en dan had ik me daar ook thuis gevoeld.

journaliste Maar denk je dat er iets typisch Nederlands is, een bepaald cultureel symbool of zo?

Django Ja, jij bedoelt zeker molens en klompen en zo. Maar dat bestaat niet meer. En dat is toch ook niet cultureel?

Key vocabulary

als het puntje bij paaltje komt	if push comes to shove
de dijk	dyke
gelden voor	to apply to
de geschiedenis	history
de handel	trade
het zegt mij niets	it doesn't mean anything to me
het homohuwelijk	gay marriage
ik kom nergens op	I can't think of anything
klagen	*here*: to moan
klompen	clogs
het koningshuis	monarchy
de mengelmoes	mishmash
de molen	windmill
ontevreden	dissatisfied
ontroeren	to move
stipt	strict
het stoomgemaal	steam-driven pumping station
ten opzichte van	with regard to
de veiligheid	safety/security
de zeurpiet	whinger

Oefening 1

Televisiefragment met Katie

1 Wat is volgens Katie een belangrijk aspect van haar nationale identiteit?

2 Is ze daar alleen positief over?

3 Waar denkt Katie aan als ze aan Nederland denkt?

4 Waar is ze trots op?

5 Wat ontroert haar?

Televiefragment met Fred

1 Welke twee karakteristieke eigenschappen noemt Fred over Nederland?

2 Wat is zijn visie op de monarchie?

3 Welke twee sporten spelen volgens Fred een belangrijke rol bij het Nederlandse nationale gevoel?

Televiefragment met Ineke

1 Is Ineke tevreden dat ze in Nederland woont?

Televiefragment met Sylt

1 Waarom zegt Sylt dat Nederland eigenlijk niet bestaat?

Televiefragment met Django

1 Betekent Nederlander zijn iets voor Django? Leg uit.

2 Vindt Django dat molens en klompen typisch Nederlandse culturele symbolen zijn? Leg uit.

Oefening 2

Speel de bovenstaande dialoogjes na en probeer zoveel mogelijk de intonatie van de acteurs op het bandje te benaderen.

Oefening 3

Maak een overzicht van de punten die de verschillende geïnterviewde mensen noemen over Nederlands-zijn, over culturele symbolen en wat wel of niet typisch Nederlands is. Onderstreep de hoofdpunten en geef ook voorbeelden aan als die genoemd worden. De eerste is al gedaan.

Katie, 58	**geschiedenis: bijvoorbeeld de Gouden Eeuw. Maar dat betekent ook negatieve dingen zoals slavenhandel.** **water: dijken, molens en stoomgemalen, de Deltawerken** **de Nederlandse vlag**
Fred, 49	
Irene, 35	
Sylt, 18	
Django, 17	

Oefening 4

Bespreek in kleine groepjes of er overeenkomsten en/of tegenstellingen zijn in de verschillende visies van de geïnterviewde mensen. Bespreek dan of je een verklaring zou kunnen geven van de verschillende ideeën die mensen hebben over hun nationale identiteit.

Oefening 5

Een cultureel symbool is iets wat een bepaalde (nationale) cultuur vertegenwoordigt. Welke culturele symbolen worden door de Nederlanders in de bovenstaande fragmenten genoemd?

Oefening 6

In Oefening 3 heb je een lijstje gemaakt van punten die wel of niet de Nederlandse identiteit beschrijven. Maak nu een lijst van sleutelwoorden die jouw nationale en/of regionale identiteit zouden kunnen beschrijven.

Oefening 7

Kijk op de volgende websites
http://sinterklaas.pagina.nl/en

http://www.sint.nl en zoek informatie op over het sinterklaasfeest. Bespreek als groep wat het sinterklaasfeest is, wat de oorsprong is van sinterklaas, wat het specifieke sinterklaas-snoepgoed is, en wie Zwarte Piet is.

Cultuur

DELTAWERKEN

For many people abroad, one of the most striking facts about the Netherlands is that 50% of the country is below sea level. Water control, protection from the sea and land reclamation have been, and continue to be, important issues in the Netherlands. Since the floods of 1953, when nearly 2000 people lost their lives, the huge engineering works of the Delta Project were set in motion – an extensive network of water barriers, dams and dykes aimed at protecting the worst hit areas during the floods of 1953 against the sea. The construction works were not without controversy, particularly as the environmental movement gained momentum during the second half of the 20th century. The powerful environmental lobby managed to halt and alter some of the original plans to ensure that some of the ecosystems were preserved.

For more information see www.deltawerken.com

KONINGSHUIS

The Dutch royal family is relatively popular in the Netherlands, particularly since the wedding of crown prince Willem-Alexander to the Argentinian Máxima Zorreguieta in 2002. The wedding was represented in the Dutch media as an event on a par with the wedding of Prince Charles and Lady Diana Spencer in the UK some decades earlier. However, despite the fact that the Dutch royal family is often represented abroad as the cycling monarchy who are open and accessible to the general public, the royal family remains somewhat aloof of the population at large, and keeps its distance from the press, who tend to treat the royal family with a certain amount of deference. Queen Beatrix presents herself to the outside world as a hard working woman.

The most visible task of Queen Beatrix, as head of state, is to open parliament every third Tuesday in September, **prinsjesdag**. On this day, she delivers the **Troonrede**, an important speech that sets out the government's goals, plans and budget for the coming year. For more information see www.koninklijkhuis.nl/welkom.htm and www.oranje.pagina.nl

DE GOUDEN EEUW

During the seventeenth century, the Netherlands experienced its so called Golden Age, or **Gouden Eeuw**. Despite the fact that it fought several wars, the fledgling Republic was powerful politically, economically and culturally. Overseas trade with areas such as the East Indies (present day Indonesia), brought the Netherlands immense wealth.

In addition, many educated people and artisans had immigrated to the Republic – from what is now Belgium – often to escape religious persecution, and contributed to the cultural development. Well-known painters of the era are Rembrandt, Vermeer and Jan Steen.
For more information see www.history-netherlands.nl, www.20eeuwennederland.nl, www.kun.nl/ahc/vg/vge, www.rijksmuseum.nl

The Netherlands in Perspective by William Shetter (London: Routledge, 2002) and Simon Schama's *The Embarrassment of Riches* (Berkeley: University of California, 1988) give more in-depth information and analysis.

MINDER MOOIE DINGEN: SLAVENHANDEL EN INDONESIË

Only relatively recently have the Dutch been able to face up to their colonial past . The Netherlands played an important role in the slave trade. Most slaves were taken to Surinam, which became a Dutch colony in 1667. The Netherlands didn't abolish slavery until 1863 and was the last European country to do so.

Equally, the behaviour of the Dutch in the Dutch East Indies, now Indonesia, has come in for much criticism, not only because of the exploitation of the people and resources, but also because of the **politionele acties** in the 1940s – the brutal attempts of the Dutch to suppress the Indonesian struggle for independence after World War II.

Communicatie

ZEGGEN DAT JE EEN BEPAALDE HOUDING HEBT

(ergens) tegenover staan	Ik sta er ambivalent tegenover.
(iets) zeggen	Het zegt me niets.
(iets) betekenen	Het betekent (persoonlijk) niet zo veel voor me.

ZEGGEN DAT JE NIETS KUNT BEDENKEN

Ik kan niets bedenken	Ik kom nergens op.

PRATEN OVER IDENTITEIT

zich voelen	Ik voel me echt Nederlander.
erbij horen	Daar horen ook minder leuke dingen bij.
meedragen	Die geschiedenis draag je met je mee.
trots zijn op	Ik ben trots op het feit dat ik Amsterdams ben.

OVER GEVOELENS PRATEN

Dat ontroert me.	It moves me.
Dat raakt me emotioneel.	I'm emotionally affected by it.
Ik maak me daar nogal druk om.	I get worked up by it.
We zijn makkelijk in de omgang.	We're easy to get along with.

Oefening 8

Werk met met z'n tweeën en stel elkaar de volgende vragen. Bij sommige vragen zijn voorbeeldantwoorden gegeven, die je op weg kunnen helpen.

1 Waar ben jij trots op?
Ik ben trots op (het feit dat) . . .

2 Vind je dat je ook de geschiedenis van je land meedraagt?

Voorbeeld

Ik ken de geschiedenis van mijn land niet.
of:
Ik denk dat vooral de Tweede Wereldoorlog erg belangrijk was.
of:
De geschiedenis van mijn land heeft niets met mij persoonlijk te maken.

3 Wat hoort er voor jou bij de identiteit van jouw land?

Voorbeeld

Voor mij hoort . . . erbij.
of:
Ik denk dat de Engelse/Amerikaanse/Duitse identiteit vooral bestaat uit . . .

4 Hoe sta je tegenover een monarchie?

Voorbeeld

Ik vind het belangrijk.
of:
Ik vind het maar niks.

5 Zijn er dingen die met jouw land te maken hebben die je ontroeren of je emotioneel raken?

6 Wat betekent jouw nationaliteit voor jou?

Oefening 9: Discussievragen

Bespreek de volgende vragen in kleine groepjes.

1. Zijn er dingen die je herkent in de meningen die de Nederlanders gaven over het Nederlander-zijn? En wat dan precies?
2. Is het bij nationale kampioenschappen belangrijk als jouw land wint? Waarom wel/niet?
3. Betekent de vlag iets voor jou? Zo ja, wat betekent de vlag? Staat het ook symbool voor minder leuke dingen?
4. Bestaat er een typisch herkenbare identiteit van jouw land of is het een mengelmoes? Zo ja, waar bestaat die mengelmoes dan uit?

Oefening 10

Schrijf een stukje van ongeveer 200 woorden over jouw nationale of regionale identiteit. Maak gebruik van de ideeën die je in de vorige oefeningen hebt besproken en van het lijstje dat je in **Oefening 6** hebt gemaakt.

Oefening 11

Wat mis jij als je uit je eigen land/plaats of streek weg bent?

Bekijk eerst het lijstje van wat sommige Nederlanders hebben gezegd dat ze missen:

Ik mis:

- de geur van vers gemaaid gras;
- films die niet na-gesynchroniseerd zijn;
- de zoute zeewind door mijn haar als ik langs de dijk fiets;
- de sfeer van gemoedelijkheid;
- het gevoel van thuis-zijn en veiligheid;
- drop;
- de aardappelen, de boerenkool en de Hema-worst.

Of:

- Ik mis niks. Ik ben blij als ik weg ben uit dat gekneuter.

NB: Doe deze oefening eerst als spreekoefening met een partner en schrijf er daarna een stukje over in een life-style publicatie. Beschrijf het zoveel mogelijk vanuit je zintuigen. Kijk eventueel weer naar Tekst 4 en 5 uit het vorige hoofdstuk om je ideeën te geven. Hoe ziet het eruit? Hoe voelt het? Welke geuren, geluiden en smaken zou je missen?

gekneuter	small-mindedness	**gemoedelijkheid**	easygoing

Tekst 2 Hoe zien buitenlanders Nederland?

Ann (29)

Zij komt uit Engeland, maar woont en werkt al vier jaar in Alkmaar.

Ann Wat ik leuk vind aan Nederland? De lagere werkdruk en de vele vakantiedagen. Maar ook de spontaniteit en de openheid van de mensen. Zelfs in de supermarkt hebben ze tijd om een praatje met je te maken. En als mijn vriend jarig is word ik meteen ook gefeliciteerd. Grappig vind ik dat!

En verder . . . afspraak is afspraak. Dat is ook wel prettig. Je kunt wat dat betreft wel op mensen bouwen. Je weet wat je aan ze hebt.

journaliste En wat vind je minder leuk?

Ann Nederlanders vinden zichzelf ongelofelijk slim. Maar zijn ze nou echt zoveel slimmer?

Françoise (32)

Françoise De openheid. Gewoon je en jij kunnen zeggen tegen je baas. En die recht voor zijn raap opmerkingen van veel mensen besparen je veel tijd en frustratie: je weet tenminste waar je aan toe bent. Minder leuk is wel de keerzijde van die openheid. Vooral bij kinderen zie je dat. Ik heb soms wel moeite met hun onbeschofte gedrag. Nederlandse kinderen zijn naar mijn smaak soms een beetje té zelfverzekerd. Als ik zelf kinderen had zou ik ze beslist meer etiquette bijbrengen.

Key vocabulary

een praatje maken met	to have a chat with
feliciteren	to congratulate
het gedrag	behaviour
grappig	funny (in a positive sense)
de keerzijde	the other side of the coin
onbeschoft	rude
ongelofelijk	unbelievable
op iemand kunnen bouwen	being able to trust someone
recht voor zijn raap zijn	to call a spade a spade
slim	clever/smart
de werkdruk	workload
weten waar je aan toe bent	to know where you stand
weten wat je aan ze hebt	what you see is what you get with them

Oefening 12

Luister naar de vraaggesprekjes met Ann en Françoise. Wie van de twee vrouwen is positiever over Nederland naar jouw gevoel? Waarom?

Oefening 13

Maak nu een lijst met de positieve en negatieve punten die Ann en Françoise noemen over Nederlanders.

naam	*positieve punten*	*negatieve punten*
Ann		
Françoise		

Oefening 14

Bespreek de volgende vragen in een klein groepje.

Zou jij het leuk vinden als mensen recht voor hun raap zijn?

Denk je dat alle Nederlanders recht voor hun raap zijn?

Oefening 15

Werk in paren. Bespreek of er enige overeenkomsten zijn tussen hoe de Nederlanders aan het begin van het hoofdstuk zichzelf zien en hoe de twee buitenlanders de Nederlanders zien? Hoe zou dat kunnen komen, denk je?

Oefening 16

Schrijf nu een stukje voor een studentenkrant waarin je aangeeft wat de overeenkomsten en verschillen zijn tussen hoe Nederlanders zichzelf zien en hoe anderen tegen de Nederlanders aankijken. Je kunt zelf je eigen mening geven over hoe jij tegen de Nederlanders aankijkt en waarom.

Tekst 3

Nederlandse diplomaat

journaliste Staan we in het buitenland goed te boek?

diplomaat Tja . . . we zijn van nature geen goede bemiddelaars. Nederlanders zijn meer geneigd het eigen standpunt te verkondigen. En als een Nederlander denkt dat hij gelijk heeft, moet je van goede huize komen om hem van zijn apropos te brengen.

journaliste Hoe komt dat op internationaal gebied tot uiting?

diplomaat We vallen anderen lastig met wat we zelf mooi vinden. Of met wat we net zelf hebben ontdekt. Anti-kolonialisme bijvoorbeeld. Nederland stond vooraan in de rij van critici van het Apartheidsbewind. Terwijl apartheid toch een Nederlands woord is en we het zelf recentelijk in Indonesië niet beter hadden gedaan.

journaliste Wat wordt internationaal gezien als Nederlandse deugden?

diplomaat In Amerika zijn ze geweldig enthousiast over de Nederlandse werknemers. Een Hollander kun je om een boodschap sturen, vinden ze. Nederlanders zijn ook nogal uitvliegerig. Je komt ze overal in de wereld tegen. Ze passen zich snel aan en gaan niet bij de pakken neerzitten. Ze zijn ook heel actief in het buitenland, richten schooltjes op, gaan in allerlei besturen zitten. Ze zijn onderling ook erg solidair.

journaliste Zijn solidariteit en tolerantie onze goede eigenschappen?

diplomaat Ik weet niet waar de grens ligt tussen tolerantie en onverschilligheid. De positieve keerzijde is dat veel kan in Nederland. Je wordt niet snel ondergeschoffeld. En dan kom ik meteen op solidariteit. Een mooie eigenschap van onze feminiene samenleving. We zijn zorgzaam, hebben goede sociale voorzieningen, althans vergeleken bij sommige andere landen. En dat is heel aantrekkelijk aan Nederland.

naar: *de Volkskrant*, Janny Groen, 'We weten het altijd beter'

Key vocabulary

de bemiddelaar	negotiator
het bewind	regime
bij de pakken neer (gaan) zitten	to give up
de deugd	virtue
geneigd zijn	to have a tendency to
goed te boek staan	to have a good reputation

de grens	border
iemand lastig vallen	to bother someone
iemand om een boodschap kunnen sturen	to be able to leave someone to it
iemand van zijn apropos brengen	to unnerve someone
je moet van goede huize komen	you have to be very good
de keerzijde	the other side of the coin
net	only just
ondergeschoffeld worden	*here*: to be socially excluded
onderling	amongst one another
oprichten	to found
de samenleving	society
solidair zijn	to show solidarity
het standpunt	point of view
tot uiting komen	to be expressed
uitvliegerig	*here*: tending to travel and move to other countries
vergeleken bij	compared to
verkondigen	to proclaim

Oefening 17

Speel het vraaggesprek met de diplomaat na. Probeer zoveel mogelijk zijn intonatie te benaderen.

Vragen bij tekst 3

1 Waarom zijn Nederlanders geen goede bemiddelaars?
2 Hoe komt het feit dat Nederlanders hun eigen standpunt graag verkondigen op internationaal gebied tot uiting?
3 Hoe komt het doorzettingsvermogen van Nederlanders op internationaal gebied tot uiting?
4 Vindt de diplomaat dat tolerantie een van de goede eigenschappen is van de Nederlanders?
5 En denkt hij dat solidariteit een goede Nederlandse eigenschap is?

het doorzettingsvermogen	determination

Communicatie

STIJL EN GENUANCEERD EN DIRECT TAALGEBRUIK

The diplomat is being interviewed in his professional capacity and both he and the interviewer use a generally formal, careful and impersonal style of language. As most people in the previous dialogues are interviewed in a personal capacity, their language use is more informal and direct. Although you might also note that some of the dialogues contain a mixture of more careful, formal language and more personal and informal language.

The chart below gives you some examples of the different styles. Note though, that in most situations, people do not stick very strictly to only one style of speaking, but are more likely to use some elements of both formal and informal speech.

personal/informal/direct	**impersonal/formal/careful**
overstating and emphasis: ongelofelijk	*less overstating*: nogal we zijn meer geneigd
words or expressions talking about feelings: dat geeft me een nationaal gevoel daar ben ik trots op	*not talking about feelings, talking about ideas and attitudes*: wat wordt internationaal gezien als . . .? ik weet niet waar de grens ligt tussen . . .
direct statements with emphasis: Nederlanders zijn verschrikkelijk ontevreden zeurpieten. Ik zou ze beslist meer etiquette bijbrengen.	*use of qualifiers*: Terwijl apartheid toch een Nederlands woord is. Wij zijn zorgzaam, althans vergeleken bij sommige andere landen.
use of modal particles: Maar zijn ze nou echt zo veel slimmer? Jij bedoelt zeker klompen en molens en zo?	*indicating links between points*: En dan kom ik meteen op solidariteit.

Oefening 18

Kijk naar de dialoogjes aan het begin van dit hoofdstuk in tekst 1 en geef voor elk dialoogje aan of de spreekstijl vooral formeel, vooral informeel, of een mengeling is van beiden. Geef voorbeelden. Je kunt deze oefening alleen doen of met een partner.

Oefening 19

Geef voor elk van de onderstaande zinnen aan of het in een directe of een meer genuanceerdere stijl is geschreven.

1 Ik moet eerlijk zeggen dat ik daar wel wat ambivalent tegenover sta.
2 We hebben toch zeker niks te klagen?
3 Als je het vergelijkt met sommige andere landen, hebben we eigenlijk maar weinig te klagen.
4 Ja, ik vind gewoon dat Nederland een fantastisch land is.
5 Nederland heeft zeker z'n positieve kanten.
6 Minder leuk is de keerzijde van die openheid.

7 Dat Nederlanders je feliciteren als je vriend of zo jarig is . . . dat is toch hartstikke leuk?
8 Ik heb wel wat moeite met dat brutale gedrag.
9 Ik vind dat brutale gedrag gewoon verschrikkelijk.

Tekst 4

Lees de onderstaande songtekst van de Vlaming Raymond van het Groenewoud.

Ik hou van Hollanders

Ze zien er keurig uit
Misschien wat lang
mooie stemmen! vol subtiele klank
de vrouwen hebben . . . iets elegants . . .
zo leuk en typisch! voor dit land
zachte ogen . . . verfijnde smaken
zwoele stemmen, die door hun neuzen kwaken

Ik hou van Hollanders!
Ik hou van Holland!
Ik hou van Hollanders!
Ik hou van Hol-land!

Hun café's . . . sluiten op tijd . . .
dat is pas . . . gezelligheid . . .
Hun bitterballen, wie doet hun dat na
en vergeet ook niet hun huzarensla

Ik hou van Hollanders!
Ik hou van Holland!
Ik hou van Hollanders!
Ik hou van Hol-land!

Ze hebben gelijk . . . ze hebben gelijk . . .
alles moet kunnen . . . niets mag . . .
alles moet kunnen . . . ja toch . . .
ze hebben gelijk . . . ze lopen rood aan . . .
ze hebben gelijk . . . daar komt het op aan . . .

Ik hou van Hollanders!
Ik hou van Holland!
Ik hou van Hollanders!
Ik hou van Hol-land!

Raymond van het Groenewoud (Debbel Debbel Produkties)

Key vocabulary

de bitterbal	café snack (type of croquette)	**de klank**	sound
eruitzien	to look like	**kwaken**	to quack
de huzarensla	Russian salad (traditional dish)	**op tijd sluiten**	to close on time
keurig	neat and tidy/dowdy	**de stem**	voice
		verfijnd	refined
		zwoel	sultry

Vragen bij tekst 4

1 Wat zijn volgens dit lied de karakteristieke kenmerken van de Nederlanders en de Nederlandse maatschappij?
2 Welke ideeën over de Nederlanders herken je van de eerdere dialoogjes in dit hoofdstuk?
3 Welke andere negatieve punten noemt Raymond van het Groenewoud over Nederlanders? Denk je dat dat iets te maken heeft met het feit dat hij Vlaming is?
4 Waarom zegt Raymond van het Groenewoud 'Hollanders', denk je en niet 'Nederlanders'?
5 Hoewel het lied heel negatief is over de Nederlanders is het grappig en zullen veel mensen, ook Nederlanders, er toch om lachen. Wat maakt het zo grappig?

Oefening 20: Hoe ziet zij/hij eruit?

Beschrijf hoe de volgende mensen eruitzien. Je kunt gebruik maken van de volgende woorden of vergelijkingen, maar bedenk er zelf ook een paar.

beschaafd truttig cool modern
vlot professioneel sportief
als een echte zakenman als een zwerver
als een jonge vent
als een Victoriaanse ondekkingsreiziger als een oude hippie

1 De koningin van Engeland
2 De minister-president
3 Een popster
4 Een filmster
5 Een oude kennis van je
6 Een docent

Oefening 21

Schrijf nu zelf een lied of gedichtje waarin je een groep mensen beschrijft, bijvoorbeeld Engelsen of Amerikanen, docenten of popzangers. Gebruik een woordenboek of vraag de docent voor woorden of uitdrukkingen die je kunt gebruiken.

Cultuur

ZO LEUK EN TYPISCH

Raymond van het Groenewoud mocks the way the Dutch talk by imitating certain cliché expressions:

zo leuk en typisch,
ja toch . . .
alles moet kunnen

POPULAR MUSIC

The title of Raymond van het Groenewoud's song may be a take on *Ik hou van Holland*, a popular **smartlap** in the sixties, sung by the then child-singer Heintje. A smartlap – sometimes called **levenslied** – song about life – is a sing-along song with melodramatic and sentimental themes. They are very popular in the Netherlands. Well-known singers in this genre are André Hazes, de Zangeres Zonder Naam, Dries Roelvink, Marianne Weber and Frans Bauer, to name but a few. When André Hazes died in 2004, the football stadium where the funeral service was held, was packed out. For more information see www.smartlappen.pagina.nl

Oefening 22

Zoek informatie op het internet over Nederland. De docent kan je thema's geven. Die kunnen bestaan uit onderwerpen zoals de Nederlandse filmindustrie, het immigratiebeleid of populaire muziek. Maar het kunnen ook 'case studies' zijn van bepaalde evenementen of instituten, zoals de Pasar Malam, het Groninger Museum of een opvangcentrum voor prostituees. Als je genoeg informatie hebt verzameld kun je je een presentatie over het thema geven.

Oefening 23

Hoe zou jij jouw land representeren in woord en beeld aan potentiële Nederlandse toeristen?

Enkele voorbeelden over Nederland:
- Ik zou de cultuur benadrukken, zoals de schilders van de 17e eeuw.
- Ik zou de festivals en feesten benadrukken, zoals het carnaval, koninginnedag en de Pasar Malam.
- Ik zou een beeld laten zien van schaatsers die door een vlak landschap rijden.
- Ik zou een beeld laten zien van een drukke multiculturele markt in Amsterdam.

Cultuur

VERZUILING

Een 'typisch Nederlands' verschijnsel dat aan het begin van de vorige eeuw ontstond was de verzuiling. Een zuil in deze context betekent een leefomgeving gebaseerd op een bepaalde levensovertuiging. Er zijn, of eigenlijk waren, vier zuilen die de heersende geloofsovertuigingen en levensvisies representeerden: de protestant-christelijke (de calvinistische), de katholieke, de socialistische en de neutrale of openbare zuil. Binnen die zuilen leefden mensen grotendeels zonder contact met mensen van een andere zuil, en dus zonder contact met mensen die een andere levensovertuiging hadden. Oorspronkelijk was dit systeem ontstaan als een emancipatiebeweging, zodat de belangen van elke groep, ongeacht geloof of overtuiging, vertegenwoordigd waren. Iedere groep had zo zijn eigen scholen, universiteiten, ziekenhuizen, kranten, politieke partijen, omroepen, uitgeverijen, clubs en noem maar op.

Geert Mak schreef in zijn in 2000 gepubliceerde boek *De Eeuw van mijn Vader*: 'Men werd geacht enkel met gelijkgezinden te voetballen, toneel te spelen, naailes te nemen, boeken te lezen, op reis te gaan, feest te vieren, geiten te fokken, en de liefde te bedrijven. Toen in de jaren dertig de bewoners geselecteerd werden voor de nieuwe Wieringermeer en Noordoostpolder, werd zo zorgvuldig gelet op een evenwichtige vertegenwoordiging van alle zuilen, en in ieder dorp werden ook keurig drie scholen gebouwd: een katholieke, een protestants-christelijke en een openbare [. . .] Zo leefde iedereen vredig langs elkaar heen [. . .] Iedereen had de eigen waarheid in pacht en die waarheid was totaal.'

Tegenwoordig zijn de zuilen grotendeels verdwenen. Wel zijn restanten daarvan zichtbaar in veel scholen, omroepen en kranten. Niettemin is het idee van zuilen niet helemaal verdwenen. Men spreekt ook wel van een nieuwe, vijfde zuil: de zuil van de islam.

Key vocabulary

het belang	interest
de emanancipatie-beweging	movement of liberation/ emancipation
enkel	only
evenwichtig	balanced
fokken	to breed
geacht worden	to be expected to
de geit	goat
de gelijkgezinden	people holding similar views and values
het geloof	religion
heersend(e)	dominant
keurig	*here*: properly, according to conventions
langs elkaar heen leven	to live in close proximity with other people but without any contact
de leefomgeving	living environment
de levensovertuiging	philosophy of life, world view

de liefde bedrijven	to make love	**de verzuiling**	pillarisation
ongeacht	regardless of	**vredig**	peacefully
oorspronkelijk	original	**de waarheid in pacht hebben**	to think one's own vision is the only true and correct one
openbaar	public, *here*: neutral	**de zuil**	pillar
de uitgeverij	publishing company		
het verschijnsel	phenomenon		
vertegenwoordigd	represented		

Oefening 24

Bespreek de volgende discussiepunten met medestudenten in je groep.

1 Bedenk wat de redenen zouden kunnen zijn van het grotendeels verdwijnen van de zuilen.
2 Wat zijn de nadelen volgens jou van een verzuilde maatschappij?
3 Denk je dat het effect van een verzuiling: leven binnen een groep die jouw levensvisie deelt, alleen een typisch Nederlands verschijnsel is?

Structuren

TE + INFINITIEF

As you have seen in Unit 3, some verbs when followed by an infinitive need to have **te** inserted before the infinitive.

The full list of these verbs is too long to give here, but it includes:

achten	**beginnen**	**beloven**	**beweren**
blijken	**denken**	**durven**	**geloven**
hoeven	**hopen**	**lijken**	**proberen**
schijnen	**vergeten**	**vragen**	**weigeren**
zeggen			

You add **te** before the infinitive regardless of the tense in which the verb is used, or whether the verb is used in the passive voice.

Ik had *gedacht* volgend jaar naar Djibouti op vakantie *te* gaan.

Men werd *geacht* enkel met gelijkgezinden *te* voetballen, toneel *te* spelen, geiten *te* fokken en de liefde *te* bedrijven.

With a separable verb

If the infinitive is separable, **te** comes in between the two parts:

opbellen Ik vergeet steeds mijn ouders op te bellen

Infinitive constructions without **te**

Some verbs which can be combined with an infinitive do *not* have **te** before the infinitive. Apart from the modal verbs, the most common ones are:

blijven	**gaan**	**horen**	**komen**
laten	**zien**	**zijn**	

Ik *zag* Margot gisteren met haar nieuwe vriendje arm in arm *langslopen*.
Nita heeft haar haar *laten verven*. 't Staat leuk.

Oefening 25

Werk met met z'n tweeën. Om de beurt praat je over een van de situaties die hieronder staan beschreven. Vul daarna de kolom beneden in. Formuleer complete zinnen. Probeer zoveel mogelijk zinnen met infinitieven te gebruiken, door te beginnen met een van de volgende werkwoorden:

Ik ben gevraagd te . . .
ik heb geprobeerd te . . .
ik moet . . .
enz.
ik word geacht te . . .
ik weiger . . .
ik laat . . .

Hieronder staan een paar ideeën, die je kunt gebruiken, maar wees zo creatief mogelijk en gebruik zoveel mogelijk van de woorden en uitdrukkingen die je in deze cursus bent tegengekomen.

de dakgoot repareren **nieuwe gordijnen maken**
de keukenkastjes opnieuw schilderen **beleefd zijn**
overal voor opdraaien
je gevoelens verbergen of juist over gevoelens praten
de vrede bewaren **naar de kerk of moskee gaan**
vergaderingen voorzitten **diplomatiek zijn**
problemen oplossen

Voorbeeld

Je bent een droomvakantie aan het plannen.	Ik probeer bestemmingen uit te kiezen die heel speciaal zijn. Ik hoop een boot te huren om door de binnenlanden van Afrika te varen, maar ik wil ook een trektocht per kameel maken.
Je wilt je huis opknappen.	
Je klaagt over je werk.	
Je schept op over je werk en de belangrijke rol die je daar vervult.	
Je beschrijft de relatie met een familielid of vriend/in en wat jouw rol daarin is.	

het binnenland	interior, inland	**de kameel**	camel
huren	to rent	**varen**	to sail

Nationale identiteit: bestaat het?

Sinds de globalisering en de Europese eenwording is in veel landen, ook buiten Europa, de discussie over nationale identiteit een populair discussieonderwerp. Vaak komen in deze discussie onderwerpen naar voren zoals de karaktertrekken van de Nederlanders of de Nederlandse maatschappij en de verschillende waarden die mensen hechten aan symbolen en dergelijke. Het gaat dan meestal om wat Nederlanders delen. Om die reden vervallen mensen al gauw in stereotiepe uitspraken of generalisaties, zoals: de Nederlanders zijn tolerant of ze zijn eigenwijs of ze zijn pragmatisch.

Je kunt je afvragen of die stereotiepen ook echt door alle Nederlanders zo gevoeld worden en of die op iedereen betrekking hebben. Heeft iedereen dezelfde ideeën en herinneringen over zijn of haar land? Berusten die generalisaties op een kern van waarheid? Deze generaliserende kernmerken worden ook wel **essentialia** genoemd. Een benadering waarin (nationale) identiteit wordt beschreven als onveranderlijk, stabiel en op 'waarheid' berustend, wordt **essentialisme** genoemd.

Key vocabulary

de benadering	approach
berusten op waarheid	to be based on truth
betrekking hebben op	to relate to
de eenwording	unification
naar voren komen	to surface (a topic)
vervallen in stereotiepen	to fall into stereotypes
waarde hechten aan	to attach value to
zich afvragen	to wonder

Hieronder volgt een discussie over de Nederlandse identiteit tussen twee vertegenwoordigers van de Nederlandse cultuur in het buitenland.

Tekst 5a

Wie ooit een week op een internationale camping in Zuid-Frankrijk heeft gestaan weet precies wat Nederlanders zijn, en wie ooit in de brandende zon door de Pleistosvallei naar Delhi liep weet ook welke nationaliteit degenen hebben die hij daar tegenkwam. Maar als een afgestudeerde Amerikaan je vraagt wat Nederland is of wat Nederlanders zijn, geef je een antwoord dat past bij de wereld van je gespreksgenoot: Rembrandt, Spinoza, Rob van Gennep of Kamerling Onnes, hoewel beelden als tulpen, kaas, abortus, drugs en euthanasie natuurlijk ook bijdragen aan het beeld dat Amerikanen hebben over Nederland. Wij vullen ons beeld over Amerikanen weer aan met beelden zoals Hollywood, seriemoordenaars, getto's en Coca Cola.

Deze relativerende benadering kan natuurlijk gezien worden als een ontkenning van de eigen identiteit. Maar die eigen identiteit is ook eerder een optelsom dan een wortel, om in rekenkundige termen te spreken. Een optelsom die nog steeds groter en gecompliceerder wordt, omdat er uit het buitenland afkomstige mensen als Clarence Seedorf, Frank Rijkaard en Hafid Bouazza in kunnen worden opgenomen.

Laat ik eerlijk zeggen dat ik trots ben op zo'n niet-essentialistische identiteit. Het individu kan er dan uithalen wat hij wil.

naar: Frank Ligtvoet, *NRC Handelsblad*

Key vocabulary

afgestudeerd	*here*: post-graduate	**de gespreksgenoot**	discussion partner
bijdragen aan het beeld	to add to the image	**de ontkenning**	denial
degenen	those (people)	**ooit**	ever
een beeld aanvullen	to add further to an image	**opnemen**	to include

de optelsom addition (used as a metaphor here to indicate that various groups of people live in the Netherlands, each with a different cultural identity)

opvatten	to interpret	**relativeren**	to put into perspective
passen bij	to fit	**uithalen**	to take/get out of
rekenkundig	mathematical	**de wortel**	(square) root

Vragen bij tekst 5a

1 Als Ligtvoet zegt: 'Als je ooit een week op een internationale camping in Zuid-Frankrijk hebt gestaan weet je precies wat Nederlanders zijn', aan wat voor eigenschappen van Nederlanders denkt hij dan? (Heeft hij het bijvoorbeeld over hun filosofische opvattingen?)

2 Ligtvoet zegt dat de informatie die je over je land geeft, afhangt van je gespreksgenoot. Waarom karakteriseert Ligtvoet Nederland met namen als Spinoza en Rembrandt als zijn gespreksgenoot heeft gestudeerd?

3 Ligtvoet suggereert dat het beeld dat mensen van een bepaalde nationaliteit hebben gedeeltelijk uit stereotiepen bestaat. Welke stereotiepe beelden noemt hij over Nederland en welke contrasten geeft hij daarbij aan? En welke beelden noemt hij over Amerika en welke contrasten geeft hij daarbij aan?

4 Wat denk je dat Ligtvoet bedoelt als hij de Nederlandse identiteit als een optelsom beschrijft?

5 En waarom zou die identiteit gecompliceerder worden omdat er uit het buitenland afkomstige sporters voor Nederland spelen?

Tekst 5b

Aan het begin van zijn stuk wekt Ligtvoet de indruk dat hij tegenover zijn Amerikaanse gespreksgenoten het net breeduitwerpt als het over Nederland gaat: hij schermt niet alleen met Rembrandt en Rudi Fuchs, maar ook met Spinoza en Kamerlingh Onnes, en met tulpen, drugs en abortus. Zonder ook maar een poging te doen de vaderlandse historie en traditie enigszins analytisch te benaderen, kwalificeert onze culturele handelsreiziger de

Nederlandse identiteit als een optelsom, die bovendien steeds ingewikkelder zou worden, nu er ineens uit Suriname afkomstige voetbalspelers op het toneel verschijnen. Hij zegt trots te zijn op 'zo'n niet-essentialistische identiteit', zonder dat hij zegt wie buiten hemzelf nog overtuigd is van het bestaan van zo'n identiteit. Amerikanen mogen dan, zelfs in *The New York Times*, weinig over het buitenland vernemen, het beeld dat zeker de Oostkust-elite over Nederland heeft is redelijk scherp, bepaald 'essentialistisch' en goeddeels correct, zoals ik tijdens vijf jaar werk voor Amerikaanse werkgevers in de vroege jaren zeventig en de late jaren tachtig heb kunnen vaststellen. Ook mijn huidige Duitse werkcontacten hebben een scherp oog voor de Nederlandse 'essentialia': handelsgeest, spaarzin en flexibiliteit, gerichtheid op de wereldmarkt, praktische wereldwijsheid, pragmatische tolerantie, democratische traditie en een intens burgerlijke cultuur.

naar: Karel Vosskuehler, *NRC Handelsblad*

Key vocabulary

aangeven	to indicate	**het net breed uitwerpen**	to have a broad vision
benaderen	to approach	**huidig**	current
bepaald	certainly, definitely	**de indruk wekken**	to create the impression
bovendien	besides	**op het toneel verschijnen**	to appear on the scene
buiten	apart from		
burgerlijk	bourgeois/conventional	**schermen met**	to talk hot air
een poging doen	to attempt	**de spaarzin**	being keen to save money
enigszins	somewhat	**vaststellen**	to determine, to observe
gerichtheid	to be focused on	**vernemen**	to hear/read about

Vragen bij tekst 5b

1 Wat is de kritiek van Vosskuehler op Ligtvoets visie op de Nederlandse identiteit?

2 Vosskuehler zegt dat hoewel Amerikanen weinig over Nederland horen in de media, de elite in Amerika (en ook in Duitsland) toch een scherp en correct beeld heeft van Nederland. Waar bestaat volgens Vosskuehler dat correcte beeld uit?

Oefening 26: Discussie

Bespreek in kleine groepjes de verschillende visies over nationale identiteit. Vind je dat je een nationale identiteit kunt herleiden tot essentialistische kenmerken of komt er meer bij kijken? Hoe denk je zelf over je eigen nationale identiteit en speelt je nationale identiteit een rol in hoe je over jezelf denkt? Denk je dat in sommige landen het gevoel van nationale identiteit belangrijker is dan in andere? Vergelijk bijvoorbeeld Amerika, het Verenigd Koninkrijk en Nederland of een ander land.

Oefening 27: Schrijfoefening

Je bent gevraagd voor het studentenblad van een onderwijsinstituut in Nederland een stukje van ongeveer 300 woorden te schrijven over jouw nationale identiteit. Je kunt gebruik maken van de bovenstaande teksten om het concept identiteit uit te leggen en jouw visie over identiteit in het algemeen en jouw identiteit in het bijzonder te beschrijven. De studenten op het onderwijsinstituut zijn zowel Nederlandse als buitenlandse studenten.

Communicatie

COHESIE

Cohesion is often achieved through the use of referring words (**er**, **dat**, **deze**, **die**, **hem**, etc.) or through markers or signalling words which indicate the relation with the previous sentence (**omdat**, **ook**, **hoewel**, etc.). But cohesion can also be achieved through the word order in sentences. Frequently people start with the old information (the topic) and then add any new comment or information (the comment or focus).

Look at the fragment below to see how the sentences are linked and how that makes the text seem fluent and easy to follow.

> ***Deze relativerende benadering*** kan natuurlijk gezien worden als een ontkenning van de eigen identiteit. ***Maar die eigen identiteit*** is ook eerder een optelsom dan een wortel, om in rekenkundige termen te spreken. ***Een optelsom*** die nog steeds groter en gecompliceerder wordt, omdat er uit het buitenland afkomstige mensen als Clarence Seedorf, Frank Rijkaard en Hafid Bouazza in kunnen worden opgenomen.

Deze relativerende benadering	**Deze** refers back to the previous sentences which set out that approach.
Maar die eigen identiteit	**Maar** indicates a contrasting view of identity than the one set out in the previous sentence. **Die eigen identiteit** refers back to the previous sentence.
Een optelsom	**Een optelsom** refers back to the previous sentence.

These conventions are not always strictly followed, particularly in informal texts. Not following these conventions can create an element of surprise, emphasis or contrast, as in the two sentences which follow on from the text above:

Laat ik eerlijk zeggen dat ik trots ben op zo'n niet-essentialistische identiteit. Het individu kan er dan uithalen wat hij wil.

Oefening 28

Kijk naar de inleidende tekst over nationale identiteit op pagina 291 en geef aan wat de oude en wat de nieuwe informatie is van elke zin.

Oefening 29

In onderstaande tekst volgt de zin die begint met 'Judi Dench kreeg dat jaar wél een Oscar' niet de topic-comment regel. Wat is het effect daarvan?

De prachtige Cate Blanchett, die sensualiteit paart aan vastberadenheid, verdiende een Oscar-nominatie voor haar rol als Elizabeth I in *The Virgin Queen*. Maar zij won niet. Judi Dench kreeg dat jaar wél een Oscar voor haar bijrol van dezelfde Elizabeth I, maar dan op latere leeftijd, in John Maddens romantische komedie *Shakespeare in Love*. Die film won liefst zeven Oscars.

Uit: *Volkskrant magazine*, 14 februari 2004

Oefening 30

Reconstrueer de oorspronkelijke *original* tekst door de woordvolgorde in het onderstreepte zinsdeel te veranderen, zodat het contrast tussen de actietoerist vroeger en nu duidelijker wordt.

Nederland vakantieland mag weer, sterker nog, moet weer. <u>De bewuste actietoerist zocht het nog niet zo lang geleden in de Himalaya</u>, liep [hij] de Kilimanjaro op en af, of ging [hij] op het koudste deel van het noordelijk halfrond één worden met de eskimo's. <u>Hij zoekt zijn heil tegenwoordig steeds vaker in Nederland</u>. De wereld is er immers niet veiliger op geworden en de euro heeft alles ook nog eens flink wat duurder gemaakt.

Uit: Mar Oomen, Wereldreiziger in de polder, *Vrij Nederland*, 26 juli 2003

beïnvloeden	influence
flink	quite
het halfrond	hemisphere
immers	after all
zijn heil zoeken in	*here*: to find what he wants

Oefening 31

Reconstrueer de oorspronkelijke tekst door de woordvolgorde in de onderstreepte zinnen aan te passen, zodat ze vlotter op elkaar volgen en naar oude informatie verwijzen.

> Met de Waddenzee is iets geks aan de hand. Wie je er ook over hoort, iedereen vindt het een uniek en waardevol natuurgebied. <u>In wet- en regelgeving is dat ook vastgelegd. -In regeerakkoorden en internationale verdragen staat het</u>. En toch waren er anderhalf jaar geleden vergevorderde plannen om een enorm windmolenpark in het wad te bouwen. <u>Meer dan honderdduizend schelpdieretende vogels zijn er toch de afgelopen tien jaar van de honger omgekomen. -Om de zoveel tijd laait toch de discussie over gaswinning op.</u>
>
> <u>Dit jaar komt mogelijk een einde aan die voortdurende discussies wat wel en niet kan in de Waddenzee.</u> Na jaren van studeren en adviseren wil de rijksoverheid knopen doorhakken over de schelpdiervisserij en de gaswinning.
>
> Uit: *Natuurbehoud*, februari 2004

NB: The Waddenzee is an environmentally protected area, which is also popular with tourists. You may want to search for more information about this area on the Internet.

er is iets aan de hand	something is up	**vastleggen**	written down
de gaswinning	gas extraction	**het verdrag**	pact, agreement
knopen doorhakken	(finally) come to a decision	**vergevorderd**	far advanced
omkomen	to die	**waardevol**	valuable
oplaaien	to flare up	**het wad**	mud flat
het schelpdier	shell fish	**de wetgeving**	the law
		het windmolenpark	wind mill farm

READER QUESTIONS

Another way of producing well flowing communicative texts is through imagining your writing process as a dialogue with the reader. You then take the role of the writer and the reader at the same time. People tend to do this by imagining questions or comments a reader might have, such as: oh really? can you explain? what is the relevance? Yes, but . . .? How does that work? But what about such and such . . . By putting yourself in the role of the reader, you are likely to write more clearly and coherently.

In conversations we respond immediately to our conversation partner, we know how much we have to explain, because generally we are familiar with his/her previous knowledge and expectations. In writing we frequently don't know who the reader is, or what his previous knowledge is, so we have to take extra care in imagining the kind of responses the reader may have.

Oefening 32

Geef bij onderstaande tekst aan welke lezersvragen de schrijver beantwoordt.

Steeds meer mensen raken in de ban van het klimmen. Nee, niet in de ijle lucht op een paar duizend meter hoogte, maar gewoon in een klimhal om de hoek. Inmiddels trekt een kleine vijftigduizend mensen zich wekelijks omhoog in een klimhal. En dat aantal stijgt even snel als het aantal kunstmatige rotspartijen dat in het Nederlandse polderlandschap verrijst.

Uit: *Men's Health*, november 1999

het aantal	the number
ijl	*here*: oxygen starved
in de ban raken van	to fall under the spell of
inmiddels	in the mean time
de klimhal	climbing wall
kunstmatig	artificial
rotspartijen	rock formations
stijgen	to increase
verrijzen	rise out of

OVER POLEMIEK

The two articles about national identity earlier in this unit are a polemic argument in a quality newspaper. Vosskuehler disagrees with the first author and states this in openly critical language and a sarcastic, even derogatory tone:

- **hij schermt met**
- **zonder de vaderlandse historie en traditie proberen te analyseren**

- **die bovendien ingewikkelder zou worden**
- **zonder dat hij zegt wie behalve hemzelf nog overtuigd is van**

Oefening 33

Schrijf zelf een polemische reactie. Je kunt zelf een artikel of een brief aan de editor opzoeken van een Nederlandse of Vlaamse krant en daar een reactie op schrijven van een actuele discussie. Je kunt hiervoor op de website www.kranten.nl kijken.

Polemisch of niet, je taalgebruik moet uiteraard wel netjes blijven en je kunt mensen niet publiekelijk beledigen.

Oefening 34

Wissel nu de brieven uit met iemand anders in de klas. Lees elkaars brieven kritisch door en stel vragen die als lezer in je opkomen en die niet beantwoord worden in de brief. Maak een lijstje van die lezersvragen en bespreek die met elkaar.

Oefening 35

Herschrijf je oorspronkelijke brief en maak gebruik van de lezersvragen die je medestudent heeft gesteld. Lees nu je brief nog eens goed na. Volgen alle zinnen logisch op elkaar? Denk je nu in dat je een lezer bent. Pas de brief aan als dat nodig is.

Structuren

PASSIVE VOICE

What is it?

Passief	*Actief*
Worden die stereotiepen door alle Nederlanders zo gevoeld?	**Voelen alle Nederlanders die stereotiepen zo?**

The underlined subject **die stereotiepen** in the passive sentence is passive, i.e. not carrying out the action of **voelen**. The agent who is responsible for this action, **alle Nederlanders**, is the object in the passive sentence. In the active sentence, on the other hand, the agent is the subject. To make a passive sentence active, you change the object of the passive sentence into the subject of the active sentence.

The agent in a passive sentence is indicated by the word **door** (by).

Note that it is not necessary in a passive sentence to indicate who is responsible for the action:

***De bewoners* werden zorgvuldig geselecteerd.**
***Ze* selecteerden de bewoners zorgvuldig.**

The passive sentence doesn't tell us who did the selecting, so in the active sentence we have to use the vague and non-descript pronoun **ze**.

Sometimes there isn't a definite subject:

***Wat* wordt gezien als onze deugden?**
Wat zien *ze* als onze deugden?

***Er* werden drie scholen gebouwd.**
***De gemeente* bouwde drie scholen.**

Again we need to make up, or guess, the subject in the active sentence in order to convey the same meaning as in the passive sentence.

How do you form the passive?

present tense:

worden + past participle

Ik word gedwongen mijn ontslag te nemen.

imperfect tense:

werden + past participle

Ik werd gedwongen mijn ontslag te nemen.

NB: How to form the perfect tense of the passive is discussed in Unit 11.

Why use the passive?

There are various reasons why you might want or need to use the passive:

- *Agent already known or not important*

  Wat wordt internationaal gezien als onze deugden?

  The question above refers to a non-specific group of people abroad, although we can deduce from the context that it probably refers to business people and authorities, but the detail isn't important.

- *If required by the context (e.g. if topic needs to precede comment)*

  De Franse voetballer Thierry Henri is erg fotogeniek. Hij wordt daarom ook veel gevraagd voor reclame spots.

- *Style*

  To make a text more formal, many academic and official texts will use many passive constructions. However, too many passive constructions can make a text dull and difficult to follow.

- *Hiding the cause or not wanting to apportion blame*

  Compare:

  De gewonde man werd in de moskee doodgeschoten.
  De soldaat schoot de gewonde man in de moskee dood.

Newspaper editors are frequently faced with these kinds of decisions: an editor who supports the government actions which could have led to the incident described above, would be more likely to opt for the passive sentence. An editor critical of the soldier in question or of a government policy that gave rise to such an incident would be more likely to opt for the active sentence.

Not only newspaper editors make these decisions, we all make these linguistic decisions on a daily basis. Compare:

Het belastingformulier moet nog worden ingevuld.
Vul jij het belastingformulier in?
Ik moet het belastingformulier nog invullen.

The passive sentence tactically avoids the question of who is actually going to fill in the form.

Oefening 36

Maak de volgende zinnen actief. Gebruik dezelfde grammaticale tijd als in de oorspronkelijke zin.

1 Sinds ze die nieuwe baan heeft, is ze volkomen veranderd: haar huis werd ineens minimalistisch ingericht.
2 Haar oude auto werd ingeruild voor een snelle sportwagen.
3 En haar vriend van ruim tien jaar werd aan de kant gezet.
4 Die kinderen worden door hun grootouders opgevoed.
5 De president werd geadviseerd door belastingontduikers.
6 De kinderen worden opgevangen door de buren.

aan de kant zetten	*here*: to dump	**de belastingont-duiker**	tax dodger

Oefening 37

Je bent gevraagd een evaluatieformulier in te vullen over het onderwijsinstituut waar je Nederlands leert. Nadat je je lijst hebt ingevuld, denk je ineens dat je misschien te kritisch overkomt. Herschrijf je oorspronkelijke zinnen in het passief, zodat je geen expliciete kritiek geeft. Denk eraan dat je soms **er** moet gebruiken.

Voorbeeld

De docent praat te weinig Nederlands in de les.
Er wordt te weinig Nederlands gepraat in de les.

1 De studenten maken niet altijd het huiswerk.
2 De docent verwacht te veel van de studenten.
3 Het onderwijsinstituut moet voor een groter leslokaal zorgen.
4 De technische staf signaleert de problemen met de computers niet altijd.
5 De universiteit heeft de koffieautomaat nog altijd niet gerepareerd.
6 De secretaresse beantwoordt de telefoon nooit.
7 De secretaresse deelt de formulieren niet uit.

Oefening 38

Wat volgt? Zin a of zin b?

1 De politie heeft onlangs 113 mannen en 2 vrouwen gearresteerd tijdens een actie tegen huiselijk geweld.
  a Zeventig arrestanten werden aangeklaagd wegens zwaar lichamelijk letsel en bedreiging.
  b De politie klaagde zeventig arrestanten aan wegens zwaar lichamelijk letsel en bedreiging.

2 De arrestaties volgden op een in dezelfde week gelanceerde publiciteitscampagne tegen huiselijk geweld.
  a Via posters, pamfletten en advertenties wordt het publiek gewezen op de strenge maatregelen tegen geweld.
  b De politie wijst het publiek via posters, pamfletten en advertenties op de strenge maatregelen tegen geweld.

3 Zelfs al doet de mishandelde partner geen aangifte,
  a Daders kunnen toch worden opgepakt.
  b De politie kan daders toch oppakken.

Tekst 6a

Bom-uitbraak mafiatop verijdeld

AMSTERDAM, De 42-jarige topcrimineel Cees H., één van de kopstukken van het misdaadsyndicaat Octopus, heeft gisteravond tevergeefs getracht te ontsnappen door met het terroristenexplosief Semtex een deel van de Bijlmerbajes op te blazen.

Samen met de 24-jarige moordenaar U.K.M. bracht Cees H. gisteravond om kwart over acht een grote hoeveelheid Semtex tot ontploffing op de bovenste verdieping van toren De Schans.

Muren ontzet

Door de gigantische explosie, die met enorme rookontwikkeling gepaard ging, raakte de bovenste verdieping van De Schans zwaar beschadigd. Alle ramen sprongen en de muren raakten ontzet. Wonder boven wonder mislukte de ontsnapping, omdat uitgerekend één gepantserde ruit, waardoor de twee naar buiten wilden klimmen, heel bleef.

Groot alarm

Direct na de enorme dreun werd groot alarm geslagen en stormde een tiental bewaarders naarbinnen.

De bewaarders vonden ook een bergbeklimmerstouw met een lengte van 35 meter en enkele stalen haken. Het vermoeden bestaat dat deze materialen evenals de Semtex met behulp van corrupte bewaarders door de Octopusorganisatie de gevangenis zijn binnengesmokkeld.

Nadat de rust was weergekeerd deed zich rond tien uur een tweede ontploffing voor.

Zie verder pag. 6 kol.2

Uit: *de Telegraaf*

Key vocabulary

de bajes	*slang for*: prison	**de misdaad**	crime
het bergbeklimmerstouw	climbing rope	**de moordenaar**	murderer
beschadigd	damaged	**ontsnappen**	to escape
de bewaarder	prison guard	**ontzet**	buckled
de Bijlmer	area on the outskirts of Amsterdam	**de rook**	smoke
		de ruit	window
de dreun	bang	**springen**	*here*: to break
gepaard gaan met	accompanied by	**stalen**	steel
gepantserd	armour-plated	**tevergeefs**	in vain, to no effect
de haak	hook	**de uitbraak**	jailbreak
heel blijven	did not break (remained complete)	**uitgerekend**	of all things
		verijdeld	to foil
het kopstuk	ringleader	**het vermoeden**	suspicion

Tekst 6b

Leider hasjbende probeert uit te breken met gebruik explosieven

Van onze verslaggever

AMSTERDAM

DE 42-JARIGE hasjhandelaar Cees H., eerder dit jaar veroordeeld tot vier jaar gevangenisstraf wegens zijn aandeel in de zogenoemde Coral Sea-zaak, heeft donderdagavond geprobeerd te ontsnappen uit de Bijlmerbajes. Daarbij is gebruik gemaakt van explosieven.

Rond acht uur vond een ontploffing plaats in de toren De Schans, waarbij een gepantserde ruit uit de sponning werd geblazen. Maar de gedetineerde slaagde er niet in uit te breken.

Om tien uur werd opnieuw een explosie gehoord. Waardoor de tweede ontploffing is veroorzaakt, was gisteravond laat nog niet bekend. De politie sloot niet uit dat de tweede explosie van buitenaf is veroorzaakt.

Cees H. stond aan het hoofd van een criminele organisatie die in de afgelopen jaren vele tonnen hasj uit Pakistan naar Nederland en Canada vervoerde. De officier van justitie heeft een claim tegen hem ingediend van driehonderd miljoen euro om hem zijn vermogen dat hij in de drugshandel heeft verdiend, te ontnemen.

Bij de uitbraakpoging van gisteravond was een tweede gedetineerde betrokken, een 24-jarige man die tot twaalf jaar is veroordeeld wegens doodslag. Beide gevangenen zijn naar een geïsoleerde afdeling overgebracht.

Uit: *de Volkskrant*

Key vocabulary

de doodslag	manslaughter
de gedetineerde	detainee
de gevangenisstraf	prison sentence
de officier van justitie	public prosecutor
de uitbraakpoging	escape attempt
het vermogen	wealth/capital
veroordelen tot	to sentence to
vervoeren	to transport
wegens	because of, *here*: on the charge of

Oefening 39

Vul het werkblad in met de antwoorden op onderstaande vragen.

1 Wat zijn de verschillen die je op het eerste gezicht opvallen tussen de twee teksten zowel visueel als qua taal?

2 Wat zijn de verschillen in hoe Cees H. in de twee teksten wordt beschreven? En wat is het effect daarvan?

3 En wat zijn de verschillen in hoe zijn 24-jarige partner in de uitbraak wordt beschreven? En wat is het effect daarvan?

4 En wat zijn de verschillen in hoe de ontploffing/explosie wordt beschreven? En wat is het effect daarvan?

5 En wat zijn de verschillen in hoe het effect of resultaat van de explosie wordt beschreven? En wat is het effect daarvan?

6 Welke tekst gebruikt meer adjectieven? Wat is het effect van het gebruik van deze adjectieven?

qua in terms of

	De Telegraaf	*De Volkskrant*
1 Verschillen die je op het eerste gezicht opvallen		
2 Verschillen in hoe Cees H. wordt beschreven		
3 Verschillen in hoe de 24-jarige partner wordt beschreven		
4 Verschillen in hoe de ontploffing wordt beschreven		
5 Verschillen in hoe het effect (resultaat) van de ontploffing wordt beschreven		
6 Gebruik van adjectieven		

Oefening 40

Kies een gebeurtenis uit die je beschrijft voor zowel *de Telegraaf* als *de Volkskrant*. Je kunt een gefingeerde gebeurtenis gebruiken of je kunt een foto uitkiezen van een gebeurtenis die je vervolgens beschrijft.

Oefening 41

Doe een onderzoekje over de Nederlandse media. Welke omroepen zijn er? En welke kranten en tijdschriften worden er gepubliceerd? Je kunt op de volgende websites kijken.

- www.ned.univie.ac.at/non/landeskunde
- www.rnw.nl/nederlinks/html/media.html
- www.kranten.pagina.nl
- Hoofdstuk 12 in *The Netherlands in Perspective*, door William Shetter (London: Routledge, 2002) geeft meer informatie over de Nederlandse media.

A closer look

Onderstaande stukjes zijn fragmenten van verschillende Nederlandse kranten over het huwelijk van de Nederlandse kroonprins Willem-Alexander en zijn Argentijnse vrouw, Máxima op 2 februari 2002.

Luister eerst naar de stukjes en beantwoord de luistervragen. Doe Oefening 42 pas als je alle stukjes hebt beluisterd en gelezen.

ALGEMEEN DAGBLAD

VAN DE KOOPMANSBEURS tot de Nieuwe Kerk ontrolde zich voor Nederland en de meekijkende wereld een strak geregisseerd, en toch ontroerend sprookje met prins Willem-Alexander en vooral de nieuwe prinses Máxima in de hoofdrollen.

[. . .] In plaats van politiesirenes en geknal hoorden het bruidspaar en de kerkgangers luid gejuich opklinken na beider ja-woord. Een duidelijker blijk van steun kon het Koninklijk Huis zich niet wensen. Zelfs doorgewinterde republikeinen snotterden in hun zakdoek.

[. . .] Ster van de dag was de door Adios Nonino en Avé Maria tot tranen geroerde prinses Máxima. Nederland had haar al van harte verwelkomd, maar na zaterdag kan zij niet meer stuk. Hoe zij zich samen met Willem-Alexander als een slimme meid op de toekomst voorbereidt, is nu de vraag. Dat zal tijd vergen en die zal zij ook moeten krijgen.

[. . .] Mochten er bij Willem-Alexander of zijn moeder al veel twijfels zijn over de houdbaarheid van de constitutionele monarchie, dan moeten die zaterdag diep zijn weggestopt. Nederland heeft de monarchie immers nog steviger in de armen gesloten.

Key vocabulary

als een slimme meid op de toekomt voorbereidt — This is a well-known phrase taken from a government campaign at the time to encourage girls to continue their education

het bruidspaar	bridal couple	**ontroerend**	moving; poignant
doorgewinterd	through and through	**ontrollen**	to unfold
het gejuich	the cheering	**regisseren**	to direct
het geknal	explosive sounds	**snotteren**	to cry, to blub
het huwelijk	wedding	**het sprookje**	fairy tale
immers	after all	**stevig in de armen sluiten**	to embrace
het ja-woord	saying 'I will' during a wedding ceremony	**tijd vergen**	to take time
niet meer stuk kunnen	can do no wrong	**de twijfel**	doubt

Luistervragen bij tekst uit **Algemeen Dagblad**

1 De schrijver vergelijkt het huwelijk met een sprookje. Wie lijkt er belangrijker in dit sprookje? Willem-Alexander of Máxima?

2 Wat kon je horen nadat Willem-Alexander en Máxima het ja-woord uitspraken?

3 En wat hoorde je juist niet?

4 Heeft Nederland nu een positief idee over de monarchie, volgens de schrijver?

TROUW

ER WAS EEN PREEK die herkenbaar het stempel droeg van het bruidspaar, een omhelzing op het balkon en een huilende bruid bij de uitvoering van een door haarzelf uitgekozen melancholische Argentijnse tango voor een gestorven vader.

[. . .] Hoe het zij, het zijn deze momenten, die onderstrepen dat we in dit televisietijdperk met het koningschap een nieuwe fase zijn ingegaan. Bij de huwelijksvoltrekkingen van Juliana en later Beatrix was er veel meer afstand. Die is nu kleiner geworden. Dat brengt het risico met zich mee van een al te populair koningschap. Maar anderzijds, het werkt ook bevrijdend, zoals het in de jaren vijftig bevrijdend werkte toen Juliana gewoon op de fiets stapte.

Key vocabulary

gestorven	dead
hoe het zij	whatever way
de huwelijksvoltrekking	wedding ceremony
het koningschap	monarchy
de omhelzing	embrace
onderstrepen	to underline
de preek	sermon
het stempel dragen van	bear the hallmark of

Luistervragen bij tekst uit Trouw

1 Wanneer begon de bruid te huilen?

2 Wat was het verschil met dit huwelijk en dat van Juliana in 1937 en Beatrix in 1966?

3 Wat was zo bevrijdend in de jaren vijftig?

DAGBLAD DE LIMBURGER

HET RIMPELLOZE FEEST van zaterdag legt een stevige basis onder de opvolging straks van Beatrix door Willem Alexander. [. . .] Verheugend was dat het katholieke element in de kerkdienst veel groter was dan iedereen verwacht had. Het is tekenend voor het zelfbewustzijn van Máxima dat zij er met haar inbreng in slaagde de streng protestantse dienst van zijn scherpste kantjes te ontdoen.

Key vocabulary

de dienst	(religious) service
erin slagen	to succeed in
de inbreng	input
de opvolging	succession
rimpelloos	without hitches
tekenend voor haar zelfbewustzijn	a sign of her self-esteem
van zijn scherpste kantjes ontdoen	to take the edge of
verheugend	heart warming

Luistervragen bij Dagblad de Limburger

1 Wat was voor de schrijver verheugend aan de kerkdienst?
2 Hoe komt het dat de kerkdienst niet zo duidelijk protestants was?

Oefening 42

Vergelijk de verschillende manieren waarop de fragmenten uit de verschillende kranten het huwelijk van Willem-Alexander en Máxima weergeven.

1 Wat zeggen de verschillende kranten over het emotionele en romantische aspect van de bruiloft? Schrijf zoveel mogelijk details op. Welke krant(en) benadrukken dit emotionele aspect het meest?
2 Wat zeggen de verschillende kranten over de monarchie?
3 Welke kranten verwijzen expliciet naar het religieuze aspect van de bruiloft? Denk je dat dat iets te maken kan hebben met de levensbeschouwing (en oorspronkelijke zuil) van die kranten?

Oefening 43

Bespreek in een groepje wat de bovenstaande tekstfragmenten over het huwelijk van Willem-Alexander en Máxima zeggen over de Nederlandse cultuur en maatschappij.

Unit 10
Vlaanderen

This unit will give you more information about things which are considered to be typically Flemish, but moreover it will look at how Flemish people talk and think about themselves, particularly in relation to the Dutch. We will look at popular culture typical of Flanders and Belgium and we will read a wide range of texts, practising the language in a wide range of tasks, both practical and creative.

TOPICS

- State structure
- History and interpretation
- Clichés about nationalities
- Education
- Typical aspects of Flanders
- The monarchy
- Comic books and Belgian surrealism
- Dutch spoken in Belgium
- Differences between the Netherlands and Flanders

FUNCTIONS

- Representing a country
- Holding a presentation
- Reading literary texts
- Reflecting on national identity
- Writing down an opinion
- Using expressions and verbs with a fixed preposition in context
- Preparing and performing a radio play
- Analysing texts on fact and opinion

GRAMMAR

- Indirect questions
- Verb order in subclauses
- Use of **men**, **je**, **ze**
- Position of direct and indirect object

Cultuur

Oefening 1

Wat weet je al over het land België en de regio Vlaanderen?

Brainstorm en bespreek. Denk aan: cultuur – kunst – politiek – beroemde personen – sport – taal – mensen

Oefening 2

Doe de quiz om je feitenkennis aan te vullen. (De antwoorden vind je in de rest van dit hoofdstuk of in de key. Soms zijn er meer antwoorden mogelijk, afhankelijk van de bron die je gebruikt.)

1 Sinds wanneer bestaat België?

(a) 1830
(b) 1831
(c) 1839

2 België heeft aan het hoofd:

(a) een koning
(b) een president
(c) een minister-president
(d) een koningin

3 Op 21 juli vieren de Belgen hun nationale feestdag, wat vieren ze dan?

(a) de overwinning op de Duitsers in 1945
(b) de onafhankelijkheid in 1830
(c) de verjaardag van de koning

4 Wat zijn de officiële talen van België?

(a) Frans en Nederlands
(b) Waals en Vlaams
(c) Frans, Nederlands en Duits

5 Door wie van de volgende volkeren is België *niet* overheerst?

(a) de Oostenrijkers
(b) de Fransen
(c) de Nederlanders
(d) de Engelsen
(e) de Spanjaarden
(f) de Duitsers

6 Hoeveel procent van de Belgische bevolking woont in Vlaanderen (incl. Brussel)?

(a) 40% (b) 50% (c) 60%

7 Hoeveel regeringen heeft België?

(a) 1 (b) 2 (c) 3
(d) 4 (e) 5 (f) 6

8 Welke van de volgende bekende Belgen zijn Vlamingen volgens huidige grenzen? En wie is helemaal geen Belg?

(a) Peter Paul Rubens
(b) Pieter Breugel
(c) Sir Anthony Van Dyck
(d) Hercule Poirot
(e) Kuifje/Tintin
(f) Jacques Brel
(g) Louis Couperus
(h) Eddy Merckx
(i) Hugo Claus
(j) Adolf Sax
(k) Kim Clijsters
(l) Jean-Claude Van Damme

9 Welke van de vorige bekende Belgen ken je? Wat doen/deden ze? Ken je er nog andere?

DE BELGISCHE STAAT

Belgium became an independent state and parliamentary monarchy in 1830, when the Dutch rulers were chased out of Brussels by the unusual union of Belgian liberals and catholics, who were both unhappy about the Dutch interference into their affairs. The Dutch had only been there since 1815, after the defeat of Napoleon at Waterloo. Belgium is often seen as a buffer state between the larger European countries, France and Germany.

As a country, it contains the border between Germanic and Latin cultures, which is reflected in the languages that are spoken, i.e. Dutch, French and German.

The cultural and linguistic differences have led to a gradual federalisation of the state, which now consists of three communities and three regions, each with their own administration and government.

The communities, **'gemeenschappen'** (Dutch speaking, French speaking, German speaking), are based on language and culture and deal with matters related to these areas, such as culture, education and health. The regions, **'gewesten'** (Flanders, Wallonia, Brussels), deal with economic matters.

Belgium has a population of over 10 million people and is currently ruled by king Albert II. The successor to the throne is his son, prince Filip, who is married and has three children.

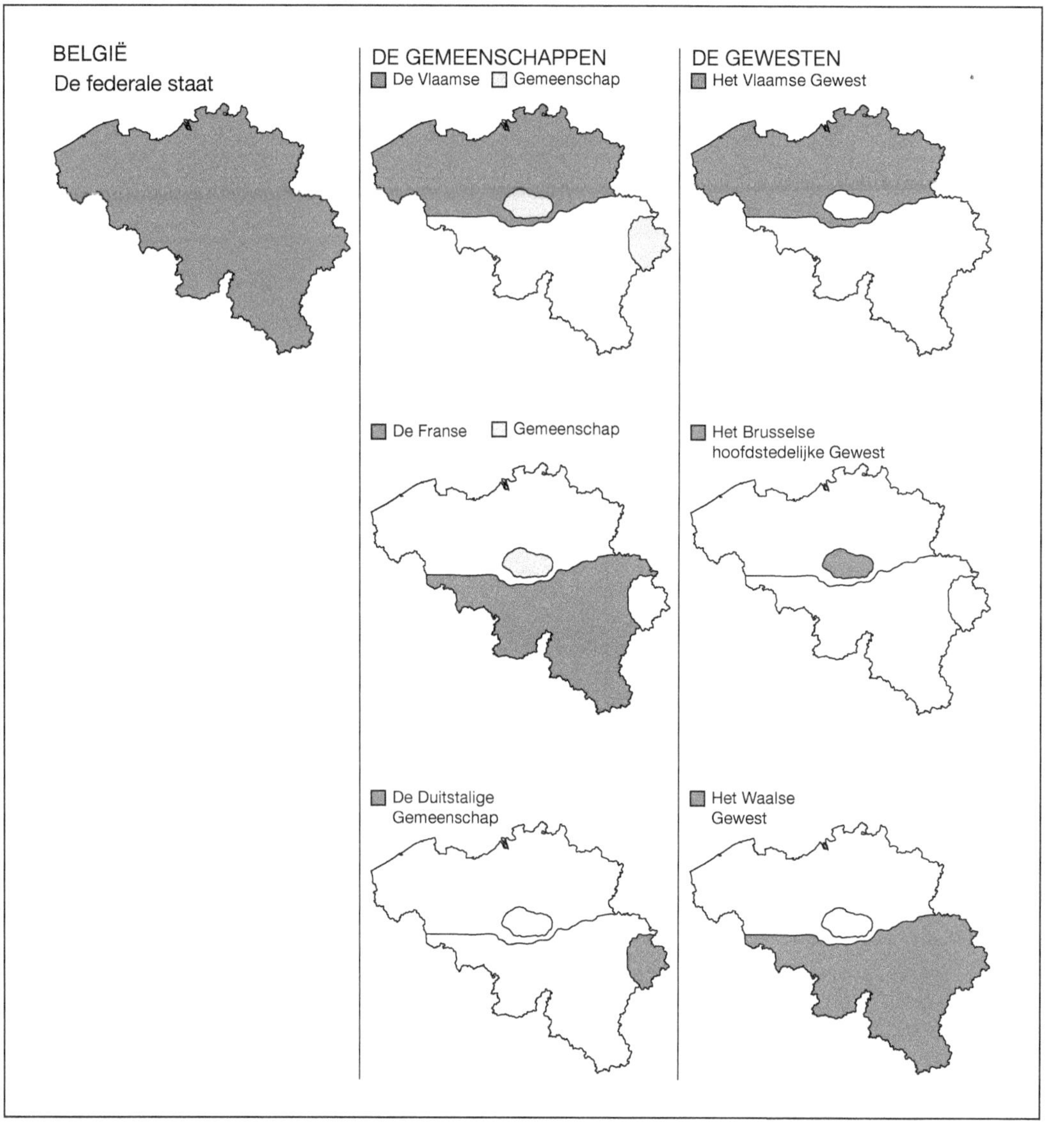

Bron: www.fgov.be

Ever since the Second World War, the Christian Democratic party had been the largest party, which reflected the large catholic majority in the country. However, this changed in 1998, when they became part of the opposition as a government was formed by a coalition of the liberal, socialist and green parties. The current federal government (2003) is a coalition of French-speaking and Flemish liberals and socialists.

For more information on Belgium, go to www.fgov.be

For more information on Flanders, go to www.vlaanderen.be

Oefening 3

1 Maak nu zelf 5 meerkeuzevragen over jouw land en leg die voor aan je medestudenten. Haal de ingevulde vragenlijsten terug op en analyseer de resultaten.
2 Presenteer de resultaten van dit mini-onderzoek aan de rest van de klas, in de vorm van een nieuwsbericht. Schrijf dit dus op voor je het voorleest.

Als je alleen werkt, kun je de resultaten verzinnen.

Voorbeeld

Onderzoek heeft uitgewezen dat slechts 5% van de ondervraagden weet wat de hoofdstad van de Oekraïne is.

Meer dan 80% wist wel dat de huidige president van Amerika George Bush heet.

Drie van de acht ondervraagden hadden geen antwoord op de vraag waarom Nederlanders zo dol zijn op de kleur oranje.

Tekst 1 De belgenmop en de hollandermop

De Nederlanders en de Belgen maken veel grapjes over elkaar, waarin je bekende vooroordelen terugvindt. Luister naar de volgende moppen en ontdek de clichés.

- Weet je hoe Belgen een champagnefabriek inwijden? Door er een schip tegenaan te gooien.
- Weet je hoe Belgen aan energiebesparing doen? Iedere keer als ze een restje warm water over hebben, stoppen ze dat in de diepvries.

Jeroen Brouwers, de Nederlandse auteur die lang in België heeft gewoond, schreef:

> Hebben Nederlanders het over 'Belgen', dan bedoelen ze Vlamingen. Belgenmoppen zijn Vlamingenmoppen. De personages in die moppen heten altijd Sjefke of Lowieke, nooit Raoul of Hercule. Afgaande op die moppen, is de Vlaming het debiele broertje van de Nederlander. (Jeroen Brouwers in *Vlaamse Leeuwen.*)

Maar hetzelfde gebeurt omgekeerd:

- Weet je hoe je rijk wordt ?
  Je koopt een Hollander voor wat hij waard is, en je verkoopt hem voor wat hij denkt waard te zijn.
- Weet je waarom een Hollander in de winter 's morgens met een ei naast de weg staat?
  Hij wacht tot de strooiwagen langskomt.

Key vocabulary

afgaande op	to go by	**de mop**	joke
de besparing	saving	**overhebben**	to have left over
debiel	retarded	**stoppen**	*here*: to put
de fabriek	factory/plant	**strooiwagen**	gritting lorry
inwijden	to inaugurate	**het vooroordeel**	prejudice

Vraag bij tekst 1

Geef aan wat de stereotiepen zijn over Belgen en Nederlanders in deze moppen.

Oefening 4: Groepsdiscussie.

Vind je dit soort moppen grappig of niet? Waarom?

Vind je stereotiepe moppen ongepast of onschuldig? Waarom?

Bestaan dit soort grappen over bevolkingsgroepen waar jij vandaan komt?

Waarom bestaan dit soort grappen denk je? Hebben ze een functie in de samenleving?

ongepast	inappropriate	**onschuldig**	innocent

Structuren

SUB-CLAUSES WITH QUESTION WORDS: INDIRECT QUESTIONS

Ik ben benieuwd *wie de nieuwe president van Amerika zal worden*.

Ik vraag me af *wat hij voor me zal meebrengen* uit Boedapest.

Zij heeft nog niet beslist *waar ze graag wil gaan wonen*.

Mark vertelde me *hoe hij zijn vrouw ontmoet heeft op vakantie*.

Mark vertelde me *hoe hij zijn vrouw op vakantie heeft ontmoet*.

Hij vroeg zich af *wie de wedstrijd zou gewonnen hebben*.

Hij vroeg zich af *wie de wedstrijd zou hebben gewonnen*.

Verbs at the end of the subclause

As you know, the verbs in a subclause all come at the end of the clause. The order in which they have to appear is the following:

1 the finite verb is the first verb;
2 modals come before other non-finite verbs;
3 infinitives such as ***gaan, komen, laten*** come before the main verb, but after the modal verb if there is one;
4 the main verb comes last.

Note that in the perfect tenses, the order of the auxiliaries **hebben** and **zijn** and the participle can be reversed without change in meaning.

	(1)	(2)	(3)	(4)
Zij heeft nog niet beslist waar ze graag	**zou**	**willen**	**gaan**	**wonen.**
	finite verb	*modal*	*other inf.*	*main verb*

Question word

In indirect questions, the question word functions as a conjunction to link the main and the subclause.

This question word is the same as the one that would be used to ask the direct question.

affirmative sentence	*direct question*	*indirect question*
Zij wil gaan wonen *in X.*	**Waar** wil ze gaan wonen?	Ze weet niet **waar** ze wil gaan wonen.
Zij houdt van *bananen.*	**Waar** houdt ze **van**?	Hij vroeg me **waarvan** zij hield.
	Waarvan houdt ze?	Hij vroeg me **waar** zij **van** hield.
Ik heb *toiletzeep* voor oma gekocht.	**Wat** heb je voor oma gekocht?	Tom vroeg me **wat** ik voor oma had gekocht.
Zij houdt het meest van *Reve.*	**Van welke** schrijver houdt ze het meest?	De journalist vroeg **van welke** schrijver zij het meest hield.

Note that *preposition* + ***wat*** becomes ***waar*** + *preposition* when forming the question word. e.g. **houden van [iets]**; → *Waarvan hou(d) je*? and not **Van wat hou(d) je?*

Tense

The tense used in the indirect question has to reflect the tense in the main clause. This may mean that the verb in the indirect question has to be put in the past tense.

Wie *gaat* er mee naar Amsterdam?
Zij vroeg wie er mee naar Amsterdam *ging*.

Wie *is* er uiteindelijk meegegaan naar Amsterdam?
Zij vroeg wie er uiteindelijk *was meegegaan* naar Amsterdam.

Oefening 5

1 Interview een medestudent over zijn/haar algemene kennis. Let op de zinsconstructie en de keuze van je werkwoorden.

Voorbeeld

hoe (ei koken)
Weet je hoe je een ei kookt/moet koken?

a wie (president Frankrijk)
b waar (Mount Everest)
c wanneer (volgende verkiezingen in jouw land)
d wat (hoofdstad van Bulgarije)
e waarom (bananen krom)

2 Vraag nu aan iemand anders of hij/zij de antwoorden weet. Doe dit op de volgende manier:

X vroeg me of ik wist hoe je een ei kookt, weet jij dat?

Oefening 6

In de volgende bijzinnen staan de woorden niet in de goede volgorde. Kan jij ze op de juiste plaats zetten?

Voorbeeld

Ik wilde weten *die vrouw / hoe vaak / had / hij / ontmoet / al*
Ik wilde weten hoe vaak hij die vrouw al ontmoet had.

1 Hij vroeg zich af *hoe lang / al bezig / zou / zijn / de vergadering.*
2 Ik wist eigenlijk niet *eieren / hoeveel / had / ik / nodig / voor een cake voor 10 personen.*
3 Ik was niet zeker *zich / mensen / hoeveel / voor die cursus / hadden / ingeschreven.*
4 Weet jij *wie / gewonnen / de presidentsverkiezingen / heeft / in de Oekraïne.*
5 Hij heeft nooit geweten *die avond / willen / vermoorden / heeft / hem / wie.*

Oefening 7

Maak van de volgende affirmatieve zinnen indirecte vragen.
Maak eerst een directe vraag zoals in het voorbeeld.

Voorbeeld

Ik kom vanavond om 8 uur naar huis.

(a) **Hoe laat kom je vanavond naar huis?**
(b) **Hij vroeg me hoe laat ik vanavond naar huis kwam.**

1 Ik erger me altijd aan haar onvoorspelbare gedrag.
Hij wilde weten ______

2 Zij houdt niet van tomaten en champignons.
De kok vroeg haar ______

3 Hij moet een cadeautje kopen voor mijn schoonmoeder.
Ik vroeg mijn man ______

4 De trein vertrekt van spoor 11!
De omroeper zal aankondigen ______

5 Deze kamer is drie meter breed.
De architect wilde weten ______

6 Voor een eenpersoonskamer moet je bijbetalen.
De toerist wist niet ______

7 De schrijver woont in een huisje aan de rand van de stad.
De vreemde man wilde weten ______

8 Waarom moet hij toch altijd zijn sokken laten slingeren.
Zij vroeg zich luidop af ______

9 Ik zou nooit op een conservatieve president stemmen.
De journalist vroeg haar ______

10 Ik zou nooit in een vieze trein vol kakkerlakken willen reizen.
Karel kwam net binnen en hij vroeg ______

Tekst 2 De homo Flandriensis en de homo Polderensis

In 2002 publiceerde de Vlaamse journalist Steven De Foer zijn observaties over Nederland in het boek *Onder Hollanders, een Vlaming ontdekt Nederland*. In datzelfde jaar komt het boek van Marko Heijl uit: *Een Hollander verkent Vlaanderen*. Steven De

Foer woonde drie jaar in Nederland, Marko Heijl is 'een in Vlaanderen geboren en getogen Hollander', zoals de achterflap ons vertelt.

Beide boeken zijn humoristische pogingen van noord en zuid om elkaar beter te begrijpen.

TEKST 2A

Een Hollander verkent Vlaanderen is een Vlaamsch-historische wandeling langs begijnhoven, Breugeliaanse pensenkermissen en de streekromans van Streuvels, en langs meer hedendaagse Vlaamse gemeenplaatsen als de frituur, de illegale villa's in natuurgebied en uiteraard de patisserie op zondagmorgen.

En als je het over Vlaanderen hebt, heb je het uiteraard ook over zijn bewoners. Een speciaal ras, waarvan heel wat trekjes worden uitvergroot in zijn literaire helden; het nonconformisme aan gezag en regels van Tijl Uilenspiegel, het Bourgondische levensgenieten van Timmermans' Pallieter, de eeuwige dorst naar het pintje van Lambik. De homo flandriensis op zijn best.

Marko Heijl. *Een Hollander verkent Vlaanderen*, p. 10

Key vocabulary

de achterflap	the back cover (of a book)	**het gezag**	authority
eeuwig	eternal	**het pintje (Vlaams) = de pils**	beer (half a pint)
de frituur	snack bar	**de poging**	attempt
geboren en getogen	born and bred	**het trekje**	feature or aspect
de gemeenplaats = het cliché	cliché	**uitvergroten**	to enlarge
		verkennen	to explore

het begijnhof	beguinage (sort of nunnery with typical architecture; tiny houses grouped around a grass patio, where the beguines/nuns lived and prayed)
Breugeliaans	as in the paintings of Pieter Breugel the Elder (Flemish Renaissance painter, ca 1525–1569)
Felix Timmermans	(1886–1947) Flemish writer from the city of Lier, made immortal by his Pallieter character
Lambik	contempory comic book hero from the *Suske en Wiske* series
het levensgenieten	the joy of life, joie de vivre
de pensenkermis	a food feast where people eat black pudding, traditionally after a pig was slaughtered, now still a popular fund-raising event
de streekroman	regional novel
Streuvels, Stijn	(1871–1969) Flemish writer whose many novels are known for their slowly developing evocations of nature and life in the Flemish country

Tijl Uilenspiegel	legendary figure from around 1500, gained fame by an anonymous writer. In 1876, the writer Charles de Coster uses this same character in a book on the 80-year war, making him a Flemish hero

Vragen bij tekst 2a

1 De schrijver maakt een onderscheid tussen meer historische en hedendaagse beelden. Wat zijn die?
2 Welke clichés over de Vlamingen vermeldt Heijl in dit stukje?
3 In de eerste alinea schrijft Heijl eerst 'Vlaamsch' in de oude spelling en daarna in de hedendaagse spelling. Kun je uitleggen hoe dit in de context past van wat hij in de eerste alinea beschrijft?
4 Welk effect creëert de auteur door een aantal literaire schrijvers en personages op te noemen?

TEKST 2B

Gedurende die drie jaar heb ik karaktertrekken aangetroffen in de homo polderensis die me totaal onbekend waren. En andere die juist overbekend zijn van de clichés en de grappen, en waarvan ik ten onrechte dacht dat ze uit de lucht gegrepen waren. Inmiddels weet ik beter: clichés overdrijven, ze liegen niet. Nederlanders zijn gierig, Belgen zijn dom. Er passen alleen een paar essentiële kanttekeningen en verklaringen bij en de wetenschap dat het oordeel van een buitenlander steeds bepaald wordt door diens land van herkomst. De mening dat Nederlanders begaafde maar overvloedige praters zijn, zal zeker niet gedeeld worden door een Fransman, want Fransen zijn nog erger. En een Duitser zal het er zeker niet mee eens zijn dat Nederland een land van stricte regels is.

Steven De Foer. *Onder Hollanders, een Vlaming ontdekt Nederland*, p. 9

Key vocabulary

begaafd	gifted	**de karaktertrek**	character trait
bepalen	to determine	**het oordeel**	judgement
diens	(old genitive form) his/her	**overbekend**	very well known
gedurende	during	**overdrijven**	to exaggerate
gierig	mean/stingy	**overvloedig**	abundant
de herkomst	origin	**ten onrechte**	wrongly
inmiddels	meanwhile	**uit de lucht gegrepen**	unfounded
de kanttekening	comment, query	**de wetenschap**	*here*: the fact

Vragen bij tekst 2b

1 Maak een lijst van clichés voor Belgen, Nederlanders, Fransen en Duitsers die De Foer noemt, of althans suggereert.

2 De Foer zegt dat clichés wel degelijk waar zijn, maar dat de betekenis van de clichés altijd relatief is. Wat maakt de waarde van clichés relatief volgens De Foer?
3 Ben je het met De Foer eens?
4 Waarom gebruikt De Foer de latijnse nonsensnaam 'homo polderensis'? Wat voor aura geeft dat aan zijn verhaal?

althans	at least	**wel degelijk**	certainly so, contrary to what you would expect

Oefening 8

Vul de woorden in de juiste vorm in.

karaktertrekken onbekend oordeel kanttekening verklaring wetenschap ongegrond herkomst bepalen het ermee eens zijn ten onrechte inmiddels

1 In de economie is het zo dat de vraag het aanbod ______ , zo zal je in de zomer makkelijker een ventilator vinden dan in de winter.

2 Alle betrokken landen hebben vorige week een ______ ondertekend die de vrede in het gebied zou veiligstellen. Maar ______ heeft een van de landen zijn beloftes al verbroken.

3 Het ______ van de Britten dat de Belgen saai zouden zijn, is ______ .

4 De Britten denken ______ dat de Belgen saai zijn.

5 De ______ van dit idee is onduidelijk voor de gemiddelde Belg.

6 Ik ______ dat roken in cafés moet worden afgeschaft.

7 In de ______ dat de meeste clichés veralgemeningen zijn, wil ik toch een ______ plaatsen bij jouw opmerking over de zogenaamd 'luie' Walen versus de 'ijverige' Vlaming.

8 Denk je dat het mogelijk is de ______ van de gemiddelde Belg of Brit te schetsen?

9 Het is mij ______ of de Ieren ook een 'beeld' hebben van 'De Belg'.

het aanbod	supply	**schetsen**	to sketch, to draft
afschaffen	to abolish	**veilig stellen**	to secure
de belofte	promise	**de veralgemening**	generalisation
betrokken	involved	**de vraag**	demand
ondertekenen	to sign		

Oefening 9

Schrijf zelf een tekstje van 150 woorden over een van je buurlanden of andere groepen in de samenleving, als column voor een nieuwstijdschrift. Probeer aan te geven wat de ideeën over je buren over jezelf zeggen.

Tekst 3 De domme Belg

Marko Heijl heeft zijn eigen verklaring voor het domme-Belg-fenomeen uit de grapjes.

> En hoe zit het met die hilarisch domme Belgen? In de twintigste eeuw sleepten de Belgen tien nobelprijzen in de wacht. Tegenover vijftien voor Nederland, wat gezien het feit dat Nederland 16 miljoen inwoners heeft en België 10 miljoen, relatief beter is.
>
> Waar komen die dommebelgenmoppen dan vandaan?
>
> [. . .] De historische grondslag van dommebelgen- of vlamingenmoppen gaat waarschijnlijk terug tot 1585, toen de intellectuele Vlaamse bovenlaag op vlucht voor de Spanjaarden massaal naar de Noordelijke Nederlanden emigreerde en in Vlaanderen de 'domme boerkes' achterbleven.
>
> Marko Heijl. *Een Hollander verkent Vlaanderen*, pp. 13–14

Key vocabulary

achterblijven	to be left behind
de bovenlaag	upper layer [of society]
de domme boerkes	country bumpkins
gezien	*here*: given
de grondslag	foundation
hilarisch	hilarious
in de wacht slepen	to carry off/to pocket
massaal	massive(ly)
de vlucht	flight/escape

Vragen bij tekst 3

1 Welk argument haalt Heijl aan om te 'bewijzen' dat de Belgen eigenlijk niet zo dom zijn?
2 Waar komen die moppen volgens hem dan vandaan?
3 Weet je ook waarom de Vlamingen in 1585 uit Vlaanderen wegvluchtten en wat er daarna met Vlaanderen gebeurde? (zoek op op het internet)

Cultuur

ONDERWIJS IN VLAANDEREN

Flanders has evolved from an impoverished rural and agricultural society to a wealthy urbanised, and densely populated region. Flanders is a knowledge-based society, where the majority of people work in the service industry.

Education in Belgium is compulsory from age 6 to 18, although nearly all children start full-time nursery at 3. Education is provided by state schools and subsidised Catholic schools, and is free. The Flemish education system is held in high regard in neighbouring countries.

Multilingualism is an important aspect of the Belgian educational system. It is compulsory for Flemish children to learn French from the age of 9 onwards and similarly for Walloon pupils to learn Dutch. Children in Brussels start even earlier with their second language. A third language, usually English, is introduced at the age of 13 and a fourth language can be taken at 15. In most jobs, language skills are essential requirements, so proficiency in three languages is considered the norm.

Tekst 4 www.flanders.be

Vlaanderen zet zijn beste beentje voor op de officiële website. Hierdoor krijg je een heel ander beeld dan dat van de grapjes.

Vlaanderen is sinds de Middeleeuwen een centrum van internationale handel. Het is erin geslaagd zich aan de tijd aan te passen en zo een van 's werelds meest welvarende regio's te blijven.

De kunststeden Gent, Brugge, Antwerpen en Brussel zijn gebouwd op de handel. Er is een merkwaardig evenwicht tussen de glorie van het verleden en de huidige dynamiek in de regio.

High-tech bedrijven en weelderige middeleeuwse stadshuizen bestaan letterlijk naast elkaar in Vlaanderen. Zij weerspiegelen allebei een drang naar vernieuwing die doorheen de eeuwen intact is gebleven. Deze drang werd versterkt door de ondernemende natuur van het volk en een opmerkelijke geografische ligging.

Een geweldige plaats om te wonen

Het is zeker geen understatement te zeggen dat Vlaanderen een hoge levensstandaard geniet. Misschien heeft de ligging nabij de belangrijkste Europese culturen het de smaak voor de goede dingen in het leven gegeven. Wat ook de reden is, bezoekers zijn altijd verbaasd over de kwaliteit van het leven in de regio.

Dit is ook te zien in de opvallende kwaliteit van zijn kunst, eten en architectuur. Het is echter ook een kwestie van deze levenstijl te onderhouden door een creatieve sfeer te creëren die gunstig staat tegenover cultuur.

[eigen vertaling]

Key vocabulary

de drang	urge	**ondernemend**	enterprising
het evenwicht	balance	**'s werelds**	of the world
gunstig staan tegenover iets	to be in favour of something	**slagen in iets**	to succeed in something
de levensstandaard	living standard	**het stadshuis**	town house
de ligging	position	**weelderig**	sumptuous
middeleeuws	medieval	**weerspiegelen**	to reflect
onderhouden	to maintain	**zijn beste beentje voorzetten**	to put one's best foot forward

Vragen bij tekst 4

1 Wat zijn de grote pluspunten van de regio?
2 Lees je ook iets over de minpunten?
3 Voor wie is deze tekst geschreven denk je? Leg uit.
4 In de eerste paragraaf krijg je een ideaalbeeld van de geschiedenis van de regio. Weet je wat er (onder andere) is weggelaten?

zich op de borst kloppen congratulate oneself

Oefening 10: Discussie in paren

Wat associeer je met een hoge levensstandaard?
Heeft jouw land een hoge levensstandaard? Hoe komt dat?

Oefening 11

Schrijf een promotietekstje in 150–200 woorden voor een toeristische website over jouw land in dezelfde stijl als het voorgaande. Denk dus eerst aan alle pluspunten, vermijd negatieve beeldvorming en gebruik relatief formele taal.

Communicatie

PRESENTATION SKILLS

If you are addressing a group of people, you want your presentation to be attractive and easy to listen to. Here are a number of tips on how to achieve this

Writing a presentation

- Write as you would speak. Try to tell your story first, before you start writing.
- Vary your sentence structure: use inversions, exclamations or commands and rhetorical questions (e.g. *Waarom is dat dan zo belangrijk?*). You can put parts of the sentence first or last for reasons of emphasis (e.g. *In Londen kan u al die dingen tegelijk doen!* or *U kan al die dingen doen, in Londen!*)
- Address and involve your audience by using **je**, **u**, **wij** (e.g. *U vraagt zich nu waarschijnlijk af . . .*).
- You can use stylistic devices such as enumerations in threes to build to a climax (think of *Veni, Vidi, Vici*! or *Ein Volk, Ein Reich, Ein Führer*) or comparisons and imagery. Bear in mind though that using imagery can be effective, but should never be forced.

Holding a presentation

- Vary your tone, this will be easier when you look at your audience. When you read, you tend to become monotonous. Be aware of which words you want to emphasize.
- Speak fluently but articulate well, and vary your speed; slowing down will attract people's attention
- Think of your body language. Move naturally and look your audience in the eye.
- Bring visual support material, but only if it is relevant to your presentation.

Oefening 12

Gebruik dezelfde informatie als voor **Oefening 11**, maar maak er nu een korte presentatie van voor een toerismebeurs. Hou een presentatie van 5 minuten over jouw land. Schrijf alleen een paar woorden of zinnen op papier. Probeer je presentatie relatief informeel te houden.

Tekst 5 Typisch Vlaams

Voormalig Antwerpse stadsdichter Tom Lanoye schrijft met een scherpe en treffende pen over Vlaanderen en zijn bewoners. Lees de volgende fragmenten uit zijn beroemde voordracht *Gespleten en Bescheten* (1997). Dit is een moeilijkere tekst omdat hij meer literair is. Je hoeft niet alle woorden te begrijpen om de tekst te begrijpen. Probeer bij een eerste lezing van deze tekst een aantal karakteristieke eigenschappen te noteren, die Lanoye de Vlaming en Vlaanderen toeschrijft. Als je de tekst beter begrijpt kan je naar de opname luisteren.

Handleiding voor buitenlanders

In Vlaanderen verschilt het culturele klimaat weinig van het atmosferische. Regenachtig, somber, onbetrouwbaar. Het archetypische prentje toont een hopeloos plat land met een bloedstollend lelijke bebouwing, elke dag zuchtend onder zware wolken die zwanger gaan van onheil en neerslachtigheid.

Plak dit prentje op de legpuzzel die België heet – een federale staat met vier regio's, drie officiële talen, tien miljoen inwoners, zes regeringen, met per hoofd van de bevolking een hogere staatschuld dan Brazilië en met meer schandalen dan Jakarta. U begrijpt meteen: dit is niet alleen een gedroomde afzetmarkt voor antidepressiva, voor donkere bieren en opknooptouwen, het is bovenal een nirwana voor schrijvers met zin voor hysterie en satire. Ik zou dan ook nergens anders willen wonen dan in mijn geboorteland.

Tom Lanoye. *Gespleten en Bescheten*, p. 71

Key vocabulary

de afzetmarkt	market
de bebouwing	buildings, housing
bloedstollend	blood curdling
bovenal	most of all
gespleten en bescheten	'split and shitty'
de handleiding	manual
de legpuzzel	jigsaw puzzle
de neerslachtigheid	depression/low spirits
onbetrouwbaar	untrustworthy
het onheil	doom, calamity
het opknooptouw	rope to hang oneself with
scherp	sharp
de staatsschuld	state debt
de stadsdichter	the city poet
toeschrijven	to attribute
de voordracht	speech
de zin voor	a sense of
zuchten	to sigh

Vragen bij tekst 5

1 Wat zegt Lanoye over de architectuur?
2 Wat vindt hij van de staatsstructuur?
3 De 'zware zwangere wolken' zijn zowel letterlijk als figuurlijk te lezen, leg uit.

4 Onderstreep de adjectieven in de tekst. Wat is het effect van deze adjectieven?
5 Lanoye gebruikt de tips voor het geven van een presentatie, kan je hiervan voorbeelden geven?

Oefening 13: Vul de woorden in

Lees de teksten eerst *zonder* en dan *met* de ingevulde woorden: wat is het verschil?

archetypische bloedstollend somber **hopeloos zware onheil**

In Vlaanderen verschilt het culturele klimaat weinig van het atmosferische. Regenachtig, ______________ , onbetrouwbaar. Het ______________ prentje toont een ______________ plat land met een ______________ lelijke bebouwing, elke dag zuchtend onder ______________ wolken die zwanger gaan van ______________ [en] neerslachtigheid.

niet alleen meteen bovenal **dan ook gedroomde donkere**

U begrijpt ______________ , dit is ______________ een ______________ afzetmarkt voor antidepressiva, voor ______________ bieren en opknooptouwen, het is ______________ een nirwana voor schrijvers met zin voor hysterie en satire. Ik zou ______________ nergens anders willen wonen dan in mijn geboorteland.

Tekst 6 Een Belg?

De Vlaamse auteur Walter van den Broeck schreef in 1980 een directe brief aan de toenmalige koning Boudewijn over de staat van zijn land. Lees de tekst en los de vragen op. Luister dan naar de opname.

> Het kan u niet ontgaan zijn dat niemand zich Belg noemt. Dat komt – daarover bestaat geen twijfel – doordat niemand zich Belg voelt. Althans niet in België. Wel in het buitenland. Maar ook dat mag niet verkeerd begrepen worden. Elders noemen wij ons zo, uit vrees dat men ons voor een Nederlander, een Fransman of – beware ons – een Duitser zal houden. Sommigen – tot wie ik mij geenszins reken – beweren zich Vlaming te voelen. Ik zal mij blijven afvragen welk deel van hun persoonlijkheid zij met die vlag bedekt weten. [. . .] Er zijn er die zich Bruggeling, Gentenaar of Antwerpenaar noemen. Hoe kleiner de groep, hoe sterker wij er ons mee verbonden voelen.

> Wij zijn wel degelijk patriotten, maar dan van een huis, een straat, een wijk, een dorp of een stad. [. . .] De grenzen van ons gemeenschappelijk *ik* – ons *wij* dus – reiken tot daar waar een ander dialekt, een andere taal wordt gesproken.
>
> Walter van den Broeck. *Brief aan Bondewijn*, pp. 279–80

Key vocabulary

aanwrijven	to blame
beware ons (God bewaar ons)	God forbid
beweren	to claim
de burgerzin	sense of public responsibility
een gebrek aan	a lack of
elders	elsewhere
geenszins	by no means
onbillijk	unfair (very formal)
ontgaan	fail to notice
reiken	to reach
uit vrees	for fear of
wel degelijk	positively
zich afvragen	to ask oneself

Vragen bij tekst 6

1. Waarom noemt geen enkele Belg zich 'Belg' volgens Van Den Broeck?
2. Wanneer doen ze dat wel en waarom?
3. Voelt Van Den Broeck zich Vlaming? Geef aan in de tekst.
4. Waaraan ontleent de gemiddelde Vlaming zijn identiteit?
5. Welke retorische middelen gebruikt Van Den Broeck, net als Lanoye, om zijn tekst ritme te geven? Luister naar de opname om het effect te beluisteren.
6. Van Den Broeck is als persoon heel sterk *aanwezig* in de tekst. Hoe komt dat?

ontlenen	derive

Oefening 14

Denk even na over jouw antwoord op de volgende vragen. Schrijf wat punten op papier. Discussieer daarna in kleine groepjes en rapporteer dan aan de hele groep over de overeenkomsten en verschillen in jullie mening.

1. Denk je dat mensen die dezelfde taal spreken ook een cultuur delen?
2. Spreek jij zelf een dialect of een andere taal thuis? Is dat belangrijk voor je?
3. Voel je je meer verbonden met je stad of dorp dan met je land? Of hangt dit af van waar je bent en met wie?

Oefening 15

Schrijf nu zelf een brief van 200 woorden aan het staatshoofd van je land over het nationalisme van je landgenoten of het gebrek daaraan. Leg uit hoe sterk de inwoners van je land zich met het land verbonden voelen en waarom dat zo is volgens jou.

Tekst 7 Het Belgische volk

Wat Vlaanderen en Wallonië verenigt is de monarchie. Dat werd duidelijk na de dood van de populaire koning Boudewijn in 1993, toen het volk massaal rouwde en het rouwregister kwam tekenen. Maar ook in België ontsnapt de monarchie niet aan de paparazzi. De toevoeging van twee 'schone' jonge schoondochters was een droom voor de roddelpers.

TEKST 7A

De laatste loodjes wegen voor Mathilde bijna niets!

Mathilde, de hoogzwangere echtgenote van de Belgische kroonprins Filip, voelde zich de afgelopen maanden zo fit en energiek dat ze weigerde verlof te nemen. Sterker nog; gedurende de afgelopen weken is ze drukker in de weer geweest dan ooit!

Overal waar ze in België verschijnt wordt de zwangere Mathilde met gejuich ontvangen. Onze zuiderburen dragen Filip's echtgenote op handen en zij wentelt zich graag in de roem en de populariteit die ze in korte tijd heeft vergaard. Mathilde heeft in de ogen van de Belgen het koningshuis weer nieuw elan gegeven en iedereen zegt dat ze Filip van een saaie en wat stille prins heeft omgetoverd in een dynamische man, die opeens veel spontaner blijkt te zijn dan men ooit had gedacht. Door de komst van Mathilde in zijn leven is hij helemaal ontdooid.

Geen zwanger-schapsverlof voor echtgenote Filip

uit: *Weekend Royalty Special* (augustus 2003)

Key vocabulary

blijken	to turn out
de echtgenote	spouse (wife)
het gejuich	cheering
hoogzwanger	heavily pregnant
in de weer zijn	to be busy
de laatste loodjes wegen het zwaarst	the last mile is the longest one
omtoveren	to change (as if by magic)
ontdooien	to defrost
ontsnappen	to escape
op handen dragen	to put on a pedestal, to adore
opeens	suddenly
de roddelpers	the gutter press
de roem	fame
rouwen	to mourn
schoon	beautiful (only used in Flanders in this meaning)
de toevoeging	the addition
verenigen	to unite
vergaren	to gather/gain
verlof nemen	to take time off
verschijnen	to appear
weigeren	to refuse
zich wentelen	to wallow
zuiderburen	*here*: the Belgians (*literally* our neighbours to the south)

Vragen bij tekst 7a

1 Wat voor beeld krijg je van Mathilde in de eerste paragraaf?

2 Geeft de tekst aan waarom Mathilde zo populair is?

3 Komt dit uit een Nederlandse of Vlaamse publicatie? Hoe weet je dat?

4 Maak een lijstje met de woorden die gebruikt worden om Mathilde en Filip te beschrijven. Wat voor beeld krijg je van ze?

Voorbeeld

Woorden om Mathilde te beschrijven

- **hoogzwanger**
- **fit en energiek**

5 Welk werkwoord (*verb*) geeft aan dat Mathilde een heel groot effect op Filip heeft gehad? En welk woord geeft Filips metamorfose weer?

6 Roepen die twee woorden naar jouw gevoel een sprookjesbeeld op? Leg uit.

TEKST 7B

In *Weekend Royalty Special* stond ook het volgende artikel over Filips broer, Laurent, die in 2003 trouwde met Claire Coombs.

'Prins Woef' is nu de populairste Belg

Hij werd de pias van het Belgische vorstenhuis genoemd en kwam regelmatig in opspraak door zijn bizarre opmerkingen. Maar sinds zijn huwelijk met de mooie Claire Coombs kan prins Laurent geen kwaad meer doen bij de Belgen.

Met Claire Coombs krijgen de Belgen een nieuw soort prinses. Net als haar Nederlandse collega's Marilène, Annette en Laurentien wil ze gewoon haar baan behouden. Claire werkt als landmeter bij de gemeente Waver en denkt er voorlopig niet aan deze baan op te zeggen. Alleen als haar representatieve functies straks te veel tijd gaan opeisen wil de prinses overwegen om te stoppen met werken. Toch is het een vreemde gedachte dat de schoondochter van een koning met meetapparatuur door de stad wandelt om eventuele veranderingen in kaart te brengen. Maar het geeft aan dat Claire een vrouw is die weet wat zij wil . . . en wat zij niet wil. En daar heeft men aan het Brusselse Hof even aan moeten wennen. Hoewel velen blij zouden zijn om met een prins te mogen trouwen, stelde Claire eisen voor haar huwelijk. Zo stond ze erop om haar meisjesnaam te behouden. Bij haar huwelijk werd ze daardoor Hare Koninklijke Hoogheid Claire Coombs, prinses van België. En voor ze haar ja-woord wilde geven eiste ze ook dat er een DNA-test zou komen om voor eens en altijd vast te stellen of Laurent al een kind had. De prins zou enkele jaren geleden een zoon verwekt hebben bij Wendy van Wanten (Vlaamse sexbom). De DNA-test, die in het diepste geheim had plaatsgevonden, wees echter uit dat de prins NIET de vader is van het kind en daardoor stond niets een huwelijk van Laurent en Claire nog in de weg. In België fluistert men overigens dat er spoedig gezinsuitbreiding te verwachten valt.

Weekend Royalty Special (augustus 2003)

Key vocabulary

aangeven	to indicate
behouden	to keep
fluisteren	to whisper
de gezinsuitbreiding	addition to the family
in het diepste geheim	in all secrecy
in opspraak komen	become the talk of the town
kwaad doen	to do harm
de landmeter	(land) surveyor
de meetapparatuur	measuring equipment
de meisjesnaam	maiden name
opeisen	to demand
overigens	by the way
overwegen	to consider
de pias	clown
plaatsvinden	to take place
uitwijzen	to reveal
vaststellen	to determine
verwekken	to father
voor eens en altijd	once and for all
het vorstenhuis	royal house
wennen aan iets	to get used to something

Vragen bij tekst 7b

1 Waarom is Claire Coombs een 'nieuw soort prinses'?
2 Vindt de auteur van dit artikel het normaal dat de prinses wil blijven werken? Welke woordjes geven dit aan?
3 Welke andere eisen stelde ze?
4 Wat is the implicatie van het zinnetje 'hoewel velen blij zouden zijn om met een prins te mogen trouwen'?
5 Wie spreekt er al over gezinsuitbreiding?
6 Wat is het ideaalbeeld van een prinses (of van een vrouw) dat naar voren komt uit deze twee artikels? Is het een traditioneel beeld of niet? Hoe komt dat, denk je?

Structuren

GEBRUIK VAN 'MEN', 'ZE' EN 'JE'

Men wordt gebruikt om over andere mensen in het algemeen te praten. Je kunt het alleen als subject gebruiken. Meestal kan **men** worden vervangen door **ze**, of door een passieve zin:

> ***Men* fluistert dat er spoedig gezinsuitbreiding komt.**
> **Er wordt gefluisterd dat er spoedig gezinsuitbreiding komt**
> ***Ze* fluisteren dat er spoedig gezinsuitbreiding komt.**

Je wordt gebruikt om algemene uitspraken te doen.

> **Het zal *je* maar overkomen, zo'n inbreker in *je* slaapkamer.**
> **Dan voel *je* je toch heel kwetsbaar, op zo'n moment.**

Met **je** creëert de spreker afstand tussen hem/haarzelf en het onderwerp, en betrekt ook de luisteraar bij het gesprek.

Oefening 16

Verander de volgende informatie in roddel. Je kan verschillende werkwoorden gebruiken (bijv. zeggen, fluisteren, vertellen, denken, vermoeden).

Voorbeeld

De eerste minister heeft een relatie met zijn secretaresse.
Men zegt dat de eerste minister een relatie met zijn secretaresse heeft.

Er wordt gezegd dat de eerste minister een relatie met zijn secretaresse heeft.
Ze zeggen dat de eerste minister een relatie met zijn secretaresse heeft.

1 De nieuwe vriendin van de prins is zwanger.
2 David Beckham heeft zijn vrouw meermaals bedrogen.
3 De actrice heeft zich met haar minnaar verzoend.
4 Michael Jackson heeft jonge kinderen misbruikt.
5 Die topatleet gebruikt pepmiddelen.
6 De minister van Defensie heeft geld gekregen van wapenhandelaren.

roddel	gossip

Oefening 17: Roddelkwartiertje

Zoek op de website van her roddelblad *Story* (www.story.nl) enkele roddels op. Vertel die dan aan je medestudenten.

Oefening 18

Schrijf een tekstje over een beroemdheid naar keuze voor een roddelblad en gebruik enkele van de volgende woorden en uitdrukkingen. (Je kunt op www.story.nl inspiratie opdoen.)

op handen dragen   geen kwaad meer doen   populariteit vergaren   met gejuich ontvangen   zich in de roem wentelen   in opspraak komen   in de weer zijn   blijken   in het diepste geheim

Oefening 19

Werk in groepjes. Schrijf met elkaar een sprookje over een prinses. Je kunt zelf beslissen of het een sprookje voor kinderen of voor volwassenen is. Bespreek wat volgens jullie de typische elementen van een sprookje zijn. Brainstorm dan met elkaar waar jullie sprookje over gaat. Schrijf dan het sprookje op.

Sprookjes beginnen met : *'Er was eens . . .'* .
en eindigen met: *'En ze leefden nog lang en gelukkig.'*

Oefening 20

Maak nu samen met je groepje een luisterspel van je sprookje. Je moet beslissen in hoeverre je in je luisterspel gebruik maakt van dialogen en/of van een verteller. Je kunt je sprookje opvoeren of op een bandje opnemen, zodat de rest van de klas het kan beluisteren.

het bandje	tape	**opnemen**	to record
een luisterspel	radio play	**opvoeren**	to perform

Tekst 8 Julius Caesar en de Belgen

Sinds de onafhankelijkheid van België (1830) leren alle Belgische schoolkinderen op school dat Caesar in zijn *De Bello Gallico* (=over de Gallische oorlog) schreef dat de Belgen de dappersten onder de Galliërs waren. De filosoof en historicus Baudouin Decharneux schreef hierover de volgende kritische noot:

De eerste bladzijde van De Bello Gallico is overbekend. Caesar schetst er de geopolitieke situatie van Gallië en noemt de Belgen het moedigste volk in dit uitgestrekte gebied. Een dergelijke vleiende voorstelling van het 'Belgische volk' deed de historici van het piepjonge België – zij het ten onrechte – glimmen van trots. Ze vonden in de woorden van de Romeinse generaal een orakel om de onafhankelijkheid van België te legitimeren.

Maar Caesars woorden moeten begrepen worden in een breder kader. In zijn ogen heeft de heldenmoed van de Belgen allereerst te maken met de grote afstand tussen hun woongebied en Rome. Daardoor worden de veroverde gebieden barbaarser en vreemder. De 'heldenmoed' van de Belgen is een onderdeel van hun barbaarsheid. Caesar, die met zijn *De Bello Gallico* politieke bedoelingen heeft, vindt hierin een zeer dankbaar argument om zijn overwinning nog waardevoller te maken.

Dat de Belgen geduchte strijders zijn, heeft dus alles te maken met de geografische ligging van hun woongebied, ten noorden begrensd door de Rijn, ten zuiden door de Seine en Marne en van noord naar zuid door de Maas; die grenzen houden trouwens geen enkel verband met de Belgische grenzen van na 1830.

(naar: Anne Morelli (red.): *De grote mythen uit de geschiedenis van België, Vlaanderen en Wallonië*, pp. 25–6)

Key vocabulary

dergelijk	such (a)	**de trots**	pride
geducht	fearsome	**uitgestrekt**	vast
de heldenmoed	heroic courage	**verband houden met**	to have a connection with
de overwinning	victory	**veroveren**	to conquer
piepjong	very young	**vleiend**	flattering
de Rijn, Seine, Marne, Maas	[rivers]	**het volk**	people
de strijder	warrior		

Vragen bij tekst 8

1 Waarom glommen de historici 'ten onrechte' van trots?
2 Waarom waren Caesars woorden een 'orakel'?
3 Wie is het publiek van deze tekst ? (Wie kent hem, die 'overbekende' eerste regel?)

4 De auteur verwacht voorkennis van de lezer. Welke dingen moet je weten om de tekst goed te kunnen begrijpen? (Welke dingen zijn voor jou onduidelijk?)
5 De auteur gebruikt aanhalingstekens (*inverted commas*) bij sommige woorden. Waarom?

Oefening 21

Zijn er in jouw land/cultuur ook verhalen die erg opgeklopt worden of uit hun context gehaald om een nationaal gevoel te versterken? Zoek er iets over op en bereid een presentatie voor van 5 minuten, waarin je kritisch kijkt naar dit soort 'mythische verhalen'.

Je publiek zijn je medestudenten, je doel is om hen te doen nadenken.

opkloppen to stir up

Cultuur

DE STRIPCULTUUR

Comic books are very popular in Belgium and the Netherlands and not only with children. Adults often collect old editions and buy new hardcover versions. The most famous Belgian comic book hero is Tintin ('Kuifje' in Dutch), drawn by Hergé (George Remy, 1907–83). Look on www.strips.be for web links about comics. For a taste of a very Dutch comic phenomenon, visit www.doorzon.nl, the site of a Dutch comic about a supposedly average Dutch family.

HET SURREALISME

An American living in Brussels once famously remarked that the surrealism of Belgian painters such as René Magritte (1898–1967) and Paul Delvaux (1897–1994) is in fact the daily reality of life in Belgium. The complicated state structure can lead to surreal situations. For example, different parts of one particular road may be the responsibility of the communal, provincial and federal authorities, which can turn road works into an administrative and organisational nightmare.

Belgian humour as a consequence can be equally absurd. A good example is the popular cartoonist Kamagurka, who daily publishes a cartoon on his website (www.kamagurka.com) and is an illustrator in the popular news weekly *Humo* (www.humo.be).

Structuren

DIRECT AND INDIRECT OBJECT

The *indirect object normally precedes the direct object* in a sentence, unless the direct object is a pronoun. The latter is the case in examples 3 and 4 below. Compare the examples. (The indirect object is in italic, the direct object is underlined.)

1 **Caesar vertelt *zijn senatoren in Rome* dat de Belgen dappere strijders zijn.**

2 **Caesar vertelt *hen* dat de Belgen dappere strijders zijn.**

3 **Caesar vertelt het *zijn senatoren* in Rome.**

4 **Caesar vertelt het *hen*.**

As you can see, the indirect and direct object pronouns always immediately follow the finite verb of the sentence.

NB: Please note that the order of the pronouns may vary in spoken language.

Oefening 22

Geef een antwoord op de volgende vragen en vervang het cursieve (*italics*) deel door een pronomen, 'pronoun'.

Voorbeeld

Vraag jij Karel of hij morgen *wijn* meebrengt?
Ja, ik zal *het* Karel vragen.

1 Vraag jij *Karel* of hij morgen *wijn* meebrengt?
2 Geef jij *Sandra* elke week bloemen?
3 Geef jij Sandra elke week *bloemen*?
4 Stuur jij de gemeente snel *een antwoord*?
5 Stuur jij *de gemeente* snel een antwoord?
6 Stuur jij *de gemeente* snel *een antwoord*?
7 Heeft de dief *de oude man* met een mes bedreigd?
8 Heb jij *de buurvrouw* gisteren dat gekke verhaal verteld?
9 Heb jij de buurvrouw gisteren *dat gekke verhaal* verteld?
10 Heb jij *de buurvrouw* gisteren *dat gekke verhaal* verteld?

Tekst 9 Het Vlaamse Nederlands

Drie verschillende visies op de taal die de Vlamingen spreken: van een Engelse historica, van een Nederlands literair auteur en van een Vlaams journalist.

TEKST 9A

Patricia Carson (ENG) (historica)

Boven de taalgrens ligt dus het Nederlandstalige Vlaanderen. De officiële taal is er dezelfde als in het Koninkrijk der Nederlanden. Vlaanderen en Nederland gebruiken hetzelfde woordenboek. Het Nederlands dat in Vlaanderen wordt gesproken vertoont, in hoofdzaak onder de invloed van het naburige Frankrijk, wel een aantal eigenaardigheden. Daarnaast leven in Vlaanderen ook veel verschillende dialecten. Die komen in het algemeen niet voor in een geschreven vorm, al zie je af en toe wel eens een dialectwoord geschreven staan, zoals een Schots woord in Engeland. De dialecten verschillen sterk van streek tot streek. [. . .] Zijn eigen taal is de Vlaming erg dierbaar. Dat komt omdat hij de hele geschiedenis door voor zijn taal heeft moeten vechten. Iemand die uit een land komt waar slechts één taal gesproken wordt, kan dat vaak moeilijk begrijpen. Een Engelsman vindt het vanzelfsprekend dat iedereen hem, tenminste in zijn eigen land, begrijpt en hij kan zich moeilijk voorstellen dat iemand die in zijn eigen hoofdstad zijn eigen taal spreekt, niet begrepen wordt. Toch kan dat in Brussel iedere Vlaming overkomen.

Patricia Carson. *Het fraaie gelaat van Vlaanderen*, p. 9

Key vocabulary

dierbaar	precious	**naburig**	neighbouring
de eigenaardigheid	peculiarity	**overkomen**	happen to
in hoofdzaak	mainly	**vanzelfsprekend**	obvious

Vragen bij tekst 9a (Carson)

1 Is volgens Carson de taal in Nederland en Vlaanderen hetzelfde?

2 Waarom is zijn taal voor de Vlaming zo belangrijk?

3 Waarom is dat soms moeilijk te begrijpen voor eentalige buitenlanders?

4 De auteur gaat voorzichtig om met gevoelige punten voor Vlamingen zoals:

   a de eeuwenlange onderdrukking door de Fransen en de Franstalige gemeenschap;

b de verschillen tussen de taal in Vlaanderen en in Nederland, waarbij het Nederlands van de Vlamingen vaak als 'afwijkend' en 'fout' wordt voorgesteld.

Kan je in hier in de tekst een voorbeeld van geven?

TEKST 9B

W.F. Hermans (NL) (literair auteur)

In Nederland spreken we – die veertien miljoen – een homogene taal. Daarnaast zijn er nog zes miljoen mensen die ook Nederlands spreken, maar dan in dertig dialecten. Vlamingen willen een eigen taal. Daar schiet je niets mee op. Ze doen het alleen maar om zich te bewijzen ten opzichte van de Walen. De Vlaamse inbreng in het Nederlands bestaat uit Franse woorden of uit met Franse woorden gemengde taal, maar dan in een soort Duitse spelling.

Willem Frederik Hermans, in een televisie-interview

Key vocabulary

ergens mee opschieten	to get somewhere	**de inbreng**	contribution
gemengd	mixed	**ten opzichte van**	with regard to

NB: The population of the Netherlands has now reached 16 million.

Vragen bij tekst 9b (Hermans)

1 Zijn er in Nederland dialecten volgens Hermans?
2 En in België?
3 Waarom willen de Vlamingen een eigen taal?
4 Wat zijn de elementen van 'het Vlaams' volgens hem?
5 Hermans werkt met het contrast tussen het 'pure' Nederlands en het 'onzuivere' Vlaams. Geef in de tabel woorden uit de tekst die het Nederlands en Vlaams karakteriseren.

Nederlands	Vlaams

TEKST 9C

Steven De Foer (VL) (journalist)

Vergelijk de taal met een fiets. De Vlaming is het kind dat pas op late leeftijd een fiets gekregen heeft. Hij is er zo blij mee dat hij hem alle dagen poetst, de reflectoren controleert en de bel doet blinken. Maar op straat blijft hij onzeker rijden en angstig om zich heen kijken, want een ongeluk zit in een klein hoekje. De Nederlander is een zorgeloze tiener, die al sinds zijn kleutertijd de wijk onveilig maakt en met gemak op één wiel kan rijden. Zijn remmen zijn versleten en zijn achterlicht is kapot, maar wat maakt het uit? Hij redt zich wel als het er opaan komt.

[. . .]

Nederlanders twijfelen er geen moment aan dat zij de taalnorm zijn, ook al wemelt die norm van de inconsequenties. De ene keer vervangen ze een buitenlands leenwoord door een eigen neologisme ('tosti' in plaats van 'croque monsieur', 'kabinetsperiode' in plaats van 'legislatuur'); de andere keer slaan ze zich op de knieën van de pret met die Vlamingen en hun 'fruitsap', hun 'haardroger' en hun 'duimspijker', omdat het natuurlijk 'jus d'orange', 'föhn' en 'punaise' moet zijn. Overigens hebben Nederlanders de neiging het gebruik van purismen zoals duimspijker in Vlaanderen te overschatten. Vlamingen spreken normaal ook van punaise. Maar omdat dit een Frans woord is, denken ze vaak dat het typisch Belgisch is en dan gaan ze om keurig te doen – zeker in een gesprek met Nederlanders – hypercorrigeren en duimspijker zeggen.

Steven De Foer. *Onder Hollanders, een Vlaming ontdekt Nederland*, p. 133

Key vocabulary

blinken	to shine	**de rem**	brake
de inconsequentie	inconsistency	**vergelijken**	to compare
keurig	proper	**verslijten**	to wear out
de kleutertijd	toddler/pre-school age-group	**vervangen**	to replace
overschatten	overestimate	**wemelen van**	to be swarming with
de pret	joy	**zorgeloos**	carefree

Vragen bij tekst 9c (De Foer)

1 In de eerste paragraaf beschrijft De Foer de typische Vlaming en Nederlander als kinderen. Verzin zelf voor elk 3 adjectieven om het kind te beschrijven.

2 Waarom zijn de Nederlanders niet consequent?

3 In de eerste paragraaf typeert De Foer Vlamingen 'onzeker' en 'angstig'. Welk voorbeeld uit de tweede paragraaf illustreert dit?

4 Vind je de fietsmetafoor van De Foer duidelijk? Zit er ook een waardeoordeel aan deze metafoor vast? Zo ja, welk?

het waardeoordeel value judgement

A closer look

De volgende twee artikels gaan over een IQ test afgenomen onder Nederlandse en Vlaamse kinderen. De ene tekst komt uit een Nederlandse krant (*NRC Handelsblad*), de andere uit een Belgische (*De Standaard*).

Kan jij zien welke tekst uit welke krant komt?

Hollands kind dommer dan Vlaams

Vlaamse kinderen scoren veel beter op intelligentietest dan Nederlandse.

Amsterdam, 19 juni. Zijn Vlaamse kinderen slimmer dan Nederlandse? Of zijn de scholen in Vlaanderen beter? Zeker is dat de Vlaamse kinderen beter scoren op een mondiaal gebruikte intelligentietest.

[. . .]

Bij het uitproberen van de test bleek dat de Vlaamse kinderen over een grotere woordenschat beschikken. Een moeilijk woord als 'mecenas' kent zes procent van de Vlaamse kinderen. Geen enkel Nederlands kind kent het.

Van de dertien testonderdelen is er maar een waarop de Nederlandse kinderen beter scoren: 'doolhoven'. Volgens de onderzoekers kan dat te maken hebben met de grote verstedelijking van Nederland. Er is ook een testonderdeel waarop de Nederlandse kinderen bijna even goed scoren als de Vlaamse. Dat is het onderdeel 'begrijpen', met vragen als 'waarom hebben we parlementsleden?'. De Vlaamse kinderen beantwoordden dit soort vragen alleen als ze het zeker wisten. Zoniet, dan gaven ze geen antwoord en kregen dus ook geen punt. De Nederlandse kinderen gaven ook antwoord als ze het maar half wisten.

De onderzoekers schrijven dit soort verschillen toe aan de wederzijdse schoolsystemen. 'Het lesprogramma op Vlaamse scholen is meer gericht op het verwerven van kennis. Nederlandse kinderen woren gestimuleerd om hun mening te geven. Ze zijn mondiger.'

Vlaamse kinderen scoren beter op IQ test

Gent. Vlaamse kinderen scoren beter dan Nederlandse op de nieuwe IQ-test die vanaf volgend schooljaar in omloop komt. Meisjes doen het even goed als jongens. Allochtone kinderen doen het enkel slechter als hun ouders tot de eerste generatie behoren of laaggeschoold zijn.

[. . .]

Uit vooronderzoek blijkt dat Vlaamse kinderen duidelijk beter scoren dan de Nederlandse. Ze doen het bij nagenoeg elke subtest beter. Bij kennisvragen blijkt bijvoorbeeld dat tweemaal zoveel Vlaamse kinderen weten in welke richting de zon ondergaat. Vlaamse kinderen beschikken over een grotere woordenschat, kunnen beter spellen en rekenen en doen het beter bij overeenkomsten.

Maar in doolhoftests doen ze het minder goed. En er gaat ook een opvallend verschil schuil achter de gelijke resultaten voor de test 'Begrijpen'. Vlaamse kinderen die een begrip moeten uitleggen, zeggen ofwel dat ze dat niet kunnen/kennen, of ze geven een perfect antwoord. Nederlandse kinderen praten veel meer, ook als ze niet zo zeker zijn.

'Concludeer daar niet uit dat Vlaamse kinderen "slimmer" zijn', zegt de Gentse hoogleraar, 'een intelligentiequotiënt is slechts het resultaat van een test, en die test blijft sterk verbonden met het onderwijs. In die zin kunnen we uit deze verschillen vooral conclusies trekken over het onderwijsniveau in beide landen. Ons systeem is duidelijk effectiever.'

Key vocabulary

behoren	to belong	**overeenkomsten**	similarities
het doolhof	maze	**schuilgaan achter**	to hide behind
gericht op	aimed at	**toeschrijven aan**	to attribute to
in omloop komen	to be introduced	**verbinden met**	to relate to
laaggeschoold	lower educated	**de verstedelijking**	urbanisation
het lesprogramma	curriculum	**verwerven**	to acquire
mondig	articulate	**het vooronderzoek**	preliminary research
nagenoeg	nearly	**wederzijds**	mutual
het onderwijsniveau	level of education	**zoniet**	if not

***Vragen bij* A closer look**

1 Welk artikel komt uit welke krant? Waarom denk je dat?

2 Kijk naar de titels. Welke titel geeft informatie, welke een waardeoordeel?

3 Vergelijk de verklaring die beide kranten geven voor de bijna gelijke score bij het onderdeel 'begrijpen'. Zit er een waardeoordeel in?

4 Hoe geven beide artikels de volgende feiten weer? Als feit of als interpretatie?

FEIT	INTERPRETATIE *NRC Handelsblad* (NL)	INTERPRETATIE *De Standaard* (VL)
Vlaamse kinderen scoren beter op IQ test	interpretatie: Nederlandse kinderen zijn dommer	feit: Vlaamse kinderen scoren beter. (De krant waarschuwt dat de lezer niet mag concluderen dat Vlaamse kinderen slimmer zijn.)
Vlaamse kinderen hebben een grotere woordenschat		
Nederlandse kinderen scoren beter op doolhoven		
Bijna gelijke score op 'begrijpen'		
Verschil in onderwijsprogramma		

5 Kijk naar de distributie van het 'goede' en het 'slechte' nieuws in beide teksten. Vind je de Vlaamse tekst triomfantelijk en de Nederlandse geschokt?

6 Lees de slotparagraaf van beide teksten. Wat is de conclusie van elk?

7 Wat is de functie van die laatste paragraaf voor de lezers?

8 Denk je dat de verschillen tussen deze twee teksten cultureel te verklaren zijn?

Unit 11
Nederland in beweging

This unit focuses on current political and social affairs in the Netherlands. We will look at various public debates taking place, and how different viewpoints shape the language people use in presenting their ideas. You will see examples of different strategies for presenting ideas, including humour. We will also take another look at making texts more coherent, by practising writing texts for different contexts. This unit also includes various revision exercises and a self-evaluation.

TOPICS

- Current debates in Dutch society
- Role of the Netherlands in the world
- Individualism *vs* collectivism
- Dutch attitudes towards Islam
- Norms and values
- Humour
- Fixed expressions
- Abbreviations
- Political parties in the Netherlands
- Revision
- Self evaluation

FUNCTIONS

- Strategies for presenting ideas
- Making texts more cohesive
- Writing for different contexts
- Recognising how a different point of view affects language use
- Using humour as a writing strategy
- Using exclamations
- Recognising main points in a text
- Recognising subjectivity in seemingly objective statements

GRAMMAR

- Linking clauses: adverbs
- Topic – comment
- Ellipsis
- Relative pronouns: **wie/wat**
- Word order amongst verbs in final position
- **Lijken/schijnen/blijken**
- Punctuation
- Revision: tenses, prepositions, **zou**, verb/subject agreement, passive voice, relative pronouns (**die/dat/wie/wat**), relative pronouns with a preposition

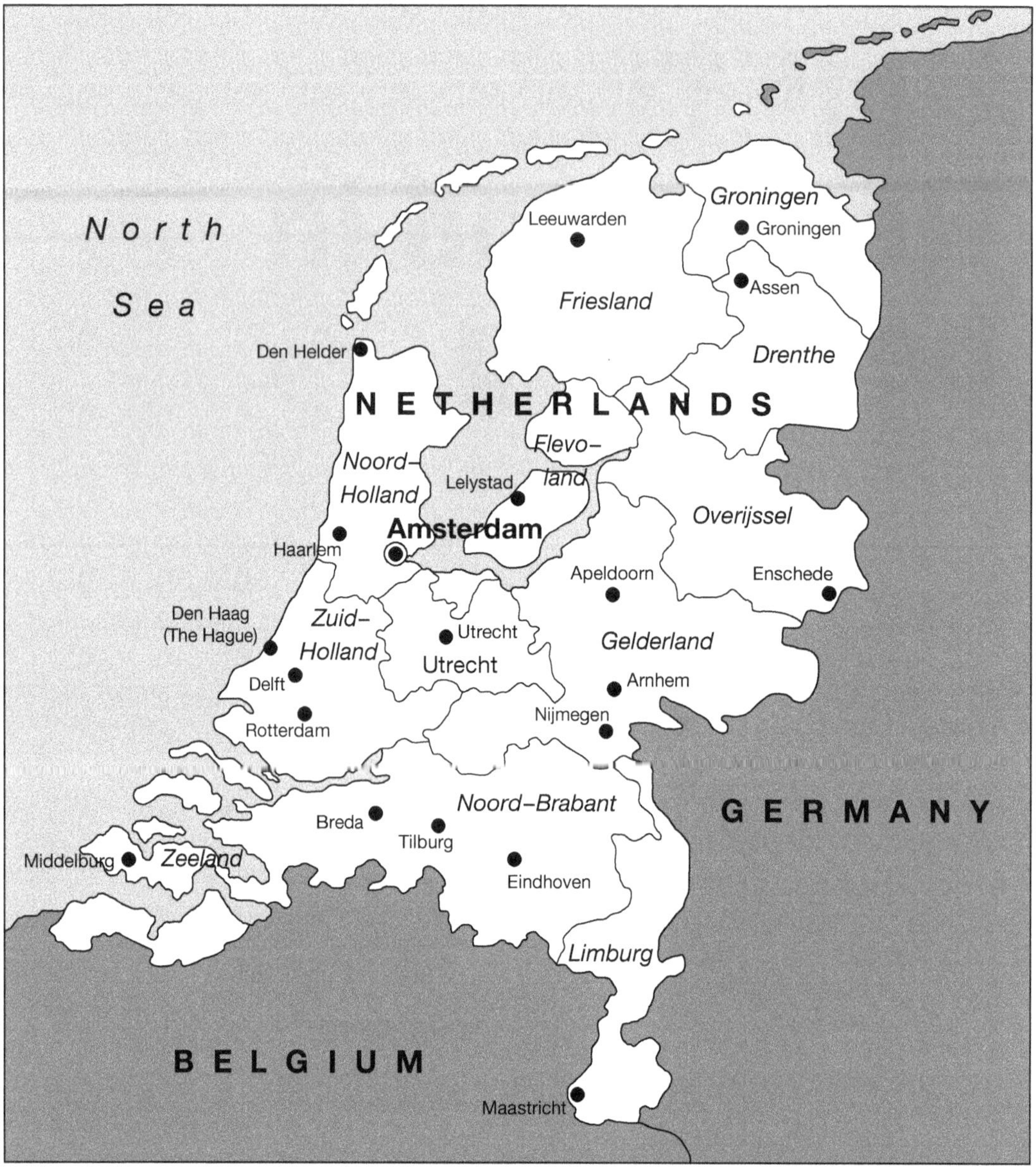
North
Sea
Groningen
Groningen
Leeuwarden
Assen
Friesland
Drenthe
Den Helder
NETHERLANDS
Flevo-
land
Noord-
Holland
Lelystad
Overijssel
Amsterdam
Haarlem
Apeldoorn
Enschede
Den Haag
(The Hague)
Zuid-
Holland
Utrecht
Utrecht
Gelderland
Delft
Arnhem
Rotterdam
Nijmegen
Noord-Brabant
GERMANY
Breda
Tilburg
Middelburg
Zeeland
Eindhoven
Limburg
BELGIUM
Maastricht

Tekst 1

De onderstaande tekst is gericht op scholieren die een project doen over de rol van Nederland in de wereld. Het is een informatieve tekst over hoe Nederland zijn eigen rol in de wereld ziet. Lees de tekst en beantwoord dan de vragen.

Nederland ziet zichzelf graag als voorbeeld voor de rest van de wereld. Wij laten ons immers leiden door het verstand, en niet door emotie. En al helemaal niet door grootheidswaan of nationalisme, zoals veel grote landen. Daarom speelt Nederland graag een belangrijke rol bij internationale ontwikkelingen.

In Irak en Afghanistan waren wij er vroeg bij. Net als bij de oprichting van de Europese Gemeenschap, de NAVO en de Verenigde Naties. En niet voor niets staat het Internationaal Gerechtshof in Den Haag, net als het Joegoslavië Tribunaal. Ook op het gebied van ontwikkelingshulp, zorg voor milieu en drugsbeleid geven wij het goede voorbeeld aan de rest van de wereld. Tenminste, dat vinden wij zelf. Andere landen zijn het daar natuurlijk niet altijd mee eens.

Deze voorbeeldrol, al dan niet ingebeeld, heeft een naam: Nederland Gidsland. Het kleine Nederland wijst de weg door ingewikkelde problemen. Dit is een lange traditie. Die heeft te maken met onze geschiedenis. Heel even, tijdens de Gouden Eeuw (zeventiende eeuw), was Nederland het machtigste land ter wereld. Daarna namen de grote Europese landen de macht snel weer in handen.

Nederland moest op zoek naar iets anders waar het groot in was. En dat was juist ons kleine formaat. Niet in militaire macht, maar juist in neutraliteit lag de Nederlandse kracht. Wij hadden geen grote machtsambities, en waren dus betrouwbaar. En omdat we een groots verleden hebben, zijn we toch gerespecteerd. En zo ontstond het idee van Nederland Gidsland.

van: www.anno.nl 1/7/04 (website over Nederlandse geschiedenis voor scholieren)

Key vocabulary

al dan niet	whether or not
betrouwbaar	reliable
er vroeg bij zijn	be/join quickly or early on
het formaat	size
het gerechtshof	court of justice
de gids	guide
de grootheidswaan	megalomania
groots	great, grand
heeft te maken met	is related to
heel even	for a very short period of time
immers	after all
ingebeeld	imagined
de machtsambities	ambitions for power
de NAVO	NATO
net als	just like
de ontwikkelingshulp	development aid
de oprichting	foundation
de Verenigde Naties	United Nations
het verstand	the mind

Oefening 1: Vragen

1 Waarom speelt Nederland graag een belangrijke rol bij internationale ontwikkelingen volgens de tekst?

2 Geef voorbeelden die aangeven dat Nederland een voorbeeldrol heeft in de wereld.

3 Onderstreep de zin in alinea 3 die een definitie geeft van het begrip 'Nederland Gidsland'.

4 In de laatste alinea zie je drie paren van tegenstellingen:

a Nederland is groot in – ons kleine formaat
b niet in militaire macht – maar juist in neutraliteit
c geen grote machtsambities – dus betrouwbaar

5 De eerste twee tegenstellingen zijn observeringen, maar de derde tegenstelling is een veel subjectievere mening. Vind je de redenering 'als je geen machtsambities hebt, ben je betrouwbaar' logisch? Waarom wel/niet?

6 De tekst verbindt het respect voor Nederland met 'een groots verleden'. Denk je dat andere landen zich bewust zijn van het 'grote' verleden van Nederland?

Oefening 2

Waarom is de zeventiende eeuw de 'gouden eeuw' voor Nederland? Zoek op Nederlandse internetpagina's naar tien dingen die de zeventiende eeuw 'groot' maakten voor Nederland (zoek bijvoorbeeld op 'gouden eeuw Nederland'). Een voorbeeld is: schilderkunst.

Structuren

PAST TENSES: REVISION

Kijk naar het volgende fragment uit de tekst en beantwoord de vragen.

> **Heel even, tijdens de Gouden Eeuw (zeventiende eeuw), was Nederland het machtigste land ter wereld. Daarna namen de grote Europese landen de macht snel weer in handen. Nederland moest op zoek naar iets anders waar het groot in was. En dat was juist ons kleine formaat. Niet in militaire macht, maar juist in neutraliteit lag de Nederlandse kracht.**

Vragen bij structuren

1 Which tense is used throughout?
2 Explain how this tense is formed with regular verbs.
3 Give the singular and plural forms for this tense for the following irregular verbs:

	singular	*plural*
zijn		
hebben		
gaan		
kunnen		
zeggen		
kopen		
schrijven		
worden		

PREPOSITIONS

Look at these prepositions from the text.

Het Internationaal Gerechtshof staat *in* Den Haag.
Wij laten ons immers leiden *door* het verstand.
Nederland speelt graag een rol *bij* internationale ontwikkelingen.
***Op* het gebied van milieu geven wij het goede voorbeeld *aan* de rest van de wereld.**

Because prepositions determine the relationships between things, it is important to use the right ones. However, prepositions are difficult to translate. They have a literal meaning, but often the way in which a preposition is used depends on the context. For instance, certain verbs or expressions combine with a specific preposition. These can be found in the dictionary under the verb, and are best learned by heart. Examples from the text:

zich laten leiden door	to be led by
een rol spelen bij	to play a part in
het goede voorbeeld geven aan	to set a good example for

Oefening 3

Wat betekenen de volgende uitdrukkingen?

1 jaloers zijn op
2 iemand betrekken bij
3 zich vergissen in
4 bewondering hebben voor
5 goedkeuring geven aan
6 zich aansluiten bij
7 voorkeur geven aan

Oefening 4

Vul de juiste prepositie in.

1 Gefeliciteerd ______ je verjaardag.
2 Hij had een voorkeur ______ de kleur rood.
3 Hij stortte zich volledig ______ zijn werk.
4 Ze voelde zich niet betrokken ______ de groep.
5 Hij viel ______ door zijn taalgebruik.
6 Laten we beginnen ______ het begin.
7 Hij was erg nauw betrokken ______ de bouw van zijn huis.
8 De groep had al eerder opgetreden ______ deze gasten.

Communicatie

LINKING CLAUSES: ADVERBS

You can give a text greater cohesive structure by linking various sentence parts together. You can use adverbs, for instance, to link clauses. (See also Unit 9)

Nederland laat zich niet leiden door nationalisme, *daarom* speelt Nederland graag een rol bij internationale ontwikkelingen.

Heel even was Nederland het machtigste land ter wereld. *Daarna* namen de grote landen de macht snel weer in handen.

Note that, whether preceded by a full stop or a comma, inversion occurs after these adverbs. With some other adverbs inversion does not take place.

Nederland ziet zichzelf als voorbeeld. *Immers*, wij laten ons leiden door het verstand.

Wij geven het goede voorbeeld. *Tenminste*, dat vinden wij zelf.

Oefening 5

Hieronder zie je informatie over de gemeente Alkmaar. Vul de gaten in met een van de volgende woorden.

althans daarmee daarnaast dan ook tenminste terwijl

Volgens de meest recente cijfers van het Centraal Bureau voor de Statistiek rijden er 34.000 auto's rond in Alkmaar. 1 ________ worden de wegen bevolkt met 4600 bedrijfsauto's en 2300 motoren. Per 1000 inwoners telt Alkmaar bijna 400 personenauto's. 2 _________ scoort Alkmaar landelijk gezien 3 _________ helemaal niet hoog.

Het gaat goed met theater De Vest. Het aantal bezoekers stijgt licht. In 2002 waren het er bijna 98.500. En dat 4 _________ het aantal voorstellingen enigszins was gedaald.

De Grote Sint Laurenskerk raakt steeds meer in trek als cultureel centrum, 5 _________ als je op het absolute aantal bezoekers afgaat: 2407. Dat waren er bijna 300 meer dan het jaar daarvoor. Het gemiddelde aantal bezoekers per voorstelling lag vorig jaar op 300, 50 minder dan het jaar daarvoor, maar er waren 6 _________ meer voorstellingen.

De Alkmaarder loopt niet warm voor de verkiezingen. 7 _________ wanneer het om de verkiezingen van de gemeenteraad gaat. Dan komt niet meer dan 55,4 procent naar de stembus. De opkomst bij de kamerverkiezingen is 78,6 procent.

afgaan op	to go by
de bedrijfsauto	company car
bevolken	populate
de bezoeker	visitor
dalen	to go down, decrease
enigszins	somewhat, a little
de gemeenteraad	local council
in trek	popular, in demand
de kamerverkiezingen	general elections
de opkomst	turnout
de personenauto	private car
de stembus	ballot box, poll(s)
stijgen	go up; to increase
tellen	to number, consist of
de verkiezingen	elections
de voorstelling	performance
warm lopen voor	take to/feel enthusiasm for (something)

Oefening 6

Combineer de volgende zinnen. Gebruik een van de volgende woorden.

daarom	**immers**	**althans**	**tenminste**	**dus**	**daarna**

Voorbeeld

Ik ben gek op het strand. Als het niet regent.
Ik ben gek op het strand. Tenminste, als het niet regent.

1 We hebben 's ochtends vergaderd. We hebben geluncht.
2 Het regende hard. We namen een paraplu mee.
3 Hij moet wel rijk zijn. Zijn hele familie is erg rijk.
4 Ze is een jonge vrouw. Ze ziet er jong uit.
5 Zij gaan skiën. Als er genoeg sneeuw ligt.
6 Het was erg druk. Ze moesten lang wachten voordat ze werden geholpen.
7 Hij had een kaartje voor de show. Hij mocht naar binnen.
8 We moeten hier niet te lang blijven zitten. We willen vanavond nog de camping bereiken.

Oefening 7: Woordenschat

Vul de volgende woorden op de juiste plaats in.

al dan niet	**betrouwbaar**	**eens**	**gebied**	**groots**	**immers**
ingewikkelde	**machtigste**	**met**	**milieu**	**neutraliteit**	**niet voor niets**
ontstond	**ontwikkelingen**	**op zoek**	**oprichting**	**voorbeeld**	**zoals**

Nederland ziet zichzelf graag als 1 ______________ voor de rest van de wereld. Wij laten ons 2 ______________ leiden door het verstand, en niet door emotie. En al helemaal niet door grootheidswaan of nationalisme, 3 ______________ veel grote landen. Daarom speelt Nederland graag een belangrijke rol bij internationale 4 ______________ .

In Irak en Afghanistan waren wij er vroeg bij. Net als bij de 5 ______________ van de Europese Gemeenschap, de NAVO en de Verenigde Naties. En 6 ______________ staat het Internationaal Gerechtshof in Den Haag, net als het Joegoslavië Tribunaal. Ook op het 7 ______________ van ontwikkelingshulp, zorg voor 8 ______________ en drugsbeleid geven wij het goede voorbeeld aan de rest van de wereld. Tenminste, dat vinden wij zelf. Andere landen zijn het daar natuurlijk niet altijd mee 9 ______________ .

Deze voorbeeldrol, 10 ______________ ingebeeld, heeft een naam: Nederland Gidsland. Het kleine Nederland wijst de weg door 11 ______________ problemen. Dit is een lange traditie. Die heeft te maken 12 ______________ onze geschiedenis. Heel even, tijdens de Gouden Eeuw (zeventiende eeuw), was Nederland het 13 ______________ land ter wereld. Daarna namen de grote Europese landen de macht snel weer in handen.

Nederland moest 14 ______________ naar iets anders waar het groot in was. En dat was juist ons kleine formaat. Niet in militaire macht, maar juist in 15 ______________ lag de Nederlandse kracht. Wij hadden geen grote machtsambities, en waren dus 16 ______________ . En omdat we een 17 ______________ verleden hebben, zijn we toch gerespecteerd. En zo 18 ______________ het idee van Nederland Gidsland.

Tekst 2

De volgende tekst gaat ook over de rol van Nederland in de wereld. Echter, deze tekst is geschreven voor studenten (de tekst komt van een website voor en door studenten) en is veel kritischer over de Nederlandse visie.

Kijken we naar Nederland dan zien we een aantal historische misverstanden die blijven bestaan. Zo zouden wij dat dappere volkje zijn die eerst de Spanjaarden een showdown gaven en vervolgens de Fransen uit ons moeraslandje hebben geknikkerd.

Daar klopt natuurlijk helemaal niets van. Wapens verkopen dat ging nog wel (aan Spanje en Frankrijk), of negers verschepen, daar hadden we ook wel aanleg voor, maar vrijheidsstrijders waren we niet bepaald. Het is enkel en alleen dankzij Engeland dat wij nu goede sier kunnen maken met ons progressieve drugsbeleid, onze zogenaamde tolerante volksaard en die lachwekkende kreet: Nederland Gidsland.

Waarom bestaat Nederland eigenlijk? Het antwoord daarop luidt kort: Engeland. Vanaf Willem III tot aan de Eerste wereldoorlog had Engeland als politiek dat de Lage Landen niet in handen mochten vallen van een continentale grootmacht. Omdat een land dat sterk genoeg was om het continent te veroveren tenslotte ook Engeland kon innemen. Laat ze in Nederland maar bloemschikken, blowtjes roken, spulletjes verkopen en spelletjes spelen; dan hebben wij ondertussen een mooie buffer tegen invasies uit Frankrijk (onbetrouwbaar) en Duitsland (expansieve driftkikkers).

Dat deden we dan ook. Binnen de kortste keren was Nederland het Drenthe van Europa en die positie hebben we niet meer prijsgegeven. Als er een top plaatsvindt in New York en er wordt een foto genomen dan staat Kok helemaal achteraan. Nog mazzel dat hij 2.93 meter is.

Wie stopte als laatste land ter wereld met het verschepen van negers? Nederland Gidsland.

Waar zijn relatief de meeste Joden overgedragen? Nederland Gidsland.

Wie heeft de eer de laatste echte koloniale oorlog te hebben gevochten? Nederland Gidsland.

Waar laat de pers terroristen uitgebreid aan het woord, alsof het een theekransje betreft? Nederland Gidsland.

Srebrenica? Laat maar. Nederland Gidsland.

van: R. van Rijswijk, www.propriacures.nl

Key vocabulary

aanleg hebben voor	have a talent for
het antwoord luidt	the answer is
binnen de kortste keren	in no time
bloemschikken	flower arranging
blowtje	joint
dan ook	therefore, not surprisingly
dapper	brave
dat ging nog wel	we managed (more or less)
Drenthe	a province of the Netherlands, traditionally consisting of rural communities
de driftkikker	hothead
een showdown geven	to defeat
enkel en alleen	only
goede sier maken met	show off (something)
de grootmacht	superpower
iets prijsgeven	give something up
in handen vallen van	fall into the hands of
innemen	take, capture
de kreet	expression (*here*: slogan or catchword)
laat maar	never mind
lachwekkend	laughable
de Lage Landen	low countries (Netherlands + Flanders)
mazzel	lucky
het moeras	swamp
neger	black person (derogatory)
niet bepaald	not exactly
onbetrouwbaar	unreliable
overdragen	hand over
tenslotte	after all
het theekransje	tea party
de top	summit
uitknikkeren	kick out
veroveren	conquer
verschepen	to ship
de volksaard	national character
zogenaamd	so-called, supposedly

Cultuur

SPANJAARDEN AND FRANSEN

During the 17th Century, an uprising in the Northern Netherlandish provinces succeeded in defeating Spanish rule and establishing the Dutch Republic. Later, the French, led by Napoleon, conquered the Netherlands but were expelled in the early 19th Century.

SREBRENICA

An enclave of Muslims in former Yugoslavia. During the ethnic wars of the late 1990s the Dutch army (as part of the UN peace force) was in charge of protecting the enclave, but failed to protect the local population against a massacre by Serb forces. The episode caused lots of soul-searching for the Dutch and caused the then coalition government to fall.

Oefening 8: Vragen bij tekst 2

1 Wat is het effect van de verkleinwoorden in de tekst? (vb: volkje, moeraslandje, blowtjes, spulletjes, etc.)
2 De schrijver doet heel extreme uitspraken over Nederland. Maak een lijstje.
3 Zijn deze uitspraken realistisch? Waarom doet de schrijver ze?
4 De tekst is geschreven voor studenten. Denk je dat dat invloed heeft gehad op de manier waarop de tekst is geschreven?
5 De schrijver heeft het over de 'eer' de laatste koloniale oorlog te hebben gevochten. Hij gebruikt het woord 'eer' satirisch. Wat bedoelt hij echt?
6 Denk je dat de verwijzing naar de provincie Drenthe positief of negatief is bedoeld? Waarom? (Kijk naar de context).
7 In alinea 4 geeft de schrijver extra kracht aan het argument dat Nederland helemaal geen Gidsland is door een lijst van negatieve voorbeelden te geven. De voorbeelden worden bijna allemaal op dezelfde manier geformuleerd, waarom denk je dat de schrijver dat heeft gedaan?

Oefening 9

Vergelijk de twee eerste teksten uit dit hoofdstuk. Maak in het schema een lijst van wat er in elke tekst wordt gezegd over Nederland.

Tekst 1	Tekst 2
Nederland ziet zichzelf als voorbeeld voor de rest van de wereld.	Het is een historisch misverstand dat Nederlanders dapper zijn
Wij laten ons leiden door het verstand, niet door emotie.	We waren geen vrijheidsstrijders. De Nederlandse volkaard is zogenaamd (= niet) tolerant.

Als je de twee lijstjes vergelijkt, wat zijn dan de grootste verschillen tussen de twee visies op het verleden van Nederland?

Oefening 10

In de twee eerste teksten van dit hoofdstuk wordt de 'gouden eeuw' van Nederland op twee verschillende manieren geïnterpreteerd:

1 Nederland was het machtigste land ter wereld, het heeft een 'groots' verleden.
2 Nederland werd rijk door het verkopen van wapens aan andere landen en het verschepen van negers, hier kun je niet trots op zijn.

Kies nu een gebeurtenis of periode uit het verleden van jouw land. Vul het schema in met drie verschillende manieren waarop je deze gebeurtenis of periode kunt interpreteren.

gebeurtenis of periode	
interpretatie 1	
interpretatie 2	

Oefening 11

Je werkt op de redactie van een landelijk dagblad. Een collega schrijft een artikel over verschillende ideeën over het concept 'Nederland gidsland'. Schrijf een samenvatting voor haar van ongeveer 60–80 woorden van de argumenten in tekst 2. Je tekst moet neutraal en zakelijk zijn.

Structuren

ZOU

Look up **zou/den** in Unit 7. Now look at the following use of **zou/den** in the text:

Zo <u>zouden</u> wij dat dappere volkje zijn die eerst de Spanjaarden een showdown gaven.

As you have seen before, this use of **zou/den** indicates that an idea, statement or fact has not been confirmed. Journalists use it a lot to indicate that a news story has not been confirmed.

Er zouden vijf overlevenden zijn van de ramp.

Consequently, because you indicate that something is unconfirmed, i.e. may not be true, you distance yourself from a particular statement or opinion, which is exactly the effect the writer of the reading text is after; he makes it clear that he does not agree with the idea of the Dutch as 'dat dappere volkje'.

Oefening 12

Make clear that the following statements are unconfirmed and/or that you do not agree with the statements, by re-writing them with **zou/den**.

1 De regering stimuleert investeringen in de IT niet genoeg.

2 Hij is de man die dat soort zaken voor je kan regelen.

3 Er leven daar nog zeldzame diersoorten.

4 Door de nieuwe regels kunnen werkgevers makkelijker personeel ontslaan.

5 Zij heeft een gave om trends te zien aankomen.

6 Onderzoekers zijn er in geslaagd om zenuwcellen met computerchips te verbinden.

7 De vrije markt is niet goed voor de wetenschappelijke vooruitgang.

8 De wereld is er nog niet klaar voor.

Communicatie

COHESION

As we've seen before, a text can be made more cohesive by linking different elements and referring back to previous information within the text.

The second paragraph in tekst 2 on page 351, for instance, starts with **daar**, which refers back to the first paragraph, and the fourth paragraph refers back to the third paragraph with **dat**.

Oefening 13

Onderstreep alle woorden in tekst 1 die (a) terugverwijzen naar eerdere informatie, en/of (b) elementen in de tekst met elkaar verbinden.

Oefening 14

Kijk nogmaals naar de samenvatting die je in **Oefening 11** hebt geschreven van de tekst. Check hoeveel verbindingswoorden je hebt gebruikt en hoe vaak je terugverwijst naar eerdere informatie. Herschrijf je tekst nu om hem grotere cohesie te geven. Geef als je klaar bent je tekst aan je buurman/vrouw en bekijk van elkaar hoe je het hebt gedaan.

HUMOUR: THE ABSURD

The text you've just read uses humour and satire to appeal to its readers. The author employs various techniques to make his text more humorous. One way is by using some extremely informal language in a text about quite a serious topic. This unexpected contrast can be humorous, although you should be aware that it can also be deemed inappropriate! Examples of extremely informal language:

op de schaats, haha

zo zouden wij [. . .] de Fransen uit ons <u>moeraslandje</u> hebben <u>geknikkerd</u>.

The author also tries to be humorous by making some outrageous suggestions. The unexpectedness of obviously exaggerated, unrealistic or ridiculous suggestions, questions or statements can make readers laugh. An obviously unexpected question is: *Waarom bestaat Nederland eigenlijk*? Its clearly exaggerated answer can also be seen as humorous: *Engeland*.

Oefening 15

1 Make a list of words or expressions from the text which you think are intentionally informal in order to make you laugh.
2 Make a list of ideas (or questions) which you believe are intentionally absurd or exaggerated.

FIXED EXPRESSIONS

Fixed expressions are often difficult to understand. Their meaning is usually not clear from a literal translation of the individual words. An example from the text is: **goede sier maken met**.

The thing to do with fixed expressions is to look up the most important word in the dictionary, and see if the expression is given as one of the examples. In the case of the example you would have to look in the dictionary under **sier**, and you would find something like:

goede sier maken met	to show off (something)

Note that Dutch/Dutch dictionaries list many more fixed expressions than Dutch/English dictionaries.

Oefening 16

Zoek de betekenis van de volgende uitdrukkingen op in een woordenboek.

1 over de brug komen
2 de mist ingaan
3 iets onder de knie krijgen
4 iemand onder de voet lopen
5 een kat in de zak kopen
6 ergens de buik vol van hebben
7 iemand kaalplukken
8 ergens geen kaas van gegeten hebben

LESS IS MORE: ELLIPSIS

Wij hebben eerst de Spanjaarden een showdown gegeven en vervolgens de Fransen uit ons landje geknikkerd.

In full, this sentence would have read:

Wij hebben eerst de Spanjaarden een showdown gegeven en wij hebben vervolgens de Fransen uit ons landje geknikkerd.

Instead of repeating the subject and verb of a sentence, often they can be left out, as long as it does not obscure the meaning of the sentence and as long as they appear in the same number, tense and position.

Oefening 17

Herschrijf de volgende zinnen. Laat woorden weg als ze niet herhaald hoeven te worden.

1 Voor volgende week moeten we een rapport indienen bij de werkgroep en we moeten een voorstel doen voor de planning van de conferentie.
2 Ze zijn eerst naar Barcelona gevlogen met het vliegtuig, toen zijn ze naar Madrid gegaan per trein, en daarna zijn ze per auto naar Toledo gereden.
3 Heb je het journaal gisteren niet gezien, of heb je de krant niet gelezen?
4 Ik heb m'n laptop nu al een paar keer laten repareren, maar ik heb nog steeds problemen met dat rotding.
5 M'n manager wil volgend jaar een bonusregeling invoeren en tegelijkertijd wil ze ons salaris met 3 procent verlagen.
6 Als ze Franse les neemt, heeft ze natuurlijk niet zo veel tijd meer om 's avonds te tennissen en heeft ze ook niet zo veel tijd meer om haar vrienden te zien.

Tekst 3

Lees onderstaande tekst en beantwoord de vier vragen onder de tekst. Probeer om te beginnen de woordenschat onder de tekst nog niet te gebruiken. Raak niet gefrustreerd als je woorden niet kent – je hoeft niet elk woord te begrijpen. Probeer uit de context op te maken wat onbekende woorden betekenen.

Wij ikken het liefst in een groep

De Nederlandse individualist bestaat niet

door Jos van der Lans

Achter de trotse gevel van ons moderne ik-beeld zijn we permanent bezig om onszelf een plek te geven te midden van anderen. Van jongs af trainen we ons fanatiek in het leren meedoen. Het voortdurend op anderen letten, is in het moderne leven uitgegroeid tot een vorm van overleven.

Het grappige is dat we deze kunst van het meedoen zien als een vorm van zelf kiezen. Als een uiterste daad van persoonlijke expressie. Daar wijzen ouders hun kinderen ook voortdurend op: je moet zelf kiezen. Dat de meeste kinderen vervolgens hetzelfde kiezen als hun vriendje is minder van belang dan de keuze zelf.

Dat patroon van uniek conformisme is alleen maar sterker geworden. Wij richten stuk voor stuk onze woningen geheel naar eigen smaak in, met als resultaat dat ze allemaal toch wel erg op elkaar lijken. We willen met de binnenkant van onze woningen iets van onszelf laten zien, maar meer nog willen we niet uit de toon vallen. Daarom is het altijd zo druk bij Ikea.

Tot een halve eeuw geleden gold in Nederland de wet: waar je woont, bepaalt wie je bent. Nederlanders woonden keurig bij elkaar naar klasse, geloof en inkomen; buren deden vergelijkbaar soort werk, deelden dezelfde ervaringswereld en hadden hun eigen voorkeuren.

Die overzichtelijke ordeningen zijn nu vervangen door een nieuwe verdeling van het land in smaakgroepen, subculturen, stijlnetwerken, etcetera. Dit heeft de individuele levens veelzijdiger gemaakt, maar ook gecompliceerder; om mee te doen en erbij te horen heb je steeds ingewikkelder sociale vaardigheden nodig. Het aantal mensen dat niet meekomt en uitgestoten wordt in dit proces van moderne gemeenschapsvorming is de afgelopen decennia dan ook fors gegroeid.

Zo ziet Nederland er dus uit: een polderlandschap vol bewegende groepen en gemeenschappen, die zich vormen op basis van leeftijden, smaken, identiteiten, mode en die voortdurend in elkaar overlopen. Er zijn grote en kleine groepen, er zijn ruzies en ongemakken, er zijn statische eenheden (eerste generatie allochtonen) en beweeglijke gemeenschappen (stadsyuppen). Het is een voortdurend bewegende verzuiling, waarbij de burgers naar elkaar kijken om zichzelf te leren kennen.

naar *Vrij Nederland* 15 mei 2004 (pp. 14, 15)

Key vocabulary

alleen maar	only
bepalen	determine
de ervaringswereld	world of experience
fors	considerable/ considerably
het ik-beeld	self image
in elkaar overlopen	fuse and mingle
inrichten	decorate, fit out (a house)
keurig	tidily, neatly
de klasse	class
letten op	pay attention to
lijken op	look like
meedoen	joining in, going along with others
het ongemak	discomfort
de ordening	structure, planning
overleven	survive, survival
overzichtelijk	conveniently arranged
het patroon	pattern
sociale vaardigheden	social skills
stuk voor stuk	one by one, to a man, every one of us
te midden van	in the midst of, among
toch wel erg	rather a lot
de trotse gevel	proud exterior
uit de toon vallen	be the odd one out, different
het uiterste	extreme, utmost
uitstoten	to expel, banish
van belang	important
van jongs af	from an early age
veelzijdig	varied
vergelijkbaar	comparable
de voorkeur	preference
voortdurend	constant(ly)

Vragen bij tekst 3

1 Lees alinea 1 tot en met 4. Geef voor elke alinea in een simpele zin aan waar de alinea over gaat.

2 Lees alinea 5. Wat zijn de problemen van de nieuwe verdeling van de samenleving?

3 Alinea 6 beschrijft de huidige situatie in Nederland. Vat die samen.

4 Geef aan (in de tekst) wat de schrijver bedoelt met:

   a 'deze kunst van het meedoen' in alinea 2.

   b 'dat patroon van uniek conformisme' in alinea 3.

   c 'die overzichtelijke ordeningen' in alinea 5.

   d 'dit proces van moderne gemeenschapsvorming' in alinea 5.

   e 'het' aan het begin van zin 3 in alinea 6.

5 Lees nu de hele tekst nogmaals met de woordenschat, en beantwoord de vragen in **Oefening 18**.

Oefening 18

1 De tekst is vrij neutraal. De schrijver gebruikt alleen wel soms vrij moeilijke 'technische' taal of jargon, zoals: ik-beeld, persoonlijke expressie, uniek conformisme, klasse/geloof/inkomen, ervaringswereld, smaakgroepen.

  a Probeer zelf nog meer van dit jargon te vinden in de tekst.
  b Als je kijkt naar deze woorden en uitdrukkingen, wat is dan de achtergrond van de schrijver, denk je? Wat zou hij bijvoorbeeld doen voor beroep?

2 Zou bijvoorbeeld een directeur bij een groot meubelbedrijf zoals Ikea het met de schrijver eens zijn wat betreft het idee dat naar Ikea gaan kuddegedrag is? Leg uit.

het kuddegedrag doing what everyone else does

Oefening 19

Werk alleen of in een groep: Je werkt voor een reclamebureau. Je hebt een opdracht gekregen, een nieuwe reclamecampagne opzetten voor Ikea in Nederland. Je hebt het artikel hierboven gelezen en gaat eerst bedenken (of in de groep bespreken) waar je je op wilt richten:

  a je wilt individueel zijn
  b je wilt niet uit de toon vallen

Maak dan een lijstje met punten die je belangrijk vindt voor je reclame. Schrijf daarna een korte tekst van 100–150 woorden die in dag- en weekbladen moet komen.

Structuren

AGREEMENT

As we explained at the beginning of this book, subject and verb have to be in agreement, i.e. a singular subject is followed by a singular form of a verb.

Hij is singular, and is therefore followed by a singular verb form, say **kijkt**, not **kijken**.

Wij is plural, and has to be followed by a plural verb form, i.e. **kijken**.

Hij kijkt naar een spannende film.
Wij kijken geen televisie als het mooi weer is.

Similarly, **de regering** is singular (even though it consists of more than one person) and must be followed by a singular verb form. In English a word like 'government' can also be used with a plural verb form, precisely because it consists of more than one person, but this is not possible in Dutch.

De regering heeft nieuwe maatregels voorgesteld.
The government has/have proposed new measures.

Oefening 20

Zet de werkwoorden tussen haakjes in de juiste vorm, op de juiste plek.

Voorbeeld

Volgende week donderdag (moeten) mijn hele afdeling klaar zijn met dit project.
Volgende week donderdag moet mijn hele afdeling klaar zijn met dit project.

1 Het kan een nadeel zijn dat de directie zich zo (afzonderen) van het personeel.
2 Het ziekenhuis (willen) dit jaar nog verder bezuinigen.
3 Het is niet duidelijk hoe de brandweer en de politie zo'n fout (hebben) kunnen maken.
4 Volgende week (moeten) de Raad van Bestuur van de hele onderneming een beslissing nemen.
5 De redactie van de studentenkrant (vergaderen) eens per week over de inhoud van het blad.
6 Het bestuur en de rest van de vereniging (hebben) de hele dag de tijd om hun stem uit te brengen.
7 De vereniging (hebben) nu 40 leden.
8 De leden van het bestuur (zeggen) niet verantwoordelijk te zijn voor de onjuiste formulering in het contract.

PASSIVE

In this final unit we will have one last look at the passive. Look at the following passive clauses:

1 Er wordt een foto genomen.
2 Relatief veel joden zijn [aan de Duitsers] overgedragen.
3 De volksaard van de Nederlander kan gekarakteriseerd worden als laf en zeikerig.
4 Die ordeningen zijn nu vervangen door een nieuwe verdeling van het land.
5 Zijn autobiografie werd pas na zijn dood gepubliceerd.
6 Het rapport was geschreven door een speciale commissie.

Indicate which tenses these clauses are in, and explain how you know this. Before doing the exercises below, study the section on the passive in Unit 9 and/or in a grammar book.

Oefening 21

Geef de tijd aan van de volgende passieve zinnen. Vertaal ze daarna.

1 Het boek wordt geschreven door twee auteurs.
2 Afgelopen zaterdag is er een man op het kerkhof aangevallen door twee honden.
3 De film werd door een buitenlandse regisseur geregisseerd.
4 De opdrachten worden door de twee mannen volgens plan uitgevoerd.
5 Het 750-jarig bestaan van Alkmaar is in 2004 uitbundig gevierd.
6 De airco was door het bedrijf zelf geïnstalleerd.
7 De boeken zijn gekocht door een antiquariaat.
8 Vrijdagmiddag worden de verdachten voor de rechter geleid.

Oefening 22

Herschrijf de zinnen uit de vorige oefening en maak ze actief.

Oefening 23

Lees het volgende tekstje. Onderstreep de passieve zinnen en maak ze dan actief (verzin een logisch subject als er nog geen subject is).

Er zijn dit jaar 25 klassieke concerten in de Ruïnekerk in Bergen. De zomeravondconcerten worden georganiseerd door de organist van de kerk. De concerten worden gegeven door professionele musici, maar ook door amateurs. Het publiek kan genieten van kamermuziek van hoge kwaliteit. Het bezoekersaantal is in de afgelopen jaren flink gestegen. De concerten zijn twintig jaar geleden voor het eerst georganiseerd door de organist. Dit jaar wordt er voornamelijk muziek gespeeld van Nederlandse en Franse componisten, vooral uit de late Renaissance.

Oefening 24

Maak de volgende zinnen passief. Gebruik de onderstreepte woorden als subject van de nieuwe zin. Als dit nieuwe subject onbepaald (indefinite) is, moet je de zin beginnen met **Er**.

1 Eileen nodigt vijfendertig mensen uit op haar feest.
2 Ze houdt het feest in haar tuin, waar ze veel tafels en stoelen neerzet.
3 Haar vriend Pedro heeft de uitnodigingen gemaakt, want hij is grafisch ontwerper en kan dat erg goed.
4 Eileen doet de catering helemaal in haar eentje, want ze is gek op koken.
5 Ze heeft al verschillende schotels klaargemaakt.
6 Een plaatselijke slijterij levert alle drank en glazen.
7 Twee van haar beste vriendinnen helpen Eileen om alles op de dag van het feest klaar te maken.

Oefening 25: Groepsdiscussie

Hoe individualistisch ben je? Ben je het eens met de auteur van de laatste tekst, die zegt dat mensen denken dat ze vrij kunnen kiezen, maar dat iedereen bang is om uit de toon te vallen? Pas jij je aan aan de norm?

Oefening 26

Write a short piece of about 150–200 words about the ways in which you see yourself conforming to and deviating from group norms. Give an idea about how individualistic you think you are.

Context: this text is meant for your personal website, and can therefore be as informal, formal, serious or humorous as you think is suitable. However, make the text as cohesive as possible, and pay special attention to the way in which you distribute your information.

When you have finished, team up with a fellow student to try and help each other to improve your texts by correcting mistakes and suggesting ways of making the texts even more cohesive.

Cultuur

Pim Fortuyn was a well-known, openly gay, political commentator, writer, columnist and media figure, not least, perhaps, due to his flamboyant, dandy-ish lifestyle. He antagonised large numbers of people with his outspoken ideas and direct ways of addressing issues and people. He had clear political ambitions, the issue of immigration being central to his ideas. In 1997 he wrote a book called *Against the Islamisation of our culture* in which he called upon the Dutch to protect their own cultural identity and cultural achievements – such as the separation of church and state, equality of women and the position of homosexuals in society – against the influences of Islam.

In 2001 Fortuyn became leader of the political party 'Leefbaar Nederland' (livable/endurable Netherlands), a collection of local parties challenging the political establishment, but without an outspoken anti-immigration agenda. After claiming in an interview: 'Islam is een achterlijke cultuur', 'Nederland is vol' and 'asylum seekers should be barred from the country', Fortuyn was forced to resign from his post as party leader. Fortuyn promptly founded his own party: Lijst Pim Fortuyn (LPF).

In the polls LPF quickly overtook Leefbaar Nederland. Early in 2002, in local elections in Rotterdam, Fortuyn gained control of the council with 'Leefbaar Rotterdam', which had invited him to head their list of candidates. With general elections coming up in

May, Fortuyn set for a big win, and the possibility of becoming the next Prime Minister, he and his LPF party dominated the news. Immigration and defending Dutch culture became the main issues of debate. Established political parties did not have a ready answer to Fortuyn and became increasingly hostile towards him and his party, denouncing them as 'extreem rechts', but at the same time not endearing themselves to the general public, as defeat in the elections loomed larger and larger.

Then, nine days before the general elections, Fortuyn was shot dead by an animal rights activist.

LPF gained 17% of the vote and became one of the coalition parties in government. The party proved ungovernable without Fortuyn, and soon started to crumble, taking the coalition government down with it. However, political debate in the Netherlands has been changed drastically by Fortuyn and his radical ideas. Ideas towards, and ways of talking about, Dutch culture, multiculturalism and immigration have been changed to such an extent that possibly Dutch tolerance and liberalism have been fundamentally changed in the process. A direct consequence of these changes was the introduction of strict new immigration legislation in 2004.

Tekst 4

De volgende tekst is een speech van Pim Fortyun. Voor Fortuyn werd er al hevig gedebatteerd over het concept 'Nederland is vol'. De discussie ging vooral over ruimtelijke ordening (*planning issues*) en het gebrek aan ruimte in een klein land als Nederland. Fortuyn richtte het debat op immigranten en buitenlanders. De slogan 'Nederland is vol' wordt nu bijna alleen nog gebruikt door mensen die immigratie een halt willen toeroepen.

Luister eerst naar de tekst. Probeer in grote lijnen het argument te volgen en beantwoord de vragen in **Oefening 27**.

Leest daarna de tekst aan de hand van de vragen in **Oefening 28**.

Nederland is vol

De oud-minister van ruimtelijke ordening, Pronk (PvdA), heeft het zelf gezegd: Nederland is vol. Dat is een subjectief begrip. Wat voor de een vol is, is voor de ander leeg. Een stadsmens kijkt anders tegen het begrip vol aan dan een boer uit Flevoland.

De open ruimte verdwijnt in ons land in hoog tempo met name in de Randstad. Pronk heeft de ruimteclaims van de departementen opgeteld en komt tot de conclusie dat we over dertig jaar de ruimte van de omvang van een provincie als Zuid-Holland te kort komen. Dat is even schrikken. Natuurlijk is dat overdreven. De ruimtelijke indeling is moeilijk te plannen en te voorspellen.

De ruimte-indeling is vooral gebaseerd op de industriële economie van dit moment. De ICT economie maakt echter een heel ander gebruik van de ruimte mogelijk. Er zijn zelfs grote ruimtewinsten mogelijk als we ICT gebruiken als concept om economie en samenleving in te richten. Daar staat tegenover dat Nederland in toenemende mate een immigratieland is geworden.

De toestroom van buitenlanders, legaal (het asielbeleid) en illegaal, gaat onverdroten voort, onder andere door het ruimhartige beleid van gezinshereniging. Iedere vijf jaar komt er een stad van de omvang van Deventer aan nieuwkomers bij. Het verscherpte asielbeleid zal daaraan weinig veranderen.

Pronk wil aan het ruimtebeslag een halt toeroepen. Een lachwekkend streven. Het in goede banen leiden van al die ruimteclaims is al moeilijk genoeg. Ontwikkelen de ruimteclaims zich in het huidige tempo dan moeten we afscheid nemen van een aantal illusies. De eerste illusie is dat Nederland een land is. Nederland ontwikkelt zich in hoog tempo tot een stadsstaat. Nederland is over dertig jaar een metropool in de Europese Unie, niet meer maar ook niet minder. Als we het goed doen, hebben we het gewicht van metropolen als groot-Londen, groot-Parijs en groot-Berlijn. Een dicht bebouwde metropool met een aantal grote parken en waterpartijen. De regering in Den Haag moet het land dan ook niet langer meer besturen als een land, maar als een metropool.

De tweede illusie waarvan we afstand moeten nemen is dat het land een asielbeleid kan voeren. Dat slaat inmiddels al nergens meer op. Een rationele oplossing voor de toestroom van vreemdelingen is een immigratiebeleid. Daarmee kan men een quota stellen en zonodig eisen stellen aan de nieuwkomers. Geen softe eisen, maar keiharde eisen waaraan moet worden voldaan. Voldoet men hieraan niet dan is de keiharde sanctie: uitzetting.

EuropoortKringen, Pim Fortuyn, 9 juni 2000, Rotterdam

Key vocabulary

het asielbeleid	(political) asylum policy
het begrip	concept
besturen	to govern, lead
daar staat tegenover	on the other hand, (but) then again
dat is even schrikken	that comes as quite a shock
dat slaat nergens op	that makes no sense at all
het departement	government department/ministry
dicht bebouwd	densely built-up
een halt toeroepen aan	to call a halt to
een streven	pursuit, endeavour
het gewicht	weight, importance
de gezinshereniging	reunification of a family
de ICT	information and communication technology
iets te kort komen	to lack something
in goede banen leiden	to steer in the right direction
in toenemende mate	increasingly
keihard	rock hard, tough
de omvang	size
onverdroten	indefatigable
overdrijven/overdreven	to exaggerate/exaggerated
ruimhartig	generous
de ruimteclaim	claim on/need for space or land
de ruimtelijke indeling	(town and country) planning
de ruimtelijke ordening	environmental planning
de sanctie	sanction
de toestroom	influx
de uitzetting	deportation
verscherpen	to tighten, make stricter
voldoen aan	to meet, satisfy
voorspellen	to predict
de waterpartij	pond, water garden
de winst	profit, gain

Oefening 27: Luistervragen

1 Wat is volgens Fortuyn de grootste oorzaak van het ruimtegebrek in Nederland?
2 Vindt hij dat de regering een goed beleid voert om het probleem op te lossen?

Oefening 28: Vragen

1 Lees alinea 1: Wat zegt Fortuyn in paragraaf 1 over het concept 'Nederland is vol'?
2 Lees alinea 2: Gelooft Fortuyn dat de open ruimte in Nederland verdwijnt? Is hij het helemaal eens met oud-minister Pronk?
3 Lees alinea 3: Fortuyn zegt dat er 'ruimtewinst' mogelijk is in Nederland, hoe? Waardoor verliest Nederland open ruimte volgens Fortuyn?
4 Lees alinea 4: Vat deze alinea in een zin samen.
5 Lees alinea 5: Fortuyn geeft aan wat de gevolgen kunnen zijn als de open ruimte blijft verdwijnen in het huidige tempo. Maak een lijstje van gevolgen die hij noemt.
6 Lees alinea 6: Volgens Fortuyn is een asielbeleid niet effectief, wat vindt hij een beter alternatief?

Oefening 29

Fortuyn doet allerlei uitspraken in de tekst over het ruimtegebrek in Nederland en de oorzaken daarvan. Een aantal zie je in het schema hieronder. De uitspraken worden allemaal objectief gepresenteerd – hij schrijft ze op als objectieve observaties. Geef aan of de uitspraken ook echt objectief zijn, of dat ze waarschijnlijk min of meer subjectief zijn.

Uitspraken van Fortuyn	Subjectief of objectief?
1 'Nederland is vol. Dat is een subjectief begrip.'	
2 'De open ruimte verdwijnt in ons land in hoog tempo met name in de Randstad.'	
3 'Natuurlijk is dat overdreven.'	
4 'De ruimtelijke indeling is moeilijk te plannen en te voorspellen.'	
5 'Iedere vijf jaar komt er een stad van de omvang van Deventer aan nieuwkomers bij.'	
6 'Het verscherpte asielbeleid zal daaraan weinig veranderen.'	

Uitspraken van Fortuyn	**Subjectief of objectief?**
7 'Ontwikkelen de ruimteclaims zich in het huidige tempo dan moeten we afscheid nemen van een aantal illusies' [. . .] 'Nederland is over dertig jaar . . . een dichtbebouwde metropool met een aantal grote parken en waterpartijen.'	
8 'De tweede illusie waarvan we afstand moeten nemen is dat het land een asielbeleid kan voeren.'	

Oefening 30: Luisteroefening

Luister naar zinnen uit de tekst. In elke zin hoor je een toon. Schrijf de juiste vorm van een van de volgende woord(en) op die je daar kunt invullen.

anders begrip besturen halt in toenemende mate schrikken verdwijnen voldoen zich ontwikkelen

Structuren

RELATIVE PRONOUNS

Relative pronouns have already been discussed in Unit 6. We will have one last look.

Die and **dat**

De man *die* gisteren naast me zat in de vergadering.
Het huis *dat* we graag zouden willen kopen.
De huizen *die* we hebben gezien, waren allemaal erg duur.

Oefening 31

Explain when to use **die** and when to use **dat**.

Wie and **wat**

Wie and **wat** can also be used as relative pronouns. Explain why they are used in the following sentences:

Alles *wat* je zegt, is helemaal waar.
***Wat* ik heb gezien, is echt niet te geloven!**
***Wie* zoiets doet is gewoon geschift.**

Oefening 32

Vul in: **die**, **dat**, **wie** or **wat**.

1 Ze gaan naar een warm land op vakantie, ______ me verbaast, want ze houden alletwee niet van de warmte!
2 Zijn vriendin, ______ nog steeds studeert, wil graag kinderen.
3 Niets ______ onze buren kopen, vind ik mooi – die mensen hebben geen smaak.
4 Het jaarrapport, ______ eigenlijk in mei gepubliceerd moest worden, komt nu uit in september.
5 ______ zijn werk af heeft, mag direct naar huis.
6 Is er iets ______ ik voor je kan doen?
7 Wat is het mooiste boek ______ je ooit hebt gelezen?
8 Zijn het mijn sleutels of de jouwe ______ je kwijt bent?

het jaarrapport	annual report	**kwijt**	lost

Wie and **waar**

When relative pronouns are combined with a preposition the following happens.

For things use: **waar** + preposition
Het project waaraan ik werk.

For people use: preposition + **wie**
De contactpersoon met wie ik heb gesproken.

Oefening 33

Maak de volgende zinnen af. Gebruik de informatie die wordt gegeven.

Voorbeeld

Ik kan het goed vinden met mijn buurman.
Mijn buurman is iemand ______
Mijn buurman is iemand met wie ik het goed kan vinden.

1 Ik hou persoonlijk het meest van rode wijn.
De drank _______

2 Ze heeft grote bewondering voor topsporters.
Topsporters zijn mensen _______

3 Ze hebben een hekel aan soaps.
Soaps zijn televisieprogramma's _______

4 Hij luistert altijd erg graag naar harde techno.
Harde techno is muziek _______

5 We hebben de grootste hekel aan grammaticaoefeningen.
Grammaticaoefeningen zijn de oefeningen _______

MORE THAN ONE VERB IN FINAL VERB POSITION

When word order changes in Dutch sentences, for instance in relative clauses, quite a number of verbs are moved into final position. When there are only two, either verb can come first. If there are two infinitives, however, the infinitive of the modal verb comes first.

Ze zegt dat ze al tien jaar *getrouwd is/is getrouwd.*
Ik heb altijd al een echt goeie stereo *willen hebben.*

In case there are more than two verbs, the rules are as follows:

A past participle can come first or last, of the other verbs the finite verb comes first and the infinitive last (and if there is more than one, the infinitive of the modal comes first).

Ik denk dat ik je voor het examen een 8 *zou moeten kunnen halen.*
Maar je snapt dat je dan wel alles goed *geleerd zal moeten hebben.*
Maar je snapt dat je dan wel alles goed *zal moeten hebben geleerd.*

Communicatie

AFKORTINGEN ('ABBREVIATIONS')

In the text written by Fortuyn, PvdA is an abbreviation for the Partij van de Arbeid, labour party in the Netherlands. The Dutch use many abbreviations, for instance within particular professions or fields, such as politics. You will find more about political parties and their abbreviations below. Here is a list of more general abbreviations.

t/m	**tot en met**	up to and including
blz.	**bladzijde**	page
p.	**pagina**	page
z.o.z.	**zie ommezijde**	p.t.o.
d.w.z	**dat wil zeggen**	i.e.
i.v.m.	**in verband met**	with regard to
m.b.t.	**met betrekking tot**	with regard to
m.a.w.	**met andere woorden**	in other words
a.u.b.	**alstublieft**	please
s.v.p.	**s'il vous plaît**	please
jl.	**jongstleden**	last (with regard to dates)
a.s.	**aanstaande**	next (with regard to dates)

Oefening 34

Schrijf de volgende afkortingen voluit. Lees de zinnen ook hardop voor.

1 Alleen te bereiken tijdens kantooruren, **d.w.z.** maandag **t/m** vrijdag van 9 tot 5 uur.
2 De winkel is vandaag gesloten **i.v.m.** ziekte.
3 Kun je me even emailen om te laten weten of je woensdag **a.s.** kunt vergaderen om 4 uur?
4 Eerst kloppen, **a.u.b.**
5 Voor verdere instructies, **z.o.z.**
6 Op **blz.** 5 vindt u een samenvatting van de maatregelen die zijn genomen **m.b.t.** de overlast van jongeren in het centrum van de stad.
7 Het bestuur heeft geen financiële middelen meer, **m.a.w.** er moet worden bezuinigd.

Cultuur

The Netherlands is a constitutional monarchy. The system of proportional representation has resulted in a large number of political parties in parliament (made up of the directly elected Tweede Kamer and the indirectly elected Eerste Kamer) and coalition governments. The differences between the political parties have tended to be relatively small, although a polarisation has been taking place on certain issues, such as immigration, but also abortion, euthanasia and drugs. However, core government policies regarding the economy and foreign policy tend to change relatively little between governments.

Here are the main political parties:

CDA:	Christen Democratisch Appèl Centre-right, with a Christian underpinning
PvdA:	Partij van de Arbeid Left of centre labour party.
VVD:	Volkspartij voor Vrijheid en Democratie Right wing, free market party
SP:	Socialistische Partij As the name suggests, a socialist party
Groen Links	Centre left, environmental 'green' party
LPF:	Lijst Pim Fortuyn Right wing, free market party, founded by and based on the ideas of the late Pim Fortuyn
D66:	Democraten '66 Centre left party
CU:	Christen Unie Right wing Christian party
SGP:	Staatskundig Gereformeerde Partij Right wing Christian party

Generally, either CDA or PvdA are the largest party.

For more on Dutch politics, political parties, government and elections, try the following websites:

www.politiekepartijen.nl (about the various political parties and politics in general many links)

www.tweedekamer.nl (lower house of parliament website)

www.postbus51.nl (government website)

Oefening 35: In paren

Onderzoek het beleid van één politieke partij. Zoek op het internet naar informatie over de partij (bijvoorbeeld op hun eigen website) en maak een lijstje met de belangrijkste ideeën van de partij. Daarna geeft elk paar een presentatie van vijf tot tien minuten over het beleid van 'hun' partij voor de hele groep.

Tekst 5 Dialoog

Je hoort nu een nagespeeld Interview met een Islamitisch geestelijk leider, Imam Haselhoef, en Pim Fortuyn. Luister een paar keer naar het interview. Probeer al zoveel mogelijk informatie op te schrijven voor **Oefening 36**, voordat je de tekst leest en de vragen in **Oefening 37** beantwoordt.

Interviewer 'Is er sprake van een fundamentele botsing van normen en waarden tussen de islam en de Westerse beschaving?'

Haselhoef 'De Nederlandse cultuur is veel islamitischer dan in vele islamitische landen. Zorg voor zwakkeren, voor zieken, gelijkwaardigheid. Dat zie ik veel te weinig terug in de landen die zich islamitisch noemen.'

Interviewer 'Meneer Fortuyn, kunt u ook iets positiefs aan de Islam noemen?'

Fortuyn 'Poeh! Eens even denken. De gemeenschapszin. Je ziet een bloeiend moskeeleven en veel verenigingen. Er is ook meer aandacht voor spiritualiteit. Als je op koranles zit, ben je niet de hele tijd bezig met je tweede hypotheek.'

Interviewer 'Waar botst het dan?'

Fortuyn 'Christendom en jodendom zijn door een proces van secularisatie gegaan. Tijdens de Verlichting zijn in ons cultuurgebied essentiële normen en waarden ontwikkeld. In de eerste plaats de individuele verantwoordelijkheid. Ten tweede de scheiding van kerk en staat. De kerk vervult een functie in het private terrein, naast de parlementaire democratie die het publieke domein stuurt. Ten derde de gelijkwaardigheid van mannen en vrouwen. Binnen het islamitisch cultuurgebied zijn vrouwen ondergeschikt aan mannen. Dat is een essentiële botsing. Dan zeggen ze wel dat die vrouwen het uit vrije wil doen, een hoofddoek, of zich helemaal bedekken. Ammehoela! Ik wil een massieve emancipatiepolitiek voor achterstandsbuurten waar deze vrouwen wonen. Vroeger sjansten vrouwen met me op straat, nu kijken vrouwen met hoofddoeken alleen nog naar beneden of opzij.'

Haselhoef, lachend 'Misschien bent u wel tien jaar ouder geworden in die tijd. Ik ben verliefd geworden op mijn vrouw tijdens de kleine bedevaart. Ze had een chador aan, helemaal bedekt, ik zag alleen haar prachtige ogen. De erotiek, die ís er in de islam. Het gebeurt alleen subtieler. Nederland is soms zo plat. Je hoeft je fantasie niet te gebruiken.'

'U neemt uw eigen cultuur als meetlat voor hoe andere culturen moeten moderniseren. Ik vraag me af of dat correct is. De grootste onderdrukking van vrouwen komt door mannen als u, die mijn zusters in de islam beoordelen alsof het wezens zijn zonder intellectuele capaciteiten. Als u eens wist hoeveel islamitische meiden hier op de universiteit studeren mét hoofddoekje. Door uw opstelling krijgen ze het idee dat ze achterlijk zijn en dat is niet zo.'

Fortuyn 'Die meiden van u op de universiteit: prima. Ik maak me veel meer zorgen over die woonwijken waar islamitische vrouwen beperkt zijn tot het huishouden en wat winkelen. Dat vind ik een grof schandaal.'

Haselhoef 'U scheert iedereen over één kam. Over één hoofddoek. U beoordeelt iemand op de wijze waarop hij of zij zich kleedt. Waar vrouwen onderdrukt worden, moet dat verbeteren, dat ben ik met u eens. Maar dat heeft niets te maken met de islam. Dat zijn stamgebruiken van degenen die zich moslim noemen. Eerwraak bijvoorbeeld, dat wordt door de islam veroordeeld, net als vrouwenmishandeling.'

Interviewer 'Wat dacht u toen na de aanslagen (11 september in New York) Marokkaanse jongens in Ede feestvierden?'

Fortuyn 'Gewoon kwajongens, waar ik om moest lachen. Ik werd kwaad om de reactie van de politie die niet optrad.'

Haselhoef 'Je om zo'n aanslag blij maken, is fout. Ik heb toen geworsteld op een excuus namens de moslimgemeenschap, maar dat wilde men niet. Ik mocht het woord "walgelijk" niet gebruiken. Bepaalde mensen vonden dat we dan zouden meedoen aan het stigmatiseren van Marokkaanse jongeren, die toch al zo vaak de schuld krijgen.'

Fortuyn 'Het vervelende is dat het vaak terecht is.'

Haselhoef 'Maar het is nog vervelender als het niet zo is.'

Interviewer 'Wat moeten we doen om te voorkomen dat hier de vlam in de pan slaat?'

Fortuyn 'Niet zoveel, onze handen thuishouden.'

Haselhoef 'Mensen met invloed moeten hun woorden op een goudschaal leggen. Ze moeten niet onnodig tegenstellingen aanwakkeren.'

deel van discussie tussen Fortuyn en Imam Haselhoef. (1/7/04)

Key vocabulary

de aanslag	attack
aanwakkeren	to fan, to stir up
achterlijk	backward, retarded
de achterstandsbuurt	disadvantaged/ underprivileged area
ammehoela	not on your life
de bedevaart	pilgrimage
beoordelen	to judge
bloeiend	flowering
botsen	to clash

de botsing	clash
dan zeggen ze wel	they may say that
degene	the one
de eerwraak	honour killing
een functie vervullen	perform a duty
de gelijkwaardigheid	equality
de gemeenschapszin	sense of community
een grof schandaal	a crying shame
handen thuishouden	to keep one's hands off
het huishouden	housekeeping
de hypotheek	mortgage
iedereen over één kam scheren	to lump everyone together
ik vraag me af	I doubt
het jodendom	Judaism
de kwajongen	mischievous boy
de meetlat	yardstick
de meid	young woman
de mishandeling	abuse
namens	on behalf of
de onderdrukking	oppression
ondergeschikt aan	inferior, subservient to
ontwikkelen	to develop
de opstelling	position
optreden	to take action
plat	coarse, vulgar
poeh	well, gee
de scheiding	separation
de secularisatie	secularisation
sjansen	to flirt
de stam	tribe
stigmatiseren	to stigmatize
sturen	to steer
de tegenstelling	difference of opinion
terecht	rightly (so)
de Verlichting	Enlightenment
veroordelen	to condemn
de vlam in de pan slaan	for a situation to get out of hand
walgelijk	disgusting
de westerse beschaving	western civilisation
het wezen	creature
de wijze waarop	the way in which
woorden op een goudschaal leggen	consider words carefully
worstelen met	to struggle with
zich bedekken	to cover oneself
de zorg	care
zwakkere	weaker person

Oefening 36

Vul het schema in met de verschillende meningen van Haselhoef en Fortuyn.

	positief over Islam	*negatief over Islam*	*positief over Nederland/ Christendom*	*negatief over Nederland*
Haselhoef				
Fortuyn				

Oefening 37: Vragen

1 Fortuyn is niet overtuigd dat Islamitische vrouwen uit vrije wil een hoofddoek dragen. Wat wil hij doen om te zorgen dat ze geen hoofddoek meer dragen?
2 Waarom vindt Haselhoef dat Fortuyn Islamitische vrouwen onderdrukt?
3 Wat ziet Haselhoef als fundamentele fout in de opstelling van Fortuyn? Geef aan waar je dat ziet/hoort in de tekst.
4 Fortuyn doet generaliserende uitspraken over negatieve aspecten binnen de Islam. Waarom vindt Haselhoef dat hij niet zo kan generaliseren over de Islam?
5 Fortuyn doet generaliserende uitspraken over de Islam, maar generaliseert de Imam ook? Zo ja, over wie?

Oefening 38

Je hebt het interview tussen Haselhoef en Fortuyn gelezen in de krant. Je wilt reageren. Schrijf een brief van zo'n 150 woorden naar de redactie van de krant. Je mag één van de twee steunen; leg uit in je brief waarom je het eens bent met de een en niet met de ander.

Structuren

TENSES: REVISION

In the interview the speakers use different tenses all the time, as you do in a lively discussion. As your level of Dutch is now good enough to listen to and also participate in quite complex discussions, this is a good point for revising some knowledge about verbs and the tenses, to help your debating skills.

Oefening 39

Beantwoord de volgende vragen

1 What is the stem of a verb, and how do you form it?
2 Explain how the various present tense forms (for ik, jij, u, hij/zij/het, wij, jullie, zij) of regular verbs are derived from the stem of the verb.
3 How is the past participle of regular verbs formed? Explain in as much detail as possible.
4 Give the past participle for the following verbs: wonen, groeien, produceren, stoppen, klagen, beven, reizen, worden, zijn, kopen, analiseren, durven, beginnen, nemen.
5 With verbs of motion, like **lopen**, **fietsen**, **wandelen**, you can use either **hebben** or **zijn** in the present perfect tense. Explain when to use **hebben** and when to use **zijn**. Give examples.

6 Name the modal verbs (and their meaning).
7 What is the main difference between a main clause and a subclause in Dutch?
8 Name five words, or conjunctions, which are used to link subclauses to main clauses.

Oefening 40

Look up the topics which you had difficulties with in the previous exercise in previous units in the book. Also do the relevant exercises. For additional practice, also look up the topics in other course books or grammar books.

LIJKEN – BLIJKEN – SCHIJNEN

These verbs have similar meanings, but it is important to know the differences.

schijnen	seem, appear
lijken	seem, appear, look like, resemble
blijken	prove, turn out

The difference between **schijnen, lijken** and **blijken** is one of certainty.

With **schijnen** you are not sure at all about what you're referring to – you have only heard about it from others:

Wouter schijnt ziek te zijn.
I've heard/It appears that Wouter's ill.

With **lijken** you are still not sure, but you have created an impression at first hand:

Wouter lijkt wel ziek.
Wouter looks/seems ill.

With **blijken** you have actual proof that something is the case:

Wouter blijkt griep te hebben.
It turns out that Wouter has the flu.

Oefening 41

Vul een juiste vorm in van **schijnen, lijken** of **blijken**.

1 De nieuwe collega ___________ een slimme vrouw. Ze kwam met goede vragen tijdens onze vergadering.
2 Alison dacht dat Ahmed single was, maar hij ___________ toch een vriendin te hebben – ze kwam hem net met de auto ophalen.

3 Ik weet het niet zeker, hoor, maar de nieuwe directeur ___________ nogal een sadist te zijn.
4 Ik vind dat de volleybalploeg beter gaat spelen. De nieuwe coach ___________ een goede invloed te hebben op de spelers.
5 Het ___________ dat Sharon alles beter heeft begrepen dan ze dacht – ze had een 9,5 voor het examen.
6 Een vakantie naar Indonesië ___________ niet zo heel duur te zijn. Ik heb gehoord dat je al een vlucht voor 500 euro kan boeken.
7 Het klaart al op. Het ___________ toch nog goed weer te worden!
8 Dat ze veel verdient, ___________ wel uit het feit dat ze volgende week alweer op vakantie gaat.

Communicatie

PUNCTUATION

Dutch punctuation is not generally a problem for speakers of English. Commas, however, can be tricky to use. The main rule to remember is: only use a comma if it makes the reading process easier. This means that a comma is generally used to indicate a pause when you are reading. It is usually also a good idea to place a comma between verbs which belong to different clauses, for instance when a subclause is followed by a main clause:

Als de vergadering niet doorgaat, ga ik vanmiddag naar huis.

For this reason, relative clauses usually end with a comma too (after all, they are a kind of subclause). However, non-restrictive relative clauses (which don't add vital new information) also start with a comma, whereas restrictive relative clauses (which add vital new information) never start with a comma.

Nederlandse vrouwen, die niet vaak fulltime werken, gaan bijna altijd tot hun achttiende naar school.

Nederlandse vrouwen die niet fulltime werken, hebben vaak jonge kinderen.

Oefening 42

Insert commas in the following sentences where necessary.

1 Het feit dat we de planning nog niet binnen hebben is erg vervelend want zo kunnen we niet beginnen.
2 De Olympische spelen die elke vier jaar worden gehouden vormen vaak het hoogtepunt van de carrière van veel sporters.

3 De meeste films die ik in de bioscoop ga zien zijn geen grote Hollywood blockbusters.
4 Hoe laat Joachim terugkomt weet ik niet maar ik zal zeggen dat je hebt gebeld.
5 Als ik je computer eerder dan aanstaande woensdag heb gerepareerd zal ik je wel even bellen.
6 Nederlandse vakantiegangers die naar het zuiden van Frankrijk gaan rijden vaak in een keer helemaal naar hun bestemming.

EXCLAMATIONS

Exclamations are words or phrases which are spoken or written with force. Obviously, they are used a lot more in spoken than in written language. Exclamations usually express an emotion, such as delight, disgust or surprise. In the interview, Fortuyn says: **Poeh!** to indicate that he is having difficulty in doing something.

Some other exclamations:

exclamation	*expresses*	*English equivalent*
jee/tjee! or **jee . . . zeg!**	surprise	really? gee!
nou! or **nou ja (zeg)!**	exasperation, disapproval or disbelief	well!, really!
nou nou!	surprise, or is used to calm someone down	my! good heavens! really!
nou en?	difference of opinion, or cynical indication of disinterest	so what? tough luck!
goh!	surprise	really?
ach!	sadness	oh dear!, really?
ach wat!	irritation	what do I care?
hè! **hè ja!**	pain or bad luck, tiredness, pain, agreement, enthusiasm	oh (dear)!, damn! phew! ouch! ah, yes!
hè?	expecting a positive reply from others	right? isn't it? don't you think?

Oefening 43

Add an exclamation to the following statements.

1 ___________ , dat is belachelijk, kun je niet maken!

2 ___________ , dat had ik helemaal niet verwacht.

3 ___________ , dat was wel genoeg. Nu ga ik even lekker zitten, hoor.

4 Ik heb de hele kamer vandaag geschilderd. Dat is niet gek, ___________ .

5 ___________ , wat kan het mij schelen? Ik doe gewoon wat ik wil.

6 ___________ , wat jammer dat hij de tenniswedstrijd heeft verloren. Hij heeft zo hard gevochten.

Cultuur

NORMEN EN WAARDEN

Ever since Pim Fortuyn's entry into Dutch politics and his outspoken ideas about Dutch culture and influences from immigrant cultures, an identity crisis has manifested itself amongst the Dutch. A collective uncertainty as to the national identity has become clear. One of the ways in which the debate about national identity has been taken up by politicians is in the area of **normen en waarden**. The Prime Minister has argued for a return to more old fashioned **normen en waarden**. The exact nature of these **normen en waarden** is hotly debated and contested.

The following text will give an idea about the areas touched by the debate surrounding **normen en waarden**. In contrast, the final text of this unit presents a different, dissenting view of the debate and ends this book on a much more cynical note.

Tekst 6 Normen en waarden

Normen en waarden zijn in het afgelopen jaar uitgegroeid tot een 'hot-issue'. In de samenleving lijken veel mensen het herstel van normen en waarden belangrijk te vinden.

Een waarde is een binnen een bepaalde groep of samenleving heersende opvatting, waaraan door de leden van deze groep of samenleving groot belang (of waarde) wordt toegekend. Bij een waarde kun je denken aan bijvoorbeeld: rekening houden met elkaar of respect hebben voor het eigendom van anderen. Deze waarden zijn uitgangspunten voor normen.

Normen zijn gedragsregels. Een informele norm is het opstaan voor een oudere man of vrouw in de bus en een formele norm is bijvoorbeeld het strafbaar stellen van diefstal volgens het Wetboek van Strafrecht.

De discussie over normen en waarden is uitgegroeid tot een maatschappelijk debat. Premier Balkenende vindt dat voor het besef en herstel van waarden en normen, het noodzakelijk is dat niet alleen de overheid maar ook de burgers hun verantwoordelijkheid kennen en nemen. Normen en waarden raken veel maatschappelijke terreinen, zoals:

- **Intergratie** ('Intergratie vereist inspanning van twee kanten', aldus S. Tak, Voorzitter, CDA-Jaarthemacommissie.);
- **Beloning topmanagers** ('Topmanagers, verbeter de wereld, neem uw verantwoordelijkheid en matig uw inkomen!', aldus G. Verburg, CDA Tweede Kamerlid.);
- **Internet etiquette** ('Voor een fatsoenlijke omgang met elkaar op internet is een cyberetiquette nodig', aldus Joop Wijn, staatssecretaris van Financiën.);
- **Opvoeding** ('Een thuis zonder liefde biedt weinig perspectief voor later', aldus M. Vroom, Voorzitter CDA-Theologenberaad.);
- **Religie** ('Geloof inspireert, richt je politiek handelen', aldus M. van Bijsterveldt, CDA Partijvoorzitter.);
- **Respect** ('Onkuis is wanneer mensen niet respectvol met elkaar omgaan. Platvloers woordgebruik vind ik ook een vorm van onkuisheid.', aldus M. de Pater, CDA Tweede Kamerlid.)

van: Steven de Jong. www.politiek-actie.net

Key vocabulary

belonen	to pay, to reward
het besef	understanding, idea, sense, consciousness
fatsoenlijk	decent, respectable
handelen	to conduct
matigen	to moderate, to restrain
onkuis	improper, indecent
de opvatting	view, belief, opinion
de opvoeding	upbringing, parenting
platvloers	coarse, vulgar
richten	to direct, to point
strafbaar stellen	to make punishable, to penalize
toekennen aan	to ascribe, to attribute
het wetboek van strafrecht	criminal/penal code, criminal laws

Oefening 44

1 Onderstreep in de tekst de definitie van 'een waarde'. Beschrijf deze definitie in je eigen woorden.
2 Hoe definieert de schrijver normen?
3 De schrijver geeft een voorbeeld van een informele norm. Kun je zelf nog andere voorbeelden verzinnen? Welke?
4 Welke maatschappelijke terreinen vind je zelf het belangrijkst als je over normen en waarden praat?

Oefening 45: Rollenspel

In een grote stad zijn er veel problemen met geweld, vandalisme, racisme, geluidsoverlast, etc. Er is overleg tussen de burgemeester en bevolkingsgroepen om te kijken hoe de situatie kan worden verbeterd. Kies een van de onderstaande rollen. De burgemeester leidt de discussie. Samen moet iedereen bepalen welke maatschappelijke terreinen de komende jaren de meeste aandacht moeten krijgen om de situatie in de stad te verbeteren. Lees voor de discussie eerst ook de laatste tekst van dit hoofdstuk. Probeer de tekst snel te lezen, en zonder woorden op te zoeken; je hoeft niet alles in de tekst te begrijpen.

Rollen:
- burgemeester
- vertegenwoordiger van winkeliers in een probleemwijk met veel immigranten
- vertegenwoordiger van Islamitische belangenvereniging (interest/lobby group)
- hoofd van de politie
- hoofd sociale dienst
- vertegenwoordiger uitgaansgelegenheden (places of entertainment, such as bars, cafés, restaurants, clubs)
- vertegenwoordiger milieuverenigingen

Oefening 46

Schrijf nu een korte tekst (50–70 woorden) met vijf concrete punten voor een brochure die in de stad moet worden verspreid. Het doel van de vijf punten is om het gedrag van mensen te veranderen, om de stad leefbaarder te maken voor iedereen. De brochure wordt verspreid in alle openbare gebouwen (gemeentehuis, stadskantoren, bibliotheken, sportcentra, etc.) en moet zo veel mogelijk mensen van de bevolking bereiken.

Tekst 7

Van de website van 'jonge socialisten in de PvdA'.

Leuk dat debat over 'de publieke moraal' in de Tweede Kamer gisteren. Tja, we hebben het verder niet zo gevolgd, maar we vinden het gewoon een prettige gedachte dat ons parlement zich bezig houdt met normen en waarden dingetjes. Eigenlijk zagen wij zelf de noodzaak van een speciaal normen en waarden debat niet zo, en dachten we dat politiek altijd al over normen en waarden ging.

Immers, elke partij, met uitzondering van D66, heeft haar gedachtengoed, bijvoorbeeld wij ons credo 'een eerlijke verdeling van kennis, welvaart en macht' en de VVD 'samen voor ons eigen'. Het zijn toch allemaal waarden en het wordt pas echt interessant als die waarden omgezet worden in concrete normen. Maar voor zo'n concretisering is 'de publieke moraal' een te breed onderwerp. Het debat deed dan ook sterk denken aan een bonte avond zoals we die vroeger op school hadden. Iedereen mocht een stukje opvoeren en ze mochten helemaal zelf weten wat. Tja, wat was er anders te verwachten, want de hele normen en waarden discussie gaat over zoveel dingen tegelijk dat het uiteindelijk nergens meer toe doet.

Iedereen heeft zijn of haar eigen waarden en iedereen, van christen-conservatief tot absoluut anarchist, zal daaruit een setje normen distilleren. Zelfs een criminele motorbende als de Banditos hebben normen en waarden, hun normen en waarden botsen alleen met die van nette burgers, Jonge Socialisten, Jan Peter en, zo af en toe, ook op dodelijke wijze met die van de Hell's Angels.

Uit: T. Rottinghuis/G. J. van Midden, www.js.nl

VOCABULARY

a.s. (aanstaande)	next (with regard to dates)
a.u.b. (alstublieft)	please
aan	at
aan: – het werk	at work
aan: – sport doen	to play a sport
aanbeveling, de	recommendation
aanbieden	to offer
aanbod, het	supply
aanbod, het	offer
aandacht, de	attention
aandacht: – besteden aan	to give attention to
aandeel, het	part, share
aangenaam	pleasant, convenient
aangestoken	lit
aangeven	to indicate
aankloppen	to knock on someone's door
aankomen	to gain weight
uitgebreid	extensively
aanleg, de	talent, aptitude
aanleg: – hebben voor	have a talent for
aanmerking: in – komen voor	to be eligible for
aanmoedigen	to encourage
aannemen	to accept
aanpak, de	approach, method
aanpassen: zich – aan	to adapt to, to integrate
aanpassen: zich – bij	to adapt (oneself) to, to integrate in
aanrader, de	something worth recommending
aanradertje, het	a must, highly recommended
aanschuiven	to queue
aanslag, de	attack
aansluiting, de	joining, connection
aanspreken	to appeal, to address
aansteken	to light
aanstoot, de	offence
aanstoot: – geven	to cause offence
aantal, het	number
aantrekkelijk	attractive
aantrekken: zich (n)iets – van iets	(not) to be bothered by something
aanvaarden	to accept
aanvaarden: de algemeen aanvaarde opvatting	generally accepted view
aanvoelen	to feel, to sense
aanvullen	to supplement, add to
aanwakkeren	to fan, to stir up

aanwezige, de	person present
aanwezigheid, de	the presence
aanwijzing, de	instruction
aanwrijven	rub against, blame
aard, de	character
aardappel, de	potato
aardbei, de	strawberry
aardig	nice
aardkluit, de	lump of earth
aarzelen	to hesitate
abonnement, het	subscription
abonnement: een – hebben op	to subscribe to, have subscription to
achten	to value, to expect
achterblijven	to be left behind
achterflap, de	the back (of a book)
achterlijk	backward, retarded
achterstandsbuurt, de	disadvantaged/ underprivileged area
achterstevoren	the wrong way round
achtervolgen	to chase
acteur, de	actor
actief	active
actiefilm, de	action film
actrice, de	actress
ademberovend/ adembenemend	breathtaking
administratie, de	administration
afbreken	to break off
afdeling, de	department
afgaan op	to go by
afgelopen	last, past (referring to days, weeks, months, years), finished
afgewezen worden	to be rejected
afhankelijk	dependent
afleiden	to distract
afprijzen	to reduce in price
afschaffen	to abolish
afscheid nemen van	to say goodbye to
afscheidsborrel, de	leaving/farewell drinks
afspraak, de	appointment
afspraak: een – maken	to make an appointment
afspreken	to arrange (to meet)
afstandelijk	distant
afstandsbediening, de	remote control
afvallen	to lose weight
afvragen: zich –	to ask oneself, to wonder
afwas: de – doen	to do the dishes
afwegen	to weigh up

afwezigheid, de	absence
afwijzen	to reject
afwisselend	varied
afzetmarkt, de	market
agenda, de	diary
agendapunt, het	discussion point for a meeting
al dan niet	whether or not
alcoholmatiging, de	reduced alcohol intake
algemeen	general
alleen	only
alleen maar	only
allemaal	all
allergisch zijn voor	to be allergic to
alles	everything
allez	come on (Flanders only)
allochtoon, de	immigrant (normally used for non-western immigrants only)
althans	at least
altijd	always
altijd: voor eens en –	once and for all
alweer	again
ambtenaar, de	civil servant
ammehoela	not on your life
amper	hardly
analfabeet, de	illiterate person
ander(e)	other
antwoord, het	answer
antwoord: het – luidt	the answer is
appelgebak, het	apple pie
apropos: iemand van zijn – brengen	to unnerve someone
arbeidsmarkt, de	labour market
arbeidsomstandigheden, de	working conditions
arbeidsparticipatie, de	level of employment
arbeidsvoorwaarde, de	term of employment
arm	poor
arm, de	arm
arm: in de armen sluiten	to embrace
armoede, de	poverty
artikel, het	article
asielbeleid, het	(political) asylum policy
atelier, het	studio
attent	considerate
auto, de	car
auto-onderhoud, het	car maintenance
avondeten, het	dinner
baaldag, de	off-day, sickie (at work)
baan, de	job, path
baan: in goede banen leiden	to steer in the right direction
babbeltje, het	chat
badkamer, de	bathroom
bajes, de	prison (slang)
bakken	to fry, bake
ban: in de – raken van	to fall under the spell of
bandje, het	tape
bankafschrift, het	bank statement
bank, de	sofa, bank
bebouwen	to build on, to cultivate
bebouwen: dicht bebouwd	densely built-up
bebouwing, de	buildings, housing
bedekken: zich –	to cover oneself
bedevaart, de	pilgrimage
bedoeling, de	intention
bedreven	skilled
bedriegen	to cheat
bedrijf, het	company
bedrijfsauto, de	company car
beeld, het	statue, sculpture, image
beeld: in – brengen	to show, to portray
been, het	leg
been: zijn beste beentje voorzetten	to put one's best foot forward
beetje, het	bit, little
beetje: een klein –	just a little
begaafd	gifted
begeleiden	to guide, to counsel
begijnhof, het	beguinage
beginnen	to begin
begrip, het	concept
behalve	apart from, except
behandelen	to deal with, to treat
behandeling, de	treatment
behang, het	wallpaper
beheer, het	management
beheersen	to master
beheren	to manage
behoefte, de	need
behoorlijk	decent(ly), adequate(ly), quite a bit
behoren	to belong
behoud: met – van	keeping
behouden	to keep
beide	both
beïnvloeden	influence
bejaard	aged, elderly
bejaarde, de	senior citizen
bejaardentehuis, het	old people's home
bel, de	bell, chime
bel: aan de – trekken	to draw someone's attention to something
belang, het	interest, importance
belang: van –	important
belangrijk	important
belastingaangifte, de	tax declaration
belastingformulier, het	tax form
belastingontduiker, de	tax dodger

beleid, het	policy
belofte, de	promise
beloven	to promise
bemiddelaar, de	negotiator
bemoeien: zich – met	to interfere with
benadering, de	approach
benieuwd	curious
beoordelen	to judge
bepaald	certain(ly), definite(ly), determined
bepaald: niet –	not exactly
bepalen	to determine
bepleiten	to advocate
bereiken	to reach
bergbeklimmer, de	mountaineer
beroep, het	profession
beroep: een – doen op	to appeal to
berusten op	to be based on
beschadigd	damaged
beschaving, de	civilisation
beschikken	to have at one's disposal
beschuit, de	Dutch crisp bakes
beseffen	to realise
beslissing, de	the decision
besparen	to save
besparing, de	saving
bespreken	to discuss
bespreking, de	discussion, meeting, review
bestaan uit	to consist of
bestellen	to order
bestelling, de	order
bestemming, de	destination
besturen	to govern, to lead
betaalbaar	affordable
betalen	to pay
beter af zijn	to be better off
betoverend	mesmerising, magical
betreffen	to concern
betreffen: wat mij betreft –	as far as I'm concerned
betrekking hebben op	to relate to
betrokken	involved
betrouwbaar	reliable
beurt: een goede – geven	to give a good clean
beurt: wie is er aan de – ?	who's next?
bevallen	to like, to give birth
bevallen: het bevalt me	I like it
bevestigen	to confirm
bevestigend	affirmative
bevolken	populate
bevrijden	to liberate
bewaarder, de	prison guard
bewaren	to keep, preserve, save
bewaren: God bewaar ons	Lord save us, good gracious
beweging, de	movement
beweren	to claim, state
bewering, de	claim, statement
bewijs, het	proof, evidence
bewijzen	to prove
bewijzen: zich –	to prove oneself
bewind, het	regime
bewust	conscious(ly)
bewustwording, de	becoming aware/ realisation
bezienswaardigheid, de	sight of interest
bezig	busy, working on
bezinnen: zich – over/op	to reflect upon, to contemplate
bezoek, het	visit
bezoeken	to visit
bezoeker, de	visitor
bezwaar, het	complaint
bieden	to offer
bier, het	beer
bij	at/with
bijdragen (aan)	to add to/contribute (to)
bijhouden	keep track
bijscholen: zich –	to take a training/ refresher course
bijstuderen	to continue one's studies
bijzonder	special, remarkable
bijzonder: in het –	in particular
binnen	inside
binnenland, het	interior, inland
binnenplaats, de	courtyard
bioscoop, de	cinema (the Netherlands)
bitterbal, de	warm snack (type of croquette)
blad, het	magazine, leaf
bladeren	to leaf through
blijkbaar	apparently
blijken	to prove to be, to turn out
blijven	stay
bliksem, de	lightning
blinken	to shine
bloedstollend	blood curdling
bloeiend	flowering
bloembollensector, de	the bulb sector
bloemkool, de	cauliflower
bloemschikken	flower arranging
bloes, de	blouse
bloot	naked, bare
blowtje, het	joint

blz (bladzijde)	page
bod: aan – komen	to get a chance
boek: een – uit hebben	to have finished a book
boek: goed te – staan	to have a good reputation
boekenbon, de	book voucher
boenen	to scrub, to clean
boerenkool, de	kale (kind of cabbage, connotation: banal, common, stupid)
boerke, het (Flemish)	country bumpkin
bollenveld, het	bulbfield
bolletje, het	roll
boodschap, de	message
boodschappen, de	shopping
boodschappen: – doen	to do the shopping
bord, het	sign, (dinner) plate
borst: uit volle –	at the top of one's voice
bos, de	bundle, bunch
botsen	to clash
botsing, de	clash, accident
bouwstijl, de	architectural style
bovenal	most of all
bovendien	besides, moreover
bovenlaag, de	upper layer (of society)
bovenvermeld	above mentioned
brand, de	fire
brandweer, de	fire brigade
brief, de	letter
broek, de	trousers
brood, het	bread
brood: – op de plank hebben	to make a living
brood: een snee(tje) –	slice of bread
broodje, het	sandwich
brug, de	bridge
brug: bruggen bouwen	to build bridges
brui: de – geven aan iets	to give something up
bruidspaar, het	bridal couple
bruin	brown
brutaal	brazen, bold
budget, het	budget
budget: een – uittrekken voor iets	to budget for something
bui, de	shower (rain), mood
buik, de	belly, stomach
buiten	outside
burgerlijk	bourgeois, conventional
burgerzin, de	sense of public responsibility
busrit, de	coach journey
buurt, de	area
buurt: in de –	around/near
buurtwinkel, de	the neighbourhood shop (grocer)

ça va	I'm fine (Flanders only)
ça va?	everything all right? (Flanders only)
campagne voeren	to campaign
campagne, de	campaign
centrum, het	centre
charmant	charming
chips, de	crisps
cijfer, het	mark
cineast, de	film maker
cinema, de	cinema (Flanders)
communicatie, de	communication
communicatief	communicative
concentreren: zich – (op)	to concentrate (on)
conferentieoord, het	conference venue
confronterend	confrontational
courgette, de	courgettes
croque monsieur, de	toasted sandwich
cultiveren	cultivate
cursus, de	course

d.w.z (dat wil zeggen)	i.e.
da's (= dat is)	that's (colloquial)
daar . . . toe	for this, to this end
daardoor	because of that
daarentegen	on the other hand
daarom	because of that, therefore
dag!	bye bye!
dag, de	day
dag: om de –	every other day
dagelijks	daily
dagtocht, de	day trip
dalen	to go down, to decrease
dan ook	therefore, not surprisingly
dank, de	thanks, gratitude
dank: nee, – je	no thanks
dankbaar	grateful
dank je wel	thank you
dapper	brave
dat klopt	that's right/correct
databank, de	database
dateren van	to date from
datum, de (plural: data)	date
debiel	retarded
deelnemer, de	participant
deels	partly
degelijk	reliable, respectable, thoroughly
degelijk: wel –	really, actually, positively
degene	she/the one who
dekbed, het	duvet
delen	to share

den, de	pine tree
denken	to think
departement, het	government department/ministry
dergelijk	such (a)
deskundigheid, de	expertise, professionalism
deugd, de	virtue
deur, de	door
deur: de – uitgaan	to leave the house
dichter, de	poet
diens	(old genitive form) his/her
dienst, de	service, department, religious service
dierbaar	precious
dijk, de	dyke
dik	fat, obese
dineetje, het	dinner
directeur, de	director, manager
doei	bye
doel, het	goal, aim
doelgroep, de	target audience
doelstelling, de	aim, objective
doemdenker, de	doom-monger
donderen	thunder, rumble
donderen: het in Keulen horen –	be stunned, flabbergasted
doodslag, de	manslaughter
doolhof, het	maze
doorgaan	to continue, to persist, to go through, to take place
doorgaan met	to continue
doorgewinterd	through and through
doorgroeimogelijkheden	possibilities for growth (usually within a career)
doorhalen: een nacht –	to make a night of it
doorsnee	average
doorvragen	to keep on asking
doorzetten	to persevere
doorzettingsvermogen, het	perseverance, determination
draaien	to turn, to show (of a film)
dragen	to wear, to carry
drang, de	urge
drank, de	(alcoholic) drink(s)
dreigend	threatening
dressoir, het	sideboard
dreun, de	bang, blow
driftkikker, de	hothead
drijvende kracht, de	driving force
dringend	urgent
duidelijk	clear
duik: een – nemen	to go swimming (lit: to take a dive)
duizend: uit duizenden	one in a thousand
duren	to last
durven	to dare
dus	so
duur	expensive
echt	really
echter	however
echtgenote, de	wife, spouse
eentje: in m'n –	on my own
eenwording, de	unification
eenzaam	lonely
eenzijdig	one-sided
eerlijk	fair
eerst	first
eerstvolgende	the first/next
eerwraak, de	honour killing
eeuwig	eternal
effen	plain (of colours)
ei, het	egg
eigen	own
eigenaardigheid, de	peculiarity
eigenbelang, het	self-interest
eigenlijk	actually
eigenschap, de	characteristic
eindigen	to come to an end
eis, de	demand
elders	elsewhere
elk(e)	each
emanancipatiebeweging, de	movement of liberation/emancipation
en	and
enigszins	somewhat, a little
enkel	only
enkel: – en alleen	only
enscenering, de	the staging, the direction
enthousiasme, het	enthusiasm
erg: – vinden	to mind
erg: iets erg vinden	to be upset by something
ergeren: zich – aan	to be irritated/annoyed by
eromheen	around it
erover	about it
eruitzien	to look like
ervaring	experience
ervaringswereld, de	world of experience
ethisch	ethical
even	just (as), (only) just
even: heel –	for a very short period of time

eventueel	possibly
evenwicht, het	balance
evenwichtig	balanced
exemplaar, het	the copy
exportbedrijf, het	export company
extralegale voordelen	additional benefits to one's salary (Flanders only)
fabriek, de	factory, plant
fase, de	phase
fatsoen, het	decency
fatsoenlijk	decent
feestje, het	the party
fel	bright
feliciteren	to congratulate
fiets, de	bicycle
figureren	to appear, to be an extra
file, de	traffic jam
filmklassieker, de	film classic
filmster, de	film star
financieel, financiële	financial
financiën, de	finances
flatgenoot, de	roommate
flink	quite
flitsend	flashy
fluisteren	to whisper
fluiten	to play the flute, to whistle, to sing (birds only)
fokken	to breed
formaat, het	size
fors	considerable/ considerably
friet, de	chips/fries
frieten	chips
frisdrank, de	soft drink
frituur, de	the chip shop (Flanders only)
fruit, het	fruit
functie, de	duty, function, position
functioneringsgesprek, het	staff review, appraisal
gaan	to go
gaan: – over	to be about (book, film, play, etc.)
gaan: dat gaat nog wel	we'll manage (more or less)
gaatje, het	small hole
gaatje: naar een – zoeken	see if you can fit it in
gas geven	to accelerate
gaswinning, de	gas extraction
geacht worden	to be expected to
gebakje, het	cake
gebakken	fried
gebied: op het – van	concerning
geboorte, de	the birth
geboren en getogen	born and bred
geborgenheid, de	security/safety
gebrek, het	lack, want, shortcoming
gebrek: – aan	lack of
gebruik, het	consumption, use
gebruikelijk	usual
gebruiken	to use
gedeeltelijk	partially
gedetineerde, de	detainee
gedicht, het	poem
gedrag, het	behaviour
gedragen: zich –	to behave (oneself)
geducht	fearsome
gedurende	during
geenszins	by no means
gefeliciteerd	congratulations
gegoede burgerij, de	bourgeoisie
gegradueerde, de	graduate
geheel	completely
geheim, het	the secret
geheim: in het diepste –	in all secrecy
gehoor, het	hearing
gehoor: geen –	no answer
geit, de	goat
gejaagd	stressed
gejuich, het	cheering
gekookt	boiled
gelden voor	to apply to
geldwolf, de	money-grubber
gelegenheid, de	place, occasion, opportunity, chance
gelegenheid: iemand in de – stellen om	to give someone an opportunity to
geliefde, de	the lover
gelijkgezinde, de	person holding similar views and values
gelijkwaardigheid, de	equality
geloof, het	religion, belief
geloven	to believe
geluid, het	the sound
gemeen	nasty, mean
gemeenplaats, de	commonplace, cliché
gemeenschap, de	community
gemeenschapszin, de	sense of community
gemeente, de	council
gemeenteraad, de	local council
gemengd	mixed
gemoedelijkheid, de	easy going-ness
geneigd zijn	to tend to
genieten van	to enjoy
genoeg	enough

genuanceerd	balanced, nuanced
gepaard gaan met	accompanied by
gepaard: de daarmee – gaande	the accompanying
gepantserd	armour-plated
gepast	appropriate, fitting
gepast: – geld	exact change
gepensioneerd	retired
gerecht, het	dish
gerechtshof, het	court of justice
gericht op	aimed at
gerichtheid	to be focused on
geringste, het	the least
gerucht, het	rumour, gossip, sound
geruchtmakend	controversial
gerust	without any fear/ problem
geruststellen	to reassure
geschiedenis, de	history
geschikt	right
geslaagd	successful, to have passed an exam
gesloten	closed
gespreksgenoot, de	discussion/conversation partner
gestadig (also: gestaag)	steadily
gestorven	deceased, dead
geur, de	smell, scent
geurtje, het	smell, fragrance
gevaarlijk	dangerous
gevangene, de	prisoner
gevangenis, de	prison
gevangenisstraf, de	prison sentence
gevarieerd	varied
gevel, de	facade, exterior
gevestigd zijn	to be located
gevoel, het	feeling
gevoel: een goed – voor humor	a good sense of humour
gevoelig	sensitive
geweldig	tremendous(ly), terrific(ally)
gewend aan	to be used to
gewest, het	region
gewicht, het	weight, importance
gewichtig	weighty, important
gewond raken	get wounded
gewond	wounded
gewoon	normal(ly), just
gewoonte, de	habit, tradition, convention
gezag, het	authority
gezellig	nice, pleasant, cosy
gezicht, het	face
gezinshereniging, de	reunification of a family
gezinsuitbreiding, de	addition to the family
gezond	healthy
gezondheidsbevordering, de	promotion of public health
gids, de	guide
gierig	mean, stingy
gisteren	yesterday
glanzend	shining
glas, het (plural: glazen)	glass
glijbaan, de	the slide
glinsteren	to shine, to shimmer
gloed, de	glow
goed	good/well
goed zitten	to fit nicely/comfortably
goedemiddag	good afternoon
goedemorgen	good morning
goedenavond	good evening
goedendag	good day
goedkeuring, de	approval
goedkoop	cheap
goedmaken	to make up
goh	gee, my (expresses hesitation, surprise)
golfbaan, de	golf course
graag	please, I like to . . .
graag: – gedaan	you're welcome
graan, het	grain
grachtenhuis, het	house on a canal
grappig	funny, amusing
grauw	grey
grauw: de grauwe massa	the masses
grens, de	border, limit
grillig	whimsical
grind, het	shingle, gravel
groente, de	vegetable
grondslag, de	foundation
groot	big
grootheidswaan, de	megalomania
grootmacht, de	superpower
groots	great, grand
GSM, de	mobile phone (Flanders only)
gunstig	favourable
gunstig: – staan tegenover	to be in favour of
gvd (godverdomme)	damn it
haar	her
haar, het	hair
hagel, de	hail
hagelslag, de	chocolate sprinkles
halen	to get, reach, fetch
halfrond, het	hemisphere
hallo	hello

halt: een – toeroepen aan	call a halt to
ham, de	ham
hand, de	hand
hand: er is iets aan de –	something is up
hand: handen thuishouden	to keep one's hands off
hand: in de – houden	to keep in check
hand: in handen vallen van	to fall into the hands of
hand: op handen dragen	to put on a pedestal, to adore
handel, de	trade
handleiding, de	manual
hart, de	heart, centre
hartje . . .	in the centre of . . .
hartstikke	very, really (very informal)
hartverwarmend	heartwarming
heden, het	present (day), now
heden: – ten dage	these days
heel erg	very
heel even	for a very short period of time
heel	intact, undamaged, very (much)
heerlijk	wonderful
heersend	dominant
hei, de	heath(land), moorland
heil: zijn – zoeken in	to find what he wants
hekel: een – hebben aan	to dislike
held, de	hero
heldenmoed, de	heroic courage
helemaal	completely
hemd, het	the shirt
herkenbaar	recognisable
herkomst, de	origin
herstellen	to repair
hesp, de	ham (Flanders only)
hetzelfde	the same
heus	real, actual
hier	here
hilarish	hilarious
hoe het (ook) zij	whatever way
hoeven: niet –	to not have to
hoewel	although, even though
hogerop	higher up
hogeropgeleid	well-educated (usually refers to having a university or college education)
hoi	hi, bye
hol	empty, without content
homohuwelijk, het	gay marriage
hond, de	dog
hoofddoekje, het	headscarf
hoofdzaak, de	main point
hoofdzaak: in –	mainly
hoog oplopen	to rise high
hoogzwanger	heavily pregnant
hooi, het	hay
hoorbaar	audible
hopen	to hope
horeca, de	catering business or hotel (*ho*tel, *re*staurant, *ca*fé)
horen bij	to belong to
horen	to hear
houding, de	attitude
huid, de	the skin
huidig	current
huis, het	house
huis: je moet van goede huize komen	you have to be very good
huishouden, het	to run the home, housekeeping
huisvrouw, de	housewife
humeurig	moody
huren	to rent
huwelijk, het	wedding
huwelijksvoltrekking, de	wedding ceremony
huzarens(a)la(de), de	Russian salad (traditional dish)
hypotheek, de	mortgage
i.v.m. (in verband met)	with regard to
ICT, de	information and communication technology
ieder	every
iel	thin
iets	something
ijl	thin, oxygen-starved
ik-beeld, het	self image
immers	after all
in trek	popular, in demand
in zijn	to be popular/trendy
inbreken	to break in(to) (a house)
inbreng, de	contribution, input
inconsequentie, de	inconsistency
inderdaad	that's right
indruk, de	impression
indruk: onder de – zijn	to be impressed
informatica, de	I.T.
ingebeeld	imagined
inhuren	to hire
inkomen, het	income
inkomensverschil, het	difference/gap in income
inmiddels	meanwhile, in the mean time
innemen	to take, to capture

inrichten	to decorate, to furnish (a house)
inschenken	to pour
inslag, de	streak, characteristic
inslikken	to swallow
interesseren: zich – in/voor	to be interested in
interimbureau, het	employment agency (Flanders only)
intimiteit, de	intimacy
invoering, de	implementation/start
inwijden	to inaugurate
inwisselbaar	interchangeable
inzet, de	effort
inzetten: zich – voor	devote/dedicate oneself to
jaar, het	year
jaar: al jaren	for years
jaarlijks	annual
jaarrapport, het	annual report
jaarverslag, het	annual report
ja-woord, het	saying 'I will' during a wedding ceremony
jazeker	yes (indeed)
jee: o –	o, dear
jl. (jongstleden)	last (with regard to dates)
jodendom, het	Judaism
jong	young
jong: van jongs af	from an early age
journaal, het	name of Dutch news broadcast
juichen	to cheer
juist	right
jullie	you (plural)
kaars, de	candle
kaartje, het	ticket
kaas, de	cheese
kameel, de	camel
kamer	room
kamermeisje, het	the chambermaid
kamerverkiezingen, de	general elections
kanaal, het	channel, canal
Kanaal, het	the English Channel
kanker, de	cancer
kans: gelijke kansen geven	give equal opportunities
kant, de	edge, side
kant: aan de – zetten	to push something aside/give someone the shove
kant: aan de andere –	on the other hand
kant: aan de ene –	on the one hand

kanten	made of lace
kantoor, het	the office
kanttekening, de	comment, query
kapot	broken
kapot maken	to destroy, to wreck
kapsel, het	hairdo
karaktertrek, de	character trait
karig	meagre
kast, de	cupboard, closet
kast: uit de – komen	to come out of the closet
kater, de	hangover
keer: binnen de kortste keren	in no time
keer: de ene –	one time
keerzijde, de	the other side of the coin
keihard	rock hard, tough
kennis, de	acquaintance
kennistoename, de	increased knowledge
kerel, de	bloke
kerk, de	church
kerngezond	in perfect health
kernwapen, het	nuclear weapon
kernwoord, het	keyword
ketjap, de	soy sauce
keurig	proper(ly), tidy, tidily
kever, de	beetle
kibbelen	to bicker
kind, het (plural: kinderen)	child
kinderopvang, de	childcare, nursery, childminder
kindersubsidie, de	child benefit
klaar staan	to be ready / to be there for someone
klaar zijn	to be ready
klaarmaken	to prepare
klaarstaan: voor iemand –	be there for someone
klagen	to complain, moan
klank, de	sound
klantenopvolging, de	customer care (Flanders only)
klantenwerving, de	recruiting new customers
klasreünie, de	class reunion
klasse, de	class
kleinburgerlijk	lower middle class/parochial
kletsen	to chat
kleur, de	colour
klikken	to hit it off
klimhal, de	climbing wall
klimmen	to climb
klinkklaar	plain, pure
klomp, de	clog

kloof, de	gap, ravine
kloppen	to be correct/right
kloppen: zich op de borst –	to congratulate oneself
knal, de	explosive sound
knelpunt, het	sticking point
knikkeren	to play marbles
knoflook, de	garlic
knoop, de	knot, button
knoop: knopen doorhakken	(finally) come to a decision
knuist, de	fist
knus	cosy, friendly
koek, de	biscuit
koek: gevulde –	almond cake/biscuit
koekje, het	biscuit
koel	cool
koffie zetten	to make coffee
koffie, de	coffee
koken	to cook
kokosmelk, de	coconut milk
komedie, de	comedy
komen	to come
komen: erachter –	to find out
komen: hoe komt dat?	how come?
koningshuis, het	monarchy
koningsschap, het	monarchy
koolzaad, het	rape seed
koopkracht, de	spending power
kop, de	head
kopen	to buy
kopstuk, het	ringleader
kordaat	firm
kort: iets te – komen	to lack something
kortaf	short, curt
korten	to cut back
korting, de	discount
kortom	in short, so
kosteloos	with no cost
kosten	to cost
kosten: op – van	paid by
kracht, de	strength, power
krachtig	powerful
krant, de	newspaper
krantenartikel, het	newspaper article
krantenwinkel, de	the newsagent
kratje, het	crate
kreet, de	expression, slogan
kritiek, de	criticism
kroeg, de	bar, cafe
kroepoek, de	prawn crackers
kroket, de	fast food snack: croquette filled with meat ragout
kudde, de	herd
kunstenares, de	artist (female)
kunstmatig	artificial
kussen	to kiss
kussen, het	pillow
kust, de	coast
kuststreek, de	coastal region
kwaad doen	to do harm
kwajongen, de	mischievous boy
kwaken	to quack
kwarktaart, de	cheese cake
kwekerij, de	nursery (garden centre)
kwetsen	to hurt (someone)
kwijt	lost
laaggeschoold	lower educated
laat	late
lachwekkend	laughable
laf	cowardly
Lage Landen, de	low countries
lakken	to varnish
landmeter, de	(land) surveyor
landschap, het	landscape, scenery
lang geleden	a long time ago
langetermijnrelatie, de	long term relationship
lastig	awkward, difficult
lastig: iemand – vallen	to bother someone
laten	to let/have (someone do something)
laten: laat maar	never mind
leefomgeving, de	living environment
lef hebben	to have guts
lef, de/het	guts, nerve
legpuzzel, de	jigsaw puzzle
lekker	nice, delicious
lerares, de	teacher (female)
lesprogramma, het	curriculum
letten op	to pay attention to
leven	to live
leven, het	life
leven: langs elkaar heen –	to live near each other without making contact
levensovertuiging, de	philosophy of life, world view
levensstandaard, de	living standard
leverancier, de	supplier
levering, de	delivery
leveringstermijn, de	ETD, estimated time (or period) of delivery
lezen	to read
lichaam, het	body
lid, het (pl: leden)	member
lidmaatschap, het	membership
lief	sweet, cute
liefde, de	love
liefde: de – bedrijven	to make love

liefdesbrief, de	love letter
liever	rather
liever (doen)	rather, to prefer to (do)
liever hebben	to prefer
ligging, de	position, location
lijf, het	body
lijf: op het – geschreven staan	to be made/cut out for something
lijk, het	corpse, dead body
lijk: over lijken gaan	to be merciless, show no mercy
lijken op	to look like
lijken	to seem, appear
lijnen	to slim, diet
lijstje, het	list
lippenstift, de	lipstick
loempia, de	spring roll
logeren	to stay/sleep over
lolbroek, de	clown, joker
loodgieter, de	plumber
loodje: de laatste loodjes wegen het zwaarst	the last mile is the longest
look, de	garlic
loopafstand, de	walking distance
lucht, de	air, sky
lucht: gebakken –	hot air
lucht: uit de – gegrepen	unfounded
luisterspel, het	radio play
lukken	to manage, to work
m.a.w. (met andere woorden)	in other words
m.b.t. (met betrekking tot)	with regard to
maag, de	stomach
maag: in je – zitten met iets	to be troubled by something
maat, de	measure, size
maat: op –	on demand/bespoke
machtsambities	ambitions for power
madame	Mrs (Flanders only)
magie, de	magic
maken	to make
maken: heeft te – met	has to do with, is related to
makkelijk	easy
maling hebben aan	to not give a damn
mannenblad, het	men's magazine
map, de	folder
marketingbedrijf, het	marketing company
markt, de	market
martelpraktijk, de	torture
massaal	massive(ly)
mate, de	measure, extent
mate: in toenemende –	increasingly
mazzel, de	luck
mazzel: de – !	see you!
medewerker, de	employee, member of staff
meedoen	joining in, going along with others
meegaan	to come along
meegenomen: dat is –	that is an added benefit
meel, het	flour
meeleven	to sympathise
meenemen	to take with you
meestal	mostly
meetapparatuur, de	measuring equipment
meetlat, de	yardstick
meid, de	young woman (informal)
meisjesnaam, de	maiden name, girl's name
melig	cheesy
melk, de	milk
mengelmoes, de	mishmash
menig	many a
mening, de	opinion
mensdom, het	mankind
merci	thank you
merk, het	brand name
merken	to notice
met	with
met z'n: met z'n vieren/vijven	the four/five of us
metselaar, de	bricklayer
middag, de	afternoon
middag: tussen de –	lunch
middeleeuwen, de	Middle Ages
middeleeuws	medieval
midden in	in the middle/in the centre
midden, het	middle
midden: te – van	in the midst of, among
mijn	my
mileuvriendelijk	environmentally friendly
minachten	to look down upon
minima, de	people on low income
minstens	at least
mis	wrong
misdaad, de	crime
mishandeling, de	abuse of women, domestic violence
mislopen	to go wrong
mislukken	to fail
mislukt	failed
mobiel, de/het	mobile phone
mobieltje, het	mobile phone
mode, de	fashion
modebedrijf, het	a fashion company
moeder, de	mother

moeite, de	trouble, effort
moeras, het	swamp
mogelijk	possible
molen, de	windmill
momenteel	at the moment
mondig	articulate
mooi	beautiful / pretty
mooi: het mooie	the beauty of it
moordenaar, de	murderer
mop, de	joke
mouw, de	sleeve
mouw: ergens een – aan passen	to find a way round something
muisjes, de	aniseed comfits
murmelen	to murmer
muur, de	wall
muziek, de	music
naartoe	to
naburig	neighbouring
nadeel, het	disadvantage
nadenken over	to think about
nagel, de	nail
nagenoeg	nearly
nakijken	to check, to mark
namelijk	as it happens
namens	on behalf of
nasi, de	an Indonesian rice dish
natregenen	get wet (with the rain)
nauw	tight, narrow
NAVO, de	NATO
Nederland	the Netherlands
Nederlands	Dutch
neerslachtigheid, de	depression, low spirits
neger, de	black person (derogatory)
nemen	to have, to take
net	(only) just
net als	just like
niemand	nobody
niet	not
niet: zo –	otherwise, if not
niettemin	nevertheless
nieuw	new
nieuwbouw, de	new(ly) built house
nieuws, het	news
niveau, het	level
nodig hebben	to need
noemen	to call
nog	still
nogal	quite
noodzakelijk	necessary
norm, de	norm
notaris, de	the notary (⊕a lawyer, solicitor)

nu	now
nuchter	sober
ober, de	waiter
of	or, if
officier van justitie, de	public prosecutor
ogenblik, het	moment
omdat	because
omhelzing, de	embrace
omkomen	to be killed
omleggen	to turn over
omloop: in – komen	to be introduced
omschrijving, de	description
omtoveren	to change (as if by magic)
omvang, de	dimension, size
onafhankelijk	independent
onberispelijk	impeccable
onbeschoft	rude
onbetrouwbaar	unreliable, untrustworthy
onbillijk	unfair (very formal)
onbuigzaam	uncompromising
ondanks	despite
onderdrukking, de	oppression
ondergeschikt (aan)	inferior, subservient (to)
onderhouden	to maintain, to look after
onderling	amongst one another
ondernemend	enterprising
onderscheiden: zich – van	to distinguish oneself from
onderstrepen	to underline
ondertekenen	to sign
onderweg zijn	to be on the road
onderwijsniveau, het	level of education
onderzoek, het	research
onderzoek: – doen naar iets	to do research into something
onderzoeken	to examine
ongeacht	regardless of
ongelofelijk/ongelooflijk	unbelievable
ongemak, het	discomfort
ongepast	inappropriate
ongerust	worried
ongewoon	unusual
ongezond	unhealthy
onheil, het	doom, calamity
onjuist	incorrect
onkruid, het	weeds
onmenselijk	inhuman
onpartijdig	impartial
onrecht, het	injustice, wrong
onrecht: ten onrechte	wrongly
onschuldig	innocent

ontbijt, het	breakfast
ontbijten	to have breakfast
ontdooien	to defrost
ontevreden	dissatisfied
ontgaan	to fail to notice
onthaasten	to de-stress
ontkenning, de	denial
ontlenen	to derive
ontnemen	to take away
ontploffing, de	eruption, explosion
ontplooien: zich –	to develop one's potential
ontroeren	to move
ontroerend	moving, poignant
ontrollen	to unfold
ontslaan	to dismiss, fire, sack
ontslag, het	dismissal, redundancy
ontslag: – nemen	to resign
ontsnappen	to escape
ontstaan uit	to originate from
ontvangen	to receive
ontwikkelen	to develop
ontwikkelen: zich –	to develop (oneself)
ontwikkelingshulp, de	development aid
ontzetten	to buckle, to free
ontzettend veel	an awful lot
ontzettend	very, terribly
onverschrokken	fearless, undaunted
onverwacht	unexpected
onweer, het	thunder and lightning
ook	too, also
oordeel, het	judgement
oorspronkelijk	original(ly)
op bezoek geweest	visited
op is op	when it's gone it's gone
op	used up, finished
op voorhand	in advance
opduiken	to arise
opeens	suddenly
opeisen	to demand
open en bloot	openly
open haard, de	open fire
openbaar	public, neutral
openbaar vervoer, het	public transport
opgaan in	to merge into, to be swallowed up by
opgeleid	educated
opgelost	solved
opkloppen	to stir up
opkomen voor	to stand up for
opkomst, de	turnout
oplaaien	to flare up
opleiding, de	training, education
opleveren	to gain
oplossen	to solve
oplossing, de	solution
opnemen	to answer (phone), to record, to include
oppervlakkig	superficial
oprecht	sincere
oprichten	to found
oprichting, de	foundation
oprotten	to bugger off
opruimen	to clear/tidy up
opschieten	to hurry up, make progress
opspraak: in – komen	become the talk of the town
opstaan	to get out of bed
opstandeling, de	rebel
opstelling, de	position
optelsom, de	addition, sum
optreden	to perform
optreden, het	action (taken)
opvallend	remarkable
opvatten	to interpret
opvatting: de algemeen aanvaarde –	generally accepted view
opvoeren	to perform, present
opvolging, de	succession
opzeggen	to cancel
opzicht: ten opzichte van	with regards to
ordening, de	structure, planning
ouder, de	parent
over: – 10 minuten	in 10 minutes
overbekend	very well known
overdekt	covered
overdragen	to hand over
overdreven	exaggerated
overdrijven	to exaggerate
overeenkomst, de	similarity
overeenkomstig	according to
overgaan	to ring (telephone)
overhebben	to have left over
overheid, de	government, state
overigens	by the way
overkomen als	to come across
overkomen	to happen to
overleven	to survive, survival
overlijden	to die
overlopen: in elkaar –	to fuse and mingle
overschatten	to overestimate
overtreffen	to exceed
overtuigen	to convince
overvloedig	abundant
overvol	completely full, packed
overwegen	to consider
overwinning, de	victory
overzichtelijk	conveniently arranged

p. (pagina)	page
paaltje: als het puntje bij – komt	if push comes to shove
paf staan	to be flabbergasted
pak, het	pack(age), carton
papa	dad
paraplu, de	umbrella
parel, de	pearl
paskamer, de	changing room
passen	to try on / to fit
passen bij	to fit
patat, de	chips/fries
patisserie, de	luxury cakes and tarts
patroon, het	pattern
patrouille: op –	on patrol
pensioenregeling, de	pension scheme
per se	necessarily, at any price
pers, de	press, media
personenauto, de	private car
persoonlijk	personal
pet, de	cap
peterselie, de	parsley
pias, de	clown
piepjong	very young
pils, de/het	beer, lager
pilsje, het	a beer (lager)
pineut: de – zijn	to be the mug
pintje, het	beer, lager
pips: er – uit zien	to look a bit pale
pistolet, de	bread roll
plaats	place
plaats: in – van	instead of
plaatsvinden	to take place
plakken	stick
plan: van – zijn	to intend to do something
plat	coarse, vulgar
platlopen: de deur –	always be knocking on someone's door
platteland, het	countryside
plezant	nice, fun (Flanders only)
plooien	to bend, fold (Flanders only)
poeh	blimey, gee
poepie, het	little darling
poetsen	to polish, to clean
poging, de	attempt
poging: een – doen	to attempt
populair	popular
potdicht	shut tight
praatje, het	chat
praatje: een – maken met	to have a chat with
praatjes hebben	to have airs, have a big mouth
pre, de/het	advantage
preek, de	sermon
prent, de	print, picture, illustration
prestatie, de	performance, achievement
prestatie: prestaties leveren	to achieve
prestatiegericht	achievement-oriented
pret, de	joy, fun
preuts	prudish
prijsgeven: iets –	to give something up
proberen	to try
probleem, het	problem
producent, de	producer, manufacturer
proeven	to taste
profileren: zich – (als)	to present oneself (as)
psycholoog, de	psychologist
pukkel, de	spot
puntje, het	(hard) bread roll
qua	in terms of
raar	strange, weird
radiospot, de	radio commercials
raken	to hit, to get, to touch
rang, de	rank
recht: – hebben op iets	to have a right to something
recht voor zijn raap zijn	to call a spade a spade
rechtzetten: iets –	to put something right, to explain something
reclame	commercial, ad
reclame maken	to advertise
redelijk	reasonable/bly
reden, de	reason
regel, de	rule
regelen	to arrange
regelmatig	regularly
regen, de	rain
regisseren	to direct
regisseur, de	director
reiken	to reach
reis, de	journey
reisvergoeding, de	travel expense
reizen	to travel
rekening houden met	to take into account
rekening, de	bill
rekenkundig	mathematical
relatie, de	relation
relativeren	to put into perspective
rem, de	brake
remedie, de	remedy, cure
remmen	to brake

rendement, het	return (on an investment)
reportage, de	report for media
reserveren	to book
resultaatgericht	result-oriented
retour	return
retraite: in – gaan	to go into retreat
rij: in de – staan	to stand in line, to queue
rijk	rich
rijst, de	rice
rimpelloos	without hitches
roddel, de	gossip
roddelblad, het	gossip magazine
roddelpers, de	gossip press
roem, de	fame
roeping, de	calling
roggebrood, het	pumpernickel bread
romantiek, de	romanticism, romance
romantisch	romantic
rondkijken	to look around
rondsnuffelen	to browse
rooien	to dig up
rook, de	smoke
rot	rotten, lousy, wretched
rotspartij, de	rock formation
rouwen	to mourn
ruiken	to smell
ruim	more than, over
ruimhartig	generous
ruimteclaim, de	claim on/need for space or land
ruimtelijke indeling, de	(town and country) planning
ruimtelijke ordening, de	environmental planning
ruit, de	window
rust, de	peace and quiet
ruzie, de	fight/argument
s.v.p. (s'il vous plaît)	please
salade, de	salad
samen	together
samenhokken	to live together in cramped conditions
samenleving, de	society
samenvatten	to summarise
sanctie, de	sanction
sap, het	juice
saus, de	sauce
schade, de	damage
schamen: zich –	to be ashamed/embarrassed
schandaal, het	scandal
schandaal: een grof –	a crying shame
scheen, de	shin
scheen: iemand tegen de schenen schoppen	to step on (someone's) toes
scheetje, het	little sweetie
scheiding, de	separation, divorce
schelpdier, het	shell fish
schema, het	table
schenken	to donate, to pour
schepen, de	alderman (Flanders only)
scheren: iedereen over één kam –	to lump everyone together
scherm, het	screen
schermen met	to talk hot air
scherp	sharp, spicy
schetsen	to sketch, to draft
schetsen: wat schetst mijn verbazing	to my own amazement
scheurkalender, de	calendar with a page a day
schijnen	to seem, to appear
schilderen	to paint
schilderij, het	painting
schoen, de	shoe
schoen: in de schoenen schuiven van	to blame on
scholing, de	education, training
schoon	beautiful (only in Flanders), clean
schoonhouden	to keep clean
schoonmaken	to clean
schrikken	to be shocked, frightened
schudden: door elkaar –	to shake
schuilgaan	to hide, to be hidden
schuld, de	debt, guilt, blame
schuld: de – krijgen van	to get the blame
schuld: de – op zich nemen	to take the blame
secretaresse, de	secretary
secularisatie, de	secularisation
sekspoes, de	sex kitten
serieus	serious
showdown: een – geven	to defeat
sier: goede – maken	to show off
sinaasappel, de	orange
sjansen	to flirt
slaan: dat slaat nergens op	that makes no sense at all
slaan: ik heb me erdoor geslagen	I got through it
slaatje, het	salad
slachtoffer, het	victim
slagen	to succeed, to pass (an exam)

slagvaardig	decisive, on the ball
slank	slim
slappeling, de	weakling
slecht	bad
slim	clever, smart
slof, de	slipper
slof: het vuur uit de sloffen lopen	wear oneself out
slordig	messy, sloppy
sluiten	to close
smaak, de	taste
smal	narrow
snel	quick(ly), fast
snelweg, de	motorway/freeway
snotteren	to cry, to blubber
soep, de	soup, mess
sok, de	sock
solidair zijn	to show solidarity
solliciteren	to apply for a job
soms	sometimes
spaarzin, de	being keen to save money
spannend	thrilling, exciting
sparen	to save money
sperzieboon, de	green bean
spier, de	muscle
spontaan	spontaneous
spontaniteit, de	spontaneity
spoor, het	platform
spoorwegen, de	rail company
sporten	to play sports
sprankelend	sparkling
spreektaal, de	spoken language
springen	to jump, to break
sprookje, het	fairy tale
spruitjes, de	Brussels sprouts
staal, het	steel
staan bij	to match
staan	to stand
staan: ergens achter –	to approve or support something
staan: erop –	to insist
staatsschuld, de	state debt
stad, de	town, city
stad: de – in	up to town
stadgenoot, de	fellow townsman/ woman
stadhuis, het	town hall
stadsdeelmanager, de	district manager
stam, de	tribe
standpunt, het	point of view
stedelijk	urban
steil	steep
stel, het	couple
stem, de	voice, vote
stembus, de	ballot box, poll(s)
stempel, het	stamp
stempel: het – dragen van	to bear the hallmark of
sterven	to die
stigmatiseren	stigmatize
stijgen	to increase, go up, climb
stijlvol	stylish
stilliggen	to lie still, to be closed down
stipt	strict, exactly
stoer	tough
stof, de	substances
stofwisseling, de	metabolism
stofzuigen	to do the vacuum cleaning
stoppen	to stop
stopwoord, het	stopgap, filler
straks	in a little while
stralend	radiant
strand, het	beach
strandtent, de	beach cafe
streefgewicht, het	target weight
streek, de	region
streekroman, de	regional novel
streven, het	pursuit, endeavour
strijder, de	warrior
strijken	to iron
stromen	to stream, flow
stroomstoring, de	power failure
stroopwafel, de	toffee waffle
studentenwoongroep, de	shared student flat
studie, de	studies
stuk voor stuk	one by one, to a man, every one of us
stuk, het	piece, part, article, hunk, play
stuk: niet meer – kunnen	can do no wrong
sturen	to steer
stuur: achter het – kruipen	to get behind the wheel
suffen	to fall asleep, not to be fully awake
suiker, de	sugar
sujet, het	character, customer (Flanders only) (in a sarcastic sense)
sukkel, de	loser
supermarkt, de	supermarket
t/m (tot en met)	up to and including
taak, de	task
taart, de	cake
tafel, de	table
talloos/ talloze	countless
tand, de	tooth

tandarts, de	dentist
tapijt, het	carpet, rug
tas, de	bag; cup (Flanders only)
tegelijkertijd	at the same time
tegen	against
tegenkomen	to meet
tegenover	opposite
tegenover: daar staat –	on the other hand, (but) then again
tegenspoed, de	adversity, misfortune
tegenspoed: voor- en tegenspoed	ups and downs
tegenstelling, de	difference of opinion
tegenwoordig	these days, nowadays
teken, het	sign
tellen	to count, number, consist of
tenminste	at least, after all
tenslotte	after all
tentoonstelling, de	exhibition
terecht	rightly (so)
terugnemen	to take back
terugtrekken: zich –	to withdraw
tevens	also (fairly formal)
tevergeefs	to no effect, in vain
thee, de	tea
theeglas, het	tea glass
theekransje, het	tea party
thriller, de	thriller
thuis	at home
thuishoren	to belong somewhere
tijd, de	time, tense (in grammatical terms)
tijd: – vergen	to take time
tijd: op –	in/on time
tijdstip, het	time (of meeting)
toch	after all, nevertheless
toch wel erg	rather a lot
toekomstig	future
toelaten	to allow
toen	when (+ past tense)
toepassing, de	application
toepassing: van – zijn op	to be applicable to
toeschrijven	to attribute
toeschrijven: – aan	to attribute to
toespraak, de	speech
toestroom, de	influx
toevallig	coincidental, here: by any chance
toevoeging, de	addition
tof	nice, cool
tolweg, de	toll road
toneel, het	stage
toneel: op het – verschijnen	to appear on the scene
tonen	to show
toon, de	tone, note
toon: uit de – vallen	be the odd one out, different
top, de	summit
topje, het	(sleeveless) t-shirt
tosti, de	toasted sandwich
tot en met	up to (and including)
tot zo	see you in a bit
totdat	until
touw, het	rope
toveren	to do magic
traan, de	tear
traan: in tranen uitbarsten	to burst into tears
tragikomedie, de	tragicomedy
traktatie, de	treat
trap, de	the stairs
treffen	to hit, strike, meet (with)
trein, de	train
trekje, het	feature or aspect
troep, de	mess
trots	proud
trots, de	pride
trotseren	to defy, to stand up (to)
trouwens	besides
tjonge	wow, my oh my
tuin, de	garden
tussen	between
tussendoortje, het	snack
twijfel, de	doubt
twijfelen	to doubt
uit	out, finished
uitbarsten: in tranen –	to burst into tears
uitblazen	to have a rest
uitbraak, de	jailbreak
uitbraakpoging, de	escape attempt
uitbreiding, de	expansion
uitdagend	challenging
uitdaging, de	challenge
uitdelen	to distribute
uitdraaien op	end in
uitdrukking, de	expression
uiteenzetten	to outline
uiteindelijk	finally
uiteraard	obviously, of course
uiterlijk, het	the appearance
uiterlijkheden	appearances
uiterste	extreme, utmost
uitgerekend	of all things
uitgestrekt	vast
uitgeven	to spend

uitgeverij, de	publishing company
uithalen	to take out
uiting: tot – komen	to be expressed
uitknikkeren	kick out
uitkomen	to end up, lead to, come out, bud
uitmaken	to break off, to finish, to matter, to determine
uitmaken: wat maakt dat nou uit?	what difference does that make?
uitnodigen	to invite
uitnodiging, de	invitation
uitproberen	to try out
uitrusten	to rest
uitschelden	to call names
uitseinen	to signal (to the world)
uitslapen	to have a lie-in
uitspraak, de	pronunciation, expression, statement
uitstaand	outstanding
uitstellen	to postpone
uitstoten	to expel, to banish
uitstralen	to radiate
uitstraling, de	radiance, aura
uitvergroten	to enlarge
uitverkoop, de	sale
uitwijzen	to reveal
uitzendbureau, het	employment agency
uitzetting, de	deportation
uitzonderlijk	exceptional
vaardigheid, de	skill
vacht, de	fur
vaderschap, het	fatherhood
vakantie, de	the holiday(s)
vakman, de	skilled worker
van . . . tot	from . . . until (to indicate timespan)
van harte	congratulations
van tevoren	in advance
vanaf	from
vanavond	tonight
vandaag	today
vandaag de dag	nowadays
vanzelfsprekend	obvious
varen	to sail
varen, de	fern
vast	fixed
vasthouden	to hold
vastklemmen	to hold on tight, to clamp
vastleggen	to write down
vaststellen	to determine, observe

vatten	to capture
vechten	to fight
veel	a lot
veelzijdig	varied
veilig	safe
veilig stellen	to secure
veiligheid, de	safety, security
vent, de	bloke, guy
veralgemening, de	generalisation
veranderen	to change
verandering, de	change
verantwoordelijk	responsible
verantwoordelijke, de	person responsible
verantwoordelijkheid, de	responsibility
verbaasd	amazed, surprised
verband houden met	to have a connection with
verbazen	to amaze
verbazing, de	amazement
verbergen	to hide
verbinden met	to relate to, to connect to
verblindend	blinding
verbrandingsoven, de	incinerator
verbrassen	squander away/waste
verder	further(more)
verdomme	damn it
verdrag, het	pact, agreement
verdrinken	to drown
Verenigde Naties, de	United Nations
verenigen	to unite
verf, de	paint
verf: uit de – komen	to live up to one's promise
verfijnd	refined
vergaderen	to have a meeting
vergadering, de	meeting
vergaren	to gather, gain
vergeleken bij	compared to
vergelijkbaar	comparable
vergelijken	to compare
vergeten	to forget
vergevorderd	far advanced
vergroten	to enlarge, to increase
vergunning, de	licence
verheugend	heart warming
verijdelen	to foil
verkeer, het	traffic
verkeersongeval, het	traffic accident
verkennen	to explore
verkiezingen, de	elections
verkondigen	to proclaim
verlangen	to want, desire
verlangen, het	desire
verlaten	to leave

verlegen	shy
verleiden	to tempt, seduce
Verlichting, de	Enlightenment
verliefd	in love
verliefd worden op	to fall in love with
verliezen	to lose
verlof, het	leave (of absence), permission
verlof: – nemen	to take time off
verloop, het	progress
vermoeden	to suspect
vermogen, het	wealth, capital
vernederend	humiliating
verontschuldigen: zich – (voor)	to apologise (for)
veroordelen	to condemn, sentence
veroordelen: – tot	to condemn/sentence to
veroorloven: zich –	to afford
veroveren	to conquer
verrijzen	rise out of
verscheidene	several
verscheidenheid, de	diversity
verschepen	to ship
verscherpen	tighten, make stricter
verschijnen	to appear
verschijnsel, het	phenomenon
verschil, het	difference
verschillend	different
verschrikkelijk	terrible/bly
verslaggeven	to report
verslijten	to wear out
verspillen	to waste
verstand, het	the mind
verstedelijking, de	urbanisation
verstoppertje spelen	play hide-and-seek
verstrikt raken in	to get ensnared in
vertegenwoordigd	represented
vertegenwoordigen	to represent
vertraagd	delayed
vertraging, de	delay
vertrekken	to leave
vervallen in	to lapse, fall into
vervangen	to replace, substitute
vervelen: zich –	to be bored
vervelend	irritating
vervoeren	to transport
vervullen	to perform
verwachten	to expect
verwarren	to confuse
verwekken	to father
verwennen	to spoil, to treat
verwerven	to acquire
verzekeringsbedrijf, het	insurance company
verzet, het	resistance, opposition
verzet: in – komen	to rebel
verzuiling, de	pillarisation
vestiging, de	branch
vet, het	fat
vieren	to celebrate
vinden	to find, to think
vinden: zich – in iets	to relate to something
vissersdorpje, het	fishing village
vlam, de	flame
vlam: de – in de pan slaan	for a situation to get out of hand
vlees, het	meat, flesh
vleiend	flattering
vlijmscherp	razor sharp
vlucht, de	flight, escape
voedzaam	nutritious(ly)
voelen: zich –	to feel (in oneself)
voeren	to conduct (a conversation)
voet: op staande –	immediately
vol	full
vol: ik zit –	I'm full
vol: zich – laten lopen	to get drunk
vol: zich – vreten	to stuff yourself
voldoen aan	to meet, to satisfy
volgens	according to
volhouden	to keep up
volk, het	people
volkomen	completely
volksaard, de	national character
volksbuurt, de	working class neighbourhood
volstrekt	completely
volwaardig	able
vooraanstaand	prominent
vooraf	beforehand
voorbereiden	to prepare
voordeel, het	advantage
voordracht, de	speech
voorhoofd, het	forehead
voorkeur, de	preference
voorlichtingscampagne, de	information campaign
voormalig	former
vooronderzoek, het	preliminary research
vooroordeel, het	prejudice
voorspoed: voor- en tegenspoed	ups and downs
voorraad, de	stock
voorraad: zolang de – strekt	while stock lasts
voorspelbaar	predictable

voorspellen	predict
voorspoed, de	prosperity
voorstel, het	proposal
voorstellen	to imagine
voorstelling, de	performance
voortaan	from now on
voortdurend	constant(ly)
voortrekkersrol, de	role of pioneer
vooruitstrevend	progressive
voorzichtig	careful
voren: naar – komen	to surface (a topic)
vorstenhuis, het	royal house
vouwen	to fold, crease
vraag, de	demand
vragen	to ask
vragen: ik vraag me af	I doubt, wonder
vredig	peacefully
vreedzaam	peaceful
vreemdgaan	to have an affair
vrees, de	fear
vrees: uit –	for fear of
vriendin, de	female friend
vrij	quite, fairly, reasonably, free
vrijgevochten	liberated
vrijkomen	to be released
vroeg: er – bij zijn	to be/to join quickly or early on
vroeger	former, past, previous
vrouw, de	woman
vuiligheid, de	dirt
vuiniszak, de	bin bag/garbage bag
waaien, het	blowing of the wind
waarde, de	value
waarde: – hechten aan	to attach value to
waardeoordeel, het	value judgement
waarderen	to value
waardevol	valuable
waarheid, de	truth
waarheid: de – in pacht hebben	to think one's own vision is the only true and correct one
waarom	why
waarschijnlijk	probably
wacht, de	watch, guard, duty
wacht: in de – slepen	to carry off, to pocket
wad, het	mud flat
wagen, de	the car (more formal word than auto)
walgelijk	disgusting
wandelen	to walk
wantrouwig	suspicious
warenhuis, het	department store
warm lopen voor	to take to/to feel enthusiasm for (something)
was, de	laundry, washing
watje, het	softie, wally
waxinelichtje, het	tea light
wederzijds	mutual
wedstrijd, de	game, match
weelderig	sumptuous
weer, het	weather
weer: in de – zijn	to be busy
weerbericht, het	weather report
weerspiegelen	to reflect
weg: uit de – helpen	to get rid of
wegens	because of
wei(de), de	field, meadow
weigeren	to refuse
weinig	little
wekken	to wake (up), create
wel degelijk	definitely
welgemeend	well-intentioned
welterusten	sleep well/goodnight
wemelen van	to be swarming with
wenkbrauw, de	eyebrow
epileren	to depilate
wennen aan	to get used to
wens, de	wish
wentelen: zich –	to wallow
wereld, de	world
wereld: 's werelds	of/in the world
wereldreis, de	trip around the world
wereldwijd	worldwide
werk, het	work
werkdruk, de	workload
werkzaam zijn	to be employed, active
westers	western
wet, de	law, legislation
weten	to know
weten: – waar je aan toe bent	to know where you stand
weten: nog –	to remember
weten: van niets –	to know nothing of it
weten: zeker –	to know for sure
wetenschap, de	science, fact
wetgeving, de	legislation
wethouder, de	alderman (Netherlands only)
wezen, het	creature
wijk, de	district, area
wijn, de	wine
wijnhandel, de	the wine merchant
wijze, de	way, manner
wildvreemd	perfectly strange
willen	to want
wind, de	wind

windmolenpark, het	wind mill farm
winkelier, de	shopkeeper
winst, de	profit, gain
wisselen	to change
wissen	to delete
woeden	to rage (of a fire)
woedend	furious
woest	furious
wolk, de	cloud
woningbouwvereniging, de	housing corporation
woord, het	word
woord: aan het – laten	to allow someone to speak
worden	to become
worstelen	to wrestle, to struggle
wortel, de	carrot, (square) root
wou	wanted
wreed	cruel
wreedheid, de	cruelty
z.o.z. (zie ommezijde)	p.t.o.
zaak, de	affair, business, firm
zaken, de	business
zaterdagochtend	Saturday morning
zedeloosheid, de	immorality
zeden, de	morals
zeggen	to say
zeggen: zacht gezegd	to put it mildly
zeiken	to whine, moan (informal)
zeikerig	whiney (informal)
zeker: u bent –	you must be
zelfbewust	self conscious, self-assured
zelfbewustzijn, het	self-esteem
zelfontplooiing, de	self-fulfilment
zelfs	even
zelfvertrouwen, het	confidence
zelfverzekerd	confident
zender, de	(radio/tv) channel
zenuwachtig	nervous
zeuren	to nag, to moan, whinge
zeurpiet, de	whinger
ziek	ill
ziekmakend	sickening
ziekte, de	illness
zielig	sad
zien	to see
zien: zie je nou wel!	see? I knew it!
zijn	to be
zin hebben in	to feel like
zintuig, het	sense
zithoek, de	sitting area
zitten: bij de pakken neer (gaan) –	to give up
zitten: iets niet meer zien –	not be able to see your way out
zo: – niet	otherwise, if not
zodra	as soon as
zoeken	to look for
zoenen	to kiss
zoet	sweet
zoet: – zijn met iets	to be occupied with something for a while
zoetigheid, de	confectionery
zogenaamd	so-called, supposedly
zolder, de	attic
zon, de	sun
zonder	without
zonsondergang, de	sunset
zoon, de	son
zorg (dragen) voor	to take care of
zorg, de	care
zorgeloos	carefree
zorgen baren	cause concern
zout, het/de	salt
zover	so/this far
zover: het is (weer) –	here we go (again)
zuchten	to sigh
zuil, de	pillar
zulk(e)	such
zwaar	heavy
zwak	weak
zwakkere, de	weaker person
zwanger	pregnant
zwart-witfilm, de	black and white movie
zweep: het klappen van de – kennen	to know the tricks of the trade
zwemmen	to swim
zwoel	sultry

Appendix 1
Irregular verbs

In this appendix you will find a list of irregular verbs. In the first column you will find a verb (the **infinitive** form) and in the last column an English translation. In the second column you will find the singular and plural forms of the **imperfect**. In the third column you will find the **past participle** of the verb – if the **present perfect** is formed with a form of the verb **hebben**, the past participle is preceded by **heeft**; if the present perfect is formed with a form of the verb **zijn**, then the past participle is preceded by **is**.

infinitive	imperfect	past participle	
aangeven	gaf, gaven aan	heeft aangegeven	to indicate, report
aankijken	keek, keken aan	heeft aangekeken	to look at
aankomen	kwam, kwamen aan	is aangekomen	to arrive
aannemen	nam, namen aan	heeft aangenomen	to accept, assume
aanvallen	viel, vielen aan	heeft aangevallen	to attack
aanwijzen	wees, wezen aan	heeft aangewezen	to point out, indicate
achterblijven	bleef, bleven achter	is achtergebleven	to stay behind
aflopen	liep, liepen af	is afgelopen	to (come to an) end
afvragen	vroeg, vroegen af	heeft afgevraagd	to wonder
bedenken	bedacht, bedachten	heeft bedacht	to think (about)
beginnen	begon, begonnen	is begonnen	to begin
begrijpen	begreep, begrepen	heeft begrepen	to understand
beschrijven	beschreef, beschreven	heeft beschreven	to describe
besluiten	besloot, besloten	heeft besloten	to decide
bespreken	besprak, bespraken	heeft besproken	to discuss
bestaan	bestond, bestonden	heeft bestaan	to exist
betreffen	betrof, betroffen	heeft betroffen	to concern, affect
bevallen	beviel, bevielen	is bevallen	to give birth, to please
bewegen	bewoog, bewogen	heeft bewogen	to move
bewijzen	bewees, bewezen	heeft bewezen	to prove
bezitten	bezat, bezaten	heeft bezeten	to possess
bezoeken	bezocht, bezochten	heeft bezocht	to visit
bieden	bood, boden	heeft geboden	to offer
bijten	beet, beten	heeft gebeten	to bite
binnenkomen	kwam, kwamen binnen	is binnengekomen	to enter
blijken	bleek, bleken	is gebleken	to prove, turn out
blijven	bleef, bleven	is gebleven	to remain, stay

infinitive	imperfect	past participle	
breken	brak, braken	heeft gebroken	to break
brengen	bracht, brachten	heeft gebracht	to bring
deelnemen	nam, namen deel	heeft deelgenomen	to take part
denken	dacht, dachten	heeft gedacht	to think
doen	deed, deden	heeft gedaan	to do
doorgaan	ging, gingen door	is doorgegaan	to continue
doorgeven	gaf, gaven door	heeft doorgegeven	to pass on
dragen	droeg, droegen	heeft gedragen	to carry, wear
drinken	dronk, dronken	heeft gedronken	to drink
eruitzien	zag, zagen eruit	heeft eruitgezien	to look (like)
eten	at, aten	heeft gegeten	to eat
gaan	ging, gingen	is gegaan	to go
gedragen	gedroeg, gedroegen	heeft gedragen	to behave
gelden	gold, golden	heeft gegolden	to apply, count
genieten	genoot, genoten	heeft genoten	to enjoy
geven	gaf, gaven	heeft gegeven	to give
gieten	goot, goten	heeft gegoten	to pour
goedvinden	vond, vonden goed	heeft goedgevonden	to approve
grijpen	greep, grepen	heeft gegrepen	to grab (hold of)
hangen	hing, hingen	heeft gehangen	to hang
hebben	had, hadden	heeft gehad	to have
helpen	hielp, hielpen	heeft geholpen	to help
hoeven	hoefde, hoefden	heeft gehoefd	to (not) have to
houden	hield, hielden	heeft gehouden	to hold, keep
kiezen	koos, kozen	heeft gekozen	to choose
kijken	keek, keken	heeft gekeken	to look, watch
klinken	klonk, klonken	heeft geklonken	to sound
komen	kwam, kwamen	is gekomen	to come
kopen	kocht, kochten	heeft gekocht	to buy
krijgen	kreeg, kregen	heeft gekregen	to get, receive
kunnen	kon, konden	heeft gekund	to be able to, can
laten	liet, lieten	heeft gelaten	to let, allow
lezen	las, lazen	heeft gelezen	to read
liegen	loog, logen	heeft gelogen	to (tell a) lie
liggen	lag, lagen	heeft gelegen	to lie
lijden	leed, leden	heeft geleden	to suffer
lijken	leek, leken	heeft geleken	to seem, appear
lopen	liep, liepen	heeft/is gelopen	to walk
moeten	moest, moesten	heeft gemoeten	to have to, must
mogen	mocht, mochten	heeft gemogen	to be allowed, may
nadenken	dacht, dachten na	heeft nagedacht	to think, ponder
nemen	nam, namen	heeft genomen	to take
onderzoeken	onderzocht, onderzochten	heeft onderzocht	to examine
ontbreken	ontbrak, ontbraken	heeft ontbroken	to be lacking, missing

infinitive	**imperfect**	**past participle**	
ontslaan	ontsloeg, ontsloegen	heeft ontslagen	to dismiss, discharge
ontstaan	ontstond, ontstonden	is ontstaan	to originate
ontvangen	ontving, ontvingen	heeft ontvangen	to receive
ontwerpen	ontwierp, ontwierpen	heeft ontworpen	to design
ophouden	hield, hielden op	is/heeft opgehouden	to stop, cease
opstaan	stond, stonden op	is opgestaan	to get up
opstijgen	steeg, stegen op	is opgestegen	to ascend, rise
optreden	trad, traden op	heeft/is opgetreden	to perform
opvallen	viel, vielen op	is opgevallen	to be conspicuous
opzoeken	zocht, zochten op	heeft opgezocht	to look up
overblijven	bleef, bleven over	is overgebleven	to be left, remain
overlijden	overleed, overleden	is overleden	to die
oversteken	stak, staken over	is overgestoken	to cross
overwegen	overwoog, overwogen	heeft overwogen	to consider, weigh up
plaatsvinden	vond, vonden plaats	heeft plaatsgevonden	to take place, happen
rijden	reed, reden	heeft gereden	to drive, ride
roepen	riep, riepen	heeft geroepen	to call (out)
ruiken	rook, roken	heeft geroken	to smell
schenken	schonk, schonken	heeft geschonken	to pour (out)
schieten	schoot, schoten	heeft geschoten	to shoot
schijnen	scheen, schenen	heeft geschenen	to seem, appear
schrijven	schreef, schreven	heeft geschreven	to write
slaan	sloeg, sloegen	heeft geslagen	to hit
slapen	sliep, sliepen	heeft geslapen	to sleep
sluiten	sloot, sloten	heeft gesloten	to close
snijden	sneed, sneden	heeft gesneden	to cut
spreken	sprak, spraken	heeft gesproken	to speak
springen	sprong, sprongen	heeft/is gesprongen	to jump
staan	stond, stonden	heeft gestaan	to stand
stelen	stal, stalen	heeft gestolen	to steal
sterven	stierf, stierven	is gestorven	to die
stijgen	steeg, stegen	is gestegen	to rise, climb
stinken	stonk, stonken	heeft gestonken	to stink
tegenhouden	hield, hielden tegen	heeft tegengehouden	to stop, prevent
tegenvallen	viel, vielen tegen	is tegengevallen	to disappoint, fall short
terugkomen	kwam, kwamen terug	is teruggekomen	to come back
toenemen	nam, namen toe	is toegenomen	to increase
toestaan	stond, stonden toe	heeft toegestaan	to allow, permit
treffen	trof, troffen	heeft getroffen	to hit, affect
trekken	trok, trokken	heeft getrokken	to pull
uitdoen	deed, deden uit	heeft uitgedaan	to take off, turn off
uitgaan	ging, gingen uit	is uitgegaan	to go out
uitgeven	gaf, gaven uit	heeft uitgegeven	to spend
uitkijken	keek, keken uit	heeft uitgekeken	to look out
uitspreken	sprak, spraken uit	heeft uitgesproken	to pronounce
uitzenden	zond, zonden uit	heeft uitgezonden	to broadcast
vallen	viel, vielen	is gevallen	to fall
vangen	ving, vingen	heeft gevangen	to catch

infinitive	imperfect	past participle	
varen	voer, voeren	heeft/is gevaren	to sail
vechten	vocht, vochten	heeft gevochten	to fight
verbieden	verbood, verboden	heeft verboden	to forbid, ban
verdwijnen	verdween, verdwenen	is verdwenen	to disappear
vergelijken	vergeleek, vergeleken	heeft vergeleken	to compare
vergeten	vergat, vergaten	heeft/is vergeten	to forget
verkopen	verkocht, verkochten	heeft verkocht	to sell
verlaten	verliet, verlieten	heeft verlaten	to leave, desert
verliezen	verloor, verloren	heeft verloren	to lose
verschijnen	verscheen, verschenen	is verschenen	to appear, manifest
verstaan	verstond, verstonden	heeft verstaan	to understand, hear
vertrekken	vertrok, vertrokken	is vertrokken	to leave, depart
vervangen	verving, vervingen	heeft vervangen	to replace
verwijzen	verwees, verwezen	heeft verwezen	to refer
verzinnen	verzon, verzonnen	heeft verzonnen	to invent, make up
vinden	vond, vonden	heeft gevonden	to find
vliegen	vloog, vlogen	heeft gevlogen	to fly
voldoen	voldeed, voldeden	heeft voldaan	to satisfy, meet
volhouden	hield, hielden vol	heeft volgehouden	to maintain, keep up
voorkomen	voorkwam, voorkwamen	heeft voorkomen	to occur, happen, prevent
vragen	vroeg, vroegen	heeft gevraagd	to ask
vriezen	vroor, vroren	heeft gevroren	to freeze
weggaan	ging, gingen weg	is weggegaan	to leave, depart
weten	wist, wisten	heeft geweten	to know
wijzen	wees, wezen	heeft gewezen	to point
winnen	won, wonnen	heeft gewonnen	to win
worden	werd, werden	is geworden	to become, be, get
zeggen	zei, zeiden	heeft gezegd	to say
zien	zag, zagen	heeft gezien	to see
zijn	was, waren	is geweest	to be
zingen	zong, zongen	heeft gezongen	to sing
zitten	zat, zaten	heeft gezeten	to sit
zoeken	zocht, zochten	heeft gezocht	to look for, search
zullen	zou, zouden		shall, will
zwemmen	zwom, zwommen	heeft gezwommen	to swim
zwijgen	zweeg, zwegen	heeft gezwegen	to be silent

Appendix 2 Pronunciation

The best way to improve your pronunciation is to listen to the recorded texts and dialogues in each unit as often as possible, and try to imitate the sounds as closely as possible. Listening to Dutch and Flemish radio and/or television and native speakers is also very useful.

Consonants

For speakers of English, Dutch consonants do not pose much of a problem, since they are generally pronounced the same as in English. There are some exceptions:

g/ch	**gek** mad	
	dicht close(d)	You should feel this sound at the back of your throat, like in Scottish *loch*. This sound softens the further South you travel in the Netherlands and Belgium.
j	**ja** yes	The same sound as *y* in English *yes*.
k, p, t	**kaal** bald	
	post post	
	taal language	These consonants sound the same as in English, except you don't exhale as much air (you can test this by holding your hand in front of your mouth to feel the difference between English *cat* and Dutch **kat**).
r	**raar** strange	Trill your tongue at the back of your upper teeth, or make some friction at the back of your mouth (like in French).
sch	**schoen** shoe	A combination of **s** (which is much less sharp in Dutch than in English) and **ch**.
v	**veel** a lot	A sound between English *v* and *f*. Particularly close to *f* at the beginning of words.
w	**waar** where	Between English *v* and *w*. Start this sound by holding your upper teeth against your lower lip.

Vowels

Dutch vowel sounds sometimes differ more from their English counterparts than the consonant sounds. We will distinguish between three groups of vowel sounds: vowel sounds formed in the front of the mouth, those formed at the back of the mouth, and combinations of vowel sounds.

1 FRONT VOWEL SOUNDS

e	**dek** deck	As in *get* but shorter.
ee	**deel** part	As in *gain*.
ei/ij	**meid** girl	Between *bite* and *train*.
	dijk dyke	Note: **ij** is usually written as one letter, like a *y* with dots.
eu	**keus** choice	No English equivalent. Make a vowel sound as in *dirt* while pouting your lips tightly and pressing your tongue down.
i	**lip** lip	As in *fit* but shorter.
ie	**vies** dirty	As in *cheat*.
u	**kus** kiss	Sounds like *dirt* but shorter.
uu	**vuur** fire	No English equivalent. Make a vowel sound as in *feet* while pursing your lips. Note: vowel sounds become longer before **r**.
ui	**huis** house	No English equivalent. Make a vowel sound as in *house* while pouting your lips tightly and pressing your tongue down.

BACK VOWEL SOUNDS

a	**tas** bag	As in *bath* but shorter.
aa	**baas** boss	As in *man* but longer.
o	**kop** cup	As in *hot* but shorter.
oo	**boom** tree	As in *boat*.
oe	**boek** book	As in *book* but with tightly rounded lips.
ou/au	**oud** old **blauw** blue	No English equivalent. Make a sound as in *shout* but start with more rounded lips and a wide open mouth.

COMBINATIONS OF VOWEL SOUNDS

aai	**saai** boring	A combination of **aa** and **ie**.
eeuw	**leeuw** lion	A combination of **ee** and **oe**.
ieuw	**nieuw** new	A combination of **ie** and **oe**.
oei	**doei** bye	A combination of **oe** and **ie**.
ooi	**mooi** beautiful	A combination of **oo** and **ie**.
uw	**ruw** rough	A combination off **uu** and **oe**.

There is one last Dutch vowel sound, 'sjwa': a sound similar to that in English sist***er***. This sound is made by simple letting air escape from your mouth. It is spelt in various different ways:

e	**de** the
ee	**een** a/an
i	**bezig** busy/active
ij	**mogelijk** possible

Oefening 1: Recognition

Recognition: listen to the recorded sounds as described above and try to imitate them. Identity for yourself which sounds you find most difficult. Then listen to the recorded texts from Unit 1, listening out in particular for the sounds you find difficult (underline them in the texts whenever you come across them).

Oefening 2: Short and long vowel sounds

Listen to the recorded sentences and repeat, paying special attention to the pronunciation of the vowel sounds.

Oefening 3: Au/ou – ui – oe – ij/ei – eu

Listen to the sentences from **Oefening 2** once more, and this time fill in the correct vowel sound in the gaps below. NB: Don't worry too much about spelling, as this is not our main focus.

1 De t___rt is lekker.
2 M___g ik iets vragen alstublieft?
3 Haar jas is r___d.
4 H___r woont jouw br___r.
5 Daar stopt de b___s.
6 Zij zingt een l___d.

7 Hij sp___lt piano.
8 Mijn man geeft mij elke m___rgen een k___s.
9 H___r zoon heet M___rk.
10 Die m___r is hoog.

Oefening 4: Au/ou – ui – oe – ij/ei – eu

Listen to the recorded sentences and repeat, paying special attention to the pronunciation of the vowel sounds **au/ou – ui – oe – ij/ei – eu**.

Oefening 5

Listen to the sentences from **Oefening 4** more, and this time fill in the correct vowel sound in the gaps below. NB: Don't worry too much about spelling, as this is not our main focus.

1 De koe staat in de w___.
2 Ik l___ster naar de lerares.
3 H___ k___kt naar de sterren.
4 W___ z___n studenten.
5 Haar tas is br___n.
6 Bl___w en groen zijn kl___ren.
7 De d___r staat open.
8 Mijn br___r is veertig.
9 Het is heel warm b___ten.
10 De tart is te z___t.

Oefening 6

Practice: say the recorded texts from Unit 1 out loud. Imitate the recorded voices as closely as possible. If possible, record your own voice and listen back to it, comparing your own pronunciation with the recorded Dutch voices.

Appendix 3
Spelling

Dutch spelling is relatively easy; most words are spelled the way they sound, so there are no difficulties to overcome like the English spellings of "Worcester" or "know". In Dutch, in general, what you hear is what you put down on paper, and vice versa: **tafel** is pronounced with a **t**-sound, an **a**-sound, an **f**-sound, an -**e**-sound and an **l**-sound. Similarly, all the letters of a longer word like **afvalverbrander** (waste incinerator) can be heard when pronouncing the word.

However, to master Dutch spelling completely, you will need to learn a few rules governing the spelling of the vowel sounds **a, e, o, u**:

Short

Look up the short vowel sounds **a, e, o, u** in the pronunciation appendix and practice pronouncing these sounds.

The short vowel sounds **a, e, o, u** are always spelt with one vowel in a closed syllable (i.e. a syllable which ends in a consonant):

bal	ball
gek	mad person
trol	troll
kus	kiss

When a syllable is added to words such as these, for instance when adding **-en** to make a plural, what was the final consonant, now becomes part of the second syllable:

***ba – len**
***ge – ken**
***tro – len**
***ku – sen**

The first syllable is now an open syllable (ending in a vowel). To make sure the syllable remains closed, as must be the case with a short vowel sound, the middle consonant is doubled. Of this double consonant, the first belongs with the first syllable, and the second belongs with the second syllable:

ballen
gekken
trollen
kussen

Oefening 1

Make the following words plural by adding **-en** and adjust the spelling where necessary.

1 **vak** (school) subject
2 **bus**
3 **trein** train
4 **fles** bottle
5 **put** well
6 **kop** cup
7 **bed**
8 **wolk** cloud
9 **pen**
10 **tas** bag

Long

Look up the long vowel sounds **aa**, **ee**, **oo**, **uu** in the pronunciation appendix and practice pronouncing them.

The long vowel sounds **aa**, **ee**, **oo**, **uu** can be spelt in two ways:

with one letter in an open syllable (ending in a vowel)
with two letters in a closed syllable (ending in a consonant).

In the following verbs the long vowel sounds are spelt with one letter in an open syllable:

slapen	to sleep	**(sla – pen)**
eten	to eat	**(e – ten)**
koken	to cook	**(ko – ken)**
vuren	to fire/shoot	**(vu – ren)**

When the final **-en** is taken away from these verbs, for instance to find the stem of the verb (the verb form for **ik** in the present tense), a single syllable is left. However, this syllable is closed, since it ends in a consonant. Consequently, the vowel sounds would be short instead of long (***slap, *et, *kok, *vur**). For this reason, long vowel sounds are spelled with two letters in closed syllables. In other words, the vowel is doubled:

slaap
eet
kook
vuur

Note that **z** and **v** often become **s** and **f** at the end of a word:

reizen	to travel	**ik reis**	I travel
geloven	to believe	**ik geloof**	I believe

This also applies to nouns and adjectives:

brieven	letters	**een brief**	a letter
poezen	cats	**een poes**	a cat

Consonants

Note that there is one important spelling rule for Dutch consonants: a Dutch word cannot end in a double consonant, so words like English 'ball', 'bell', 'I fall' are spelt **bal**, **bel**, **ik val**.

Oefening 2

Find the stem (the verb form used with **ik**) of the following infinitives by taking away **-en** and adjust the spelling where necessary.

1	**vragen**	to ask	ik ______________ .
2	**lenen**	to lend/borrow	ik ______________ .
3	**kopen**	to buy	ik ______________ .
4	**dragen**	to carry/wear	ik ______________ .
5	**herhalen**	to repeat	ik ______________ .
6	**sturen**	to steer	ik ______________ .
7	**geven**	to give	ik ______________ .
8	**roken**	to smoke	ik ______________ .

Oefening 3

Make the following nouns plural by adding **-en** and adjust the spelling where necessary.

1	**oor**	ear
2	**maan**	moon
3	**minuut**	minute
4	**banaan**	banana

5	**haar**	hair
6	**kantoor**	office
7	**uur**	hour
8	**been**	leg

Oefening 4

From the following stems of verbs (verb forms used with **ik**), find the infinitive of the verb by adding **-en** and adjusting the spelling if needed.

1	**ik leg**	(to lay)
2	**ik stap**	(to step)
3	**ik buk**	(to duck/stoop)
4	**ik schop**	(to kick)
5	**ik rek**	(to stretch)

Oefening 5

Make the following words plural by adding **-en** and adjusting the spelling where necessary.

1	**adres**	address
2	**zak**	bag, sack
3	**advocaat**	lawyer
4	**karaktereigenschap**	character trait
5	**school**	
6	**kast**	cupboard
7	**boterham**	slice of bread, sandwich
8	**dief**	thief
9	**kat**	cat
10	**muur**	wall

INDEX

Related titles from Routledge

Dutch: A Comprehensive Grammar

Bruce Donaldson

Dutch: A Comprehensive Grammar is a complete reference guide to modern Dutch Grammar, presenting a clear and accessible description of the language.

The volume is organized to promote a thorough understanding of Dutch grammar. It offers a stimulating analysis of the complexities of the language, and provides full and clear explanations. Throughout, the emphasis is on Dutch as used by present-day native speakers.

Features include:

- Detailed treatment of the common grammatical structures and parts of speech
- Extensive exemplification
- Particular attention to areas of confusion and difficulty
- Dutch–English parallels highlighted throughout the book

Bruce Donaldson retired in 2004 from the Department of German and Swedish at the University of Melbourne where he taught Dutch and German for thirty years. His most recent publications are *Colloquial Dutch, Colloquial Afrikaans* and *Mastering German Vocabulary,* all published by Routledge.

ISBN10: 0–415–15418–9 (hbk)
ISBN10: 0–415–15419–7 (pbk)

ISBN13: 9–78–0–415–15418–5 (hbk)
ISBN13: 9–78–0–415–15419–2 (pbk)